Structural Adjustment, Global Trade and the New Political Economy of Development

Structural Adjustment, Global Trade and the New Political Economy of Development

---

Biplab Dasgupta

Zed Books
London • New York

Structural Adjustment, Global Trade and the New Political Economy of Development

is published in South Asia by Vistaar Publications (a division of Sage Publications India Pvt Ltd), Post Box 4215, New Delhi – 110 048, India, and in the rest of the world by Zed Books Ltd, 7 Cynthia Street, London N1 9JF, UK, and Room 400, 175 Fifth Avenue, New York, NY 10010, USA, in 1998.

Distributed in the USA exclusively by St Martin's Press Inc., 175 Fifth Avenue, New York, NY 10010, USA.

A catalogue record for this book is available from the British library.

US cataloging-in-publication data has been applied for from the Library of Congress.

ISBN: 1 85649 595 7 hb
ISBN: 1 85649 596 5 pb

Cover design by Ad Lib designs

Contents

List of tables

List of abbreviations

ADR	American Depository Receipt
AMS	Aggregate Measure of Support
APEC	Asia Pacific Economic Cooperation
ASEAN	Association of South East Asian Nations
BSFF	Buffer Stock Financing Facility
BWI	Bretton Woods Institution
CACM	Central American Common Market
CAP	Common Agricultural Programme (of EC)
CCFF	Compensatory and Contingency Financing Facility
CEFTA	Central European Free Trade Agreement
CFCs	Chlorofluorocarbons
CIDIE	Committee of International Development Institutes on Environment
CPF	Central Provident Fund
CRS	Computer Reservation System
DSB	Dispute Settlement Board (of WTO)
DSU	Dispute Settlement Understanding (of WTO)
DUP	Directly Unproductive Profit-Seeking (activities)
EC	European Community
ECA	(United Nations) Economic Commission for Africa
ECLAC	(United Nations) Economic Commission for Latin America and the Caribbean
ECOSOC	Economic and Social Council (of the United Nations)
ECU	European Currency Unit
EEA	European Economic Area
EEC	European Economic Community
EEP	Export Enhancement Programme
EFTA	European Free Trade Association
EIAL	Early-Intensive Adjustment Lending (countries)
EMR	Exclusive Marketing Rights
ERM	Exchange Rate Mechanism

ESAF	Extended Structural Adjustment Facility
EU	European Union
FAO	Food and Agriculture Organisation (of the United Nations)
FDI	Foreign Direct Investment
G7	Group of Seven (rich countries)
GATS	General Agreement on Trade in Services
GATT	General Agreement on Tariffs and Trade
GDP	Gross Domestic Product
GDR	Global Depository Receipts
GEF	Global Environment Facility
GEMSs	Global Environment Monitoring Systems
GHG	Greenhouse Gas
GNP	Gross National Product
GRID	Global Resource Information Database
GSP	Generalised System of Preferences
HCI	Heavy and Chemical Industry
HPAE	High-Performing Asian Economy
IBRD	International Bank for Reconstruction and Development (World Bank)
ICSU	International Council for Scientific Unions
IDA	International Development Assistance
IDRA	Industrial (Development and Regulation) Act, 1951
IDS	Institute of Development Studies (of Sussex, UK)
IFC	International Finance Corporation
IIE	Institute for Internatinoal Economics (at Washington)
ILO	International Labour Organisation
IMF	International Monetary Fund
IPCC	Inter-governmental Panel on Climatic Change
IPR	Intellectual Property Rights
IRPTC	International Registry of Potentially Toxic Chemicals
ITO	International Trade Organisation
LDC	Less Developed Country
LPG	Liberalisation, Privatisation and Globalisation
MFA	Multi-fibre Agreement
MFN	Most Favoured Nation
MITI	Ministry of International Trade and Industry (of Japan)
MNC	Multinational Corporation
MOSS	Market Oriented Sector Sensitive (Talks)
MOU	Memorandum of Understanding
MRTP	Monopolies and Restrictive Trade Practices (Act)
NAFTA	North American Free Trade Association
NEP	New Economic Policy
NIC	Newly Industrialised Country

NIEO	New International Economic Order
NNP	Net National Product
NPE	New Political Economy (of Development)
NRI	Non-resident Indian
NTB	Non-tariff Barrier
NTM	Non-tariff Measures
ODA*	Overseas Development Administration (of UK)
ODA	Overseas Development Assistance
ODI	Overseas Development Institute (of London)
ODM	Own-design and Manufacture
OECD	Organisation for Economic Cooperation and Development
OECF	Overseas Economic Cooperation Fund
OEM	Original Equipment Manufacture
OPEC	Organisation of Petroleum Exporting Countries
OTC	Organisation for Trade Cooperation
PBR	Plant Breeders' Rights
PDS	Public Distribution System
PFP	Policy Framework Paper
PL480	Public Law 480
PSU	Public Sector Unit
PTA	Preferential Trade Area (for Eastern and Southern African countries)
R&D	Research and Development
SAF	Structural Adjustment Facility
SAL	Structural Adjustment Loan
SAP	Structural Adjustment Programme
SDR	Special Drawing Rights
SECAL	Sectoral Adjustment Loan
SII	Structural Impediments Initiative
SOE	Smaller Open Economies
SSA	Sub-Saharan Africa
START	System for Analysis, Research and Training (on Global Change)
TCDC	Technical Cooperation among Developing Countries
TFP	Total Factor Productivity
TINA	There Is No Alternative
TNC	Transnational Corporation
TPRM	Trade Policy Review Mechanism (of WTO)
TRIMs	Trade Related Investment Measures
TRIPS	Trade Related (aspects of) Intellectual Property Rights
UDEAC	Union Douaniere et Economique de l'Afrique Centrale
UK	United Kingdom
UN	United Nations

UNCTAD	United Nations Conference on Trade and Development
UNDP	United Nations Development Programme
UNEP	United Nations Environment Programme
UNICEF	United Nations Children's Fund
UNIDO	United Nations Industrial Development Organisation
UNRISD	United Nations Research Institute for Social Development
US/USA	United States of America
USSR	Union of Soviet Socialist Republics
USTR	United States Trade Representative
VER	Voluntary Export Restraint
VIE	Voluntary Import Enhancement
WCED	World Conference on Environment and Development
WDR	World Development Report (of the World Bank)
WHO	World Health Organisation
WMO	World Meteorological Organisation
WTO	World Trade Organisation

Prologue

The idea of a book on structural adjustment was originally prompted by the decision of the new Indian government, led by Narasimha Rao, to introduce structural adjustment in India in July 1991. At that time the objective was a modest one, of a book exclusively on India, examining the post-1991 developments in the context of what had happened earlier to the Indian economy, and then to conclude whether and how far this package was good or bad for India.

As I began reading the extensive literature, the similarities between the package applied to India and those implemented in other countries by the World Bank and the International Monetary Fund were hard to ignore. It was clear that an understanding of what structural adjustment can or cannot do to India would not be complete without a careful examination of the global experience since 1980 when it was first introduced.

A two-month Visiting Fellowship to the Institute of Development Studies (IDS), at Brighton, United Kingdom, the institution with which I had been associated during the 1970s, gave me the first opportunity to read the vast global literature on this theme, particularly that emanating from the World Bank and International Monetary Fund. This was followed by several visits to the British Library located at the British Museum in London over the next three years, which provided me with the raw material for the book.

As it happens with all researchers, one thing leads to another. East Asia entered my horizon first as a glittering example of the success of market-based policies prompted by structural adjustment. Later, in-depth studies by some eminent researchers, including my former IDS colleague, Robert Wade, established the interventionist role of the state in these countries beyond doubt.

Then came the World Bank study, *The East Asian Miracle* (1993), claiming that state intervention in East Asia was an exceptional case and not amenable to replication by other less developed countries. The New Political Economy explained the success in East Asia in terms of the authoritarian nature of the state and the competence and impartiality of its bureaucracy. This then led me to the proliferating literature on the New Political Economy that provides the theoretical prop to structural adjustment.

The emphasis on external orientation in the structural adjustment package made it imperative that this study be linked in some ways with the world trade system. In fact, the two Bretton Woods Institutions, along with the World Trade Organisation, now form a global holy economic trinity with a common economic philosophy. Then came environment, mainly to answer the question whether structural adjustment protects the interests of the future generations.

What has emerged, after several years of hard work, is an attempt at a comprehensive critical analysis of the Fund–Bank approach on development in less developed countries. While critical of these agencies and their approach, this book mainly draws on the material and research produced by their staff. It is replete with references to research papers prepared by Fund–Bank staff members that are critical of some aspects of their formal position on structural adjustment.

A negative consequence of this exercise is that the proposed book on India's experience with structural adjustment still remains to be written.

I am grateful to the Institute of Development Studies, University of Sussex, for a two-month fellowship in 1994, to the staff of the British Library located at the British Museum (London) for help during the next three years, to my friend Dr Yoginder Alagh, Minister of Planning at that time, for organising a seminar on my paper on New Political Economy at the Planning Commission, to Oxford University's Queen Elizabeth House, Sussex University's Centre for African and Asian Studies and Institute of Development Studies and London University's Birkbeck College, for seminars on various parts of the book during 1995–97. I am also grateful to the Vice Chancellor of Calcutta University for permitting me to take time off for research, to *Economic and Political Weekly* for printing some articles based on this research, and to my colleagues at the Centre for Urban Economic Studies at Calcutta University for organising a series of seminars on various chapters of this book.

BIPLAB DASGUPTA

one

Introduction

For a majority of the less developed countries (LDCs) of the world today, structural adjustment is a fact of life. Sponsored by the World Bank in 1980, this package of policies is supplemented by the stabilisation package sponsored by the International Monetary Fund (IMF). To make life easier, in this book we are subsuming 'stabilisation' under the label 'structural adjustment', though, as we shall see in Chapter 3, there are important differences in their policy prescriptions.

These packages were originally introduced as short-term remedies to rectify severe imbalances in external and internal accounts in a large number of countries. However, once initiated, very few countries have succeeded in growing out of them, as one lending programme has followed another. For some countries, their association with the World Bank and IMF has continued, off and on, for nearly 17 years. This is long enough to assess the viability or effectiveness of any package of policies; more so, because structural adjustment has been applied uniformly to a wide variety of conditions.

Adjustment involves both some finance and a set of conditionalities. These conditionalities have provoked many controversies. Some see them as a perfectly normal banking practice to guarantee repayment. Some others see, in these conditionalities, an attempt to retain the recipient countries as perpetually dependent client-states of the rich nations operating at a low level of development. Still others see structural adjustment as an attempt to transfer the burden of the oil crisis of the 1970s to the backs of the poor countries. Those taking a positive view argue that such conditionalities should have been adopted by the countries concerned in any case, as these reflect good economics, irrespective of whether these are accompanied by funding. The conditionalities help to 'get the basics right', to avoid trade and price distortions, make resource allocation rational and optimum, and link production decisions to the comparative advantage of the countries concerned.

In this book, we are attempting to study and analyse various implications of structural adjustment for the economies of the LDCs. In Chapter 2 we begin with the New Political Economy (NPE) of development, that provides the theoretical basis of structural adjustment. NPE argues that self-interest and group interests, along with broader distributional coalitions of a number of groups, lead to a situation where perfectly rational individual decisions produce irrational economic outcomes. Since distributional coalitions thrive in controlled economies, a solution is to remove entry barriers, to make resources mobile and the market free and perfectly competitive. One interesting aspect of NPE is its emphasis on rent-seeking behaviour that characterises controlled economies and produces welfare losses in terms of diversion of resources from more productive activities for lobbying, etc. Another solution is to rely on impartial and competent bureaucrats for overseeing resource allocation. NPE holds a poor view of the political leaders of the LDCs, and would prefer them to leave economic issues in the hands of the private agents operating in a market without barriers.

Chapter 3, on structural adjustment, begins with the two Bretton Woods Institutions (BWIs), and traces their changing role in the world economy up to the stage where these have become largely irrelevant as far as the developed countries are concerned, but wield enormous influence in the economic life of the LDCs. After a discourse on the political economy of these two institutions and on the genesis of structural adjustment, the chapter discusses in detail the main conditionalities in both stabilisation and structural adjustment programmes (SAPs). The chapter also discusses how these conditionalities become incorporated in the Policy Framework Paper (PFP) that defines the relationship between the BWIs and the recipient countries. This is followed by a detailed examination of the performance of countries under structural adjustment, sector by sector, and then by summaries of major evaluations of these programmes by Fund–Bank sources and independent scholars.

Chapter 4, on global trade, begins by pointing out the essential similarity of views on trade related issues, between BWIs on the one hand and the newly established World Trade Organisation (WTO) on the other. This is followed by an examination of the General Agreement on Tariffs and Trade (GATT) system—its principles and practices, achievements and constraints—as it operated over eight rounds, first as a temporary outfit pending the formation of the International Trade Organisation (ITO), and later as a regular feature of the world trade scene until 1995, when it was replaced by the WTO. Then comes a detailed examination of trade-restricting practices of the rich countries, such as voluntary export restraint (VER); the Multi-fibre Agreement (MFA); Super 301; and the use of safeguard, the anti-dumping legislation and subsidies to keep competitors out and to promote their own industries. The part on the Uruguay Round deals with new features such as agreements on patents, services and investment, and then with agriculture and subsidies for agriculturists as a separate issue. The chapter concludes with an extensive discussion on multinational corporations (MNCs), their distinguishing features and their implications for the economies of the host countries.

Chapter 5, on the relationship between structural adjustment and environment, mainly deals with how far the adjustment package takes account of interdependence between different sectors of the economy and of the interests of the future generations. The implications of the environment debate of the 1970s on the time-bound and project-bound project analysis based on private cost and benefit considerations have been explored. This has been followed by a discussion of various environment-friendly solutions emerging from the economics of structural adjustment—rational pricing of resources, clear identification of private property rights and their rearrangement through free bargaining, and the 'polluter pays' principle of taxation supplemented by tradable emission permits. The chapter then deals with global issues such as the relationship between trade and environment and the use of the environment standard as a protectionist measure and the problems that arise when attempting to apply the environment economics of structural adjustment to solve global level issues. One section deals with the interesting question of the relationship between environment and development, as it has been debated over the past two-and-a-half decades.

Chapter 6, on East Asia, deals with issues relating to Japan, South Korea and Taiwan, the three countries with a reasonably large internal market, where the state has played an interventionist role in the course of development. A wide range of explanations for the astounding growth of the region, that has been sustained over more than three decades, has been considered, including land reform, repression of labour, human development in terms of high literacy and health levels, state role in promoting indigenous industries and exports, and a variety of other cultural and political factors, including the role of the bureaucracy. One section deals with the technological aspects. Another section examines in depth, the World Bank study on this region's development, and the related controversies, the main one being whether their success can be attributed to doing the opposite of what the Bank theology advocated.

Chapter 7 looks at the experiences of a cross-section of countries from three continents, most of them operating under structural adjustment for a certain period of time. First, it looks at the two island cities of East Asia, left out of the previous chapter because, without a land mass and an internal market of some size, their policy options are different. Then come the countries of Southeast Asia—Thailand, Malaysia, Indonesia and the Philippines—three of them having done well over the past two decades, while the fourth one has hardly grown. In the case of the first three, we ask whether there are explanations other than adjustment for their success, and for the fourth one we ask why, despite considerable support from BWIs, it has failed to show results. The next section deals with countries in Sub-Saharan Africa, which have a long association with structural adjustment, but seem to have become poorer over these years. The Latin American section deals with Chile, Brazil and Mexico; Chile being the only one with some measure of success with adjustment. Brazil is presented as a puzzle, particularly in the course of 25 years of high growth during 1955–80, when it was accompanied by a high level of inflation. The chapter ends with an examination of the Indian case, and attempts to answer two questions: (*a*) why India has failed when East Asia succeeded, though both followed more or less similar policies and (*b*) what has been its experience with adjustment since 1991.

All these issues have been critically analysed and the broad conclusions summarised in Chapter 8.

two

The new political economy of development

The main objective of this chapter is to present an outline of the main ideas of the New Political Economy (NPE), that provides the theoretical underpinning to the structural adjustment programme (SAP) of the World Bank which shall be discussed in the following chapter, and then, to subject these ideas to a critical examination.

The literature on NPE is vast and is steadily growing, and as one would expect in the case of a school of thought, veering round the main theme are interesting variations as also subtle, and not too subtle, differences on some of the major issues within the school. Some describe it as the neo-classical economic theory of politics (Toye, 1993: 324). Some see it more specifically as a political cousin of structural adjustment, setting out political preconditions for its success. According to some others it is a cocktail of the Marxist concept of the state without its class analysis, with the Liptonian theory of urban bias thrown in and blended with neo-classical economics (Toye, 1993: 321). Some even object to its description as a new theory while some others, mainly political scientists, see in it a fudged understanding of the political world and its processes by ignorant economists. Indeed, NPE contains various shades and colours, such as public choice, collective choice, social choice or rational choice theories, all of which attempt to provide explanations for the paradox of what they consider are irrational economic outcomes of rational political or social choices (Grindle, 1991: 43).

We begin our discussion with a summary presentation of the main ideas of the NPE school, followed by a critical analysis of these. Then follows a comparison of these ideas with those of the development economists and the Marxists, the two competing schools, which in turn is followed by an attempt at a political–economic analysis of NPE itself. Finally, we present the main conclusions of this chapter.

The new political economy

Self-interest, group behaviour, distributional coalitions

At the base of NPE, following the footsteps of Hayek, is the concept of rationality that choices are made in accordance with the perceived self-interest of an individual (Hayek, 1949). In the formulation of Downs, a father figure of this school of thought, the type of economic reasoning applied in the neo-classical economic models based on self-interest can be applied to every institution run by men (Downs, 1957: 283). Transition from individual self-interest to group interest, a major concern of Olson and NPE in general, takes place when these two are not in conflict, that is, 'if the individuals in some category or class had a sufficient degree of self-interest and if they all agreed on some common interest' (Olson, 1982: 17). Generally speaking, a rational self-interested individual has no incentive to contribute to the provision of public good if he can do without it. This is more likely to be the case where there is no close and direct connection between his contribution and the social good that results (Hindess, 1988: 14). He will not join a union or pay taxes and would rather enjoy being a free rider of higher wages from collective action or contribution by others, unless not being a member or tax-payer confers some disadvantages (e.g., social exclusion or imprisonment) that are, in his reckoning, more costly than the amount he will have to pay as union subscription or taxes.

Perception of common interest becomes easier when the group is small in size and has a clearly defined goal. Otherwise, there would be an inevitable tendency to enjoy a 'free ride' (Olson, 1982: 18). Further, the larger the number involved, the greater would be the heterogeneity of interests, and the more difficult it would become to bargain and negotiate among members within a special-interest group for agreeing to a common position. A cartel of a very small number of oligopolists is likely to function more coherently in its group interest, when dealing with bureaucracy or the consumers, than a multitude of rice farmers facing mill-owners or traders. In other words, the smallness of a group, which also implies a greater homogeneity of interest and approach, makes it more effective than the larger 'catch all' types.

An interesting feature of NPE analysis is its emphasis on 'distributional coalitions' and their implications. An interest group, to succeed, would engage in various types of lobbying and campaigning in order to influence public policy in its favour. Every interest group seeks to raise its share in the national product, and for this purpose it is prepared to undertake any type of action, legal or illegal, moral or immoral. One way it can succeed in its endeavour is to form coalitions with other interest groups on specific issues, so that their aggregate strength and vigorous campaign can overwhelm those in authority to change the rules or legislation in their favour.

A major question raised by NPE is whether such pursuit of self-interest by individuals and interest groups operating in an economy, with conflicting aims and with unequal access to decision-makers, brings about a desirable optimum allocation of resources for the country as a whole. Until NPE, an assumption underlying neo-classical micro-economics was that the sum of individual welfare and utility maximisation adds up to social welfare. Olson, however, disagrees. Indeed, as his analysis attempts to show, the former would lead to an irrational economic outcome. The special-interest groups will only cater to the interests of their members, and thus, will reduce the efficiency and aggregate income of the society as a whole in which they operate (Olson, 1982: 47).

Coalitions, because of the diversity of interests they represent to achieve a common aim, would tend to have a crowded agenda and, thus, would be rigid and slow in decision-making. Once a bargain has been struck, it would be difficult to change the terms within a short period, even if that becomes necessary because of altered market or technology conditions (Olson, 1982: 59). Further, distributional coalitions, once big enough to succeed, will tend to limit the diversity of interests and values of their membership, and make themselves more and more exclusive (Olson, 1982: 69). In other words, the politically rational goals of private interests and public officials will 'lead to ends that are economically irrational'

(Grindle and Thomas, 1991: 25). While economic competition in the market generates efficiency in resource allocation, competition in the political market based on self-interested behaviour generates a negative outcome (Grindle and Thomas, 1991: 25–26).

On balance, special-interest organisations, collusions and their coalitions will reduce efficiency and aggregate income and make political life more divisive (Olson, 1982: 47). Their lobbying will look after their own segmental interest and not that of population as a whole. They will induce the government to make rules and pass legislation that would benefit them exclusively. As a consequence, over time, laws and regulations would become more complex, bringing lawyers into the field to find loopholes in the laws for the benefit of interest groups or to find ways of plugging these on behalf of the government. 'There can be an unending process of loophole discoveries and closures with the complexity and cost of regulation continually increasing.' The coalitions will strive to capture the largest possible share of national income at the cost of the vast majority who are poor and unorganised (Olson, 1982: 69–73).

The only exceptions to this are 'encompassing organisations', such as unions representing most earners in a society, or a lobbying organisation representing all firms, who, because of the sheer number of those they represent, would have an interest in national well-being that would also further their own interests (Olson, 1982: 63). In some cases, a special-interest group that is small, in terms of the size of the economy of the population, can be quite large and significant in the context of a particular society or factory or industry, e.g., a union of all engineers in an industry. But in case of encompassing organisations, the success of the organisation will depend largely on its ability to frame rules that benefit the vast majority of its members or avoid conflicts, for instance, the seniority rule in promotions. To be effective, a cartel has to fix both price and quantity, but in this situation the encompassing organisations tend to fix only the price of a product, in case of a cartel, or wages in case of a union, leaving the quantity to be determined by the market (Olson, 1982: 48–59). In the case of the labour market, that would imply the presence of unemployed on the one hand and the prevalence of high wages for the employed on the other. Wages would not be adjusted downward to allow the market to be cleared and to make unemployment disappear.

Olson favours free entry and absence of all types of barriers, as it eventually eliminates all shelters and monopoly profits, but takes the view that this by itself would not bring about perfect competition or Pareto efficiency (Olson, 1982: 60–67). He gives the example of British India as a country operating completely according to the principles of laissez-faire, whose rate of growth was also one of the lowest among the countries, particularly when comparison was made with Japan where the state was interventionist. The laissez-faire ideology, therefore, left something out—the negative impact of 'distributional coalitions' (Olson, 1982: 179). The larger the number of such distributional coalitions, the greater would be the complexity of regulations to protect their interests and therefore, the role of the government (Olson, 1982: 73).

Interest groups in traditional Western political analysis

In the traditional Western political analysis it was held that competition between interest groups, for a share of the state resources and privileges, was desirable as it made the polity plural and sensitive to diverse views and opinions. The outcome of lobbying by various pressure groups, i.e., the formation of a coalition of interest groups and bargaining between them to arrive at a consensus, all part of a democratic political process, was a political equilibrium that brought about a balance between those interests. Participation, in a broad sense, implied as much a high turnout in elections and a choice in favour of parties or individuals holding preferred views, as membership in a variety of interest groups—from 'save the whale' campaigners to business groups demanding a ban on certain imports—each campaigning, lobbying and otherwise trying to influence decision-making in its favour.

In this literature, such competition between interest groups in the political arena was taken as analogous to competition between economic agents in a market place in the neo-classical framework. The interest groups—of consumers, unions, production groups, civil servants, political parties, regional, ethnic, and other political formations—were seen as agents (like individual enterprises in the field of economy) operating in a free political market and being involved in bargaining for power and access to resources. Liberal economic views corresponded with liberal political views, and competition—in economic or political markets—for a share of

GNP or some specific resources or privileges was seen as desirable and welfare maximising. It was held that to the extent a person might belong to more than one interest group, and these groups might overlap in their areas of concern, the conflicts would be minimised (Grindle, 1991: 46–47). In contrast, since such free expression of views would not be tolerated under an authoritarian regime, these would not be known to the decision-makers and hence, there would be every likelihood of the sum total of decisions by such a regime being opposed to the welfare of the country as a whole.

Where NPE departs from this pluralist tradition is in its view that lobbying by interest groups with the objective of influencing decision-making in its favour is not a positive feature of a political–economic process. Here rational political choice is seen as an impediment to achieving the collective economic good (Grindle, 1991: 49; Olson, 1982: 47). As Olson shows, for such lobbies to succeed, the interest groups would have to be small, relatively homogeneous, and powerful, and the decisions in their favour are unlikely to be in the overall interest of the economy (Olson, 1982: Chapter 3). They are likely to form 'distributional coalitions' and seek various types of state intervention in the economy, e.g., controls against imports and other competitors and licences and permits for themselves for more lucrative activities, at the cost of welfare loss for the economy as a whole (ibid., 1982: 59–73).

The high cost of acquiring information by an individual makes him vulnerable to lobbying. A voter is 'rationally ignorant' because the cost of acquiring relevant information for decision-making is too high in relation to the impact a single voter can make to the electoral outcome. A lobbyist brings to him processed information in a summarised form which an individual cannot easily acquire for himself by going back to the data source, and, in the process, helps to influence the latter's decision. On the other hand, some individuals can gain from intimate knowledge, such as politicians, journalists, and social scientists (Olson, 1982: 26).

An important distinction is made in the discussion between the state and the civil society. It is held that the civil society has deep roots in the history of the developed Western democracies. Articulation of diverse demands and interests, by way of lobbying, campaigning and voting in the elections is, for this reason, an important component of the political system in these states. In this historical and cultural context, interest groups play a positive rôle and help to bring about a balance between different interests as also between the ruler and the ruled. In contrast: 'The modern state can be thought of as a contrivance or invention of administrative technology, capable of being transported or imported into societies that did not possess it.' But when such a transplant is undertaken, the state without roots in the history of its country, interacts differently with its civil society, and tends to assume an increasingly authoritarian character as one moves away from the citadels of civil society (Findlay, 1991: 17–18).

While critical of all types of 'distributional coalition', the main targets of NPE are organised trade unions. Olson raises the question: Why is there more unemployment among groups with lower skill and productivity (e.g., teenagers, or disadvantaged racial minorities) while it is the least among the highly skilled workers? He then seeks an explanation that should be consistent with both 'boom' and 'bust' and also with the substantial difference between societies. He concludes: 'The main group that can have an interest in preventing the mutually profitable transactions between the involuntarily unemployed and employers is the workers with the same or competitive skills.' Though he also adds that 'the only other group that could have such an interest would be a monopsonistic [or buyers'] cartel or lobby of employers: it would need to block mutually advantageous transactions between individual employers and workers to keep wages below competitive levels', the emphasis here and in many other parts of his study is on the negative role of the organised workers. They are made responsible for the stickiness of wages, and for not letting the market be cleared. When wages are set above market-clearing levels, the argument goes, it is inevitable that the employer will choose and attract the more skilled, and, inevitably, the less skilled and young would go without jobs (Olson, 1982: 195–205).

However, wage agreements are usually for a three-year period. This implies that in periods of inflation, wages would not rise correspondingly and prices will be closer to the level for market clearing. 'An unexpected inflation therefore reduces the losses from monopoly due to cartelization and lobbying and the degree of involuntary unemployment. In a period of unexpected inflation an economy with a high level of special-interest organization and collusion will be more productive than it normally is.' Unless, of course, the rate of inflation is so high, as also uncertainty about future inflation, that workers insist on indexing their wages (Olson, 1982: 206). The fact that the impact of inflation is inequitable and that it makes the society more unequal does not concern Olson.

Rent-seeking behaviour

The question then arises: What is the cost of such distortions induced by interest groups on the economy as a whole? For those who hold special-interest groups guilty for these distortions, the disappointing finding by a highly respected neo-classical trade theorist, Arnold Harberger, was that social losses from monopoly and tariffs and certain other distortions are relatively small—only a 0.5 per cent loss from 100 per cent distortion—in relation to national income (Taylor, 1995: 40; Toye, 1993: 327). Olson, however, disputes this and argues that such a loss can be colossal, as decision-making will be slow and the economy will not quickly adapt to change and new technology (Olson, 1982: 46).

A more substantial intervention in this debate comes from Anne Krueger, in terms of what she describes as rent-seeking behaviour. She argues that, in addition to the static welfare loss due to, say, import control, there would be another kind of welfare loss, from the process of lobbying for import licences themselves. Lobbying would involve diversion of manpower and resources from other, more productive activities. These rent-seeking activities—for licences and permits, for example—would distort allocation of resources and make the economy inefficient (Krueger, 1990: Chapter 7).

However, the NPE theorists take care to distinguish rent-seeking from rent creation; the latter being seen as a positive feature. Economic rent is, to put it simply, receipt in excess of opportunity cost. In other words, even without such economic rent the resource concerned would have been deployed to that particular employment. Economic rent is a genuine social surplus, over and above what would have attracted that particular factor in any case, and plays a dynamic role in the economy. The economic reward paid to an inventor for his machine is essential for progress. Attracted by economic rent, entrepreneurs undertake resource relocation that prompts economic growth. On the other hand, negative economic rent induces resources to be converted to alternative use and will ensure that no additional resource is shifted in its favour. Eventually, with no barrier to entry, and increasing competition, economic rent disappears. Here economic rent creates added value in the economy, rather than diverting the value that already exists (Buchanan, 1980: 3–7).

Rent-seeking, in contrast, appears when entry to the market is restricted and the rent, rather than getting dissipated by way of competition, perpetuates. A firm seeking a barrier to entry is rent-seeking. The presence of rent in such a restricted market will, therefore, induce firms seeking entry to invest efforts, time and other resources to influence the government in their favour. However, barriers necessary to protect individual rights, persons and property and for enforcing voluntarily negotiated private contracts, are justified and are not construed as rent-seeking by the protagonists of NPE (Buchanan, 1980: 7–9).

The analysis of rent-seeking can be extended to a variety of fields, e.g., preparation for the civil service examination, spending time and money in acquiring knowledge, most of which would not be relevant to the work if appointed. In the latter case, the temptation for such socially unproductive investment is the higher level of expected earnings—from both legitimate and less legitimate sources. In contrast, in the 'ancien regime' in France or in the pre-1860 British army, jobs could be purchased. Tullock justifies such job purchase on the ground that the government got some money by selling positions and the countries concerned had not done badly because of this. The job was tradable; a person in a job could eventually sell the job to someone at a high price if he performed well and got a high enough income (Tullock, 1980: 20–22).

Sometimes, according to this view, the damaging impact of rent-seeking can be reduced, if not entirely eliminated, by suitable policies, e.g., when tariff replaces import licensing, when flow of information about who benefits from it is increased, when moral sanction is applied, or, more decisively, when the government opts for liberalisation and privatisation. Enlightened technocrats insulated from the influence of interest groups have also been proposed as a solution. Some others take the view that catastrophes like a military coup, revolution, invasion or war are some of the major means of getting rid of rent-seekers (Grindle, 1991: 57–58). While rent-seeking is directly linked with the scope and range of governmental activity, it is possible to visualise political allocation without rent-seeking, where all persons have an equal access to the scarcity value created by barriers to entry and state intervention, e.g., by way of lottery or auction (Tullock, 1980: 9–11).

Bhagwati, in his extensive work on this subject, has added Directly Unproductive Profit-Seeking (DUP) activities as a variation to the 'rent-seeking' theme, emphasising on tariff, revenue or monopoly-seeking activities as well as tariff evasion and smuggling (Bhagwati, 1991: 129). In his studies, Bhagwati discusses three types of DUP: policy-triggered (e.g., Voluntary Export Restraints [VERs] or rent-seeking activities), policy-evading (e.g., smuggling) and policy-influencing (e.g., demanding tariff on certain imports). However, unlike the analysis of rent-seeking by Krueger and others, Bhagwati is willing to accept even wasteful activities as beneficial in certain situations, e.g., in case of immiserisation (Bhagwati, 1991: 129–31).

Further, as his co-author in a number of publications, T.N. Srinivasan argues, referring to Krueger's recommendation for replacing import licences by tariff in order to minimise rent-seeking: 'To the extent open and free play of interest-groups in political arena is part of a democratic process that has systemic value, the resources spent by individuals and groups in lobbying for their interests can not be viewed as wasteful' (Srinivasan, 1991: 145). In their work, both he and Bhagwati disagree with Krueger's view that rent (or revenue)-seeking, by its very nature, plays a negative role and causes welfare loss. Srinivasan argues that 'resource-using political scramble for tariff revenues need not always result in an additional welfare loss over and above the primary welfare loss imposed by the tariff and in fact can reduce the latter'. Unlike import quota,

> a price-based intervention such as tariff leaves the quantity of import to be determined by the market . . . . To the extent the diversion of resources to revenue seeking reduces the resources devoted to the production of costlier import-substitutes (compared to the situation with tariffs but no revenue seeking), clearly the deadweight loss due to the tariff is reduced. The reduction in the output of import substitutes may even be large enough to bring it below its level under free trade (Srinivasan, 1991: 129).

In other words, to the extent such rent (or revenue)-seeking diverts resources away from efforts towards import substitution, it helps to avoid some welfare loss. We can see, from what we said above, that even the protagonists of NPE differ amongst themselves as to what constitutes rent-seeking (or DUP) and whether rent-seeking (or DUP) is always undesirable.

Justifiable coalition of potential beneficiaries of reform

However, not all interest groups or coalitions are decried by NPE. Its proponents argue for mobilising support for structural reform by bringing together the potential and actual beneficiaries of such reform. To quote a World Bank publication: 'Adjustment programs should thus be designed and presented with an awareness of the importance for political sustainability of building a coalition of groups benefiting from and expanding as a result of the reform process' (Webb and Shariff, 1992: 84).

A considerable amount of literature exists that identifies such beneficiaries of reform—mainly two, not mutually exclusive groups—the rural–agricultural masses and those producing exportables. Structural reform takes the position that the policies in most third world countries favour the urban better-off while discriminating against the agriculturists and the rural population in general. The policy of food procurement at low, state-prescribed prices and its sale at subsidised prices to urban consumers, according to this view, is a reflection of 'urban bias', the influence of the urban middle class and the rich over the decision-making process. Such bias against agricultural/rural areas is inequitable and inefficient and distorts the allocation of resources. Structural reform calls for the withdrawal of such price regulations and controls and favours paying a price for the produce to the agriculturist that emerges from a free play of demand and supply.

The second aspect of this view is that the policies of import control and export promotion operate against the tradables, making them costlier than these would be otherwise. These regulations and subsidies take away advantages of the commodities that would otherwise enjoy a comparative advantage while pushing those items for export that do not enjoy such an advantage. What NPE prescribes is the formation of an alliance of all these potential beneficiaries of reform—agriculturists and traders in items enjoying comparative advantage—to provide the regime with a political base (Nelson, 1988: 107–18).

The theory of the state

NPE does not take the state as a neutral or a benevolent institution. This constitutes a serious break with the pluralist political tradition in the West. To pluralists, the state is more or less neutral, and in its functioning, no group is systematically discriminated against. State institutions and rules help to organise competition between interest groups, to establish modes for conflict resolution, and to arbitrate between competitors. In this conception of the state, the initiative lies with the interest groups, who mobilise people, form coalitions, and attempt to influence decision-makers (Grindle and Thomas, 1991: 23). Economists generally looked upon the state as 'that agency in the division of labour which has as its proper function the maximisation of social welfare' (Downs, 1957: 282) and, excepting for the Marxists, avoided political analysis. Public policy was given exogenously and the economy had to operate within it. The development economists went a step further than treating the state as neutral; to them the state was benevolent and had the welfare of the citizenry at heart

NPE, in contrast, takes a great deal of interest in politics, because, according to it, any economic policy, to be effective, has to be politically sustainable. In the specific context of NPE, the policies its protagonists have in mind are those incorporated in the SAP. The question, therefore, arises, what kind of political regime, system or leadership is likely to be committed to structural adjustment, to vigorously attempt its implementation, and to ensure its success by sustaining it long enough through the twists and turns of the economic and political life of the country.

However, the NPE analysis of the state begins with a negative premise, that elected leaders are principally interested in remaining in power (Downs, 1957: 28), and in deriving rent by providing access to public goods, services and regulations. They have no principled position on any issue, and will take a policy position that increases their chances of remaining in power (Grindle, 1991: 49). They are, thus, no longer detached from the market, and are endogenised (Bhagwati, 1991: 141). Earlier, governments were taken as 'platonic guardians' of national interest, but 'now the governments are depicted as centres of corruption, policy failures, rent-seeking, ignorance etc., while the Bank has acquired a self-confident position of being in possession of the Holy Grail of good policies and an ability to sort out the "good boys" from the "bad boys"' (Singer, 1995: 21). While earlier the development economists of the 1950s to the 1970s held as if the state could do no wrong, under NPE the state can do nothing right (Streeten, 1995: 176). In contrast with the Adam Smithian 'invisible hand' of the market, which balances demand with supply at a certain price and optimises allocation of resources, the 'invisible foot' of the state encourages DUP activities that distort allocation and make the economy inefficient, according to NPE (Grindle, 1996: 5). The state uses the legal monopoly of the use of violence (Lal and Myint, 1996: 263) in favour of dominant interest groups. It is the fountain of privileges of all sorts, which are marketable in exchange for payments to the political leaders and bureaucrats.

The protagonists of NPE differ amongst themselves with regard to the form and content of state power. Some see the state as standing only for the dominant interest groups, but some others attribute a certain amount of autonomy to the rulers in making decisions and implementing them (Lal and Myint, 1996: 11). The latter do not see the state simply as a passive agent of the society at large, nor as an executive committee of the ruling class, as Marxists would see it, but as an independent and dynamic force. With interest groups or classes locking their horns in an inconclusive battle, the state—a dynasty, a dictator, or a ruling clique—can pursue independent policies of aggrandisement that may diverge from the interests of each of the classes themselves (Findlay, 1991: 15). Bhagwati introduced a third category: puppet governments who choose objective functions on the guidance of technocrat–bureaucrats (Bhagwati, 1991: 153). But in almost all these formulations, the predatory character of the state is emphasised: those running the state at various levels, from the political ruler at the top, through bureaucrats and technocrats, to those at the bottom of state hierarchy, are only aiming at furthering their own specific or group interests. The interest of the country and the welfare of its people do not figure in their agenda.

The case for authoritarian regimes

Between different types of states, according to NPE, the authoritarian ones can make things work, while those with too many competing interest groups at loggerheads with one another, and each indulging in rent-seeking behaviour, might find decision-making slow and nearly impossible in certain situations. Moreover, democracy generates demands on the state and tends to favour consumption over investment, thus stifling growth. Further, in most of the LDCs articulated interest groups covering a wide spectrum of interests are conspicuous by their absence, while a small number of privileged minority groups are better placed to impose their will on the decision-makers. In the NPE literature, trade unions of organised workers seeking wages that are much higher than the average earnings of the multitude of unorganised workers, industrial interests seeking import control to keep foreign competitors out, urban dwellers seeking price control on food to keep their own living costs low while denying the rural agriculturist his share of GDP, are some of the more frequently mentioned interest groups holding sway in the LDCs. In this situation, free play of interest groups would lead to large-scale rent-seeking at an enormous loss of welfare to the economy.

To the extent an authoritarian regime can more effectively keep the privileged groups in control and can rise above them, the welfare loss from rent-seeking would be minimised. There would be less distributionist pressure and greater ability to extract resources for development and cope with short-term costs of adjustment (Hoggard, 1996: 209). Comparing authoritarian and democratic societies, Grindle takes the view that in the case of countries with histories of political instability where democratic institutions have been recently introduced, leaders face a more risky and constrained environment of political competition, and, therefore, changes are slower to emerge than in the authoritarian ones (Grindle, 1996: 193–94).

Another justification for the authoritarian solution is the painful process of structural reform itself. There is a consensus that the process of adjustment is likely to be painful, involving low income and unemployment for a number of years. To sustain reform despite these factors, the ruling elite would have to show a significant degree of political determination or even ruthlessness and a capacity to withstand unpopularity for a time. A democratic regime exposed to public criticism and subjected to voting is unlikely to succeed in such a political environment, while an autocratic regime can have the capacity to ride over those difficult years. Lipsett was among the traditional political scientists working on LDCs who took the view that authoritarian regimes, by suppressing civil liberties and preserving distributional inequality (which promotes saving) help to sustain the drive towards growth, and are more capable of curtailing public expenditure and using it for productive purposes (Lipsett, 1959).

The role of the bureaucratic and technocratic elite

However, NPE concedes that not any authoritarian state is capable of rising above interest groups and sustaining structural reform in the initial difficult years. A precondition for the success of such a regime is that, not only the political rulers but the bureaucrat–technocrat elite too is somewhat insulated from the interest groups and is capable of taking an objective view in the overall interest of the economy. Better still, if these bureaucrat–technocrats have been exposed to global experience, e.g., spending some time with the World Bank or IMF, and, thus, can take a macro, global view of the issues involved. Their success would be largely based on their ability to promote saving and investment, to establish and maintain ground rules for open market competition, and to set up an objective performance criteria for firms and industries. Export performance is adjudged as an important, objective criterion as the efficiency of a firm would be tested in a highly competitive arena without the comfort of state support.

This view regarding the role of the bureaucrat–technocrat elite complements the Fund–Bank contemptuous view of the politicians and the political parties as narrow-minded, self-serving and rent-seeking. Insulation from the political pressure groups is seen as a necessity to establish objective indicators of performance and to take a wider view of the issues at stake (Mosley et al., 1991: 15).

Some proponents of NPE focus on the competition that exists between various departments of the same government. The state is far from a unitary actor with clearly defined goals; much of the struggle on policies and implementation is within the government, between agencies and departments (Nelson, 1991: 274). One model depicts the conflict between the finance and spending departments; the former attempting to impose adjustment on the latter. It concludes that the adjustment programme has a great chance of success when budget authorities have a veto over spending (Hoggard, 1991: 273).

Some studies also focus on contradictions that exist between the executive, taking a broader view of national interest, and the legislature in a majoritarian state, which is dominated by sectional interests. This contradiction often forces governments to formally adopt measures that they themselves never mean to implement. Bhagwati refers to porous protection models where protection is not intended, but the government, for political reasons, does not wish to antagonise the industry seeking protection, e.g., footwear and textiles in the case of the United States. Here it is easy to cheat on rules of origin, and imports can be passed on as products of countries not covered by VER or the Multi-fibre Agreement (MFA). From the point of view of the government, 'that is precisely its attractiveness'. If the executive favours free trade but the legislators are keen to protect sectional interests, the former would prefer porous protection (Bhagwati, 1991: 172–73). There can be other situations where the government itself ditches a formally adopted popular policy to appease sectional interest, e.g., non-implementation of land reform despite public rhetoric in its support. Another interesting example of the latter comes from Olson; the government's formal decision to make the tax system as progressive as it is popular, coupled with porous legislation that provides the rich with good lawyers to avoid tax payment (Olson, 1982: 27).

In other words, liberal neo-classical economics requires, for its success, its political obverse—an illiberal, authoritarian political structure—a ruling party (or leader) which can rise above interest groups, make decisions and impose them on the rest of the society, and sustain unpopular but desirable policies over what is likely to be a number of difficult years. While more politically liberal regimes do not necessarily associate themselves with market-oriented and economically competitive pricing policies (Healey et al., 1992: 18), the authoritarian regimes, for their own reasons, are likely to be more market-friendly than the democratic ones.

Timing and pacing of structural reform

There is some dispute among the adherents of the NPE view as to the timing and pacing of structural reform. Some take the view that 'reforms should be introduced as quickly as is economically and technically possible' to take advantage of the honeymoon period following the takeover by a new regime (Webb and Shariff, 1992: 84). Two further arguments are advanced in support of such a 'big bang' approach. First, improvements brought about following temporary dislocation during the change over of the regime would be attributed to the structural reform and would enhance the credibility of the reform and the regime. Second, the quicker the reform and the achievement of a certain degree of success, the more difficult would it be for the opponents of reform and the regime to coalesce and undermine reform (Webb and Shariff, 1992: 84; Grindle, 1996: 194). Further, such reform should yield results pretty fast; a slow and painful adjustment process might alienate the population and play into the hands of the opposing forces.

On the other hand, there are those, the gradualists, who argue that the reform, to be successful eventually, should be carefully implemented, counting every step and not attempting a short cut that does not exist. Any failure resulting from fast-track action in the early stage might jeopardise the reform process as a whole. To quote Dornbusch: 'Avoiding a key battle over immediate credibility and spending the political capital to broaden the reforms (even with moderate and rising inflation) seem preferable to losing the battle early on.' He further adds: 'The credibility, I would argue, comes from the accomplishment of reform, not from a decisive recession showdown' (Dornbusch, 1992: 114). The shock approach can work if there is excess capacity in the economy and the possibility of a high level of financial inflow within a short time; if that is not the case, the shock treatment might produce its opposite—a revolution, or a coup, or, at the least, a massive outburst of protest, perhaps leading to the abandonment of the adjustment programme by the leadership (Nelson, 1988: 125). A longer term also implies the opportunity for phasing and for mid-course adjustment, taking into account the performance and its perception by the people (Nelson, 1988: 84–85).

The concept of ownership

The SAPs suffer from a high mortality or interruption rate and the progress is at best patchy (Killick, 1994: 1–2), but 'the most common of all the reasons for failure are internal political pressures, which lead the government to postpone coercive action until the economic crisis is acute and/or dilute or abandon programs before the necessary economic adjustments are completed' (Nelson, 1988: 82). Structural adjustment is not understood intuitively, and it carries a high risk when it offends powerful interests including bureaucrats; political leaders tend to assess the risks from stabilisation and structural adjustment with possible gains and can get easily scared.

One way forward, according to some political economists at the World Bank is to devise the programme in such a way that it is owned by the political leaders; so that no feeling is generated that it has been imposed from outside (Corbo et al., 1992: 13). The idea behind the Policy Framework Paper (PFP), which incorporates the conditionalities as declarations or decisions by the governments applying for support themselves, and which is prepared in 'consultation' with the World Bank and IMF and is approved promptly after its submission, is to carry such an impression (see Chapter 3).

Structural adjustment, given its character, as we have already noted, is bound to be a painful process. The important question is, how to sustain such reform over a long period in the face of the hostility such a programme is likely to encounter. Further, such pain is unlikely to be distributed uniformly—for most it would be relatively more painful, while the potential long-term beneficiaries are likely to be in the minority, at any rate at the beginning of the adjustment process. In this situation, it is inevitable that various interest groups will try to outwit one another, if possible to secure a free or less costly ride than others. Such a 'war of attrition' can eventually reach a stage where the government, unable to reconcile various conflicting interests, would be forced to abandon the programme (Kiguel and Liviatan, 1992: 109). One way of obviating this is to provide, in the words of John Williamson, 'a sweetener that will help the reformers to retain political support during the difficult and perhaps lenghty period before the reform starts to bear fruit' (Williamson, 1992b: 21). A wide variety of sweeteners have been deployed in the past, such as the safety net or renewal programme to help the unemployed to get re-trained for another job. Williamson also suggests loans by Western governments to bribe bad governments in order 'to get off the backs of their long suffering citizens' (Williamson, 1992b). The emphasis on equity, tax reform and bigger allocations for health and education are some of the others, though land reform, a more obvious one, is generally not prescribed by the Fund–Bank doctors (Williamson, 1992b).

Crisis leading to adjustment

In many cases a heavy dosage of structural reform follows a severe economic crisis. Such a crisis enables the regime to change course or make way for the entry of another, more authoritarian regime, more determined and capable of undertaking and implementing such reform in the face of popular resistance. To quote an important World Bank publication: 'Crisis can increase the likelihood of reform, by raising the perception within and outside the government that policies must change, by weakening anti-reform interest-groups and by increasing the willingness to rely on the technocrats' (Webb and Shariff, 1992: 84).

In these situations it is possible for the succeeding regime to put the blame for all the economic ills on the previous one and to project its own harsh measures as ones that are unavoidable under the circumstances (Nelson, 1988: 99). To quote the same World Bank publication again:

> When new economic teams or governments have come to power and the policies of the previous team or government have been discredited, there is more leeway to undertake reform measures . . . . Often the strongest political asset of the new teams and governments is people's dissatisfaction with previous policies and their willingness to try something fresh (the honeymoon effect), as exemplified in Poland and Argentina (Webb and Shariff, 1992: 84).

NPE and conditionalities of structural adjustment

This, in a nutshell, is what NPE is all about. It is not difficult to derive the link between this theory and the specific conditionalities contained in standard SAPs including the one operating in India. One major objective of these conditionalities is to eliminate or minimise rent-seeking. Since the latter is associated with controls and other restrictive measures, doing away with all controls in a liberalisation package is a major way of handling such behaviour. Rent-seeking, according to this analysis, is associated with the strategy of import substitution and corresponding import licences and high tariffs; so this should also go. Integration with the global market, the entry of foreign competitors, and the parity between internal and external prices for various commodities, would force the internal economic agents to sharpen their competitive edge and to shift production towards those items for which the country enjoys a comparative advantage. Globalisation or export orientation is, therefore, a must for success. Another added argument is that, such globalisation will provide the economy with an objective test of success with various lines of production. If globalisation results in the closing down of an industry, that will establish that the country does not enjoy comparative advantage in that industry. Pruning of such inefficient industries will help to divert resources to others that are in line with that country's comparative advantage.

Further, since rent-seeking is promoted by the existence of a large public sector which has a tendency to grow over time, privatisation is a way of reversing this trend. Compulsion to keep fiscal deficit below a certain percentage point in relation to GDP would be another way of keeping the government slim and fit. Coming to distributional coalitions, such as trade unions or hawala operators, anything that obstructs the clearing of a market should be done away with, whether it is labour legislation which is not permitting closure of factories, or directed credit or investment in banks or rigid exchange rates for the local currency. Prices should be right, flexible in both directions, and should succeed in balancing demand with supply, whether they are for commodities, labour, land, foreign exchange, credit or what have you. Market, and not the state, should rule, in order to go as far as possible near Pareto optimality in the allocation of resources.

A critical analysis of NPE

Self-interest: Not the sole determinant of human behaviour

Let us begin our critical examination of NPE with its most basic assumption: that human behaviour is solely guided by self-interest, and that is what constitutes rationality. According to this school, 'through the lens of self-interest, politics becomes endogenous to policy choice and can be modeled along with more traditional economic variables' (Grindle, 1991: 44). While not disputing the role of self-interest in motivating individual, group or class action, one can dispute whether it is the sole determinant of human behaviour even in a largely selfish society. The history of mankind abounds with examples where people have risen above their own narrow interests to sacrifice a great deal, including their lives, for a cause. NPE does not explain philanthropy, martyrdom, nationalism, ethnicity, giving and taking life in ugly communal outbursts, or fights between two groups of football fans not involved in gambling. People can and do go beyond their immediate self-interest quite regularly. Further, the joining of a group (e.g., the 'save the baby seal' campaign) is not merely prompted by the desire to get a share of the national cake. Emotions, sentiments, concern for others and enjoyment in being a part of a larger group are matters that go beyond personal book-keeping and cost–benefit analysis. One can even go to the extent of saying that if rationality is defined only in terms of self-interest, the most rational behaviour should be an irrational one.

Taking the case of the 'rationally ignorant', half of the voters who do not visit the polling booth mentioned earlier; self-interest does not explain why the other half goes, when their own individual vote is a miniscule factor in the outcome. When the NPE analysts talk of bureaucrats and technocrats who can see beyond their own self-interest, they never explain how this is consistent with their own concept of rational choice. In another context, Olson includes 'moral satisfaction' from, say, contributing to a cause, in 'self-interest' as it provides the person with some sense of utility. He also mentions, while explaining why people join groups, that they value companionship and respect those with whom they interact (Olson, 1982: 19–23). However, in these cases, as Grindle observes, the concept of self-interest becomes effectively meaningless

(Grindle, 1991: 60). If doing good makes one feel good, to describe do-gooding as utility maximisation from a self-interested concern would be stretching the concept of 'self-interest' too far. It would also make the entire analysis of Olson irrelevant. Olson was not consistent and obviously self-contradictory when he tried to introduce moral arguments into a neat analytical framework based on individual self-interest.

Who is to undertake reform if all politicians are corrupt and rent-seeking?

Similarly, the idea that all politicians are corrupt and rent-seeking and are only interested in self-aggrandisement is highly simplistic. There are indeed politicians, perhaps many or even most, who are selfish, greedy and corrupt, but then there are also others who are selfless, with a vision or an ideology that motivates them and sustains them through tortures, incarcerations, humiliations and financial disasters. Here again one finds a logical inconsistency between this generalised characterisation of the political leaders and the expectation that the same leaders can be induced to carry out the reforms desired by NPE. How can the same narrow, selfish, amoral politicians be motivated to undertake policies that would take the country along the growth path, and through the pains and tribulations that accompany structural adjustment, with determination? Here NPE seems to have reached a dead-end (Toye, 1993: 323). As Streeten puts it: 'If the will to action is absent, there is no point in asking for the will to have the will' (Streeten, 1995: 178). Nelson more or less makes the same point when she says, 'Either the government has sufficient political will or it does not. If it does, political analysis is unnecessary; if it does not, there is not much to be done about it' (Nelson, 1988: 84). This negative and rather cynical attitude towards politics 'makes the task of explaining the potential for economic reform extremely difficult and limits the applicability of policy-relevant advice' (Grindle, 1991: 44).

Assuming that structural adjustment is beneficial for the country, why should a ruling elite introduce and implement it if this is not in line with its own self-interest? Why should a state, so far under the influence of rent-seeking urban dwellers, import substituting industrialists and rigid wage-protecting trade unionists, suddenly change course and opt for structural adjustment? Why should the individuals in control of the state stop milking it for their own good and suddenly get seized with policies that promote saving and investment? Or, for that matter, why should the people in general acquiesce to policies that would, at least in the short run, according to the protagonists of structural reform, involve hardship and deprivation for them while producing enough profit for the capitalist minority to make the reform a success?

Given this interpretation, the only way out is, as suggested by Olson and others, a catastrophic event or 'the appearance of wise statesmen or technocrats who, for unexplained reasons, exhibit behaviour that is politically irrational' (Grindle and Thomas, 1991: 26). But even after such a change, where is the guarantee that rent-seeking will not return (Grindle, 1991: 59)? Some, including Srinivasan, put an enormous amount of trust in the political leaders who, becoming increasingly aware of the negative economic and political consequences of rent-seeking, would do something to contain it. But they offer no explanation for the appearance of such leaders or 'their ability to escape the logic that binds ordinary mortals' (Grindle, 1991: 60).

How can an authoritarian state insulate itself from rent-seeking interest groups?

Similarly, it does not follow from the NPE analysis how an authoritarian state can insulate itself from rent-seeking special-interest groups. As the experience with the military and other types of authoritarian regimes shows, every regime has to seek and find coalitions of political support for survival. It has to favour some groups and oppose some others in order to work out a balance of forces that favours its continuance in power. The absence of parliamentary institutions does not necessarily obviate the need for such a balancing act, though the correlation of political forces, resulting coalitions supporting or opposing the regime and their character might be changing over time (Hoggard, 1994: 105; Toye, 1991: 117; Rapley, 1996: 140). In fact, regimes divorced from civil society become more dependent on external agencies, such as the World Bank (e.g., Rawling's Ghana), than those with a secure support base in the civil society (Toye, 1991: 117). Authoritarian regimes are no less corrupt or allocation-distorting as other types of regimes

(Taylor, 1995: 42). On the other hand, people living under corrupt and brutal regimes tend to disengage themselves from the state, parallel markets emerge and new, underground relationships are forged that run parallel to the formal state structure (Grindle, 1996: 7).

A recent study on Chile, a country that actually did well under structural adjustment and that too under a strong authoritarian rule, takes the view that 'free market economic reforms were not solely the creation of technocrats isolated from society by a strong state', and indeed involved close interaction between the state and capital. The change from the 'Chicago boy' regime of undiluted neo-liberalism in the early post-Allende years to a pragmatic neo-liberalism since the early 1980s came about only because the indigenous capitalists threatened to join the opposition if that policy was continued. The Chilean capitalists maintained cohesion and supported Pinochet, and the latter responded to capitalists and landlords and included them in the policy-making process (Silva, 1996: 206–16). Normally an indigenous capitalist class would not support a regime that is unresponsive to its demands unless they perceive a severe threat from below. In this case, given the background to the emergence of the Pinochet rule and the existence of a strong opposition, one would expect the indigenous capitalists to reconcile themselves to such authoritarian rule, but, as Silva shows, Pinochet did not stand above them when framing policies (Silva, 1996: 206–16).

The NPE is not consistent when it places high hopes on a high quality, objective and impartial bureaucratic and technocratic elite for initiating and sustaining structural reform. The inevitable question is, why the latter should be free from concern with self-interest and why should not they too seek to strike a bargain with interest groups for self-aggrandisement? There is also some ambiguity in the NPE literature as to the question whether the bureaucracy and the state should be neutral between various interest groups or should throw their weight behind the potential beneficiaries of reform in order to make the reform politically sustainable. Quite frequently one comes across NPE-based studies that do not hesitate to make both points without realising that these are not consistent with each other. If it is possible for the elite to become fully insulated from interest groups, and for the regime to sustain its programme through ups and downs, then why should it bother to build a coalition of supporters of reform? And if it does, would these be simple coalitions without distributional implications or would not these also be 'distribution coalitions'? In the latter, why would this distributional coalition of agriculturists and traders not behave like other distributional coalitions, i.e., slowing down decision-making, not letting the market be cleared and seeking rent?

Further, as Taylor argues, if the authoritarian generals, because of their total control over the country, are so efficient in keeping the government out of the market, what prevents them from taking over the market? 'The record of the Third World authoritarian states in avoiding corruption and distortions is not encouraging in this regard', he concludes (Taylor, 1995: 42). Generals ousting corrupt politicians in a coup, and making trains run in time at the beginning, usually end up being worse than those they replace, as the experience of many countries—from Pakistan and Bangladesh in Asia to Central American Republics through Africa south of the Sahara—confirms.

No less surprising is the idea that the political leaders, being what they are according to NPE, would actually stand aside and allow the technocrat-bureaucrats to work on their own, free from interference. It is not clear why the top leaders should relinquish control over allocation of resources which is so essential for maintaining the loyalty of their factions, irrespective of whether these are majoritarian or authoritarian states (Nelson, 1988: 102). As Grindle admits, NPE provides 'no logically apparent means of moving from bad to better' (Grindle, 1991: 58). Why should the political elite abandon import licences and replace them by tariff, as recommended by Krueger, if the former are in its interest?

Not every one belonging to the NPE school agrees on this point. Little et al., despite their overall support for NPE, are sceptical about the analysis of interest groups in most of the NPE literature. Like pre-NPE political scientists of the Western society, they look upon interest groups as inevitable and necessary components of democratic societies. The function of politics, according to them, is to reconcile diverse and often conflicting interests among the citizens. 'Who gets what, when and how?' is the core of the study of politics. Their implications for macro-economic management are 'surprisingly little' according to them. Most people want growth and low inflation, and get confused when growth is accompanied by inflation. Macro-economics is not well understood even by the relatively well-informed elite (Little et al., 1993: 381–82).

Alongside 'rent-seeking' as defined by Krueger and Buchanan, Amsden has introduced the concept of private rent-seeking which involves 'buying cheap and selling dear, or realizing profit "upon alienation" rather than through investment in new plant, equipment, and human resources'. It connotes speculation and arbitrage in stocks or existing assets (Amsden, 1991: 127). The 'private rent-seeking', according to Amsden, stands in the way of the most socially efficient use of resources, and is no less serious than rent-seeking associated with public/political patronage. Further, private rent-seeking behaviour forces the governments to offer concessions, subsidies and support in various other forms in order to induce private entrepreneurs to invest in manufacturing. Once the existence of private rent-seeking is recognised, privatisation can no longer be taken as synonymous with efficiency (Amsden, 1991: 229–30).

Is democracy incompatible with development in LDCs?

The argument that development and democracy are incompatible in the LDCs has been disputed. Obviously, its obverse, authoritarianism, cannot be a sufficient condition for development; had this been the case, Zaire under Mobutu with three decades of unalloyed authoritarianism would have become one of the most developed countries in the world. Is this a necessary condition? One detailed research, based on cross-country data, has actually found that not only is the relationship between democracy and development a positive one, they are mutually reinforcing (Healey et al., 1992: 3).

Another study, based on data for 104 countries, concludes that developing countries achieving high levels of development are more likely to establish and sustain democracy, while democratic political institutions are more likely to facilitate growth. Political pluralism acts to release energies and foster conditions conducive to change, entrepreneurial risk, and economic development (Healey et al., 1992: 2; Pourgerami, 1991). Still another study, by Przeworski and Limongi, based on 21 countries, shows that in eight countries democracy and wealth are correlated, in another eight authoritarianism and wealth, but in five there is no clear association. The study concludes that the form of government is not important (West, 1996: 4). Hoggard takes the view that there is no conclusive evidence, over the long run that the economic performance of democracies is either better or worse than those of authoritarian regimes. In fact, taking all the countries of the world into account, while poor countries tend to be ruled by authoritarian regimes (India being an exception) and the better-off ones by the democracies, the middle layer show no relationship (Hoggard, 1996: 200).

However, there is another way of looking at this relationship. One can take the view that while, generally speaking, democracy is compatible with development, it is not in case of development induced by structural adjustment, particularly in view of the pain the economy has to undergo, at least at the initial stage. Huntingdon and Dominguez, like many others before and after them, took the view that democracy encourages more of consumption and less of investment. Adam Smith himself was aware that in a democracy simple majority might try to limit competition and enjoy rent-seeking, and that interest groups would pursue their own group interest in various ways, including lobbying. Nor was he interested in voting rules, and preferred a combination of democracy with monarchy. He also associated democracies with thoughtless extravagance. But the main thrust of his writings was for restricting the coercive powers of the state. There is reason to believe that Smith had doubts about 'a simple harmony of egoisms through laissez-faire and the invisible hand'. In several places one gets the impression that he was concerned about the 'alienation' of people from the production process without actually using the word, and sought education as a corrective (West, 1996: 4–12). Not all the proponents of NPE favour authoritarianism for development. Little et al., in their study based on 18 countries, found no evidence that authoritarian governments can quash opposition and carry out a coherent long-term programme. 'A cursory examination of our eighteen countries does not support this frequently expressed view. Neither the form of government nor the degree of political freedom seems to have had a significant bearing on the adaptability of our countries to external shocks and their subsequent performance.' They found tradition and history as more powerful explanations. However, they admitted that 'New governments, whether democratic or authoritarian, are more likely to make drastic changes in economic policy—macroeconomic or structural—than are incumbent governments' (Little et al., 1993: 362–70). Bhagwati, another strong advocate of structural adjustment and a strong opponent of DUP activities, also finds no correlation whatsoever, positive or negative, between democracy and growth rates (Bhagwati, 1991: 20).

Gerd Nonneman concludes that democracy fosters economic liberalisation (Nonneman, 1996: 307). Healey et al. find no strong empirical relationship between regime type and policy performance in relation to stabilisation and adjustment policies implemented under conditions of economic crisis (Healey et al., 1992: 3). A detailed examination of LDC budgets and policies shows that, since late 1970, there is no evidence that democratic regimes face more difficulty in restraining public expenditure; in fact, fiscal deficits are smaller in the more democratic ones. The more democratic regimes are less likely to resort to inflationary financing via credit from monetary authorities. However, at the same time, they are not so efficient or keen to increase taxes or to reduce the share of indirect taxes. On the other hand, they are more likely to reduce the share of expenditure on defence or security, and to raise that on health and education (Healey et al., 1992: 18). Further, governments brought about unconstitutionally tend to be more prone to fiscal deficits or to the promotion of inflationary tendencies (Healey et al., 1992: 9).

Snider, a political scientist, takes the view that economic adjustment has a better chance of succeeding when it is preceded by political adjustment. Political adjustment, beginning with secure property rights and contract enforcements, does not involve taking the state out of the economy, but provides a new role for the state. Democracies are more capable of adjustment and in the restriction of rent than the authoritarian ones. The political capacity to carry out adjustment depends on the ability to extract human and material resources from society, the explicitness or directness with which these resources are mobilised and the credibility of political and economic institutions—all of which would be easier to carry out in a democratic environment. The issue is not about the size of the public sector but about the capacity of the society and the regime to make an optimal extraction of human resources (Snider, 1996: 219–21). The state need not be authoritarian to impose unpopular measures, as it needs close interaction with the civil society to make its policies work (Rapley, 1996: 142).

Economistic interpretation

The economistic interpretation of the state and its role in the NPE analysis has also been heavily criticised. Politics, according to this view, is 'the central means through which societies seek to resolve conflict over issues of distribution and values', and should not be viewed as a constraint on economic welfare (Grindle, 1991: 45). The market cannot be the be all and end all of state policy. Nor can self-aggrandisement be the only motivating force behind the action of political leaders. History, tradition and culture play an important role in their decisions, and even the most authoritarian or predatory regimes can find it difficult to overlook these. Their attitudes, outlook, and world-view are considerably shaped by the values and beliefs of the society they grow up in.

Further, maximising the national product need not be the sole objective of a political regime. For a country, at a particular juncture of history, nation-building can be a legitimate goal to aim at, even at some economic cost. As Little et al. admit: 'Expenditures to strengthen national cohesion, or to build political coalitions, may in the minds of political leaders take precedence over the maintenance or restoration of macroeconomic equilibrium—as long as the expenditure can be financed somehow, or until inflation imposes risks to cohesion or coalition that appear to outweigh gains from expenditures' (Little et al., 1993: 373). Similarly, external threats also usually get priority over economic considerations (Little et al., 1993: 374). One has to recognise that a political entity like a state can have multiple objectives, a major one, and certainly not the only one, of them being economic progress.

Bates, while not averse to the application of economic reasoning to politics, a la Downs, questions the concept of political market, with demand for and supply of public policy. The political arena does not generate alternative mixes of public programmes in response to prices, nor does that price, however defined, move up and down to eventually equalise demand for public policy with supply. Obviously, one can take the view that politics should operate like the market, or that, while deciding on policies, the citizenry should be aware of the opportunity costs associated with particular policy packages, so that the decision is rationally made. But NPE does little to enlighten one as to how the preferences of citizens are translated into public policy. Nor is it right to assume that the state is a single agency with a clearly defined objective function (Bates, 1991: 264–65).

Even some of the leading protagonists of NPE now admit, that the vehemence of the neo-classical attack on the state has been carried too far (Grindle, 1996: 5). They recognise that the state alone can provide a set of conditions essential to economic development—law, order, effective macro-economic policy, infrastructure development, investment in human capital, enhancement of equity (Grindle, 1996). Further, the policy elite is not merely interested in staying in power and in adopting whatever policy would make it cling to power; it does have some explicit notions of what constitutes good policy. Still further, the coalition partners it seeks for staying in power are usually historically and ideologically given, while it will not seek support from some forces even for the sake of staying in power. Power is a means to an end, and not the end itself (Grindle and Thomas, 1991: 54–55).

Lacking historical and social perspective

Some have argued that the NPE approach is ahistorical (Taylor, 1995: 43). The nine propositions of Olson are supposed to work universally, irrespective of the social, cultural, political and historical context. Development does not seem to be affected by differing initial conditions under NPE (Colclough, 1993: 110). These are expected to work as well in India as in UK, despite the fact that the former had to spend nearly two centuries under colonial rule, and had to begin, as an independent nation, with an enormous lag in economy, education, technology, share in world exports and institutions conducive to development. NPE would not be concerned with the concrete historical and global location of East Asia when the process of development picked up.

The ahistorical aspect of NPE is illustrated by Olson's comparison of pre-independence India with Japan, mentioned above. Olson argues that laissez-faire alone cannot explain growth; had this been the case, British India working under laissez-faire should have done better than Japan, an interventionist state. He then puts forward his explanation, in terms of distributional coalitions working differently in these two countries, without elaborating on this highly important point.

One wonders what kind of distributional coalition could have constrained India's growth despite free trade? Obviously, the organised workers—the whipping boy of NPE—cannot be the explanation; their number was small and their organisation had limited influence during the colonial days. Nor could it be the peasantry, which was, on the whole, passive, but for some struggles here and there. The three main 'distributional coalitions', in the Olsonian sense, in those days were—the British industrialists and planters, the landlords—an ally of the colonial rulers—and the newly emerging indigenous capitalist class. The conflict was mainly between the first and the third, and it was at the latter's insistence, after the first world war, that some protection was given to Indian industrialists, prompted also by the compulsion of the British government to develop some defence capability within India in the event of another world war. As the history of the period shows, the Indian capitalists were not competing with their British competitors in a level playing field. The entire administration, culture of the Raj and the overall political environment made it extremely difficult for the indigenous interests to thrive. Nor were the British industrialists interested in building industries in India. The colonial market was a captive one for the British manufacturers, while raw materials from the colonies supplied the needs of the British industry.

Nor is it correct to say that entrepreneurs from all over the world were free to buy and sell, but for some favouritism for the British firms (Olson, 1982: 79). The world in those days was run on the basis of some mutual understanding among the imperial powers; the primacy of a colonial power in its colonies was recognised. British goods were not easy to sell in Dutch-held Indonesia, while the Royal Dutch Oil Company could get an entry into the Indian market only after merging with the British-owned Shell Transport and Trading Company. Laissez-faire mainly applied to the operation of British companies, and the public sector was largely absent, but it was not easy for a non-British foreign company to gain access to the Indian market.

Such explanations, for limited industrialisation and development during the British rule despite a formal proclamation of free trade, do not find a place in NPE. Nor does Olson find space to examine the 'distributional coalitions' in Japan—like *Zaibatsus*, the giant industrial conglomerates or their rural counterparts—and then to show that their action was less distorting and damaging for growth than of those in India. In his study, Olson favours simpler explanations—parsimonious and having power—that explain a large number of phenomena (Olson, 1982: 13–14), but still, in this case, he does not go for the one that is the simplest and amenable to generalisation for all countries subjected to colonial rule; that Japan thrived because it was independent, had the power to take autonomous decisions and to experiment with a variety of ventures, while India was under the thumb of the colonial masters and had few options of trade, production and development.

Similarly, the theory lacks social dimension. NPE's attitude on this is probably summed up in an interesting one-liner from Olson: 'The best macroeconomic policy is a good microeconomic policy' (Olson, 1982: 233). Micro rules over macro. One can contrast this with the approach of the classical economists, from Adam Smith, whose concept of the 'invisible hand' of the market occupies such an important position in NPE theory, to Ricardo and Marx among others. Like the NPE school they too were interested in the way the national product was divided, but they dealt, not with payments to 'factors' or 'inputs', but with 'social classes' such as landlords, capitalists and workers, and their shares in terms of rent, interest-dividend and wage, respectively.

Like colonialism, social and institutional factors are conspicuous by their absence in most of the NPE literature. Landlordism or usury are not examined as serious constraints to growth. Land reform does not figure in their agenda; except as a way of making structural adjustment somewhat less painful in some cases. Recording of tenancy rights appears only as a part of the process of privatisation of natural resources, not for bringing security to cultivators or reducing the oppressive monopoly power of the local gentry. The institutional constraints to growth are not taken as relevant, nor even the factors that limit the role of money and market. Issues like poverty, disparity or unemployment are not considered as resulting from some structural constraints, as if the magic wand of market and price can produce anything that is needed. Such a view ignores the obvious, that markets cannot function without institutions.

The issue of resource allocation and avoidance of distortions

The main objective of NPE is to achieve Pareto optimality. The conditions for Pareto optimality are as follows:

(*a*) For different commodities, the marginal rates of transformation in production are equal to their marginal rates of substitution in consumption;
(*b*) For any two factors, the marginal rates of substitution between them are the same in all industries in which they are used; and
(*c*) For any two commodities, the marginal rates of substitution between them are the same for all individuals consuming both goods.

In case of internationally traded goods one can add another condition: that their marginal rates of transformation through foreign trade are equal to their marginal rates of transformation in domestic trade, and both are also equal to their marginal rates of substitution in domestic consumption.

These stringent conditions are not known to have worked anywhere in the world, for any pair of commodities or factors. They work in a world with perfect information, constant or increasing returns to scale and without externalities; the theory of welfare economics provides no guidance as to what happens when such conditions are only partially met (Mosley et al., 1991: 92). One can look upon Pareto optimality conditions as useful abstractions from reality because they set bounds within which a certain economic situation can be assessed. But in a world with some distortions, it does not logically follow that one should try to make these conditions hold as much as possible. Distortions have their own logic and may only be rectified with other distortions in the opposite direction, and not by conforming to optimality in all but those areas affected by distortion.

When driving in London one expects every driver to conform to rules, e.g., looking at the mirrors and giving signals before changing direction, not driving on the wrong side, not overtaking the car in front from the left, and so on. For a driver, not to conform to these rules there is always a serious risk of getting involved in a multiple car crash, as the other drivers expect him to obey the rules. But it is a different matter for someone trained in driving in London to follow London driving norms in Calcutta, where, despite a formal similarity in norms between the two cities, the operation rule is not to obey any rule, where mirrors are irrelevant and where the only motto of driving is: 'Look ahead, cars behind you and by your side will take care of themselves.'

If all distortions can be removed, we are in an ideal situation. Removing some and leaving others in place will not produce even a second best solution, even if all but a few distortions have been removed (Toye, 1995: 71). In such a situation a search for the 'best' can be only at the cost of the 'good', and 'optimum' can become an obstacle to 'improvement' (Streeten, 1995: 179).

A country, operating in a world plagued with trade distortion, with scarce foreign exchange, with private and social costs not aligned, and with rampant 'private rent-seeking' in an Amsdenian sense in vogue in the internal market, cannot afford 'the luxury of an unregulated transfer mechanism' (Taylor, 1995: 44–45). As our reference to 'private rent-seeking' indicates, not all distortions are due to the government. However, there is a tendency in the NPE literature to make the assertion, not backed by arguments or facts, that 'government failures' are more serious than 'market failures' (Taylor, 1995: 40). Further, as an UNCTAD study of four countries—Egypt, Tunisia, Morocco, and Turkey, countries that have been following liberalisation since the mid-1970s—shows, liberalisation alone does not succeed in rooting out rent-seeking. It cannot, as long as the state collects taxes, regulates urban land-use, spends money by using contractors, and sets priorities. If it is controlled in some areas, new areas of rent-seeking are opened up, e.g., privatisation deals, fictitious exports, etc. (Boratav, 1993: 10).

NPE and development economics

We have already noted that a major shortcoming of NPE is its failure to comprehend the importance of institutional factors, and of distribution and participation to make development work. Implicit in NPE is the belief that growth alone takes care of other problems, such as distribution. The possibility that maldistribution and absence of popular participation in the development process can inhibit growth itself is not treated by NPE as worth considering. Nor does it accept that market and prices may not work in the institutional context of the LDCs.

These points, in addition to a lack of sense of history, make it difficult for NPE to comprehend factors that gave birth to the Development Economics of the 1950s, and sustained it until the end of the 1970s. The main theoretical issue confronting the development economists was whether the same economic prescriptions were valid for both developed and less developed countries. Leaving aside a Peter Bauer here and a Harry Johnson there, the consensus among the economists in this field favoured a separate policy package that took into account the institutional and social handicaps of the backward countries. Exclusive reliance on market and price signals was not considered viable as these countries lacked developed market structures and accompanying institutions (Colclough, 1993: 2).

Some asked, pointing to a low level of monetisation of the economy, how price signals alone could bring about the desirable allocation of resources. The importance of prices in resource allocation was not disputed. The argument was that price alone would not work without a proper institutional infrastructure. A whole range of bottlenecks, constraints or obstacles were mentioned that were hindering market functioning, some of them sociological or historical in orientation. It was admitted that, given the right opportunities, a farmer would show price-responsiveness in choosing the cropping pattern, a la Schultz, but would landlordism, widespread usury, or his societal framework allow him to make the appropriate response? No one denied that even the most backward peasants would pick up their bags and move across the border and seven seas in search of better earning opportunities—but how was a Bhojpuri rural folk to know of a country called Guyana and its immense opportunities until this important piece of information was passed on to him, and his transport cost was paid in advance by a sirdar, a recruiting agent representing a sugar plantation in the Caribbean?

Under colonial rule, land, labour, credit and commodity markets began developing, replacing the feudal or pre-feudal production relations, but only up to a point. Private property in land allowed large foreign-owned plantations to be established. The creation of a labour market enabled the colonial regime to procure workers for their mines or plantations from distant areas. The commodity market allowed products of their industries to be sold to the captive colonial markets. The credit market was only partially developed to allow the foreign firms to function. Rail and road networks radiated from colonial ports, many of which later became metropolises, for facilitating the import of goods and from the industries of the ruling country and the export of raw materials out of the country to feed the latter's industries; otherwise communications remained poor. Commodity-marketing boards in export crops met the consumption and industrial needs of the ruling country. Over the ruins of the old industries and urban centres was built a new urban–industrial–agricultural pattern that furthered colonial interests. Indigenous capitalist development was not permitted in the colonised market.

It was against this background that the newly independent countries began their journey towards industrialisation and development. Poor in capital, skill and management experience, in income and education, and with a large, grossly under-utilised labour force, many of these countries were rich in land, forest and mineral resources. But who would harness these for the country's interest? The richer classes were either parasitic landlords or traders interested in immediate return. Business and industrial classes were either absent or weak and small, without necessary skill and resources or risk-bearing capacity, with no capability to take on the multinational companies (MNCs) in a competition. In this situation, the newly elected governments had two options: one, to become a client state of the erstwhile colonial country and play a comprador role, and two, to chalk out a path of autonomous indigenous capitalist development. The vast majority of the countries chose the first option, opened up their economy to MNCs for exploiting their mines and plantations, but some, mainly the bigger ones, among them with large internal markets and a wide natural resource base, like India or Brazil, opted for the second.

In these countries, the role of the state was to remove various institutional bottlenecks and to lead the country towards development. Their leaders, like Nehru, Nasser, Nyrere or Sukarno, were not in the business of making money out of rent-seekers. They had a dream which went beyond their own self-interest—unless the sense of self-satisfaction for doing a good job was also counted as self-interest—to make indigenous capitalism flourish. The state undertook activities its nascent capitalists wanted but were unwilling to undertake on their own account—mainly setting up capital- and knowledge-intensive industries with long gestation periods and protecting these from foreign competitors. Whereas industries evolved over centuries in the developed countries and the economy grew slowly, these latecomers sought to bridge the gap between themselves and the former rapidly (within a generation or two), with a high growth rate.

The main task of development economics was to make that dream feasible. Issues discussed were: how to transform the vicious circle of poverty, low growth and under-utilisation of manpower into a virtuous one; how not to let scarce skill, management, capital and other resources dissipate without a trace; how to focus on a few, selected areas of growth and give a big push; how, with a given capital-output ratio, to mobilise necessary capital to produce a certain predetermined growth rate; how to transfer largely under-utilised surplus rural labour to industries and urban areas and promote industrialisation; what critical minimum effort was needed to scale some thresholds; how to evade the negative implications of cumulative causation and convert them into positive ones; how to promote industrialisation around growth poles with interrelated industries by way of forward and backward linkages and then make their 'spread effects' stronger than 'backwash effects' in the hinterland. Only the state was capable of responding to these issues, or of operationalising, planning and implementing them. The indigenous capitalists were not capable, the MNCs were not wanted, the international agencies like the World Bank did not wish the LDCs to 'squander' their resources on industrialisation when they could get what they wanted (provided they could pay for it) through trade.

There can be endless arguments as to whether the alternative of leaving everything to the market would have been better for these countries. History cannot be recreated. No one can claim that public enterprises in these were models of efficiency, or even remotely resembled those in East Asia, but was the private sector any better? Indeed, a part of the reason why the public sector expanded and made losses was because many of the failed private sector units were passed on to the former. Comparing like with like, for instance, the balance sheet of the entire public sector with that of the entire private sector, including both the efficient units and those which were sick or closed down, would probably leave the matter inconclusive, or even in favour of the public sector.

As admitted by a major World Bank document: 'The key factor determining the efficiency of an enterprise is not whether it is publicly or privately owned, [but] how it is managed' (World Bank, WDR, 1983: 50). It adds that once barriers to entry—which can be erected by the state, or by the monopolists or oligopolists—have been removed, there can be no a priori presumption as to whether better management will be found in the public or private sector. Lessons from the market-friendly countries where public sector units maintain a low profile (the vast majority including India's neighbours such as Pakistan or Bangladesh and the Central American republics), are anything but inspiring. At least countries like India, Brazil, Argentina, or Egypt, pursuing import substitution, have managed to build some industries and have achieved self-sufficiency in quite a few, something that cannot be said about those following laissez-faire.

Perhaps these economies could have done better but for two types of problems they faced. First was the perennial problem of capitalist development in a semi-feudal set-up with a strong feudal presence in politics and society. The dichotomy between the rhetoric of land reform and its non-implementation reflected the dependence of the political elite on these feudal elements, without whose support, elections could not be won in a parliamentary system. Even the authoritarian regimes could only ignore their importance in the civil service and army at their peril. In India, the highly influential second Five Year Plan put heavy industries on the agenda, but not land reform. As a consequence, agriculture was not modernised and not enough of agricultural surpluses were available for sustaining the working non-agricultural population or for exports. Most of these LDCs even failed to produce enough food for their population, and, paradoxically, became dependent on the most industrialised countries—such as USA or the European Community—for food. However, this very important component of development—land reform—is conspicuous by its absence in the World Bank scheme of things under structural adjustment (see comments of John Williamson in Corbo et al., 1992: 21).

The second was the other perennial problem, their relationship with the world capitalist system. Their quest for independent capitalist development brought them in conflict with the West, and made some of them dependent on the Soviet Union for building industries, including armament industries under public ownership, for non-traditional exports and imports and for technology. Yet, despite this and their occasional socialist rhetoric, they strove to build a society that was closer to the West. In the case of India, in the later years, priorities in industrialisation shifted to consumer durables for the rich and middle classes, a small proportion of the population, but still a very large number in absolute terms; 5 per cent of India's better-off population being nearly as large as the population of UK or France, large enough to make industries producing fridges, washing machines, televisions and VCRs viable. Industries, responding to price incentives, produced for the 5 per cent privileged minority with purchasing power, and not goods for mass consumption for the other 95 per cent. Slogans such as 'redistribution with growth' proliferated in a situation of low growth and widening income and wealth disparity in India, Egypt, Indonesia, Brazil and elsewhere. In the ultimate analysis, dependence on the West prevailed over conflict in the relationship.

At the same time, the East Asian experience conclusively proves the hollowness of a particular subset of Marxists: the dependency school. Mainly inspired by the works of Samir Amin and Andre Gundar Frank, they attempted to explain every policy in an LDC in terms of the global capitalist system and its interests. Writing in the 1970s when the world market was not as integrated as it is today, they treated all governments in LDCs as alike, as compradors and as subservient to world capitalism, irrespective of their levels and patterns of development. What the experience of East Asia underlines is that, even the politically and militarily most subservient and economically most integrated regimes are not devoid of nationalist aspirations and the capability to seize the opportunity, when it comes, for indigenous capitalist development (Amsden, 1988: 143).

The Marxist perspectives

A number of scholars have pointed to a formal resemblance of some aspects of NPE, to the Marxist analysis of the state, though the overall thrust of its conclusions is anti-Marxist. For instance, like Marxists, NPE disagrees with the view that the state is benevolent or impartial. Both agree that the most important attribute of the state is its power of coercion; the latter being described in

NPE as legal monopoly of use of violence, though carrying more or less the same meaning. Such coercive power is used to promote the ruling class in the Marxist framework and some interest groups favoured by the state in NPE. The ruling classes, or interest groups with influence, operate, with state support, for their own interest, and not for the welfare of the population as a whole. Both the Marxists and the proponents of NPE agree that individual welfare does not add up to social welfare, and in both ruling class or dominant group interests act negatively on social welfare. Both agree that the richer sections are more aware of their interests than the poorer ones, and, being smaller, they are more cohesive and active in promoting and protecting their interests.

In both schools, some variations of the main theme suggest the possibility of an autonomous state, independent of classes (or interest groups) in certain situations. In the case of the Marxists this can happen if the major classes have locked horns with no clear winners in a transitory phase, e.g., as it happened in France in the 1850s and 1860s, with landed gentry and the emerging capitalist class engaged in a major battle for capturing political power. In the case of NPE, this can happen more regularly, under authoritarian regimes, with no section of the population sufficiently organised to pose a threat to its continuation. There is even a touch of dialectics in the conclusion that economic liberalism, to succeed, needs its opposite in politics, viz., authoritarianism. Or even in the fact that, though using Marxist jargons and methods quite generously, they reach just the opposite conclusions. It is almost like what Marx did with Hegel, turning Hegelian dialectics on its head and deriving opposite conclusions.

Both the schools talk about the need for 'structural change', though they mean entirely different things by that expression. In the NPE scheme of things land reform and forcible takeover of large firms under state control would be out of the question. Structural reform, in the NPE sense, despite the word 'structure', is geared to create an incentive structure that is conducive to production and is responsive to market signals. Financial, fiscal, and public enterprise reform, along with changes in trade, industry and agricultural policies, as covered by the usual SAPs, are the sorts of things meant to be covered by the term 'structure' under NPE. Some of the NPE protagonists, however, even talk of 'revolution' as a means of getting rid of rent-seekers, since other routes out of a society seething in rent-seeking are closed.

Obviously, there are many qualitative differences. To start with, Marxists will never agree with the basic premise, that self-interest is the driving force of human behaviour. They would take the view that if a person is self-interested in a class society, that is precisely because otherwise he would not survive. But, even in a class society, alongside individual incentives, people do respond to social incentives in many situations. Otherwise there would have been no struggle or change. A socialist society is also a class society and is not free from selfishness, greed, jealousy and other vices of a class society, having been born in the womb of a capitalist society. But the success of a socialist regime would lie in transforming popular attitude and outlook, in making them respond increasingly to social incentive. As the state takes care of livelihood, education, health, shelter and other basic requirements of life, there would be increasingly less need for selfishness. Why the Soviet Union failed to live up to that expectation is an important question but to discuss this will take us beyond the scope of this book.

The Marxist concept of 'class' is a social category, while the NPE definition of 'interest group' is a generalised one with overlapping membership. According to the rigorous definition of 'class' given by Lenin, a class is understood with reference to its location in the mode of production and in the distribution of surplus. 'Class' is also a way of life and a group of people identifiable by their dress, attitude, beliefs, morals and values. One can recognise a 'worker' distinctly from a 'peasant' or a 'factory owner'. 'Interest groups' of NPE are not so distinct or easily identifiable, nor do they depict a particular way of life. The only thing that brings together people in a special-interest group, according to NPE, is to attain a common aim. Again, while Marx took a keen interest in rent, his concept was land-based. The NPE concept of rent is of a more generalised kind, viz., the excess of receipt over opportunity cost for the employment of a resource. Rent-seeking, as understood by NPE, has no parallel in Marxist theory, except in the sense of the trend towards 'commodification' of everything in a capitalist society.

Perhaps the biggest difference lies in the treatment of the working class. To NPE protagonists, from Olson onwards, trade unions of organised workers are responsible for most of the economic ills: for keeping the wages, and hence costs of production, high; for their downward inflexibility, thereby not allowing the market to be cleared; and for disparities between themselves and the unorganised workers and peasants. The Marxists, in contrast, look upon the working class as the one with the highest revolutionary potential, under whose leadership class struggle will be fought in a capitalist society. While NPE will welcome a fall in the share of wages in national income and the rate of growth of wages that lags behind labour productivity increases to make room for profit and capital accumulation, the Marxists will be worried with the tendency for the share of wages to fall in a capitalist society with increase in the organic composition of capital.

The missing link: The role of BWIs in NPE

While not spoken of in the NPE literature, implicit in most of the discussion and formulations of NPE is the pivotal role of the international agencies such as the World Bank and IMF in the economics and politics of the LDCs. As the 'universal guardian of the rational-legal order', they lurk somewhere in the shadows (Findlay, 1991: 19). Sometimes they prefer not to be too conspicuous, lest this be resisted openly or by way of subterfuges (Findlay, 1991: 19). Nor would they like to be too closely identified with the government, as that might become a politically sensitive issue, erode the credibility of the adjustment programme and make the government concerned vulnerable to accusations of subservience to the West.

Their role is partly fulfilled through indigenous bureaucrats and technocrats trained by and/or having worked with the World Bank at some stage in their career, who are now in charge of implementing SAPs in various countries. It is more directly fulfilled by way of conditionalities that force the state to withdraw from the market and to refrain from what the World Bank sees as distorting activities. In this way the outside agencies help to prop up those in favour of the desired policies so that they can take decisions independently of the rent-seeking interest groups. These two international agencies are seen as a major determinant of the success of a government in neutralising rent-seeking wasteful activities. By coaxing, cajoling, browbeating and threatening, and in numerous other ways, they can mould the opinion of the political leaders and their bureaucrats towards what the BWIs would consider as desirable policies. As Nelson puts it: 'Commitment to stabilisation on the part of the top political leaders is indeed crucial. But the commitment itself is a *variable* on which outside agencies can have some influence' (italics by the author) (Nelson, 1988: 84).

Nelson admits that IMF and the World Bank 'play [a] more direct role in evolving economic policy, through their programs of training and technical assistance and through policy dialogues'. She considers this as positive and useful and urges dialogue with a broader group of officials to allay 'misgivings' as also to help with designing and implementing adjustment programmes (Nelson, 1988: 98). Little et al. argue that external agencies, such as USAID, the US government and the World Bank, play influential roles 'by holding out carrots and sticks', or through foreign experts, e.g., the 'Berkeley Mafia' in Indonesia or the 'Chicago boys' in post-Allende Chile (Little et al., 1993: 386–87).

Within these institutions two types of approaches towards LDCs are discernible regarding their own role in the implementation of structural adjustment. The tougher approach recommends the release of loan in tranches conditional to the fulfilment of a set of performance criteria, and withdrawal or postponement of funding in case of non-compliance (Mosley et al., 1991: 45). The lenient view, shared by Nelson among others, is to discard such minimum-level support and short leash in favour of assistance on a generous scale, so that institutions can be built for sustaining adjustment over a longer term. However, both approaches share a common view that the level and management of aid should be such as to retain pressure on the government, since otherwise things would not move, though the second approach would not favour putting pressure to such an extent that it leaves the government with little room for manoeuvre vis-à-vis internal political opposition. It argues that the support should be on an optimal level, above which painful correctives should not be undertaken, and below which political risks would 'look too high or economic gains too low to warrant a serious stabilisation attempt'. External assistance should be seen as an insurance for the fulfilment of conditionalities. According to this view, IMF should be responsive to the difficulties facing a government following a changed exogenous condition, but it notes with dismay that often in these situations IMF does just the opposite: it calls for more austerity (Nelson, 1988: 122–23).

Grindle argues that such pressure to comply with adjustment requirements might come in conflict with the other pressures on them: to respond to diverse interests and to mediate over societal conflicts. The open compliance with the former might erode the legitimacy of a government that is essential to handle the pressures of the second type. Further, austerity budgets might also impair the administrative capacity of these states. In many such cases the governments concerned might not be willing or capable of sustaining structural adjustment in the face of such internal opposition. However, as some argue, the decline in the administrative capacity of the state, in this situation, while leading to popular disaffection in many cases, might not be necessarily bad—it might also help revitalise the civil society and the autonomous functioning of voluntary groups (Grindle, 1996: 180–83).

All these views—whether tough or lenient, and emanating from those who are on the whole on the side of structural adjustment—confirm the overriding role of the BWIs in the formulation as well as implementation of structural adjustment. These also clarify why the NPE protagonists contended that structural adjustment was feasible despite the tendency towards rent-seeking among the LDC's leaders. The BWIs were expected to work on them and to put them in their place. They were the 'invisible hands' that would make structural adjustment work by alternating bullying with good counselling. They were the ones to force political commitment for adjustment out of those reluctant leaders and then to force them again to own it as their own, independently thought-out programme (Killick, 1993b: 109).

Let us also add, to make the picture complete, that a powerful view among the international trade theorists in the United States, led by Charles P. Kindleberger, is that a liberalised world trade system can only operate with a hegemon, obviously the United States, in command. The theory purports to show, on the basis of historical data, that whenever the leading power became weak and lost its control, anarchy prevailed and the entire system went into disarray. The hegemon, in a sense, takes the responsibility of producing public goods, in this case an ordered world trade structure, and pays for those, while permitting others to enjoy a free ride. In other words, a strong command structure is needed to keep the world market free (Kindleberger, 1986; Webb and Krasner, 1989). There are others, such as Keohane, who argue that an open liberal economy can exist independently of the configuration of power among member states (Keohane, 1984; Grunberg, 1990; Low, 1995: 16–19).

Conclusions

Our analysis shows that the New Political Economy of development is internally inconsistent, ahistorical, is oriented towards justifying market-centred economic policies under authoritarian regimes, is dependent on the rich world institutions for its success and ignores the importance of institutional factors in the development process. While self-interest is a powerful motive, its attempts to explain all types of behaviour solely in terms of selfishness is not only wrong but has led to serious inconsistencies in the NPE theoretical structure. Its poor opinion of political leaders, for helping rent-seeking behaviour and for other failings, has raised the question of, whether, if that premise holds, there is any basis for hoping that the same leaders would implement an SAP that runs counter to their own self-interest. Its high opinion of the 'impartial' bureaucrats with national interest at heart and the ability to rise above interest groups and their conflicts, similarly, leaves the question of where this particular breed would come from and whether their presence would qualify the Olsonian premises of self-interest as the sole motivating factor in human behaviour, unanswered. More important, why should these nationally interested bureaucrats be allowed to implement structural adjustment by self-interested politicians if that is not in their interest?

Similar confusion abounds in relation to other aspects of the theory. Distributional coalitions, particularly the trade unions, are blamed for producing irrational economic outcomes, because they seek to maximise their own share of national cake, and yet NPE urges the possible beneficiaries from structural adjustment to form coalitions in its support in order to make it politically sustainable. The theory does not reveal why such a coalition would be any different from other types of distributional coalitions seeking to maximise their share of the national cake, and in that case how they can avoid inefficiencies and irrationalities associated with distributional coalition in general, as discussed by Olson himself.

At the end of the analysis, NPE comes out with the paradoxical conclusion that, for sustaining a liberalised market-oriented economy, a country needs its obverse in the political arena, an autocratic regime, which, like the enlightened bureaucrats, can rise above interest groups and can get things done, quickly and flexibly, in the national interest. This analysis too misses out a simple point that, even these autocratic regimes need, for their survival, a certain balance between different interest groups, and can never be shielded from rent-seeking and other distorting behaviours. While the basis for such a startling conclusion is the economic success of the East Asian countries which are mainly governed by autocratic regimes, this is a mere coincidence and cannot be generalised. We will examine, in Chapters 6 and 7, when discussing the East and Southeast Asian development experience, the complex mix of factors—national and international, historical and contemporary, social, political, ethnic, as well as economic, along with the very decisive role of the interventionist state—that gave rise to the East Asian phenomenon. This will also provide us with the occasion to examine this particular issue in depth—of the role of autocratic regimes in development—in the East Asian context.

A simple linear relationship between economic success and the political form of the government is hard to establish. In fact, taking all the countries of the world into account, generally speaking, the better-off countries tend to be more democratic than the poorer ones. On the contrary, autocratic governments—whether ruled by Mobutu, Trujillo, Batista, Duvalier, Idi Amin, Rhee, or Ayub Khan, just to name a few with long records of governance, all generously supported, financially/militarily, by the West, the World Bank and IMF—do not seem to have done much for the economic upliftment of their people.

We have examined the superficial resemblance of some formal features of the NPE analysis with Marxism, along with its essentially anti-Marxist conclusions, and also its failure to comprehend the historical conditions that gave rise to the Development Economics of the 1950s to 1980s and its emphasis on the role of the state. We have also drawn the conclusion that, implicit in NPE, though never formally stated, is the role of the World Bank, IMF and the government of the United States, in making the reluctant governments accept structural adjustment conditionalities and then in making them project these as their own policy decisions.

Perhaps the only redeeming feature of this theory is its analysis of 'rent-seeking behaviour', that has a certain relevance to the contemporary LDCs' political economy. This explains in formalised form what had been known in India for the past five decades as 'licence–permit raj', and, perhaps, with similar expressions, in the vocabulary of many other LDCs. Apart from the economic costs involved in 'rent-seeking', what it can do to the political environment of a country is amply illustrated by the voluminous documentation of corruption at high places, over the past decade or two, in a large number of countries, including India, South Korea, Japan and Italy. While open and competitive economy is a myth, unbridled state control also cannot be a recipe for success, human material being what it is in a class society. There is a serious need to critically examine the overwhelming system of controls and regulations that breed inefficiency and corruption and stifle individual initiative, but, at the same time, it would be nothing short of wishful thinking to assume that a no-control regime can deliver development to a poor country. While excessive controls should be done away with, it would be equally wrong, as the saying goes, to throw the baby out along with the bath water. Paradoxically, however, the highly negative experience with corruption at high places also contradicts the NPE claim that an open economy is more capable of handling corruption. In India's case, the era of sleaze and scam largely coincides with increasing liberalisation since the mid-1980s and the introduction of structural adjustment, dismantling of controls, privatisation, integration with the global economy, and the entry of the MNCs in the economy. Whether in the notorious Bofors gun case, or in the share-market scam, to mention only two, the foreign-owned private enterprises or banks operating in India have been identified as being mainly responsible for promoting corruption in their drive for securing contracts or making money.

three

Structural adjustment

Introduction

Having critically examined and analysed the theoretical structure of the New Political Economy of development in the previous chapter, we will now examine the structural adjustment package itself in this chapter. Balassa defines structural adjustment as 'policy responses to external shocks, carried out with the objective of regaining the pre-shock growth path of the national economy'. The expression 'structural', according to Balassa, reflects the need for discrete, as compared to marginal changes in policies in response to discrete shocks. During the period of adjustment, growth was to take precedence over distribution and production over social justice (Balassa, 1981: 1–2).

The shock the adjustment programme was primarily concerned with, when it was introduced in 1980, was the oil crisis of the 1970s. And the treatment was not expected to run for a period longer than three–four years. It was expected that the growth rate would slow down during the period of adjustment, but only up to the mid-1980s, after which there would be an upward trend. This was the expected time horizon for adjustment. Adjustment was not expected to be the sole concern of the LDCs who were finding it difficult to balance their internal and external accounts. Along with the poor countries, the industrialised countries were expected to play their role by liberalising trade, increasing aid, importing more from LDCs, saving energy, and increasing capital flows to the LDCs.

The package that is being implemented now as 'structural adjustment' bears no resemblance to this original conception. Far from being a discrete response to a discrete shock, this has been turned into a standard bunch of policies, applicable anywhere anytime, without any reference to any shock. One loan follows another as a continuous exercise, and the entire package has become solely the concern of the poor countries of the South. The role of the North is almost exclusively as the guiding force behind the World Bank and IMF, and not as a group of countries sharing the burden of adjustment as a global problem (Balassa, 1981: 1–2; World Bank, WDR, 1980: 3–12).

We begin our discussion with an examination of the changing roles of the World Bank and IMF, the two BWIs that have been instrumental in the formulation and monitoring of the implementation of this policy package at the global level. In a sense, this is going to provide a vital link with the previous chapter where we discussed NPE. In that chapter we pointed to a paradox, that while NPE holds a poor opinion about the political leaders of the LDCs, as being self-interested and seeking rent, it expects the same leaders to implement structural reform that is not likely to be in their interest. The answer we came up with, towards the end of that chapter, was that, though not explicitly stated, implicity, NPE expects the World Bank, IMF and the US, to play a role in inducing (or rather coercing) these political leaders to adopt structural reform. Such inducement/coercion would come about mainly in three forms—through bureaucrats having close Fund–Bank connections, by forcing on them appropriate conditionalities in exchange of loans at a time of crisis, and by using the sheer military might of the West, if need be. This section carries the thread of that conclusion, and asks the question: What prompted these organisations to introduce this package, and whether any motive other than doing good for the poor countries dominated their thinking and action. What is the political economy of structural adjustment?

Following this, we take a look at the genesis of structural adjustment; how it was originally conceived and how its character changed in the 1980s. Then we examine the conditionalities imposed by the Bretton Woods Institutions (BWIs, or simply the twins), and the manner in which the performance of a country under structural adjustment is monitored. This is followed by an examination of the major consequences of this package for the recipient countries, including those on GDP, trade, industry, agriculture, public enterprises, macro-economic management and their social dimension. We then attempt an evaluation of the performance of the package in various countries.

Fund and Bank: The twins

In this section, we are examining the evolution of the role of the International Monetary Fund (IMF, or simply Fund) and the World Bank (International Bank for Reconstruction and Development, in short, IBRD, or simply, Bank). To make life easier, in this chapter, the stabilisation programme of IMF will be treated as a part of the structural adjustment package, though, at a formal level, these two organisations prescribe somewhat different policies.

Keynes' proposals and the final outcome of Bretton Woods

In his original proposals, in 1942, contained in three memoranda, written in response to the call by the German Economic Minister, Walter Funk, for a post-war new world economic order, Keynes suggested three post-war international institutions to meet three specific purposes, with clearly delineated areas of operation. First, an International Clearing Union, a central bank of central banks, with its own currency (to be named 'bancor') to help ease the balance of payment difficulties of the member countries. This bank, contrary to the current practice, was to penalise countries holding trade surplus, with a global tax of 1 per cent per month, on the grounds that they were keeping the world effective demand low by their under-purchase of goods produced by other countries. The proceeds of such global taxation were to be utilised for international buffer stock operations in primary goods. Second, a fund for the economic reconstruction of war-devastated Europe, based on his Plan for Relief and Reconstruction. Third, a Commodity Buffer Stock, to be operated by an International Trade Organisation (ITO), which would maintain and operate this buffer stock of primary goods, in order to stabilise their prices. The buffer stock operation was supposed to be anti-cyclical; ITO making purchases when the world prices were low and selling when the prices became high (Singer, 1995: 17).

The final outcome of the deliberations of the 1944 Bretton Woods Conference, where, along with Keynes, Harry Dexter White, supported by Jacob Viner and Alvin Hansen, representing the US, also played an important role, was somewhat different from these proposals. The 'fund' that was established resembled Keynes' 'bank' but without some of his proposed features, while the 'bank' approximated the 'fund' in the Keynesian scheme of things (Singer, 1995: 18). The differences were not merely in the nomenclature. No common world currency was floated by IMF and, in contrast with the Keynesian view, the deficit countries were now penalised as if they alone were responsible for their trade deficits. The World Bank never had to engage in the task assigned to it by the Conference; European reconstruction was carried out by the US-sponsored Marshall Plan with a huge budget of $13 billion (Lateef, 1994: 18). ITO, to be discussed in the following chapter, was never born because of US opposition, though its charter was drawn up and other formalities were completed.

It is important to remember, in the context of our own discussion and also of the role the Bretton Woods twins came to play in the later years, that in the original conceptions of Keynes and White, the development of the LDCs was not on the agenda. Both the twins were to operate, nearly exclusively, in the interest of the developed countries alone. Though colonies like India, Iraq, Iran and the Philippines were represented in the Bretton Woods Conference that was only to provide the British and US governments with some supporting voice. Although USSR and some other socialist countries took part in the Conference, they were, on the whole, silent spectators, their attention focused on the battlefields in Central Europe, and showed little interest in what was, to them, principally a matter for the capitalist countries to sort out. The word 'development' associated with the name of IBRD was an afterthought as the task of reconstruction was not required to be performed, and did not really mean development in the sense the term is used today. Further, if Keynes was advocating for a buffer stock of primary goods that was only because these were often a destabilising factor in the world market and affected industrial growth in the developed capitalist countries. In the original conception, these were to be rich country institutions catering to the rich country needs of project funding and temporary assistance for balancing external accounts.

Changes up to 1980: Abandonment of gold standard and oil crises

In the course of the following five decades, both organisations underwent significant transformation in the scope and manner of their functioning. The Soviet Union and its allies opted out of both with the onset of the cold war following the conclusion of the second world war. This, plus the fact that the voting power in these was linked with the contributions or 'quotas' of the members, brought the twins under the clear domination of the rich Western countries and gave them a pro-market and anti-state-intervention focus.

Despite their sharing a common philosophy, the twins differed in the scope and time span of their programmes. IMF's main role was to guard the gold standard under which the value of a country's currency was defined in terms of ounces of gold. Countries facing imbalances in their external account usually sought IMF's financial support to tide over temporary difficulties. If the imbalances persisted and reflected a fundamental disequilibrium, the IMF prescription was for devaluation—to encourage exports at a cheaper price and to discourage imports now available at a higher price. In both cases, the time span was short and the medicine was expected to work immediately. The organisation's brief was specific and well-defined. From early days, conditionalities had been a part of IMF loans, but these were few and not rigorously enforced. The conditionalities were oriented towards improving macro-economic management and operated from the demand side.

Those seeking long-term financial support for a project went to the World Bank, which acted as an international banker. It assessed the viability of a project in terms of its capability of repaying the loan with interest and offered loans on the basis of guarantees provided by the governments. While IMF was concerned with macro-economic management and operated on the demand side, the World Bank's concern was micro, project-based lending. In its country reviews, the World Bank's approach was supply side-oriented, and it urged the governments to get the prices right, to make the private sectors the main actors in the economic scene, and to reduce the role of the state in the economy to the minimum.

Over the past two to three decades, both have undergone important changes. With the abandonment of the gold standard and the floating of currencies in 1971, IMF's role as supervisor of the gold standard was over. Its role as a world body also declined, as the rich countries found other ways of funding their deficits, e.g., from the global capital market. The last occasion when a rich country took an IMF loan was more than two decades ago when, in 1975, UK and Italy were loanees. Since then, IMF's activities have remained exclusively confined to the LDCs, a 180-degree deviation from the original concept (Bird, 1993: 5). Though IMF regularly publishes world surveys, etc., it plays no global surveillance role in the world economy and carries no influence with the rich country governments (Killick, 1993b: 109).

Thus, only 10 per cent of the global liquidity, for which the poor countries were responsible, remains within the control of IMF (Huq et al., 1995b: 4). Keynes' expectation that about half of the world's imports would be backed by IMF funding never materialised; the current level of IMF support covers only about 2 per cent of world imports (Huq et al., 1995b: 4). While bancor, the international currency proposed by Keynes, was to be linked with average prices of 30 primary commodities, including gold and oil, in order to stabilise world commodity prices, neither was any such international currency put into circulation, nor was the role these bodies could play in stabilising primary product prices ever discussed, except in terms of some facilities for adjusting to unforeseen changes in the world market. GATT, the main international trading agency until the formation of WTO in 1995 (to be discussed in Chapter 4) excluded primary commodities from its agenda (Huq et al., 1995b: 6). The World Bank too, now operates exclusively in the LDCs. With the emergence of an integrated global capital market, backed by modern means of communication, rich countries with good credit ratings face no difficulty in mobilising required project funding from that source. Only countries with low credit rating, having no other source of funding, now come to the World Bank as a last resort.

Though Keynes suggested a soft loan window, to be operated through the United Nations' International Development Assistance (IDA), the agency providing such soft loan and accounting for around 12 per cent of all concessional assistance worldwide, is a subsidiary of the World Bank. IDA offers loan at a low, subsidised rate, but both the quantum of loan offered through IDA and the category of recipients are rigorously defined (Singer, 1995: 24). IDA loans are interest free, but carry a 0.75 per cent service charge a year. Until the mid-1980s, these were repayable over 50 years with a one-year grace period before payments had to start. Recently, the repayment period has been reduced to 40 years for the poorest and 35 for others. The trend is towards further reduction in concessional loans (Lateef, 1994: 5–8).

Fund–Bank ascendance over the United Nations

While their global role has diminished with the dissolution of the gold standard and the emergence of a well-integrated global capital market, the importance of the twins has grown more than proportionately in the economic life of the LDCs. The conditionalities accompanying their loans now shape the economic policies of the poor recipient countries who have virtually no influence over the decision-making process of the twins.

In their charters, these were recognised as international institutions affiliated to the United Nations, and were expected to send their reports to the Economic and Social Council (ECOSOC) of the United Nations. Their heads were expected to attend the meetings of ECOSOC which, rather than either of the twins, was supposed to be the agency coordinating the economic activities of the nations, and was to play a role in the world economy that was parallel to the role of the Security Council in political and military affairs. In practice, neither the World Bank nor IMF ever played this subordinate role vis-à-vis ECOSOC, and in time the BWI twins came to loom much larger than the latter. Today, the Secretary–General of the United Nations is not even allowed to address the annual meetings of the BWIs. By an informal understanding among the rich countries, the 'hard' instruments of development, such as finance, macro-economic policies, balance of payments and growth, are now the exclusive preserve of the twins, while they are happy to leave human and social issues for the attention of the UN agencies (Singer, 1995: 23–24).

With the beginning of the cold war, the rich countries played down the role of the ECOSOC and patronised the World Bank and IMF. While ECOSOC was perennially short of funds, the twins were generously funded by the rich Western countries. One reason for the favour shown was that the twins were seen as instruments in the cold war and as being more amenable to their influence than the less orderly United Nations (Gwin, 1995: 98). A related reason for the Western preference for the World Bank and IMF, over ECOSOC, was its decision-making procedure. Unlike the United Nations, where every country, big or small, has one vote, in the case of the twins, voting is linked with their contributions to the initial fund, which again is linked with the size of their GDPs. Over the past five decades the 'quotas' for various countries have been revised, each revision raising the share of the rich countries. Such revisions are not simply based on key national and international economic variables, but reflect the bargaining strength of various countries and groups of countries in the executive bodies of these organisations (Bird, 1992: 24). At present, the G7 countries (US, UK, France, Germany, Canada, Italy and Japan) account for roughly half the voting power and virtually control the World Bank and IMF (David, 1985: 15). Based on an informal arrangement, from which the LDCs are excluded, the presidentship of the World Bank and the post of Managing Director of IMF are rotated between the US and Western Europe.

Twins working in tandem

These two agencies operate in close understanding with each other. In fact the article of agreement for the Bank makes it obligatory for its members to be members of the Fund too (Polak, 1994: 1). The relationship between the two is governed by periodic concordats, e.g., those of 1966 and 1989, that delineate their respective jurisdiction, e.g., IMF leads on exchange rates, balance of payment problems and restrictive trade systems, while the World Bank leads in development, financial institutions and capital markets (Polak, 1994: 5; Mosley et al., 1991: 36, 53). The regular meetings of the Development Committee, involving senior officials of the two organisations and ministers of member countries, is a forum where common issues are raised, discussed and resolved. Not that they do not quarrel. From time to time they engage themselves in 'turf battles' to protect their own territories or to advance into the domain of the other, sometimes surreptitiously, or in quarrels when something goes wrong in relation to a country, but these are not serious and are more in the nature of temporary matrimonial friction (Polak, 1994: 4–5).

Each takes a representative of the other in its own country missions, and follows, to quote Polak, a 'you twist their right arm and we'll twist their left arm' kind of cooperative strategy (Polak, 1994: 5, 27). Since 1986, both work together with the country concerned to produce what is known as the Policy Framework Paper (PFP) which forms the basis of support given by either. The PFP projects the country's major issues, the objectives and priorities of a three-year programme, the broad thrust of macroeconomic and structural policies and makes out a case for external financing. In most cases, the LDCs lack the competence to design and prepare PFP and quite willingly delegate these functions to the Fund and Bank staff (Polak, 1994: 28–30). As the saying goes, IMF prepares the draft on PFP, the World Bank concurs and the country concerned signs (Mosley et al., 1991, Vol. 1: 53–55; Killick, 1992a: 23; Lancaster, 1991: 39). Once the PFP emerges from 'joint' discussion between the country and the two agencies, which implies that all the outstanding issues between them have been resolved, approval of the loan application becomes a matter of formality.

Though these two agencies deny operating cross conditionality, the manner of formulation and implementation of PFP suggests a very high degree of cooperation on the conditionalities in a specific country case. In fact, a supplementary note sent by the World Bank to its board (and a corresponding one by IMF to its board), in April 1992, states that: '. . .the Bank expects to receive a policy letter that sets out the Government program for structural adjustment, set in a macroeconomic framework which would be based on understandings reached with the Fund [as spelled out in the Letter of Intent for Fund arrangements].' This, indeed, amounts to an admission of de facto cross conditionality (Polak, 1994: 44). Further, an understanding exists that, for a country, structural adjustment would be preceded by a stabilisation package under the IMF umbrella (Polak, 1994: 16; Mosley et al., 1991: 56).

While the twins were set up to perform two distinct tasks, over time, they have come closer in their mode of functioning and treatment of issues. IMF, which was supposed to be concerned with short-term remedies to balance of payment difficulties, is offering 10-year term Extended Fund Facilities (EFF) since 1974, and structural adjustment loans since 1986, while the World Bank, specialising in micro issues, has now graduated from project-based lending to policy-based programmes (structural adjustment loans and sectoral adjustment loans [SALs and SECALs]) and is taking a close interest in macro-economic management, including balance of payments (Killick, 1992a: 17; Mosley et al., 1991, Vol. 1: 37, 40). With these shifts in policy, 'the former distinctions between the roles of the Fund and the Bank—macro versus micro, demand versus supply, adjustment versus development, financial versus real, program versus project loans, short term versus long term—have been severely eroded' (Williamson, 1983b: 619; Polak, 1994: 7). To quote Polak again: 'The conditionality applied by the two institutions in these lending operations, while not becoming identical, has converged into a large common area, and in general the countries borrowing under these conditions have been the same' (Polak, 1994: 11).

When structural adjustment was introduced by the World Bank, making a complete break with narrow, project-based lending, the argument advanced in support of such a change was in terms of fungability. That is, such project-based loans were often spent on activities that the governments would have undertaken in any case with their own money even without Bank lending, and the Bank provision for this only allowed the country concerned to spend on other activities that were not always in accordance with World Bank priorities. Further, the task of project assessment was made difficult by the divergence of internal prices from their scarcity values or world prices. In this situation, the argument went, it was necessary to have an overall view of the country's economy and to influence its overall policy direction (Mosley et al., 1991: 29–30). A third argument was that the Bank, endowed with a highly qualified staff, was seeking to make a more optimal use of its skill in planning design and performance assessment, by taking into account the entire economy of a country (Singer, 1995: 21). Now that their activities and conditionalities have largely converged, and they work in close cooperation in relation to a given country, a strong view is aired from time to time that the two bodies should be merged (Polak, 1994: 46; Mosley et al., 1991, Vol. 1: 56; Rafter and Singer, 1996: 207).

Special drawing rights (SDRs)

While bancor, the proposed international currency, was never floated, in 1969 an amendment was made to IMF's Article of Agreement to give it the right to supplement its existing stock of gold and dollars with its own Special Drawing Rights (SDRs), an accounting currency with no physical existence and based on the weighted average of the values of a basket of currencies. Armed with this provision, SDR was created in 1970–72 and again in 1979–81. The value of outstanding SDRs accounts for about 3 per cent of the world's non-gold reserves today (Polak, 1994: 2–3).

The Fund authorities wished to make SDR the principal reserve asset in the international monetary system, in view of its capital value and liquidity. However, after the collapse of the gold standard, reserve adequacy was no longer seen as a relevant issue and no fresh SDR allocation was made, while the dollar took over that function of reserve currency. As capital mobility permits settlement of current account imbalances, more important than reserve constraint now is credit-worthiness constraint (Williamson, 1992a: 87).

In recent years, with the failure of the global banking system in meeting the balance of payment financing requirement, and the low credit rating of the LDCs, again interest has been focused on the possibility of fresh SDR allocations. Such allocation, based on membership quotas, was expected to help countries with low credit-worthiness but without implying a permanent real transfer of resources. Such allocations were not to be tied to conditions or a fixed repayment schedule, and were to stand as a proxy for the long-term demand to hold international reserves (Williamson, 1992a: 91; Bird, 1992: 21). Some take the view that SDR should be regarded as an international public good, and used to supplement foreign exchange reserves in poor nations. Some have even suggested a special SDR issue to cancel all debts of the poorest African countries (Huq et al., 1995b: 12).

All the proposals have been heavily resisted by the rich countries as, according to them, augmentation of international liquidity would not be in their interest (Bird, 1993: 23). One proposal for the creation of SDR for financing development by routing it through IDA was killed in 1986, when an interim committee of the Fund expressed its opposition to the use of SDR as a 'means of transferring resources' (Polak, 1994: 3). The rich country opposition to increasing international liquidity by way of SDR, is based on the ground that there already exists sufficient liquidity in the international market. The difficulties encountered by some countries, according to this view, are primarily a reflection of their lack of credit-worthiness; and SDR allocation is not the appropriate tool for compensating them for this handicap which is, by and large, their own making (Griffith–Jones, 1993: 102–3).

What motivates the twins to introduce and implement structural adjustment?

To summarise the discussion so far, here we have two rich country-controlled institutions that are exclusively operating in the poor countries. In some instances the Fund–Bank teams visiting a country involve themselves in the details of budget-making, even going to the extent of 'analyzing the budget line by line', to implement the cut in government expenditure (Killick, 1992a: 19–20). The question that naturally arises is: With what objectives do these institutions operate in LDCs? To put it in another way, in the context of this chapter and also of NPE, discussed in the previous chapter, what is the political economy of structural adjustment? There can be three possible answers to this:

(*a*) In their operation they are inspired by the concern for the well-being of the LDCs, or by a strong ideological commitment to free market because of their belief that it is good for mankind;
(*b*) Their actions in the LDCs, motivated by rational self-interested behaviour, further the economic (and maybe also political) interests of the rich countries; and
(*c*) The interests of the two—the rich and the poor countries—converge, and, therefore, while acting in the interests of the rich countries, their policies also benefit the poor ones.

Of these three, (*a*) would be irreconciliable with NPE, with its emphasis on self-interest as the motivating force, that provides the theoretical basis for structural adjustment (Olson, 1982; Dasgupta, 1997b). And (*c*) appears improbable given the known contradictions of interest between the two sets of countries on a wide range of issues. But if one accepts, for the sake of argument, that, in the long run, their interests are compatible, the fact would remain that, even in that situation, the self-interest of the rich countries would be paramount, and its convergence with that of the poor countries would be a matter of coincidence. By all accounts, (*b*) would come closest to NPE.

In the past, the behaviour of these two institutions has been consistent with (*b*). Generally speaking, the interests of the Fund–Bank management regarding a country complemented the cold war requirements of the West (Stiles, 1980; Lancaster, 1991: 9; Killick, 1992a: 25; Bird, 1993: 22). There have been numerous examples of a hardened attitude on the part of these two institutions towards countries not favoured by the West (e.g., Chile under Allende or Ghana under Nkrumah). The hostile attitude changed dramatically after these regimes were toppled and were replaced by a pro-US government, e.g., Chile under Pinochet, or Ghana under Busia. The Soviet Union under Gorbachev was denied loan, and was told by the G7 leaders that more important than money was good policy, but a more generous approach was adopted when the Soviet Union disintegrated, and Yeltsin took over the reins of Russia. The latter was promised a loan of $40 billion on the eve of a crucial election for the presidency. Similarly, a massive loan package was put together for Mexico in a matter of days, during 1995–96, something that is unlikely to be done for India unless its foreign policy changes. The Fund–Bank attitude towards the rich and the poor countries is explicitly asymmetrical, as also that between left-leaning and other deficit states (Killick, 1992a: 6).

Structural adjustment: The genesis

The oil crises of the 1970s

The SAP, as a loan package, was introduced by the World Bank in 1980, and IMF began offering SALs from 1986. However, to understand how this programme came into being and evolved as it did, we need to go back to the 1970s. The decade of the 1970s was one of massive economic upheavals, prompted by two oil crises—in 1973 and in 1979–80. The sudden and steep rise in oil prices created, on the one hand, an unforeseen opportunity for growth for a group of LDCs exporting oil, and on the other, at least for while, a feeling of despair in the West, as it was going to involve a massive outflow of resources from the rich countries located in that part of the globe.

The oil exporting countries led by the Organisation of Petroleum Exporting Countries (OPEC) were wholeheartedly supported by the other LDCs ('Nopecs', to use the terminology of Hans Singer) on the basis of two major expectations: (*a*) that it would make possible for other groups of primary producing and exporting countries—specialising in copper, bauxite, jute, tea, etc.—to bring about a similar reversal of terms of trade through collective action, and (*b*) that a substantial part of the resource flowing into OPEC would become available to them in the form of a cheap loan. However, as it turned out, the OPEC model was not amenable to easy replication, as the other primary products were more easily substitutable and lack of contiguity and political–cultural cohesion made collective action politically infeasible (Barker and Page, 1974; Dasgupta, 1974). On the other hand, while the OPEC-led oil exporting countries amassed enormous wealth, and within a short time, the last thing they wanted was to dissipate it in the form of aid to LDCs.

If these two sets of LDCs had agreed to work on the basis of a common understanding, the problems of both could have been solved, perhaps at the cost of the developed West, by transferring the surplus investible fund from the former to the capital-starving LDCs of the South. That was not to be, mainly because of the political economy of these oil-rich tiny kingdoms, dependent as their ruling elites were, for their political survival, on the military might of the West. The petro-dollar was recycled back to the West, much to the relief of their economic managers, more specifically to the private international banks located in the West (Mosley et al., 1991: 6–7), while the oil-consuming countries (Nopecs) faced a severe balance of payment crisis, only partly mitigated by a special IMF facility set up for compensatory and contingency purposes.

International banks: Lending petro-dollar

This, again created a new situation; the international banks were now flush with funds and were willing to lend to anybody. The

LDCs—mainly in Africa and Latin America—were now induced to borrow from these banks to ease their balance of payment difficulties. Within a few years, an enormous amount of loan was dished out by these banks—who were competing with one another to find borrowers—to a very large number of countries, mostly poor and backward, ruled by authoritarian governments with virtually no popular participation in, or organised opposition to, administration. In this practice, they threw the usual conservative banking norms to the wind. The LDCs, on their part, apart from various inducements, preferred this source of borrowing: unlike IMF, these banks asked few questions and were quick with their paperwork (Polak, 1994: 6). Quite a few borrowed more than was prudent in view of the precarious conditions of their own economies, their crucial dependence on only one or two export items with records of volatile price fluctuations in the global market, and low levels of macro-economic management efficiency. Between 1970 and 1980, public and publicly guaranteed loans to LDCs, from this and other sources increased from $46 billion to $410 billion, that is, almost nine times (Lateef, 1994: 25).

The commercial banks insisted on repayment guarantees by the governments, and usually operated through Loan Syndicates that worked with cross-default clauses to reduce the risk of non-payment. The Syndicates charged 1 per cent commission, paid in advance (which was free from risk), which induced the Syndicates in many cases to 'push loans on to borrowers' (Vas, 1994: 133). The bank business appeared to be lucrative and risk free, and every year between 1973 and 1980, many new European banks entered this field of international lending, thus intensifying oligopolistic competition among themselves. Hardly any country was left in Africa and Latin America that did not take huge loans during this period, in many cases lured by competing banks. Many countries borrowed in total indifference to the future repayment obligations or the capacity of the economy to repay such loans.

International banking, despite the fact that the number of banks was growing due to the influence of the petro-dollar, was highly concentrated. The top 100 banks accounted for three-quarters of the total assets and the top 20 banks accounted for half the international lending. Further, 70 per cent of total assets of the top 10 banks was held by only six US banks. By the end of 1982, nine US banks controlled 60 per cent, and the top 25 US banks controlled

80 per cent of private international bank lending. The fact of the dominance of international banking by the US banks, as we shall see later, had a decisive influence in the course of events that was to follow (Vas, 1994: 133–34).

The bonanza lasted for only a few years. While lending on a massive scale, the international privately owned banks were influenced by a herd mentality. Then, as it happens with international finance quite regularly, the same banks suddenly woke up, began calculating the risks they had taken, and became parsimonious with their money. This too reflected their herd mentality as they tried to extricate themselves from the LDCs (Williamson, 1983b: 615; Bird, 1992: 6–7). Unfortunately, this coincided with a slump in the world demand for agricultural exports and their prices, landing many of the mono-crop LDCs in serious trouble. Ironically, this was the time when they needed most to borrow from these banks, but by then the traditional conservative attitude of the bankers had returned.

The international banks, rather than extending further loan, operated pro-cyclically, wanted their money back with interest, and were not willing to take any further risk in this volatile financial situation. The credit-rating of the LDCs took a nosedive and further loan was denied (Bird, 1992: 7; Vas, 1994: 118). Lending by private international banks to LDCs, rising dramatically from $14 billion in 1973 to $57 billion in 1980, plummeted in subsequent years, reaching a negative figure of −$6 dollars in 1987 (Vas, 1994: 127). While private bank lending, as a proportion of the disbursed public and publicly guaranteed external debt of all LDCs, increased from 38 per cent in 1973 to 55 per cent in 1982. during the slump that followed, the net resource transfer to them became negative, causing a 3–4 per cent loss of GDP, and jeopardising the long-term development strategy of these countries (Griffith–Jones, 1993: 101–13). To make things worse, the coming to power of monetarist regimes in the West, particularly in UK and the US, under Margaret Thatcher and Ronald Reagan, respectively, resulted in a rise in interest rates accompanied by a fall in prices because of tighter monetary control, thus accentuating the debt burden as most loans were subject to variable interest rates (Mosley et al., 1991, Vol. 1: 7–8). Government-to-government assistance was also severely curtailed, particularly between 1980 and 1986, to add to the growing burden of the LDCs (Mosley et al., 1991: 8–9).

The international debt crisis: The rescuing operation to save international banks

The inevitable debt crisis that followed, beginning with a public proclamation of bankruptcy by Mexico in August 1982, gravely undermined the international banking system, with a high and increasing risk of large-scale default on the part of the LDC borrowers. At that stage IMF stepped in, offered fresh loans, with the understanding that, with that support, loan repayments to private international banks would be continued. During 1983–88, in three years, $12.7 billion of adjustment loan was given to six countries by the Fund, and another $2.3 billion by the Bank (Polak, 1994: 12). Such loans were tied to stabilisation and structural adjustment conditionalities. The latter were expected to bring LDC imports in-line with their dwindling foreign exchange earnings from exports and whatever little they could get from the outside world in the form of assistance (Mosley et al., 1991: 9). Exports and imports were sought to be equalised, as also domestic revenue and expenditure, by constraining demand in the 'stabilisation' stage and later, through the complementary Bank package by way of privatisation and inflow of foreign investment.

Initially, in the late 1970s, the idea of 'structural adjustment' was not meant for the LDCs at all. The objective was to restructure the economy of the Organisation for Economic Cooperation and Development (OECD) countries, the most developed countries of the world, following oil crises, the emergence of huge deficits in the balance of payments of the US and the expected dismantling of the multi-fibre agreement (MFA) and the European steel price ring. Only afterwards, the emphasis was changed, and the burden of adjustment to the new world economic situation, arising from a variety of developments in the 1970s, was shifted to the not-too-broad shoulders of the LDCs (Mosley et al., 1991: 22–23).

The formal, official motive for giving support to structural adjustment was to rescue the hard-pressed debtor countries, but a less charitable explanation is that the main concern of the BWIs was to save the global private banking system from bankruptcy. To quote Polak: 'In the first phase of this crisis, from August 1982 to late 1985 . . . the primary concern of the major industrial countries was the protection of the international banking system' (Polak, 1994: 12). Under this interpretation, the fund that was supplied by

IMF, through its 'stabilisation programmes', to the indebted LDCs, was intended to ensure repayment of bank loans, so that the grave crisis facing the international banking system could be resolved. While the governments of the LDCs were asked to give guarantees of loans taken, no corresponding obligation was put on the developed country governments. 'An asymmetry thus arose in debtor and creditor government actions, as regards private capital flows' (Griffith–Jones, 1993: 111–12).

Structural adjustment accompanied debt rescheduling under international agreements, by waiving a part and stretching the rest over a longer period, which further guaranteed repayment. In both the Paris Club and the London Club meetings held for this purpose, a precondition for rescheduling was that the country concerned would undertake a stabilisation programme and avoid defaulting bank loan payments (Lancaster, 1991: 33–54). According to the United Nations' Economic Commission for Latin America and the Caribbean (ECLAC), the debt rescheduling process under the guidance of the OECD countries was far from even-handed, as the cost of the crisis was passed on to the debtors (ECLAC, 1994: 195). Another study by the Overseas Development Institute (ODI), at London, concluded: 'The Fund insisted that recipients of Fund loans remained current with their commercial debt obligations and hence, in some quarters, [was] viewed as a debt collector for the banks' (Bird, 1993: 17). The Brady Plan of 1989, involving a reduction in the real value of debt to banks, was accompanied with a strong commitment on the part of the LDC governments to loan repayment; in the case of Mexico, this was reinforced by a further guarantee of the government of the US itself (Lancaster, 1991: 48).

All these measures helped the private international banks to stave off the crisis. Between 1984 and 1991, with interest and principal repayments far exceeding new loans, their net transfer was negative to the tune of $20 billion. Debt–equity swap and other debt-conversion mechanisms reduced debt owed to commercial banks by $25 billion, while debt-servicing and debt reduction accounted for another $80 billion between 1987 and 1991 (Development Committee, 1992: 39). Further, the rescue operation was on the basis of the nominal value of the debt, but the growth of secondary market for the external debt papers showed that the real value of the debt was much lower than its nominal value (ECLAC, 1994: 194–95). Thus, the private international banks got much more than the lendings were worth at market price, because of the support they received from the BWIs and the Western countries. There was another way they were over-compensated: the crisis they faced was, in a great part, their own contribution, as they threw traditional banking caution to the winds during the 1970s in their quest for profit (Sarkar and Singer, 1992: 12–13). 'Where it happens that the commercial banks rush in, tempt a country to overborrow, and do not assure themselves that the borrowing country will be in a position to repay . . . they deserve to forfeit a part of the value of their loans' (Wiliamson, 1983b: 654).

However, loan repayment by LDCs, with the support of the BWIs, was undertaken without any assurance that further loans from this source would be forthcoming. In fact, given their low credit rating, it is highly unlikely that, for a long time to come, the global banking system would take any notice of them as borrowers (Development Committee, 1993b: 49). Once in the lap of IMF, few countries have managed to grow out of it. The Bank–Fund programmes, once initiated in a country, as a time-bound measure to solve all problems, tend to continue for ever. Even if interrupted for one reason or another, external or internal, the country reverts back to it after a few years, usually after a coup or some other less orderly form of change of guards. Evidently, the amount offered at a time has not been adequate to meet the balance of payments and other needs of the countries concerned (Bird, 1993: 33–34).

US balance of trade deficit: Another possible motive for structural adjustment

The other motive, consistent with rich-country self-interest, could be the urge to find markets in the LDCs, especially for the MNCs based in the US. The soaring US balance of trade deficits, in particular with Japan, Germany and China, reaching a dizzy figure of $162 billion in 1987, impelled these MNCs to look for markets elsewhere, particularly in those countries where the government and the competition were weak (Krugman, 1991: 1–3). Finding access to markets in various countries also became a matter of urgent priority in the Uruguay round of the GATT negotiations to be discussed in the following chapter.

A measure of the success, from the point of view of the economies of the US and some other Western countries, is the fact that, despite lending by these two agencies, there has been a consistent net outflow of financial resources from the countries operating under the SAP since 1980. Between 1984 and 1991, the net transfer out of the LDCs amounted to $20 billion per year. IMF net lending was negative during most of the 1980s (Development Committee, 1992: 39; Bird, 1993: 7). As for the World Bank, by mid-1983, net transfer to developing countries became zero, and became −$30 billion by 1987. Both IMF and the World Bank were getting back more than they were lending (Mosley et al., 1991, Vol. 1: 47).

We have already noted that the expansion of SDR was opposed by the rich countries, while the terms of trade, we shall see below, moved against the primary producers during this period. Expansion of SDR and/or improvement of terms of trade could have gone a long way towards resolving the difficulties the LDCs were facing with their external accounts. But this was not to be.

The package with conditionalities

The conditionalities accompanying the loans of these two organisations reflect their common market-oriented approach, but, as we have already noted, while IMF emphasises on demand constraint, the World Bank operates on the supply side, and there is a broad consensus that the former would precede the latter in the sequencing of programmes. Sequencing has become a major source of controversy inside both the organisations, but that is a different story and need not concern us here.

Policy framework paper and the concept of ownership

Both the organisations incorporate the conditionalities in the loan package in the PFP which, as we have noted earlier, though formally signed by the country concerned, is drafted by the BWIs. Once the negotiations are over and PFP is drafted, the formalities, such as submission of loan application and its approval, are completed very quickly. There is seldom, if ever, any discussion between the lending organisation and the applicant country between the submission of the application and its approval, which are taken as mere formalities.

One reason why so much care is taken to formulate PFP in this particular way is linked with the Fund–Bank idea of ‘ownership’ of such programmes, discussed in Chapter 2. The theory is that the success of a programme is closely correlated with the feeling in the country that it was developed by it on its own and without outside interference. However, such feeling about 'owning' a programme sponsored by either of the twins is qualified by the way the financial assistance is dished out. The total quantum of loan is usually sliced into a number of tranches, each specific to a time period, and payment for each tranche is conditional on the fulfilment of the performance criteria specified for the preceding period (Mosley et al., 1991: 45). In case of non-fulfilment of some or all of the performance criteria, following discussion with the government, the twins usually take one of the following positions: (*a*) the performance is on the whole satisfactory, despite non-fulfilment of some criteria, and, therefore, the fund is released; (*b*) the fund is released, but with a warning, asking the government to adhere to agreed norms if it were to receive payments for following tranches; (*c*) the fund is withheld pending the fulfilment of conditions; (*d*) funding for this particular loan programme is allowed but no further loan is going to be considered for the future; and (*e*) the programme is scrapped.

Whether publicly acknowledged or not, coercion is often applied to make a country accept what, in the opinion of the country, is not in its interest (Killick, 1992a: 10; Mosley et al., 1991: 38). Needless to say, this coercion, an inherent element in a conditionality package, undermines 'ownership' (Berg, 1991: 216–17; Killick, 1993a: 5). One World Bank study found government 'ownership' of the adjustment package high only in one-fifth of the programmes (Killick, 1993a: 110). Some studies have commented on the arrogance of the Fund–Bank staff visiting a country, their 'take-it-or-leave-it approach' and the 'judgemental nature' of their reviews of the performance of that member (Cooper, 1983: 576; Killick, 1992a: 24–27). Apart from coercion, the weak administration in most LDCs tends to fold under the pressure of mounting outside commitments, and permits them no sense of ownership (Killick, 1994: 11–14).

Sometimes a country on its own anticipates these conditionalities, and undertakes policy reforms even before the formal negotiation with these funding bodies begins. In some cases such policy changes are imposed as preconditions by the Fund or the Bank for entering into negotiations. This fulfilment of anticipated (or front-loaded) conditionalities helps the country concerned to claim that its policy changes have not been dictated by the lending bodies and have preceded loan negotiations (Webb and Shariff, 1992: 82; Mosley et al., 1991: 45). In the case of Thailand, half the conditionalities were implemented prior to signing the agreement, as a kind of down payment (Sahasakul et al., 1991: 102).

Varying conditionalities

Generally speaking, for both the World Bank and IMF, the package of conditionalities varies according to the quantum of loan sought, the economic position of the recipient country, the purpose for which the loan is being asked for and the character (political and otherwise) of its government. The larger the loan, other things remaining the same, the greater is the number of conditions and the rigour with which it is monitored. Further, the kind of conditionality imposed on Sub-Saharan Africa would be unthinkable in the case of countries with stronger economies but with some temporary difficulties, and would most certainly not be tolerated by developed countries (Killick, 1993a: 109). If the government concerned is already ideologically and otherwise market-oriented in its approach, the conditionalities are less and the twins tend to take a more lenient attitude in cases of violation of norms or non-fulfilment of some criteria. If, on the other hand, the lending organisations suspect that the government concerned is not basically market-friendly, the conditionalities and their implementation become harsher. Often countries with weak bargaining strength buy conditionalities, even though these are not necessarily the countries that need reform from a Bank point of view, and even though they do not mean to implement them (Mosley et al., 1991: 40). Most studies reveal a high degree of slippage in the implementation, largely arising from lack of political will (Killick, 1993a: 106).

Loan types and conditionalities

Much depends also on the type of loan sought. In the case of IMF, a loan is linked as a percentage of the 'quota' of a member. The first credit tranche, equivalent to 25 per cent of the quota of the country, is made available more easily and with fewer conditions, but the next three upper credit tranches (each of 25 per cent), involve more stringent conditions. A reserve tranche, equivalent to the difference between its quota and current holding by the IMF of its currency, is offered without conditions and is in fact not treated as a loan. In all cases, the permissible quantum of loan is calculated as a percentage of 'quota'.

The Compensatory and Contingency Financing Facility (CCFF) takes care of sudden declines in export earnings which may be due to an adverse movement in terms of trade or a shortfall in remittances from out-migrants, or a sudden increase in import costs, as it happened with oil prices in the 1970s. Earlier, the only requirements for this type of assistance were that the change was unforeseen, was beyond the control of the country concerned, and support was needed. In recent years such CCFF assistance is being made available only for a short period and only to countries which have agreed to a high conditionality IMF programme (Killick, 1992a: 13). As a consequence, this source has become practically dry, accounting for a mere $1 billion throughout the 1980s, and only another $0.50 billion during this period from Buffer Stock Financing Facility (BSFF, a similar facility) (David, 1985: 18; Bird, 1993: 11). In contrast, loan under Structural Adjustment Facility (SAF) or its extended version (ESAF), can fetch up to 350 per cent of the quota under a three-year arrangement, repayment beginning after five-and-a-half years and ending in 10 years, the instalments being paid twice a year. While these loans carry a low rate of interest—of around 0.5 per cent—the conditionalities accompanying them encompass the working of the entire economy and are subjected to strict monitoring as tranches are released.

Generally speaking, IMF conditionalities prescribe the following: (*a*) devaluation to bridge the gap between official and market exchange rates of the currency of the country concerned; (*b*) demand management, mainly by way of reducing government expenditure, to reduce domestic effective demand and consequent inflationary pressure; and (*c*) reduction of fiscal deficit, as a proportion of GDP, below 4 per cent, in phases. Here (*b*) and (*c*) are complementary, as both require curtailment of public expenditure, and both also help to reduce domestic demand for imports. The objective behind these measures is to bring imports in line with export earnings and to take the steam out of the inflationary pressure. Devaluation has become virtually a compulsory requirement for getting IMF assistance since 1983 (Bird, 1993: 20).

Never-ending dependence on loans

One perennial problem with IMF or World Bank assistance is that once dependence on them begins, it seldom ends. One programme is followed by another and loanees, in particular low-income countries, find it difficult to disengage themselves from these funding bodies. Figures show that 21 countries had their support for 14 years or more, and Mexico has continuously been on the agenda, one programme succeeding another, from the beginning of structural adjustment in 1980. During 1979–89, no less than eight had used a minimum of six programmes over a period of six-and-a-half years. There is, thus, strong evidence that IMF policies do not allow a country to graduate away from their reliance on these organisations. All this, despite the idea incorporated in the Articles of Agreement of IMF that such assistance would be temporary and the funds would be revolving (Bird, 1993: 12–13; Killick, 1992a: 17).

Regression models on the demand for IMF loans give inconsistent results with low explanatory power, possibly because of the arbitrary nature of decisions on assistance (Bird, 1993: 22–26). Countries suffering from balance of payment problems initially resist the idea of borrowing from IMF with attached conditionalities, but once a threshold has been passed, they become less resistant to future borrowing (Bird, 1993: 27). In the case of IMF-sponsored structural adjustment facilities, IMF conditionalities come very close to the World Bank ones, as discussed in the following sections (Killick, 1992a: 21–22).

The stabilisation model

The stabilisation programme of IMF rests on a monetarist perspective, a la Milton Friedman and Polak, that the changes in the stock of money are the primary determinants of total spending and, therefore, of the overall level of economic activity. A second aspect is also the Friedmanian view that the demand for money is a function of total wealth and the expected future streams of money income that can be obtained from holding wealth in alternative forms. The third aspect is the view that there exists a close relationship between nominal money and the price level. Taking the three together, movements in the quantity of money tend to provide the most reliable measure of monetary impulses, and these are transmitted to the real sector of the economy via relative prices. Thus, a policy aiming at influencing the real sector of the economy has to find ways of keeping control over changes in the quantity of money, including bank credit.

According to this view, in the long run, growth of output and employment are determined by society's resources. The price level is simply the rate at which money can be exchanged for this output. Since the behaviour of prices over time is determined by the growth in the money stock relative to the growth in output, total spending and the rate of inflation are uniquely dependent on money supply. What is needed, according to this view, is a long-term monetarist policy. A steady and moderate growth in money supply is important as also judicious management of money. Fiscal solutions alone will not work, according to this view, without a monetary policy.

According to this theory, under fixed exchanged rates, the balance of payment is essentially a monetary phenomenon. In the IMF stabilisation programme, based on Polak's model, heavy reliance is placed on the familiar quantitative theory identity, in which national income or output equals the money supply multiplied by the velocity of circulation of money. In that model, money supply is defined as being equal to domestic credit plus foreign exchange reserves. The balance of payment is taken as equal to balance of trade and capital imports, with the behaviour of the latter assumed as independent of money stock and money incomes. The model further assumes that the trade balance depends on income, via the propensity to import and not on expenditure while nominal income is determined by the money stock, with changes in the latter dependent on changes either in domestic credit creation or foreign exchange reserves. The implication is that, if money supply is held constant, any growth in domestic credit will be offset by a reduction in foreign exchange reserves, with any reduction tantamount to balance of payment deficit. Lastly, the transmission process takes place in terms of the influence of the money stock on the level of money income. An increase in domestic credit raises the money stock and therefore money income. This leads to a reduction in international reserves and a balance of payment deficit. In future rounds the deficit leads to a decrease in the money stock, and hence money income, until the initial equilibrium is restored. The main point that emerges from all these is that balance of payment deficit can be corrected by controlling domestic credit expansion (David, 1985: 52–69).

The theory also assumes the law of one price, that there is perfect arbitrage in the international goods market, and that the domestic price level is determined by the international price level or exchange rate. In this situation, imbalances between aggregate demand and aggregate supply arise when the domestic rate of absorption is too high in relation to its income and wrong macro-economic policies are being pursued. When domestic prices and costs are out of line with international prices, the overall competitiveness of the economy is reduced as also the efficiency of the allocative process. In this situation, adjustment of exchange rate or devaluation becomes a remedy. Similarly, the theory assumes only one interest rate.

This monetarist approach has been challenged on a number of grounds. The first question raised is how to measure money in an LDC situation where the level of monetisation is low and a large number of economic transactions are carried out without the exchange of money. The problem is essentially structural in character and an attempt to address it chiefly by means of demand restraint is liable to a high-cost solution (Killick, 1992a: 6). Second, the postulated relationship between changes in money supply and the behaviour of variables in the real sector of the economy, such as current output, is disputed. According to Killick, the monetarist expectation that credit restrictions would have few or no adverse consequences for output and employment have been decisively disproved (Killick, 1993b: 17). In fact, in its quest for external balance, the Fund puts internal balance out of gear. In the middle of the deepest depression for half-a-century, in 1982, IMF sought demand constraint. Under this policy, exports and imports are equalised, but only at a low level of economic activity, as recession is compounded by the deliberate deflationary policies under stabilisation (Williamson, 1983b: 640).

Third, it is contended that, in a situation where the economy is operating below full capacity, increase in money supply will not necessarily lead to inflation. Inflation arises less from an increase in money supply than from supply bottlenecks; in a situation of excess capacity and supply bottlenecks, what are needed are more funds (and not less) and institutions that free supply (Avramovic, 1983: 595). Fourth, the monetarist view that unemployment cannot be pushed below a 'natural rate' and most unemployment is voluntary, is challenged on the ground that it ignores the structural factors that operate in the labour markets in the LDCs (David 1985: 54–60). The projection of devaluation and other adjustments in exchange rate as a cure for all ills has been questioned; partly because of the possibility of competitive exchange rate depreciation by competitors, partly because it often leads to higher prices for goods with high import content, and partly on the ground of low price elasticities of import and export in most LDCs (Killick, 1993a: 16).

No less important is the relationship between exchange rate and fiscal policies. Changes in exchange rate can influence the size of the budget deficit through changes in the revenue generated by customs duty and export duties, foreign debt service, transfers to enterprise and subsidies. If the impact of devaluation on the budget is likely to be adverse, it may be counter-productive to recommend free floating of the currency. In such a situation, 'movements in the exchange rate and the budget deficit might reinforce each other in a destabilizing manner', as it happened in Bolivia, Sierra Leone and Zambia (Chhibber and Khalizadeh-Shirazi, 1991: 30).

The main criticism of this approach is that, in its obsession to control inflation, the policy of demand constraint goes so far as to become self-defeating. It often leads to a contraction of supply, because of its overpowering deflationary impact, which aggravates inflationary pressure (Avramovic, 1989: 15). There is also the risk of devaluation, by transferring real purchasing power to those with a high propensity to save, resulting in raising saving above investment, thus leading to contraction of the economy (Krugman and Taylor, 1978).

World Bank conditionalities: LPG model

The conditionalities imposed by the World Bank tend to be many more in number, less specific and aiming principally at reorienting the incentive structure in tune with a market-centred economy.

These are also less easy to monitor (Polak, 1994: 15). While such conditionalities seek to trade distortions and to produce an optimum allocation of resources, the measures of such distortion vary widely, and often produce confusing and contradictory results. One highly regarded index of distortion, the David Dollar index, finds Japan, Taiwan and South Korea much more trade distorting than India, a result that would be contested by many, no less by the free market diehards in the World Bank itself (Rodrik, 1994: 36–37). The three main components of World Bank conditionalities seek to achieve liberalisation, privatisation and globalisation, described by some as the LPG model (World Bank, WDR, 1994; Webb and Shariff, 1992).

Liberalisation

The core of the idea is that economic management should be left to the market. The prices determined by the interaction of demand and supply forces—whether for commodities, labour power, capital, land, or foreign exchange—should be flexible in either direction and should be capable of clearing the market. The resulting allocation—of resources, commodities, labour power, foreign currency, etc.—would be optimal and efficient, while any deviation from it would involve avoidable social costs. To ensure that markets are allowed to do their jobs, all controls and regulations should be done away with as also measures that constitute barriers to entry (Balassa, 1981: 13–15).

It follows from this that the state should take a back seat in economic matters. Any intervention by the state—in the form of controls, subsidies, selective protection, etc.—would distort prices and make the resulting allocation inefficient, thus hindering economic growth. Controls, by restricting flows of commodities or capital, involve high social costs, distort priorities, and involve rationing in some form or the other. Further, controls create opportunities for rent-seeking and bribing on the part of licence-seekers or for accumulation of social/political power. In the case of the LDCs, such controls operate in favour of the better-off, mostly urban dwellers, including the bureaucrats, at the cost of the rural poor. For instance, food tends to be under-priced in order to satisfy the vocal and powerful urban–industrial sector.

Privatisation

It follows from this economic philosophy that whatever public sector economic activities are in operation should be closed down, phased out or trimmed or passed on to the private sector. Public ownership should be allowed only in cases of natural monopolies and strategic industries, e.g., in defence and research establishments, and should not be allowed to become a drain on state resources. These would operate under a memorandum of understanding that delineates the state's financial commitment and other responsibilities. Privatisation of such enterprises would improve their efficiency and bring in much needed funds for reducing fiscal deficit.

Globalisation

The third major objective is globalisation. Here the core idea is that more trade is better for all the parties concerned—some may gain more than others, but all would gain. Any action that interferes with the free flow of capital, goods and services, would produce sub-optimal results. Import substitution and consequent protective measures, e.g., tariffs, controls and restrictions, raise the cost of domestic production. Such a policy, by reducing their competitiveness, discriminates against those export items that could be traded in the global market on the basis of the country's comparative advantage. Import substitution, in this way, hinders exports, makes the economy inward-looking and increasingly backward, and isolates it from worldwide technical and other changes.

Further, the goal of self-sufficiency makes no sense in a closely integrated world economy with free buying and selling. A country should specialise in production and exports only in those items where it enjoys a comparative advantage, that is, given its factor endowments, where it can produce best. Earnings from such exports should be able to pay for the required imports. In most poor countries such comparative advantage lies in labour-intensive production such as food products and textiles, and not in large-scale capital- and knowledge-intensive industries involving long gestation periods such as steel, oil refining, petrochemicals, or shipbuilding.

Multinational corporations

A corollary of the third is an open door policy with regard to the multinational enterprises—many of which are vertically integrated, operate with numerous affiliates and subsidiaries spread over the world, and maintain close and tacit understanding with fellow oligopolists while also engaging in non-price competition with them. Under structural adjustment, such enterprises should be treated on par with the local enterprises and should not be discriminated against. In particular, local content requirement—e.g., to deploy local labour, to purchase local goods and services, to reinvest a part of the profit within the country or to export a proportion of total production, and so on—should be discontinued. Foreign competition, according to this view, would improve the efficiency of the indigenous producers and would drive them towards production of goods that are in-line with the country's comparative advantage. Further, the vast experience, skill and new technologies of the MNCs would facilitate global integration of the national economy.

The role of the state

This world-view is reflected in specific provisions in the conditionalities of these two organisations. Their insistence in bringing down inflation first to a single-digit level and then further to a figure of around 3–4 per cent reflects their concern for macro-economic stability. The concern for a low fiscal deficit leads them to insist on elimination of subsidies. Privatisation, by improving efficiency and eliminating subsidies for public sector activities, they hope, would reduce fiscal deficit and inflation, while the selling of the government's share in public sectors is expected to contribute further towards the effort to reduce deficit.

Not that the state has been left with no role under this new regime. The main economic task of the government, under the SAP, is to promote human capital formation. Universalisation of literacy, priority extension of technical education and access to safe drinking water and health facilities by all, are seen as major areas of governmental activity. Natural monopolies and areas of security concern are also admitted as exclusive preserves of the state, as also its role in rectifying market failures. Another major task of the state is to create and maintain an incentive structure and environment that is conducive to production under private ownership. All these are in addition to the traditional functions of the state—to maintain law and order and to defend the country. Otherwise, the government is expected to retreat and to allow the market to take over.

Financial and fiscal reform

The Fund–Bank package relies heavily on the financial sector to provide necessary incentives to the private agents of production. Financial reform is, therefore, an integral part of the overall reform package. State-directed credit for certain favoured categories including the poor and the weak, usually along with subsidised interest rates, is frowned at. The interest rate is expected to be flexible and market-determined, while allocation of credit is to be subjected to forces of demand and supply. A corollary of this objective is to keep the real interest rate positive, that is, to keep nominal interest rates ahead of inflation, in order to encourage saving. The concept of 'development banking' is rejected in favour of the view that banks too should aim at profit-maximisation. Uneconomic parts of bank functioning—such as branches in backward and inaccessible areas at a loss—should be discontinued. The state enterprises should not have privileged access to bank finance and should not 'crowd out' private sector investment. Further, banks too should be under private ownership, and foreign ownership should not be discouraged(Chhibber and Khalizadeh-Shirazi, 1991).

Further, bank funding of investment should be coupled with other forms of saving—in equities and bonds. Development of a capital market is seen as a logical progression, which, ultimately, leads to the integration of the domestic capital market with the global capital market. To achieve this, the Bank advises withdrawal of restrictions on capital inflows from foreign sources, and, eventually, full convertibility of currency in capital accounts, which is the ultimate in global integration. Once such integration is achieved, interest rates and exchange rates no longer remain under government control, and emerge from the interaction of demand and supply forces in the world market.

Fiscal reform too is an integral part of the adjustment package. A major objective of such reform is to reduce fiscal deficit below, say, 4 per cent of GDP. Control on fiscal deficit is expected to bring inflation under control and to allow for stable growth. At the same time, given the link between two deficits, this is also likely to reduce trade deficit, and to maintain exchange rates at stable and competitive figures. Between the two ways of reducing fiscal deficit—pruning expenditure and raising revenue—the emphasis is on the expenditure side, particularly curtailment of public expenditure. This is accomplished by reducing the level of subsidies, making public enterprises charge fees and prices that cover their costs, and cutting public expenditure in general. A measure that both cuts government expenditure and liability and augments revenue is the selling of equities in public enterprises. However, here the two objectives of selling shares in public sector units can come into conflict. The revenue-augmenting objective would necessitate the selling of the most efficient and profit-making enterprises that are likely to be in demand, while the efficiency-augmenting objective would require the offloading of the least efficient ones.

Under fiscal reform, the tax structure is expected to be transparent and simple, not arbitrary and/or dependent on the whims and caprices of the taxing authorities and also not oppressive. The rates of taxation should be low enough to encourage compliance and to avoid the growth of 'black money'. Even with lower rates, along with a stricter enforcement, a higher level of compliance is expected that would raise the level of revenue collection. The tax system should be conducive to saving and investment and productive asset accumulation and should not be, as far as possible, discriminatory and selective in its incidence. Linked with trade liberalisation in general, the fiscal reform under structural adjustment expects customs and excise duties to be lowered, which may or may not lead to a fall in revenue collection. If accompanied by better compliance and stricter enforcement, as in the case of direct taxes, this may even lead to an increase in overall tax collection. The streamlined tax system is expected to widen the tax net and improve collection.

Adjustment with a human face

The proponents of structural adjustment do not claim that adjustment can be achieved without pain. The easing of price controls might, at the initial stage, lead to a sudden jump in prices, and inflation might continue at astronomical rates for several years, but, eventually, as prices settle to new, higher levels, inflationary pressure would be brought under control. The Fund–Bank prescription does not rule out growing poverty, inequality or unemployment during the process of adjustment, but, they argue, this would be the price to pay for past follies and for future prosperity. During the 1980s, poverty alleviation was not seen as an area of primary concern in the SAPs, the argument being that a high growth rate would take care of poverty-related problems. State subsidies for the economically poor or socially backward, or for underdeveloped regions were frowned upon while they prescribed whittling down and eventual abolition of public distribution systems (except limited ones targeted at the poorest).

This stern view was somewhat modified after UNICEF pleaded for a 'human face' in structural adjustment (Cornea et al., 1987). Some 'social component' is now added to SAPs, such as a 'renewal fund' or a 'safety net' for severance pay and re-training of a retrenched worker.

This is a bare outline of the Fund–Bank fundamentals and conditionalities. Most of these conditionalities are present in most of the agreements, explicitly or implicitly, though not all the agreements include all the components discussed above.

Consequences: The global experience

In this section we are examining some of the major consequences of the SAP for the economies of the loan recipient countries. These are broad generalisations, based on the reading of available data at the global level, and do not rule out countrywise variations on some specific points.

Banking reform

A major objection to the World Bank-induced banking reform is that it denies the banks any role in the development process, and takes a narrow view of viability and profitability, while a broader social cost-benefit analysis may help in taking policy decisions that conform to national interest. Even if a branch of a bank, located in a distant and backward area, is making losses, that alone cannot be an argument for closing it down, if for the following reasons, the social benefit arising from such location far exceeds the private costs to banks: (*a*) that the branch keeps loan-sharks away and helps to transform the semi-feudal agrarian system into a modern one; (*b*) that the branch mobilises local saving that would have otherwise gone to informal, and often illegal, financial companies who were likely to invest in socially less productive areas such as smuggling or real property; and (*c*) that, taking a long-term view, the initial losses should be taken as an investment for the future generation, that would in time be more than fully repaid as the local economy develops with bank support and working with banks becomes a part of the daily chore of the people.

As for the Development Finance Institutions (DFIs), despite Fund–Bank opposition, these play a social role that the commercial banks are unwilling to undertake, by extending credit to vulnerable sections of the population, backward regions and sick industries. As a consequence, they are unlikely to be as profitable as the commercial banks, but should still be allowed to operate (comment by Maxwell J. Fry in Gelb and Honohan, 1991: 101). To liquidate them because they do not make as much profit as their commercial counterparts, would deprive the backward sections of the population and areas from vital support that is in the overall interest of the national economy.

One controversial issue is whether insolvent banks should be allowed to fail. Going by the 'survival of the fittest' logic of free market, they should be, but considering its consequences, particularly its impact on depositors, and the risk that it would undermine the banking system as a whole, even the most ardent market-oriented governments have shied away from such an attitude. 'Deposit insurance' has been suggested for the protection of depositors in such an eventuality, but this has not made much progress (Gelb and Honohan, 1991: 82–83). As for the cause of insolvency of banks in general, this can arise as much from wrong government controls and policies, as from market failures. In the LDCs, one cause of insolvency is the considerable spread of 4 per cent to 6 per cent, between borrowing and lending rates, that can only be reduced with a higher level of efficiency.

Contrary to monetarist expectations, credit restrictions imposed by stabilisation tend to have adverse consequences for output and employment, particularly because of the undeveloped nature of the financial market. Further, liberalisation of interest rates and credit markets, and the resulting higher interest rates, do not always lead to higher aggregate saving, as the experience of five countries—Indonesia, Malaysia, the Philippines, Korea and Sri Lanka—shows (Cho and Kahtkhate, 1989; Singh, 1995: 87). To quote another study: 'Higher real interest rates and increased financial assets brought about by liberalization of the domestic financial system, or reduced uncertainty or lower inflation stemming from successful stabilization, often have ambiguous or at best minor positive direct effects on private saving' (Schmiddt–Hebbel and Webb, 1992: 139). In several instances it has been found to make a substitution of one form of saving by another, while gross saving ratio appears to be more responsive to GDP growth. Even positive real interest rates fail to have a significant impact on private saving, as the comprehensive econometric study by Schmiddt–Hebbel and Webb reveals; here the resulting income and substitution effects seem to cancel out each other (Schmiddt–Hebbel and Webb, 1992: 152). Such liberalisation, in poor countries with large agricultural sectors, is likely to have adverse growth and distributional implications in the short and long periods. Even if in the short period the balance of payments situation improves due to a reduction in the level of economic activity, over a long period its balance of payment implications are likely to be adverse (Dutt, 1995: 21–22).

Further, market-determined interest rates do not always allocate credit efficiently. This is largely because of asymmetry of information between the suppliers (banks) and the users of finance (corporations) (Singh, 1995: 87). In fact, even in the rich industrialised countries, credit is not allocated to the highest bidder, who may also be the most risky client. There too, lending institutions including banks consult and exchange information amongst themselves, to avoid default, a behaviour that does not conform to World Bank financial guidelines (World Bank, 1993: 91). Where quantitative controls are imposed on credit, the banks tend to prefer bigger customers and active competition from the new customers is discouraged (Killick, 1993a: 17–18). As an influential World Bank document admits: 'In practice, and for a variety of reasons, however, most countries choose to retain some degree of control over financial resource allocation and some degree of subsidy in the financial system' (Gelb and Honohan, 1991: 84).

On a more practical plane, certain difficulties arise in the implementation of banking reform, the foremost being lack of auditing and accounting skills. To the extent the reforms seek upgradation of skills, better record-keeping along with strong computer use, a better definition of efficiency by taking non-performing assets into account, redefinition of capital adequacy to make the banking operations viable, the cleansing of the balance sheets of banks as a once-for-all exercise, suitable measures for debt recovery, improved legal and other measures for regulation, and a service-oriented attitude on the part of the employees; these are usually held as non-controversial (Gelb and Honohan, 1991: 81). A more serious difficulty arises with political patronage, that is responsible both for a large share of bad loans, and also for obstructing loan recovery by legal means, but on this too there is broad consensus that such undue political influence should be resisted.

Capital market and capital account convertibility

The ultimate test of global integration, in the eyes of the BWIs, is the full convertibility of all currencies, and the removal of all restrictions on capital movement. The Feldstein–Horioka hypothesis states that perfect capital mobility across country borders would make domestic savings and national investment uncorrelated. However, the data show that, contrary to the hypothesis, these two are indeed highly correlated, thus proving that capital mobility is still of a low order. There is also a clear North–South divide on this issue. While the correlation is declining in the North, indicating increasing integration, it continues to be high in the South, which shows that mobility of capital is relatively much lower in the LDCs (Feldstein and Horioka, 1980; Vas, 1994: 129–30).

The study by Griffith–Jones shows that in the private international capital markets, periods of over-lending alternate with periods of under-lending. Generally speaking, the private capital market tends to operate pro-cyclically, and comes to no help, and even makes matters worse when things go wrong (Griffith–Jones, 1993: 101–13). Given their pro-cyclical nature, the commercial bank-lending to the LDC markets has ‘proved to be an unstable source with a systemic risk of producing debt crises’ (Vas, 1994:

276). Further, the private capital market, reluctant to take avoidable risk, generally concentrates lending on the bigger and economically stronger among the LDCs. The East Asian countries, and the big ones like India, Brazil and Mexico are favoured, but not the smaller and/or poorer ones such as the Sub-Saharan African countries with low credit rating.

Frankel takes the view that the Feldstein–Horioka hypothesis rests on the crucial assumption that, with perfect mobility, real interest rates would become equal everywhere. If real interest rates are high, investment flowing in from other areas would eventually bring these down. If, on the other hand, real interest rates are low, low saving will crowd out investment, thus forcing the interest rates to go up again. Recent IMF studies show that, leaving aside differentials arising from exchange rate changes interest rates within the industrialised world are converging. However, this is far from true in the case of the LDCs. A major obstacle in the way of interest rate convergence is fluctuation in exchange rates which can put off movement of capital towards high interest areas. In a situation of exchange rate volatility, the capital markets will remain segmented even when there are no restrictions on capital movement, and a forced capital market integration might give rise to, or at any rate add to, interest rate and exchange rate instability (Frankel, 1991; Vas, 1994: 131).

Looking at their history, the industrialised countries of the North have been quite slow to liberalise their capital accounts. It was not until 1958 that the process of liberalisation of capital accounts was initiated and then, in 1961, OECD decided on a code of liberalisation. Still, most industrialised countries were cautious in opening their capital accounts. In the 1970s, several countries, including UK, introduced restrictions on capital movements in the aftermath of the oil crisis. In fact, most of the liberalisation took place in the 1980s, only a decade-and-a-half ago. The progress towards capital account convertibility was slowest in the Southern European countries: at the beginning of the 1990s, France, Portugal, Spain and Ireland still maintained some restrictions on movement of capital across the border. In other words, the twins are now asking the poor countries to do, and immediately without delay, what the rich countries took many decades to carry out even after their economies had become industrialised. In several instances, premature opening up of capital account has been followed by hasty retreat from convertibility when the experiment has made the economy of the country vulnerable, e.g., in Argentina, Chile and Mexico in the mid-1970s (ECLAC, 1994: 234).

Most experts on international finance advise the LDCs not to rush into making capital account convertible. To quote John Williamson:

> It is now generally agreed that the capital account is the last thing that should be liberalized. Failure to heed this advice in an era when funds were readily available on the international capital market led to overvalued currencies, erosion of the productive capacity of the tradable goods sector, and excessive build up in foreign debt [much of which was used to finance capital flight] (Williamson, 1995: 60; Fischer, 1995: 26).

Another word of caution comes from ECLAC:

> It should be recalled that Latin American history has been marked by periods of large-scale capital inflows, followed on a number of occasions by periods of debt crisis. This has sparked a wide-ranging debate on the dynamics of the process of opening up the capital account . . . . The process must be tailored to the economy's capacity to absorb and efficiently allocate external resources (ECLAC, 1994: 21).

In view of the fact that capital movement contributed to disaster in several LDCs, some argue that until the banking system has been strengthened, 'control should be retained over the acquisition of foreign assets and liabilities by residents. This is consistent with giving non-resident Indians and foreigners guarantees of convertibility at the market rate when they buy assets in India' (Joshi and Little, 1995b: 67).

One major advantage with capital account convertibility is that it eliminates the gap between official and unofficial exchange rates, as also allows a thriving business (known as hawala market in India) in illegal transactions in foreign and local currencies. It facilitates business transactions and, in general, makes life easy. The question always is, can such convertibility be sustained in case of a weak currency? Would these currencies not be vulnerable to speculations by some of the mightiest economic forces at work in the world, the international dealers in foreign exchange? As experience shows, these dealers tend to be very sensitive to political changes, weather variations, epidemics, riots and a variety of other factors. Their subjective assessment about the relative strength of a currency, irrespective of whether it is right or wrong, becomes an objective reality as speculation turns against a currency. UK had to opt out of the Exchange Rate Mechanism (ERM) of the European Union several years ago when, despite frantic attempts to shore up the value of sterling by buying pound in the global market, which led to a loss of £7–8 billion in a matter of a few days, the slide of the currency driven by powerful speculation could not be stemmed. In case of a poor and weak country, such adverse speculation can do incalculable and perhaps, irreversible harm to the economy. If UK and Spain had to come out of ERM unable to handle speculation, what chance would poor countries have (Killick, 1993a: 15)? As ECLAC observes, full convertibility on capital account is a high risk strategy as it takes control over money supply out of the hands of the government and leaves it entirely to the market (ECLAC, 1994: 227–28).

Another serious problem is related to the earlier point raised about interest rates. Capital account convertibility would imply that even the domestic investors would be able to borrow from foreign sources at low interest rates. In this situation, domestic banks in the LDCs would be forced to lend at a low rate of interest that is comparable with rates in the developed countries. But that would require the banks in those countries to borrow at rates that are even lower. Here the critical question is whether adequate domestic saving would be forthcoming at that low interest rate, or whether there would not be a risk of more of domestic saving getting diverted to non-banking, informal, financial institutions that offer higher interest rates and then lend, at still higher rates, to low priority, often illegal activities such as financing real property speculation or movies with black money. Some take the view that a dual exchange rate regime can act as a shock absorber of changes in the capital account, if the premium does not exceed 15 to 20 per cent (Dornbusch and Kuenzler, 1993).

A related question is about the functioning of the stock markets that the BWIs are keen to foster, on the grounds that it logically follows the development of a country's financial sector, and it helps integration of a country's economy with the global market.

Though after the 1982 debt crisis there was a fall in private capital flows, these again began increasing in the late 1980s. Total bond issues in international security markets by developing countries increased from $5 billion per year during 1987–90, to $12 billion in 1991 and then to $23 billion in 1992. Figures show that placements by developing country companies in international equity markets also grew rapidly, from $1 billion in 1990 to $7 billion in 1992. However, such participation is limited to a very small number of countries: Argentina, Mexico, Brazil and Venezuela in Latin America; China, Korea, Turkey and Hungary in Asia and Europe. But low-income countries, particularly those with unresolved debt burdens, and most former socialist countries have had virtually no access to the international securities market (Development Committee, 1993a: 39–40).

Under Fund–Bank persuasion, a number of countries have opened stock markets, and are offering fiscal benefits of various types to encourage people to buy shares and bonds, e.g., exemption from wealth taxation. The stock market is supposed to encourage saving by providing households with additional instruments—in the form of equities or bonds—for saving, which may better meet their risk preferences and liquidity needs. However, it is not clear how much of additional saving is generated from stock market operation, and how much of it is merely substitution of some other forms of saving, while leaving the aggregate saving unaltered (Singh, 1995: 89, 100). In some of the high-saving East Asian countries, such as Singapore, institutional sources, such as provident fund, account for the bulk of the saving. In the rich countries too, institutional savers, e.g., pension funds, are more important in mobilising saving than the non-institutional sources in the capital market. In the US, in 1989, pension funds amounted to a mind-boggling sum of $7.5 trillion, and grew at the rate of 15 per cent per year (Singh, 1995: 90, 101). In any case, progress in this direction has been slow and patchy, and concentrated in a small number of countries: seven countries—Taiwan, South Korea, Thailand, Malaysia and India from Asia, and Brazil and Mexico for Latin American—together accounting for 90 per cent of the capitalisation among 30 LDCs listed by the International Finance Corporation (IFC) (Singh, 1995: 72–79).

Another question deals with what role the foreign capital is likely to play in the stock market. One advantage often cited is that the flow of foreign capital spares the need for external borrowing, which, in any case, is becoming hard to get. Over time, the flow of concessional country-to-country overseas development assistance (ODA), has declined, though still it accounts for 40 per cent of all flows to LDCs. 'In real terms, however, growth has been zero and ODA flows have fallen as a share of donor economies over the past decade, to 0.34 per cent of GNP compared with the 0.7 per cent target. Relative to per capita income of recipient countries, ODA flows have fallen in real terms' (Development Committee, 1993a: 47).

To the extent this capital comes by way of Foreign Direct Investment (FDI), it contributes to the growth of industries, often based on highly sophisticated technologies, and bears the risk of investment. In recent years, FDI in developing countries has increased: from $17 billion per year during 1987–90 to $29 billion in 1991 and $37 billion in 1992. But, making the same monotonous statement again, it tends to be concentrated in some of the more privileged among the LDCs, such as those in East and Southeast Asia and the big countries in Latin America (Development Committee, 1993a: 39). As we will see in Chapter 6, Japan, suspicious of foreign capital, kept the domestic capital market in tight control and insulated it from the world capital market for a very long time. Only the government sector had access to international borrowing and lending, and FDI was heavily circumscribed (Singh, 1995: 87). Here the fear was that an excessive flow of FDI might harm the nascent domestic industrial producers.

Recently, more fear has been expressed in relation to capital flows other than FDI. Lured by high interests and high returns from the share market, this flow tends to be speculative in motive, and can leave as quickly as it comes when the relative conditions change. Even when such capital flow comes from the nationals residing abroad, their patriotism is severely tested when the relative return declines for one reason or another. The latter are usually first to invest in their mother country, as they are more knowledgeable than other international investors, and are also usually the first to take their money out as they are more likely to come to know of an impending crisis than others, thus aggravating the crisis (ECLAC, 1994: 212). Foreign institutional investors, such as pension funds, are likely to be more stable and less susceptible to short-term fluctuations.

Non-FDI equity flows usually take three forms: (*a*) depository receipts that trade on industrial country markets; (*b*) direct purchase of equity shares on local developing country markets; and (*c*) country funds. The American Depository Receipts (ADRs) are negotiable equity-backed instruments that are traded on the US securities market. Global Depository Receipts (GDRs) are similar but can be traded on several industrial-equity markets. Country funds are close-ended; once an initial public offer is made, the amount available for investment is fixed. This is usually the first step towards opening the local stock market to foreign investors. The International Finance Corporation (IFC), a subsidiary of the World Bank, plays a major role in promoting these. Equity purchase depends on local laws; it is permitted in some countries and not in others, while, where permitted, it is subjected to some restrictions (e.g., percentage of foreign capital permitted in the equity of a company) (Development Committee, 1993b: 41–43).

The case of Latin America shows that GDP rate is negatively correlated with dependence on external finance. During 1950–65, only 1 per cent of GDP came by way of external finance and the net transfer was negative, but still Latin America managed a rate of growth of GDP of around 5.5 per cent. Whatever external finance came, was either FDI (60 per cent) or medium- and long-term loans by foreign governments or multilateral agencies (40 per cent). Speculative capital played no role. In contrast, during the period from the mid-1960s to the early 1980s, external finance, partly induced by recession in OECD countries, and then the availability of the petro-dollar, accounted for 3 per cent of regional GDP but the region managed growth rates of around 4–5 per cent of GDP. By the early 1980s, external debt had reached a staggering figure of $300 billion, three-quarters of which was from private international banks, exceeding the critical level of solvency of 200 per cent of export earnings. Debt-servicing took away one-third of export earnings, while interest on external public debt accounted for 10–25 per cent of tax revenue. This led to the debt crisis, with Mexico's declaration in August 1982 that it could not continue to service its bank debt. Though the subsequent international rescue operation made it possible for Mexico to repay its debts, it came about at a high economic cost. The recession engineered by IMF's stabilisation programme brought down imports to the level of low exports, and caused an outflow of resources of the order of 4 per cent of regional GDP during 1982–86 (ECLAC, 1994: 191–94).

Again in the early 1990s, the outflow was turned into inflows, largely because of slow growth in the developed countries and the persistent high yield on capital in Latin America. A great deal of the external fund also came to take advantage of the privatisation of public sector enterprises or by way of the debt–equity swap. The foreign investors were also aiming to diversify and reduce risks on their investment by spreading it to many countries. ECLAC had been warning that a great deal of what was coming was short-term (51 per cent of the total in 1991), speculative and volatile, but its warning was not heeded. While some experts discounted the possibility of massive withdrawals, ECLAC warned in early 1994 that a crisis was brewing. Its observation,

> However, the financial influence of investors and externalities on the stock exchange is so great that we must not underestimate the risk of possible stampedes by foreign investors and systemic crises for events on the stock or foreign exchange markets may induce a massive liquidation movement in an attempt to cut losses sustained as a result of additional price declines

turned out to be prophetic when Mexico faced the second, and even more serious, crisis in 1995, and had to be rescued with emergency lending mobilised with the help of the President of the United States (ECLAC, 1994: 204–16).

It has also been pointed out, referring to the East Asian experience, that banks are more stable and reliable than stock markets in providing funds for industrial investment. On the other hand, the 'takeovers' and 'mergers', which are regular features of stock market operations, often reflect a company's success more with financial engineering than with production. Share prices do not always reflect the long-term expected earnings, since the operators in the share market typically take a short-term view of the affairs of a company, and, basing themselves on the present discounted value of future earnings, ignore the earning potential beyond, say, a period of 10 years. Banks, generally, take a longer-term view, but also suffer from 'crony capitalism' (that is, favouritism), particularly when industrial and financial interests get merged, and political patronage gives rise to imprudent and non-viable lending (Singh, 1995: 104–6).

Strict legislative and administrative control of both banks and the capital market by the government and the central bank is a must for their successful operation and for avoiding illegal and wasteful transactions. The drive towards computerisation, the setting up of depositories of shares, and of statutory authorities for controlling capital issues in order to keep fly-by-night operators out, and a more orderly conduct of stock market operations in place of haggling on the floor, has been a feature of capital market reform in recent years. Governments are also adopting measures to restrict capital flows to those committed to somewhat longer terms. It is still too early to say whether such measures would make the capital markets thrive in the LDCs.

One major difficulty in the functioning of the capital market is the lack of access to vital information on the part of the potential purchasers/sellers of shares. The operation of stock markets, as these are run, is a highly specialised area, with its own vocabulary, practices and conventions, with which ordinary investors are unfamiliar. In such a situation, its operation becomes manipulable by unscrupulous influential brokers, which can lead to heavy losses incurred by the ordinary investors, which in turn can cause a serious erosion in their confidence, making them withdraw from the stock market, as it happened in India during 1991–96.

GDP growth, saving and investment ratios and export earnings

One major consequence of demand management under the IMF stabilisation programme has been, for most countries, a decline in saving and investment ratios associated with or leading to a decline in GDP growth rate, even when trade deficits have been eliminated and inflation has been bridled (Corbo and Fischer, 1992: 14). This is largely because, contrary to the Fund–Bank fundamentals, a decline in public investment, carried out in order to reduce fiscal deficit, has not been compensated by a corresponding rise in private investment. Rather than crowding out private investment, as the World Bank would make us believe, public investment in an area signals government priorities and commitment and willingness to share risks, that encourages private investment. One study shows that across the world, the government size is positively associated with growth (Ram, 1986: 16). The complementary nature of these two types of investment, in the context of the LDCs, is not understood by the voluminous World Bank literature and its prescriptions (Muzulu, 1993: 31; Stevens and Solimano, 1992: 132). Perhaps the only major exception is Chile, where private investment has made up for the decline in public investment (Stevens and Solimano, 1992: 120).

Further, when a government is forced to reduce its expenditure, the axe tends to fall on capital expenditure, e.g., on irrigation, power and other major rural infrastructure, to the detriment of production (Killick, 1992a: 19–20). In many cases, social expenditure on education or health is also curtailed (Mosley et al., 1991: 101–2). The global experience shows that a fiscal adjustment that falls disproportionately on capital expenditure tends to reduce private investment and hinders export promotion by leading to exchange rate appreciation in some cases (Foroutan, 1993: 29). The balance achieved between imports and exports, in this situation, often reflects a low capacity to import because of a slow rate of growth of GDP. As two scholars from within the World Bank once pointed out, 'There is little merit in having a low budget deficit and a low external account deficit if the outcome is a low level of saving and investment in the economy' (Chhibber and Khalizadeh–Shirazi, 1991: 28).

The stabilisation programme, by constraining growth, also reduces the capacity of the economy to export, thus, making it harder to restore external balance. One econometric study, by El Farhan, using data of 32 countries of Sub-Saharan Africa, finds a close positive correlation between GDP growth and export earnings and a negative one with debt-service ratio (Killick, 1992b: 12–14). As the experience of Sub-Saharan African countries shows, despite following the IMF and World Bank prescriptions more truthfully than most recipient countries, they are yet to recover from deflation induced by the IMF package. Repeated devaluations have failed to boost demand for their exports, though the external accounts are in better balance now than they had been in the past. In several cases, competitive devaluation has brought collective ruin for countries exporting the same range of products, as the prices have steeply declined. One study shows that per capita income declined in 17 out of 23 countries undertaking structural adjustment in Africa and 11 out of 13 adjusting countries in Latin America, during the 1980s, which is now described as the 'lost decade of the eighties' (comments by Frances Stewart, in Corbo et al., 1992: 67).

and, with a few exceptions, no effort has been made to increase tax revenue. One dominant argument against such policy, a la Donald Please, is that, such transfer of resources from the corporate and rich private sector to the public sector by way of taxation might reduce aggregate saving in the country, as the propensity to save is relatively lower in the latter. However, as the East Asian experience shows, it is possible to raise tax revenue to finance public investment, which in turn can raise aggregate saving and investment in a country (Chhibber and Khalizadeh-Shirazi, 1991: 27).

Justification of such an attitude on the ground that it operates as a disincentive, again, looks at the issue from one side—that is, the requirement to induce the rich to make an effort to become richer by producing more—but not the other one, no less important, of providing incentive for the vast majority of workers who would actually turn the wheel. In fact, the literature on structural adjustment and NPE is replete with policy prescriptions that would keep wages within limits, even by way of repression of organised labour, while allowing the industrialists and traders to maximise profit.

Some have questioned the Fund–Bank obsession with fiscal deficits. Fiscal and budget deficits do not necessarily give rise to inflation. The high and continued budget deficits in the US in recent years have not given rise to a high rate of inflation. In Pakistan, a 7 per cent fiscal deficit during the 1980s, accompanied an inflation rate of 7 per cent and a GDP growth of 6.5 per cent per annum (Zaidi, 1994: 2–11). If output is below capacity levels, an increase in money supply may be non-inflationary and output-augmenting (Dell, 1983: 37). It all depends on how the money created is spent; if this is moved in the right direction and the production grows, the deficit alone may not give rise to inflation or crowd out private investment. Further, high budget deficit need not necessarily influence current account deficit. As the experience in Thailand and Malaysia shows, it is possible for a government to maintain a high budget deficit without prejudicing the current account if the private sector is willing to generate additional net saving surpluses at reasonable rates of inflation and real interest rates (Chhibber and Khalizadeh-Shirazi, 1991: 27–39). Some have even asked whether inflation alone is a debilitating factor. The years of high and sustained real growth in Brazil witnessed astronomical inflation levels of around 40 per cent (Dornbusch, 1992: 114; Stevens and Solimano, 1992: 122; Stein 1995: 14–15). The 'secret' of an elaborate and structured system of wage indexation and price mark-ups, with a high degree of predictability, was no secret and was, in a sense, 'a more transparent way of grappling with falling real wages' (Dornbusch, 1992: 114).

Trade reform and export orientation

There is an implicit understanding in much of the Fund–Bank literature that export orientation, openness and competition are universal good things that benefit everyone (Balassa, 1981: 3–9). The assumption underlying the argument is that global trade is free and competitive, there are few barriers to entry and all that a country needs, in order to reap its benefits, is to identify commodities in which it enjoys a comparative advantage.

This formulation has been challenged. As John P. Lewis commented: 'The neoclassical alternative of a completely open international market is not a viable alternative because it is not available' (Lewis, 1995: 34). A recent OECD document observes that there is no free world market, and that the global market is typically dominated by large oligopolistic firms engaged in mostly non-price, and sometimes price competitions amongst themselves (OECD, 1995: 209). As we will see in Chapter 4, exports from LDCs are subjected to a variety of trade restrictions in the developed countries. Further, as we will see in Chapter 6, the concept of comparative advantage need not be a static one, based on resources and history; a dynamic interpretation of that concept is that comparative advantage can be created in certain situations, by investing in heavy industries, as indeed has been done in East Asia. To quote Helpman and Krugman: 'Competition in the international markets is typically imperfectly competitive and that trade is, to a considerable degree, driven by economics of scale rather than comparative advantage.' Therefore, it makes sense for a government to favour industries that generate externalities (Helpman and Krugman, 1985 quoted in Corbo and Fischer, 1992: 10).

Nor can the world prices for various commodities be taken as objective prices reflecting their scarcity values. As we will see in Chapter 4, such prices embody high rich-country subsidies and market manipulation. These, therefore, cannot be taken as objective measures to decide on the comparative advantage of a country in world trade. Further, there is no conclusive statistical evidence that liberalisation boosts exports (Agosin, 1981: 21). Perhaps, more important than any other policy change at the global level for the benefit of the LDCs, could have been some restructuring of global trade in order to reverse the unfavourable shift in terms of trade in favour of primary producers. Chapter 4 shall discuss this point further.

Agriculture

Agriculture was expected to benefit from structural adjustment which, in the LDC context, is distinctly biased in favour of that sector. With the dismantling of controls that favoured urban–industrial interests, agriculture was likely to take off and its exports were supposed to be the main earner of foreign exchange (along with light industries such as textiles) for meeting the costs of imports of other goods. Agriculture was taken as an area where the LDCs possessed a comparative advantage, and with the dissolution of controls that kept domestic agricultural prices low and the costs of agricultural inputs high, this advantage was supposed to take the economy to new heights. Further, the agriculturists, identified as potential beneficiaries from structural reform, were expected to form the core of a political coalition in support of reform, in order to make it politically feasible in the face of stiff opposition from vested interests in industries and urban areas (Knudsen and Nash, 1991; Dasgupta, 1997a; 1997b).

Despite these expectations, agriculture has, generally speaking, done badly under structural adjustment. In most cases, with the dissolution or dilution of the working of the commodity marketing boards under the World Bank directive, and the adverse terms of trade effect mentioned above, prices have become lower and unstable. Where agriculturists have gained from higher prices of their produce, either because of withdrawal of price control or because of a rise in government-administered support prices, this has been outweighed by higher input prices they have been asked to pay because of cessation or lowering of subsidies for inputs. In several instances, only the larger, surplus-producing farmers have gained from higher agricultural prices, given the highly skewed land distribution in most of the LDCs (Dasgupta, 1997b; ILO, 1993: 5; Toye, 1991: 190–97). The rural producers have also suffered more than they have gained from higher crop prices, due to the curtailment of public expenditure on irrigation, power, roads, education and health, undertaken in order to reduce fiscal deficit as already discussed (Webb and Shariff, 1992: 77–78).

Perhaps most serious has been the withdrawal or dilution of fertiliser subsidies. Such subsidies compensate for the imperfection in the capital market and for all the risks associated with the adoption of a high-risk technology, stimulate trial and error in fertilisers and offset initial high costs of distribution and transport when the use of fertilisers is low, mainly from the point of view of the poor majority (Islam, 1991: 154). Nor should one grudge subsidies that help to stabilise agricultural prices, e.g., by way of price support schemes, and thus, protect the investment of the farmers and of those engaged in downstream activities. Agricultural production remaining dependent on the vagaries of nature, and the system of crop insurance being undeveloped, governments cannot absolve themselves of the responsibility of intervening in the market for bringing about stability of prices and supply. Nor can access to the international market be a solution for occasional sellers and buyers, who are unlikely to get good prices or to find the required amount for importing (Islam, 1991: 155–56).

On balance, the influence on agricultural output has been more negative than positive. Politically also, there is no evidence anywhere of the agriculturists marching to the capital with waving flags in their hands to express their support or gratitude to the governments for implementing structural adjustment. In any case, the high level of agricultural protectionism in the US and Western Europe, far exceeding that in LDCs, has undermined the credibility of Fund–Bank prescriptions favouring liquidation of agricultural subsidies and controls in these countries (Development Committee, 1992: 93–94). On the other hand, these SAPs have ignored the most basic structural issue in agriculture: that is, land reform. On the contrary, in several cases, the process of land reform has been reversed under structural adjustment, as in Chile, Peru and Ethiopia (Knudsen and Nash, 1991: 137).

Industry

The main thrust of the industrial policy under structural adjustment has been towards elimination of control and subsidies, support to private agents, rolling back of the state from economic affairs, and 'getting the prices right'. The removal of entry barriers, under adjustment, allows both domestic and foreign private companies to move in, while attempts to impose 'local content requirements' on foreign firms are frowned upon. The programme discourages investment in heavy industries and prefers production in line with the 'comparative advantage' of a country, which in effect implies specialisation in light industries such as textiles and garments. The conditionalities imposed by the World Bank reflect its strong opposition to a national strategy of self-reliance based on import-substituting industrialisation.

There is no evidence that domestic industries have bloomed under structural adjustment anywhere. Developing countries responded to economic crisis by substantial reductions in the domestic market's share of manufactured imports, especially in Africa and Latin America. In a sample of 50 developing countries, examined by Tybour, growth in manufacturing value added dropped during 1982–83, but that occurred along with the decline in the rest of the economy, while in Africa it shrank more than proportionately. There was a distinct preference for policies that insulated industrial producers and urban workers and consumers. A sub-sample of adjusting loan receiving countries showed better than average growth in their respective regions. The evidence of import penetration during the adjustment period was weak (Tybour, 1991: 159–79).

As we will see in Chapter 6, in East Asia, where a group of LDCs have sustained a high rate of industrial growth for three decades, the influence of Fund and Bank was conspicuous by its absence during the course of their growth. Perhaps the 'southern tier' of three Southeast Asian countries; Thailand, Indonesia and Malaysia, two of which operated for a long time under structural adjustment, is the best example of industrial success under this package (see Chapter 7). But the record gets somewhat soiled when one recalls that the fourth country in the region, the Philippines, which was at one time the most advanced of the four, and which has been showered with more blessings by the Bretton Woods twins than the other three, has failed to take off despite being under BWI tutelage ever since structural adjustment was initiated (Mosley, 1991). One possible explanation for their success lies in the flying geese model, or some of its variants such as the neighbourhood effect, that attributes industrialisation in this area to the shifting of Japanese (and then East Asian) capital to this region in order to evade restrictions placed upon their own investments by the West (Chapter 7).

Issue of privatisation

Since state intervention in economic affairs is considered to be bad per se, two types of issues are handled in relation to public sector units in SAPs: first, how many of these public sector units can be transferred to private hands to make them more efficient, and, second, how those remaining in the public sector can be made more efficient and less burdensome for the government. As for the first, we have already noted that in the privatisation programmes, concern for bringing down fiscal deficit makes the state sell mainly those public sector units which are running well, but which also have a good demand in the market. On the other hand, units that are not performing well and might possibly benefit by being transferred to private ownership, generally fail to find buyers, partly also because the domestic capital markets are unwilling to fund such transfers, and the governments continue to run these at a loss. Shutdowns are not seen as a preferred alternative in this situation as these lead to increased unemployment and provoke strong opposition.

Even in countries where public sector units have been sold in dozens, e.g., in Chile or Mexico, potential buyers often collude and offer low prices. Sleaze is a regular companion of such transactions (Webb and Shariff, 1992: 80; Nash, 1991: 503; Boratav, 1993: 31, 34). A senior economist with pro-privatisation views like Arnold C. Herberger, has cautioned: 'Even people as generally market-oriented as myself are advising governments to move carefully, to go slowly and to think about the prices they are getting and alternate terms on which to achieve privatization. Governments should, in particular, try to have a saleable asset before putting it for sale' (Corbo et al., 1992: 182). As someone has commented, the World Bank 'should continue to move away from specifying the number of public enterprises to be sold by a particular date; this approach is counterproductive' (Nellis, 1991: 125).

Many states, goaded by the World Bank, tend to dismantle the public sector hastily, even when the private sector is not ready to offer services that were until then delivered by the state-owned units (Mosley et al., 1991: 112). As one Bank document concludes: 'When the immediate alternatives are limited, however, it is not always advisable to dismantle public agencies' (World Bank, 1990a: 39). Another World Bank document takes the view that privatisation is not always a necessary strategy; in China or South Korea, the private sector grew without privatisation. More important is to stress on restructuring and upgrading public administrative capacities. It also admits that the attitude regarding privatisation has been changing in the light of the East Asian experience (Development Committee, 1993a: 69–70).

It is instructive to make note of the following observations on divestiture of public enterprises by a World Bank staff paper, that are usually overlooked:

> First, the ultimate goal should be efficiency—not divestiture in itself. Monopoly rights, favorable financing terms, and protection from imports will attract buyers, but they will also curb competition and reduce the efficiency gains from divesting. Second, successful divestiture takes time. Attempts to privatize quickly without due process and without transparent, orderly procedures can lead to transferring firms to buyers that lack the capability to operate or finance the enterprises. Third, adequate preparation is essential. Experience shows that prior restructuring of the enterprise (for example, rationalizing the labor force or financial restructuring) may be essential for the negotiation of an agreement that is politically acceptable and that also produces an efficient firm.

It then goes on to add: 'Finally, although most countries have focused on sales and liquidation, other mechanisms—such as management contracts, leases, asset stripping (selling peripheral assets of a state firm), and contracting out billing, maintenance, and so on—can also bring important efficiency gains and may be less politically contentious' (Development Committee, 1990b: 41).

Although about 31 countries are involved in privatisation, supported by the World Bank, the success achieved in this programme so far has been quite modest. A 1991 study of eight Commonwealth countries shows that, of about 2,000 public enterprises, only 80, mostly small, have been privatised, mainly by way of direct sale; only in Jamaica and Trinidad and Tobago, sales proceeds exceed 1 per cent of GDP. And, in nearly all, the public property has been under-priced. In Kenya, through privatisation, foreign control has expanded, as also in several Latin American countries under the debt–equity swap arrangement. In Chile, the number of public enterprises was brought down from around 500 to only 13 between 1973 and 1978, after the coup led by Pinochet, but raised only $585 million because of under-pricing, while the auction of forests and national parks led to environmental degradation. In Bangladesh, in 1982, under General Ershad, privatisation of a majority of 544 public enterprises led to deterioration in terms of output and financial performance, particularly of jute and cotton textile mills (Bhaskar, 1992: 12–31).

Drive towards privatisation under the Bank's mandate fails to take into account the circumstances that led to the proliferation of public sector units in many of these LDCs. Very few of these were set up by way of takeover of private units, and a large number of these were transferred from the private sector at its request as the unit concerned was making losses and was unable to keep going. A number of these, the bigger ones with high capital and knowledge intensity and long gestation periods, were brought into being because the domestic private sector was unwilling to undertake the task, while the government was unwilling to accept the foreign concerns in control over those commanding heights of the economy. If these units are not running with a desirable level of efficiency, there is no guarantee that private ownership would do any better.

Public enterprise reform

Public enterprise reform turns out to be the most difficult of all reforms incorporated in structural adjustment (Development Committee, 1993b: 42). We have already referred, in the previous chapter, to the admission by a World Bank document that once barriers to entry have been removed, there is no a priori presumption as to whether better management will be found in the public or private sector (World Bank, WDR, 1983: 50). Allocative efficiency is a function of market structure and not of the form of ownership (Muzulu, 1993: 31). In East Asia, public enterprises manage to show good profits, and produce a saving that helps domestic investment. Some of the public enterprises in that region are among the best in the world in their fields. Obviously, the East

Asian case cannot be generalised. In most LDCs, public sector units are seldom models of efficiency; but are the private sector units any better? It is generally found that many of the loss-making public sector units were earlier in private hands and were passed on to the former in order to save jobs. If the public sector as a whole is doing badly, in terms of conventional performance criteria, this is at least partly because it is saddled with many such sick, erstwhile private sector units.

Comparing like with like is not easy. The tendency to compare the most efficient private sector units with the most inefficient public sector ones can only produce biased results. Further, any comparison should take into account many social responsibilities the public sector units carry out, which privately owned units, operating solely on profit considerations, would never undertake, e.g., crop insurance, power transmission or banking in sparsely populated vast rural areas, or oil exploration in untested areas with unknown possibilities. While the private sector is allowed to be money-minded, public opinion is more alert and vigilant when it comes to the functioning of the public sector, as it expects the latter to play the role of a model employer, e.g., under-payment or casualisation of the workforce is not on. Further, when competing in the same area with the private sector, they are by no means operating on a level playing field, as they lack autonomy and are saddled with an administrative culture that permits regular bureaucratic interference in their functioning, forcing inefficient decisions. Despite all these, there is no harm in repeating what we have already mentioned in the previous chapter, a comparison of the balance sheet of the entire public sector with that of the entire private sector including both the efficient units and those which were sick or closed down, would probably leave the matter inconclusive, or even turn out in favour of the public sector.

Obviously, public enterprises should try to cover their costs, and even to earn a return that is comparable with returns to investment in other activities, by offering their goods and services at appropriate prices. There can be no argument on the point that less subsidy is better than more; no subsidy and even a substantial surplus over costs is even better. The question is, when fixing prices, should the enterprise completely ignore the linkages between the supply and price of its goods and services on the one hand, and the rest of the economy, on the other, and take a narrow enterprise-based approach? For instance, what are the implications of high, non-subsidised fertiliser prices for the adoption of modern agrarian technologies by poor farmers or even on aggregate food production? Does the rate of exhaustion of a natural resource, following a time-bound and project-bound policy of profit maximisation, safeguard the interests of the generations yet to be born? Such issues would probably make no impression on private enterprises, unless forced by legislation and regulations, but can these be ignored by the publicly owned ones? Even a privately owned unit—whether a cafeteria cooking many items or a multinational enterprise involved in many activities and in many countries—seldom seeks profit maximisation on each and every slice of activity and fixes prices accordingly; what counts in its case is the overall profit taking all the items and operations into account. Extending this analogy to publicly owned units, what would be the difference in principle if the owner, the government, attempts to base its policies on optimising overall profit (which is defined as achieving a target rate of growth of GDP, while also creating a certain amount of employment and reducing disparity) taking all its enterprises and activities into account? Much depends on who is optimising what and how.

Labour, employment and social issues

The protagonists of structural adjustment seek reform of the labour market too, by rescinding labour legislations that inhibit dismissal of employees, and reduce factor mobility and substitution, but in most countries, because of strong local opposition, have not been able to make much headway in this area. As one World Bank document puts it, 'the Bank has acquiesced in the desire of the governments to avoid the politically sensitive issue of labour retrenchment' (Corbo and Fischer, 1992: 11; Webb and Shariff, 1992: 78). Only in a country like Ghana, where ghost workers constitute a significant proportion of the public pay roll, a substantial public saving has been achieved by removing many (not all) of these from the list (Toye, 1991: 175).

In general, structural adjustment leads to a freeze in public employment. The organised private sector employment also seldom grows because of the low level of private investment and high capital intensity of what takes place. Most of the unemployed fall back on the low productivity informal sector which acts as a natural safety net. The organised sector also takes full advantage of the surplus labour situation by opting for contract labour and casualisation, and for putting out systems that avoid establishment costs and make it easier for them to offload surplus workers as demand falls. This high social cost of SAPs has been a recurrent theme in studies by UNICEF and ILO among others. In Sub-Saharan Africa structural adjustment has destabilised many poor households, which have been hurt by inflation and food scarcity (ILO, 1993: 4–9; Cornea et al., 1987).

For a long time, social issues were ignored by the World Bank, but from the early 1990s, thanks to a campaign launched by UNICEF, a 'social dimension' is now added to SALs, e.g., with a safety net and renewal programmes that cushion the impact of retrenchment in non-viable industries by offering some funding and training for self-employment and other jobs (Development Committee, 1993b: v). However, the amounts available for these activities have usually proved to be inadequate. On this issue, there appears to be a serious contradiction between the Bretton Woods twins and ILO, which views provision of social insurance and social protection both as a human right and as an essential element to be embodied in concepts of international labour standards (Development Committee, 1993b: 123). There is a strongly held view, and not only by the trade unionists, that long-term labour contracts, with tenure systems and the like, are an important feature of well-functioning labour markets in many developed countries; Japan as a country and IBM as a company being two good examples of such a policy (Corbo and Fischer, 1992: 20).

In recent years, through the offices of WTO, attempts are being made to impose some 'labour standards' on the LDCs which despite the high moral posturing by the Trinity (including WTO with the twins), are in effect concealed protectionist measures against LDC exports. The latter have now begun raising the issue of labour mobility (paralleling the rich country demand for mobility of capital) and the easing of immigration laws in the rich countries to allow poor country labour export as a countervailing measure.

Most studies show that structural adjustment gives rise to poverty, unemployment, lowering of wages and a lower level of access to health and education, as government social spending and subsidies are reduced and wages are held back in the face of inflation

(Muzulu, 1993: 32). One Bank study admits that 'Little is known about how poor people at large are affected when countrywide subsidies have to be cut back to reduce the government deficit'. But then adds hastily: 'But experience with adjustment programs has already shown clearly that failure to adjust is likely to hurt the poor' (Development Committee, 1990a: 31). Another World Bank study, evaluating the performance of the adjustment programmes in the 1980s, admits that calorie intake had stagnated or declined during the 1980s, and the poor had been hurt by the pruning of government activities or privatisation of health and other services; in the latter case the richer are targeted by those providing services (World Bank, 1992: 6; Zuckerman, 1991: 254). On the other hand, on the basis of evaluations undertaken by the World Bank, some take the view that adjustment lending is not associated with misery, and is less costly, in social terms, than disorderly adjustment without Bank support would have been (Corbo and Fischer, 1992: 14). Some protagonists go so far as to argue that a country has no choice but to go through this pain because of past follies and the future it promises. There is a view that even 'social safety nets' should be privatised, while the more dominant view is that, in view of limited fund-management capability and the virtual non-existence of a regulatory mechanism, such a measure might expose the pensioners and other beneficiaries to a high risk (Development Committee, 1993b: 5, 69–74).

The 'social safety net', as a concept, has been in circulation for a long time, but it is not sufficiently precise to be amenable to the operational thrust. Informal sectors are often described as natural safety nets because this is where those having no other option usually go. In the world of the Bank the range of safety net instruments is described as follows: (*a*) targeted public delivery of basic goods and services—food, education, health, housing, water, etc., subsidised, free or work-exchanged; (*b*) cash transfer or payments; (*c*) employment services and re-training; (*d*) consumer subsidies on basic goods; (*e*) infrastructure development in poor areas; (*f*) support to basic need suppliers; and (*g*) public information and knowledge transfers. Those being rescued through such safety nets are in turn classified as follows: (*a*) permanently unable to earn income from market economy (old, disabled, etc.); (*b*) temporarily unsupported, e.g., children, students, nursing mothers, sick, inadequately educated; (*c*) those who temporarily do not earn because of their environmental circumstances (lack of access, discrimination, undeveloped formal sector); (*d*) those with inadequate income from market economy (large family); and (*e*) those under temporary shock (due to recession, natural disaster). Targeting has a three-way classification: (*a*) means-tested individual assessment; (*b*) indicative targeting; and (*c*) self targeting (Jayarajah et al., 1996: 104–13).

On the issue of the public distribution system, the overwhelming opinion inside the Fund–Bank establishment is in favour of trimming it to its minimum size and targeting it in favour of the rural poorest. The opinion on the other side is that, in a situation where the administration is not equipped to identify recipients and perform such targeting, such a policy does hurt the most vulnerable section in a poor country. Further, the higher administrative cost associated with targeting may significantly exceed the benefit it derives from reaching the poorest (Knudsen and Nash, 1991; Islam, 1991: 157; Development Committee, 1993b: 75).

It has been found that the breakdown of the adjustment programme and a policy reversal is more likely in cases where the social cost is high, in terms of its impact on vulnerable sections, e.g., in Zambia in 1987 and in Madagascar in 1991, leading to a suspension of adjustment programmes (Foroutan, 1993: 31). A food riot here and a strike there, or, in the case of democracies, a few election debacles, are likely to unnerve the government in power and to lead to a rolling back of the economy from structural adjustment.

The rationale for World Bank conditionalities

Several scholars have questioned the rationale behind World Bank conditionalities. Where the recipient countries are convinced about the need for these policies, such conditionalities amount to pushing an open door. Where the recipient countries are reluctant, and such policies are forced down their throat, the political will tends to be missing (Foroutan, 1993: 9). The government concerned always compares the political cost of compliance with conditionalities with the financial costs of non-compliance (Mosley et al., 1991: 77). Sometimes conditionalities are formally accepted without meaning to implement them. The very high mortality rate of the structural adjustment and stabilisation programmes is, at least partly, a consequence of such coercion. As Berg (1991) reminds us, conditional lending began in Latin America in the 1960s under the Alliance for Progress programme. Its conditionalities were similar to those imposed by IMF now, under the stabilisation programme, but 'few traces of the exercise in conditionality were visible by the end of the decade'. Conditionalities generally have a 'poor track record' (Berg, 1991: 216). 'Half of all programmes broke down before the end of their intended life in 1980–90; two-thirds in 1987–90. Three-quarters of World Bank adjustment loans have installment tranche releases delayed because of non-implementation of policy condition in 1987–88' (Killick, 1993a: 104).

One interpretation of conditionalities is that while insisting on the implementation of conditionalities, BWIs are functioning like any other lending agency, except that in their case conditionalities have taken the place of collateral. This view may be contested on the ground that these conditionalities go far beyond what is needed to ensure loan repayment; these attempt to shape government policy in a particular direction, which becomes a goal in itself independent of whether it helps loan repayment or not. In fact, conditionalities can be seen as the outcome of a bargaining process, between the rich and the poor countries, whose severity or otherwise reflects the power relationship between the two (Mosley et al., 1991, Vol. 1: 66–67, 90). Another major argument in favour of conditionalities associated with structural adjustment is that, despite the evident rich country self-interest in it, the conditionalities only force the poor countries to do what they should have done in any case in their own interest. This is based on the argument that export orientation, openness and competition are universal good things that benefit everyone (Balassa, 1981: 3–9). We will discuss this issue in detail in the following chapter.

Another major criticism of the conditionalities is that these standardised packages are imposed without taking account of the diversities and specificities arising from history, resource endowment, and popular attitudes and perceptions. 'The programmes are too much inspired by a common theory or ideology and as a result take insufficient account of country specificities and country differences' (Singer, 1994: 178). Further, conditionalities, by telling the governments what to do and what not to do, take away initiative from the governments and 'undermine the development of indigenous policy-making capacity', apart from undermining their legitimacy (Killick, 1994: 11).

Evaluation of structural adjustment programmes

Over these years, both experts from the World Bank and IMF and also many independent scholars having some association with the Fund–Bank, have carried out a number of evaluations of the structural adjustment and stabilisation programmes. In this section, we are examining these and attempting some broad generalisations about the global empirical evidence on the performance of these programmes in the 1980s and the 1990s (so far). To be fair, the sponsors of these programmes warned, when these were launched, that there were no painless remedies, but once an initial period of adjustment was over, the economies would be on their growth path, propelled by high investments and savings, with balances in external and internal accounts and with better control over prices. By now many countries have been on these programmes, off and on, for nearly two decades, a sufficiently long time to measure the success or otherwise of a given, clear, unambiguous set of policies.

Corbo and Fischer (1992)

This Bank study summarises two reviews on adjustment lending undertaken by the World Bank in 1968 and 1990. It concludes from the 1988 study that adjustment lending was moderately successful in improving economic performance. Thirty countries that received adjustment loans before 1985 did better than the 63 that did not; 12 countries with three or more loans before 1987 did better and countries exporting manufacture even better. However, it was not successful in Sub-Saharan Africa. In a sample of 50 adjustment loans to 15 countries, 60 per cent of the conditionalities were fully met and another 24 per cent were met partially. Those who 'owned' the programme appeared to be more committed.

As for the 1990 study, it concluded: 'After adjusting for initial conditions, external shocks and the amounts of external financing, the countries that initiated full-fledged adjustment programs (called early-intensive adjustment lending or EIAL countries) experienced a larger increase in the average rate of GDP growth' (Corbo and Fischer, 1992: 7–20). Nigeria, the Philippines, Cote d'Ivoire and Mexico were among the countries with slower-than-expected growth, but South Korea, Mauritius, Morocco, Ghana and Thailand did better before and after adjusting for external shocks and the amounts of external financing. However, 'the picture was less positive in the case of investment. After adjusting for the same factors, investment fell on average as a share of GDP in EIAL countries'. The study concluded that 'resumption of public investment in infrastructure was important to stimulate private investment and restoring growth'.

Corbo and Rojas (1992)

In this Bank study, three approaches were adopted: (*a*) before–after comparison; (*b*) control group comparison; and (*c*) modified control group comparison (which included control for country characteristics that helped determine the decision to participate in an adjustment programme). Four indicators were used: rate of growth of GDP, ratio of saving to GDP, ratio of investment to GDP and ratio of exports to GDP. Figures for 1985–88 were compared with those for 1970–80 and 1981–84. Comparison was made for the following three groups of countries: (*a*) Early Intensive Adjustment Lending (EIAL) countries starting in 1985 or before, with at least two SALs or at least three SALs/SECALs; (*b*) Other Adjustment Lending (OAL) countries, after 1985; and (*c*) No Adjustment Lending (NAL) countries.

The study concluded that adjustment lending programmes usually increase the rate of growth in GDP and ratios of exports and savings to GDP, but show a decline in the investment–GDP ratio, compared to the 1970s. The decline in investment arises partly because of a reduction in inefficient public investment, while private investment is still feeling uncertain to move in and fill the void (Corbo and Rojas, 1992: 23–37).

McCleary (1991)

Between 1980 and 1987, the World Bank made adjustment loans totalling $15 billion to 51 countries, of which SALs amounted to $5.90 billion, and SECALs, $9.35 billion. Almost half the number of loans went to Sub-Saharan Africa (SSA), but more of the amount to other countries. Of these 51, 15 (five from Africa, four each from Latin America and Asia and one each from the Middle East and North Africa) were selected, not randomly, and not proportionately to the number of countries from various regions under the SAL programme for evaluation. According to McCleary, performance ranged from successful (Ghana, Korea, Thailand, Turkey, Cote d'Ivoire) and moderately successful (Pakistan, the Philippines and Senegal) to outright failure (Zambia, Bolivia and Guyana). About 60 per cent of the conditions had been fully implemented and 80 per cent substantially. Performance was better in relation to price changes and reallocation of public expenditure and worst for institutional reform, particularly in relation to the industrial sector, taxes and public enterprises. Factors that influenced performance were macro-economic policy framework, tranche-release conditions, government commitment, the quality of World Bank advice and the economic environment. It was found that a rapid rate of adjustment involved high social and economic costs (McCleary, 1991: 212–14).

Faini et al. (1991)

This study compared 30 pre-1985 SAL countries with 63 non-adjusting countries for 1982. It found that countries with adjustment loans improved their external position but fiscal and inflation indicators deteriorated, and growth rate also fell, mainly due to deterioration in terms of trade and the difficulties in achieving the required reduction in absorption. Overall, adjusting countries did better than their comparators on several indicators (Faini et al., 1991: 222–39).

Stevens and Solimano (1992)

This study of the adjustment experience of the 1980s, based on a sample of 78 developing countries, shows that the average share of investment in GDP, at constant prices, increased from 22 per cent in 1970 to 25 per cent in 1981, but declined after 1982. The drop was quite drastic in the case of Mexico (8 per cent), and Bolivia (from 15.7 per cent in 1978–81 to 4.9 per cent in 1985–89), but in Chile the decline in public investment was compensated by an increase in private investment. The regression analysis, based on

15 developing countries, indicates that growth in output and public investment strongly influences private investment. On the other hand, the foreign debt burden, variability of prices and real exchange rates and the reduction of external financing affect private investment adversely. External debt burden and credit rationing had the most adverse impact on private investment. 'Even if policy changes are perceived as permanent, insufficient public investment (particularly in infrastructure) that is complementary with private investment may hamper the recovery of the latter' (Stevens and Solimano, 1992: 118–32).

Overall evaluation of Bank evaluations

Questions have been raised about the methodologies adopted in these studies to vindicate Fund–Bank conditionalities. In almost all cases countries have been selected arbitrarily, without concern for the randomness of the sample, which makes the statistical validity of their conclusions dubious (Berg, 1991). One major objection is that, in these cross-country studies, 'success' is often defined in terms of their degree of conformity with conditionalities, e.g., openness, export-orientation and so on, rather than in terms of a set of objective economic criteria (Marshall et al., 1983: 321). Second, countries operating under these conditionalities are compared with those which are not, as if conditionalities alone account for the differences between these two sets of countries, ignoring a whole variety of intervening factors including initial conditions, historical and political context and also the specific conditions prevailing in the world market during that period (Killick, 1993b: 104). In many cases such assessment tends to be subjective (Berg, 1991: 217). Third, some of these evaluations try the before–after method, but these do not tell us what could have happened to these countries without structural adjustment (Mosley et al., 1991: 182). Fourth, lack of weighting of countries, by their population size, GNP or some such indicator, also makes such comparisons somewhat meaningless. It was asked whether one would get a fair idea of what is happening around the world by putting Botswana on par with China, a thousand times bigger, without any weighting, in these exercises (Behrman, 1992: 65). Fifth, even where success has been achieved with structural adjustment, it is never clear how far this is due to conditionalities and how far to the additional funding made available along with it (Killick, 1993a; 1993b; Mosley et al., 1991: 182–205).

Often, the conclusions derived by these evaluations do not necessarily follow from their data. Working on the same set of data as used by the World Bank, the UN Economic Commission for Africa (ECA) has reached the opposite conclusion: that countries with 'strong' SAPs recorded an overall negative average annual growth rate (about −1.5 per cent) during the period 1980–87, while 'weak adjusting' countries and 'non-adjusting' countries achieved an overall average annual GDP growth rate of 1.2 per cent and 1.3 per cent, respectively, during the period 1980–87 (Muzulu, 1993: 62). Most independent researchers, from Berg to Williamson, through Killick and Mosley, all having close relations with the World Bank and/or IMF, have greeted the findings claiming high success with adjustment lending with unconcealed scepticism. To quote Williamson: 'I doubt if the case made in the paper will convince a determined skeptic that adjustment lending has been an enormous success . . . .' Adjustment lending is not yet, however, nurturing a new generation of newly industrialised countries (Williamson, 1992b: 22).

At the same time, these evaluations admit that, generally speaking, investment has declined, including private investment which, contrary to the Bank view, tends to move together with public investment, and growth has been sluggish, while in Sub-Saharan Africa it has been negative. Foreign debt has grown but not foreign equity participation in industrial enterprises. Though the programmes have been relatively successful in reducing balance of trade deficit, the success with price control has been modest. Wherever some growth has been noticed, it is never conclusively established whether it has followed from the conditionalities and consequent structural changes, or from the external finance made available by the sponsors, or because of other factors unrelated to either. The list of 'successful' countries keeps on changing from one study to another, without any consistency.

From time to time, several miracles have been projected outside East Asia, such as Turkey or Mexico, that have not stood the test of even half-a-decade. A deep search of the literature reveals only two country cases of consistent performance over a reasonably long period: Ghana under Rowling and Chile under Pinochet. Even in these two countries, 'successes' are only in relation to the immediately preceding period, post-Nkrumah and post-Allende periods, respectively, until structural adjustment was vigorously pursued (Chapter 7). When comparison is made with periods under Nkrumah and Allende, in terms of saving and investment ratios and growth rates, the period under structural adjustment does not appear in a positive light even in the case of these two countries (Leechor, 1991: 327; Moran, 1991: 478, 490–93; Agosin, 1981: 27).

Even these studies point to some of the social costs of adjustment, largely because of a sharp decline in the rate of growth of the LDCs, from an average of 5.6 per cent during 1970–79 to 2.3 per cent during 1980–87, and the associated problems of mounting debt and the net outflow of resources for repaying debts. Another is the decline or stagnation in calorie intake, particularly in Sub-Saharan Africa. These admit that the poor are being hurt by reduction in government expenditure, high agricultural prices, and withdrawal of subsidies, except in some countries like Chile and South Korea (World Bank, 1992: 2–33).

Killick (1993)

Killick summarises the overall performance of the stabilisation programmes as follows:

(*a*) These strengthen balance of payments but fail to bring down inflation;
(*b*) Programmes do not make much difference to economic growth. Results for various countries are in conflict with one another;
(*c*) Programmes are associated with reduced public investment and sluggish private response to improved policy instrument;
(*d*) Outcomes tend to be less favourable for low-income (or African) countries than for middle-income countries;
(*e*) On balance, adjustment programmes have only a modest capacity to improve economic performance; and
(*f*) The absence of strong results is partly because conditionality has a modest revealed capability for achieving improved policies (Killick, 1993b: 104–6).

Mosley et al. (1991)

According to Mosley et al. (1991), for 1980–86, adjustment lending adversely affected GDP growth rates, particularly in those countries which have more faithfully adhered to conditionalities and are guilty of few slippages (Mosley et al., 1991: 204). Further, adjustment lending plus IMF stabilisation conditionalities have reduced investment as a share of GDP. A favourable aspect of SAP has been the decline of current account deficit as a percentage of GDP, and the halting of deterioration in export performance (Mosley et al., 1991: 205).

The regression-based results, for 17 countries operating under structural adjustment, show that compliance with conditionalities had a weak effect on GDP growth. For IMF finance, the impact on GDP growth is negative, though weak and statistically insignificant (Mosley et al., 1991: 216). Terms of trade and weather seem to have a positive impact on GDP growth. Inflow of SAL and SECAL, lagged by two years, has a positive effect on export growth, though negative in the current period (Mosley et al., 1991: 217). Compliance with Bank policy reform has a negative impact on GDP growth (when lagged by a year, mainly because of the negative impact of compliance on investment) and positive impact on export growth during the current year. As for IMF finance, results are mixed and disappointing (Mosley et al., 1991: 218). As for the impact on import growth, its relationship is negative with SAL and SECAL finance in periods t and t-1 but positive in t-2. Compliance with Bank policy (removal of quantitative restrictions, reform of the tariff regime and the liberalisation of the foreign exchange allocation mechanism) has a positive effect, but for t-1 and t-2 it is negative. IMF finance has a positive effect, more than counter-balancing the adverse impact of demand-deflationary policies (Mosley et al., 1991: 220). As for the impact on investment, as a share of GDP, the results are inconclusive. Bank finance has a two-period lagged negative effect (that is, with t-2) with investment. Further compliance with Bank policy has a negative effect on investment (Mosley et al., 1991: 221). Similarly inconclusive is the impact of SAL on inflow of private foreign finance. The study does not show that either Bank finance or its conditions has attracted foreign private investment (Mosley et al., 1991, Vol. 1: 217–22).

Where the performance is good, the direction of causation is not always clear. It may be that where it has worked, it is because high growth has made liberalisation possible, rather than its being the other way round. In the case of Malawi and Thailand, export growth occurred after trade liberalisation. In Kenya and the Philippines the results are ambiguous. In both, programme finance was followed, with a one-year lag, by export collapse and a continued decline in GDP growth. In both, peak in export growth was followed by liberalisation. Further, in the case of the Philippines, improvement in GDP and exports followed the 1986 reimposition of trade control, but more important was the surge in private foreign investment following a change of regime. But in Kenya, trade liberalisation and high export coincided in 1986. There was a stronger link between programme aid and GDP and exports in the cases of Malawi and Thailand (Mosley et al., 1991, Vol. 1: 224–25).

The views of other international agencies

The views propagated by the World Bank and IMF are by no means shared by all international agencies. Indeed, various other international agencies have, from time to time, raised important questions regarding different aspects of structural adjustment. Experts working with UNICEF have focused on the misery inflicted on the people, particularly the poor, by such programmes (Cornea et al., 1987), those with ILO have opposed the idea of trimming labour legislation in the name of letting the market work, those with FAO have challenged the idea that food security is not important and countries running a deficit in food need not strive for food self-sufficiency, those with UNCTAD (Agosin, 1981) have questioned the view that trade is the cure for all third world ills, while those with UN's regional ECA (Adedaji, 1993; Berg, 1995) as well as ECLAC, have expressed their opposition to the package in its entirety.

Conclusions

At the very outset in this chapter, we have pointed to a paradox, that while the agencies sponsoring, financing and monitoring structural adjustment are controlled by the rich countries in terms of voting rights, they operate exclusively in the poor countries. Neither the World Bank nor IMF carries any clout with the rich countries, nor plays any role in monitoring their policies or programme or otherwise attempts to influence their policies. On the other hand, these agencies are now the single biggest influence in shaping the economic policies of the poor countries, which were not on the agenda when these two agencies were brought into being in the mid-1940s.

The question that inevitably follows is whether in their decision to introduce and implement structural adjustment, the very rich countries have been prompted by an altruistic motive or whether their self-interest is involved in this exercise. We then ask, more specifically, how far and to what extent the adjustment package had been introduced to rescue the international banking system from bankruptcy in the aftermath of the second oil crisis and debt crisis and/or to find markets for the MNCs of US origin in order to rectify its massive balance of trade deficit. In other words, whether structural adjustment is an instrument through which the burden of adjusting the trade deficit of the US has been passed on to the fragile shoulders of the LDCs.

We then examine IMF and World Bank conditionalities: how these are incorporated in the PFP in order not to hurt national pride, the particular manner in which the negotiation is carried out including the economic coercion it accompanies, and how, despite their imposition from outside, these are 'owned' by the government concerned, as the sovereign autonomous decisions of that government.

A detailed examination of specific conditionalities is followed by a sector-by-sector examination of their performance in the course of the past 17 years. These are, by their nature, broad generalisations, based on the totality of experience, as revealed by numerous studies, many undertaken by the World Bank and IMF staff members themselves. These show that, to say the least, the results are far from inspiring. In Latin America and Africa the 1980s have been dubbed as the lost decade, as GNP has failed to take off, investment has taken a nosedive, while poverty, unemployment and disparities of all kinds have mounted. Results available so far for the 1990s do not suggest any turnaround. Ironically, the countries that have been the most subservient to the World Bank and IMF, those of Sub-Saharan Africa, seem to have performed the worst, becoming significantly poorer after several rounds of structural adjustment and stabilisation loans. The plight, deprivations and misery of their population, suffering under adjustment, have prompted several scholars and one UN agency, UNICEF, to question whether adjustment wears a human face.

The only major success with industrialisation in recent years, that of the East Asian countries, has been accomplished without World Bank/IMF conditionalities or financial assistance, but for one instance (see Chapter 6). On the contrary, as we shall see in Chapter 6, they have flouted virtually each and every norm of the SAP in the course of development and yet have managed to maintain a very high rate of growth for more than three decades. If they are liberalising now, that is precisely because, by following an independent policy, they have reached a stage from where they can take on the economic might of the rich countries with impunity. Their recent phase of liberalisation follows their growth, and not the other way round. Ironically, while they had been protecting their industries from foreign predators for most of the time in their recent history, now the table has turned against them, and the rich countries, worried by their competition, are busy erecting a variety of non-tariff barriers against their exports (to be discussed in Chapter 4).

Leaving aside East Asia, and to a certain extent Southeast Asia, one is hard put to come across cases where the structural adjustment model has proved to be a success. Miracles have been projected from time to time, but these have failed to withstand the test of time. The only two notable cases of success, Ghana and Chile, are 'successes' only in a qualified sense, that is, in comparison with the immediately preceding period; per capita income and investment ratios, to pick only two of the major variables, are lower in these two countries now than they had been under Nkrumah and Allende. On the other hand, the SAP, rather than injecting funds from outside, has actually reversed the net flow of resources in favour of the rich countries, as voluminous evidence available from the World Bank and IMF sources shows.

The biggest flaw of the package is that it expects the LDCs to 'adjust' to the world economic environment, by which they imply the environment created by the rich countries themselves, while placing no obligation on the rich countries to orient their own economies in tune with poor country interests. It blames the governments in the LDCs for all their economic ills, but fails to take into account the real 'structural' factors that inhibit their exports, a structure that has been created by the rich countries themselves. Further, it attempts to impose a standardised format on all poor countries, irrespective of the historical, social, political and other roots of their present condition, and of the specificities of their natural endowments, ecologies and social–economic–political institutions. While the recent Rio conference on global environment calls for biodiversity, no plurality or deviation from the Fund–Bank understanding of what is rational or optimum is permitted.

Such unilinear, nearly theological understanding of world development, emanating from Fund–Bank sources, is not necessarily accepted by the international institutions under the umbrella of the United Nations. UNICEF, ILO, UNCTAD, ECLAC and ECA are among those agencies that have, from time to time, through their publications, challenged the implicit economic philosophy of the package as a whole or some of its major aspects, or have pointed out its negative implications in their own fields of specialisation. Some of the most serious concerns have been expressed by staff members of both the World Bank and IMF, in their occasional papers (which are not taken as the views of their organisations) to which ample references have been given in this chapter. In fact, most of the data used here have their origin in Fund–Bank sources.

Dependence on structural adjustment tends to become never-ending, and more so for countries that have been most faithful in implementing these, e.g., countries in Sub-Saharan Africa. What was originally planned as an emergency surgical operation, has now become a routine treatment, irrespective of the specific conditions of the patients. Once admitted, it becomes a life-long patienthood in the Fund–Bank hospital. Seventeen years is a long time for testing a package of policies, and there can be no doubt that structural adjustment has failed the test of time. On the other hand, the success of the East Asian countries on the basis of a strategy of import substitution, led from the front by a strong intervening state, points to an alternative route of indigenous capitalist development in a late developing country that has a proven record of success.

four

GATT, WTO and the world trade system

Introduction

The past few years have witnessed dramatic changes in the world economic regime, beginning with the intense and heated debate on the so-called Dunkel draft, in December 1991, following which the April 1994 Marakesh agreement was reached. This was followed, logically, by the establishment of World Trade Organisation (WTO), in January 1995, for monitoring the implementation of the Marakesh agreement, for settling disputes between nations on various trade issues, and for taking further steps to hasten the flow of trade on commodities, services and what have you. Both have brought into being a global patent regime and agreements on services, investment, agriculture, subsidies and other aspects of trade liberalisation.

On each of these issues questions have been raised, how far and to what extent these agreements and measures are in accord with the present and future development possibilities in the LDCs, or whether they simply reflect the political–economic reality of a world with a single superpower, or a 'hegemon' as noted in Chapter 2.

The discussion on the world trade system in this chapter complements that in the preceding chapters. The convergence of views between GATT/WTO on the one hand, and the World Bank and IMF on the other, on major trade issues, is anything but accidental. All of them share a common economic philosophy, and an identical view on trade-related issues. The latter were active proponents of the global trade system that eventually emerged (Development Committee, 1994: 19–22).

The following is a brief summary of these common ideas on trade:

(*a*) Trade benefits every participant, though some benefit more than others.

(*b*) The productivity and efficiency of a country's economy are linked with its outward orientation. The rate of growth of an economy is positively correlated with its degree of integration with the global economy. In contrast, the inward-looking economies tend to be inefficient and generate low growth.

(*c*) The theory of comparative advantage determines what a country can produce and export best. For instance, an LDC is more likely to enjoy a comparative advantage in producing and trading in agricultural products and/or some light industries. On the other hand, the developed countries are likely to perform better with industrial goods which are capital- and knowledge-intensive.

(*d*) Any barrier to trade in the name of self-sufficiency based on a strategy of import substitution promotes inefficiency. Import controls and regulations, by making imports costly, make the production of tradables costlier, thus taking away any comparative advantage in producing them. They impose heavy welfare costs on consumers in terms of higher prices of import-substitutes. Further, such controls encourage rent-seeking activities that cause further diversion of resources for an unproductive pursuit and impose further welfare loss on the economy.

(*e*) Even if import liberalisation results in the closing down of some lines of domestic production, it is inevitable and is welcome as it helps to determine which of the domestic products are or are not in tune with comparative advantage. Armed with this knowledge and the weeding out of inefficient industries, domestic resources would now be diverted to industries that enjoy comparative advantage, thus leading to growth.

(*f*) Subsidies distort allocation of resources and do not allow market forces of demand and supply to equalise and thus determine the desirable levels of price and output at which the market is cleared. Any restraint on the free functioning of market forces, particularly by an interventionist state, is bad per se. There should be no interference with the entry of the MNCs in the domestic market, or of their capital and remittances. The government should be neutral and non-discriminatory in its attitude towards them.

(*g*) The world trade is, on the whole, free and competitive, and the prices ruling in the world market emerge from the interaction of the forces of demand and supply, and hence, are rational and objective, and reflect the scarcity values of the products in question. A country would do well to take these prices into account in deciding which products to promote and which not to promote for both production and exports.

We will have occasion, in the pages that follow, to critically examine some of these views. Sufficient to say at this stage that a free, competitive world market with objective, rational prices is a fiction. Nobody believes in these, not even their propagandists, the Western countries. While they advise the LDCs not to obstruct flow of trade by imposing non-tariff barriers, as we will see below, this is exactly what they do when confronting low priced poor country exports in their own markets. In fact, both the quantum and the quality of trade-inhibiting and trade-distorting protection measures have significantly increased since 1980. If the LDCs are advised not to offer subsidies, the developed countries turn out to be the ones that provide massive subsidies, incomparably more than what their poor counterparts can afford for their agriculturists and other producers, so much so that they create their own comparative advantage in the world market in these products (e.g., wheat) and corner a large slice of the market with low prices.

The prices ruling in the world market are not objective or rational, and cannot form the basis for policy decisions in the LDCs. If the developed countries stop giving astronomical subsidies to their farmers, their production costs would become so high that not only would they be unable to export their wheat at competitive prices any more, at prices that would come to rule in a world without subsidies, their domestic production would also collapse. Further, a great deal of what passes as world trade is actually intra-company transfer between affiliates and subsidiaries of the same parent MNC entity, and takes place at a price that has no bearing on either demand or supply. Those transfer prices or accounting prices can be fixed at any arbitrary level without any prejudice to their global profits or without having any influence on the amount transacted. If the real price of oil in the world market declined steeply between 1949 and 1973, the MNCs had a role in this, while the current much higher oil prices, providing a better approximation of the scarcity value of this non-renewable resource, came about not by way of the interplay of market forces but through determined cartel action by oil-exporting countries.

Further, while the developed countries are opposed to self-sufficiency and would prefer every country to rely on the world market for selling what they produce best and for buying what they cannot produce at international prices (plus local transport costs), they themselves have always assigned the highest priority to a concern for national security. The generosity of the European Community (EC) (or Japan or US) with subsidies for agriculturists, a tiny proportion of its population, largely stem from its reluctance to depend on any country outside the region for something as important as food. Though their drive for self-sufficiency eventually took them beyond that goal and made them a major player in the world wheat market, that was a bonus. If the US is keeping a large part of its oil reserve as a shut-in capacity, while importing oil from West Asia and North Africa, that is largely because of this concern for adequate supply at the time of war. Similarly, huge investments in shale rocks and tar sands to produce oil at a high cost, when plenty of oil is available at quite low prices in the world market, can only be justified on the ground that such deposits are mainly located in the western hemisphere and would come in handy during a war. Here, as also in a wider perspective, in the formation of regional economic blocks such as EC or NAFTA, import substitution emerges as a major objective, though it is considered a sin when practised by the LDCs.

In this chapter, we begin with a critical review of the work of GATT, which began as a stopgap arrangement pending the establishment of the International Trade Organisation (ITO), but, by the early 1950s, became a regular feature of the world trade structure, and remained so until its replacement by WTO in 1995. Then we examine how far the Western countries dominating GATT were indeed serious about free flow of goods and services across international borders. This is followed by an examination of the main features of the Marakesh agreement of April 1994, which followed the eighth round of GATT negotiations, and the establishment of WTO. Then come issues relating to world trade in agriculture and the MNCs (or Transnational Corporations [TNCs]).

General Agreement on Tariffs and Trade (GATT)

For about 48 years after its establishment, GATT was the single most important institution regulating world trade and determining the quantum and direction of trade flows, until its activities were taken over by WTO. In its original concept, GATT was no more than what its title suggested: a forum for bringing the countries together and to reach agreement on trade and tariff issues, pending the constitution of ITO. The first agreement, launched in Geneva in April 147, came into force on 1 January 1948, with some parts of the Havana Charter written into it, and with only 23 signatory countries (Low, 1995: 39). No one could visualise in those early days that GATT would complete eight rounds and carry on for nearly five decades. Negotiations for the second round began at Annecy in France in 1949, under a cloud of doubt whether the proposed organisation would take off. By the time the third round was launched in 1951 at Torquay (UK), GATT was functioning more or less as a permanent structure while ITO was out of the reckoning.

International Trade Organisation (ITO)

It is not commonly known that the Bretton Woods Conference of 1944, in addition to the World Bank and IMF, also decided to set up an international trade organisation. In his original concept, Keynes made this organisation responsible for the stabilisation of the prices of primary products by maintaining buffer stocks, and by a policy of buying when the primary product prices were low in the world market and of selling when the prices were high. One can even go further back to the Atlantic Charter of 1941, whose 'proposal for expansion of world trade and employment' contained the idea of an international trade organisation. In the 1946 UN conference on Trade and Employment in London, a preparatory committee was formed with 18 governments which met in New York (1947), Geneva (1947) and Havana (1948). The ITO negotiations were completed in March 1948 in Havana and the Charter was submitted to the US legislature in April 1949 for ratification (Low 1995: 36–40; Agarwal, 1994: 15–16). In line with the Keynesian view, the primary objective of the new organisation, as laid down in the Havana Charter, was of stabilising commodity prices by buffer stocks, commodity agreements and direct intervention (Singer, 1995: 22).

After a year, hearings were held by the US House Committee on Foreign Affairs on President Truman's request for a joint resolution permitting US participation in the ITO. The Committee never reported, nor did the issue ever reach the floor of the House. In 1950, the request of the President was withdrawn. It was never put to vote in Congress, because the negative outcome was easy to predict. Without the US, by far the largest trading nation in the world, other countries did not consider it worthwhile to form the organisation. In 1955, a GATT review session, which had been convened to take stock of the situation in the light of the demise of ITO, suggested an Organisation for Trade Cooperation (OTC), but that too failed to get the approval of the Congress (Low, 1995: 36–42).

The explanation for this decisive shift in the policy of the United States could be found in the changes that had taken place in the international correlation of forces in the intervening years, as also in the dawning of the McCarthy era in the US (Singer, 1995: 22). With the onset of the cold war, any association with the communist countries was now to be shunned, and certainly in international fora where the former was likely to gang up with the LDCs against the West (Low, 1995: 42). This was also the era when the protectionist attitude was strong and intervention by outside institutions was resented. Some also found in ITO a deviation from the market principle, and a control by bureaucrats that they disliked. All these, a combination of a changed international political landscape, domestic witch-hunting and economic nationalism, operated to prevent the formation of a world body on trade (Low, 1995: 36–42).

If, eventually, after nearly f··e decades, the United States agreed to the establishment of a multilateral trade organisation, albeit with a different name, that was largely because of the profound changes the international politics had undergone since 1991, particularly since the dismantling of the Soviet Union. In the changed political scenario there was no longer the fear of the socialist and the third world countries uniting against the West. This was the time for the hegemon (discussed in Chapter 2) to assert its authority (Webb and Krasner, 1989).

Tariffication, lowering of tariff barriers and MFN

Five more GATT rounds followed Torquay: the Geneva Round (1956); the Dillon Round at Geneva (1960–61); the Kennedy Round at Geneva (1964–67); the Tokyo Round (1973–79); and the Uruguay Round (1986–93). Each round was named either after the place where it was launched or after a dominant US political personality (indicating the importance this country always enjoyed in trade negotiations) who took interest in that round of negotiation. Each round of negotiation was followed by an agreement that lasted for a given number of years, and before it came to an end another round of negotiations was completed. In this way, GATT moved from round to round, each round further reducing tariffs and further easing international flow of goods. With time, more and more countries joined GATT, issues became more complex and it took much longer to complete negotiation and reach agreement. While the first round, with 23 participants, took only a few months, the last round, with 108 members on its roll, went on and on for more than six years. The Dunkel draft, on which the Marakesh agreement of April 1994 was based, was a document with a 450-odd page text and contained 28 proposed accords.

The declared objective of GATT was to augment trade by removing barriers to trade in various forms. More specifically, it aimed first at 'tariffication', that is converting non-tariff barriers (NTBs) into tariffs and then lowering the existing tariff levels. However, as we shall see below, the GATT negotiations were, generally speaking, more effective in reducing tariffs than in controlling the proliferation of NTBs. In the 1980s, the NTBs mushroomed in the rich countries which more than outweighed their tariff concessions.

A third objective was non-discrimination and universalisation of trade relations by way of the most favoured nation (MFN) concept. Simply defined, under this concept, the trade concessions agreed upon between any two countries would be automatically extended to other member countries of GATT. The superlative made it clear that there could not be any country more favoured than the GATT members, who were the most favoured. If any member chose to make an agreement with another state that provided more concessions than were hitherto available to the members, the former immediately became applicable to all other members. In other words, a member could not discriminate against another member when entering into trade negotiations with a third country.

Exceptions to MFN: Regional economic blocks and GSP

However, this principle was subject to some important exceptions. The biggest were the regional customs unions, like the European Union (EU), Andean Pact, Central American Common Market (CACM). Caribbean Community (Caricom), Mercado Caomu del Sur (Mercosur), Association of South East Asian Nations (ASEAN), and in Africa, Preferential Trade Area (PTA) for Eastern and Southern Africa, Union Douaniere et Economique de l'Afrique Centrale (UDEAC) and West African states, which were permitted to extend additional concessions to intra-region members of those bodies that were denied to other GATT members. It was never made clear how such concessions given to regional trade bodies were compatible with the MFN concept (Low, 1995: 27).

While the Uruguay Round discussions were in progress, NAFTA was signed, as also the Agreement on European Economic Area (EEA) to cover relations of the European Union with European Free Trade Association (EFTA) countries, and, the Central European Free Trade Agreement (CEFTA), and Europe progressed towards a system based on a single currency under the Maastricht Treaty. It has been asked whether these regional groupings are 'building blocks' or 'stumbling blocks'. The argument in favour of the former view is that, by making the economies stronger and more competitive, while working within a region, it makes it easier for them to accept global integration outside the region. The other view is that it stands opposed to MFN and non-discrimination principles (UNCTAD, 1994b: 31).

Second, some concessions were also given to the poor countries from 1955 onwards. Part IV of the Treaty on Trade and Development formally introduced the principle of Special and Differential

Treatment, that allowed for safeguard actions (used more by the rich countries including the United States, to be discussed later) and balance of payment measures, and waived the reciprocal obligation of trade liberalisation (Watkins, 1992: 33). Under article XVIII, GATT permitted withdrawal of concessions for protecting domestic infant industries (Hoekman, 1993b: 487). The treaty also asked for greater access of the LDCs to rich country markets. Perhaps the timing had something to do with the global trade offensive launched by the Soviet Union that offered balancing of trade, loans at highly subsidised interest rates and technological support along with the construction of turnkey infrastructure projects, more or less at the same time. However, from the time of the Tokyo Round, that is, the 1970s, the rich countries began saying that the LDCs should grow up and forego such concessions (Watkins, 1992: 33).

Another major concession was in the form of Generalised System of Preferences (GSP), which was negotiated under the auspices of the United Nations Conference on Trade and Development (UNCTAD, 1994b) in the late 1960s, when the poor countries of Africa had begun emerging from under the colonial yoke. However, given that GSP was concentrated in manufactures, 44 per cent of GSP trade benefits accrued to just four beneficiaries—Hong Kong, South Korea, Taiwan and China. One reason for this was the condition imposed by US and EC that at least 35 per cent of the value added in manufacturing should originate in the exporting country, which most LDC manufacturers found difficult to fulfil. Further, trade in steel, machine tools, etc., was hedged with import quotas in the rich countries (Watkins, 1992: 34). In many instances, GSP was offered or withdrawn without consistency, largely on political grounds. GSP for Nicaragua under a left-wing regime was withdrawn on 'human rights' grounds, but not for Zaire, Guatemala and Haiti, countries ruled for very long periods by brutal, autocratic regimes. In any case, GSP paled into insignificance when compared with preferences given within regional economic blocks such as EC, EFTA or NAFTA (Watkins, 1992: 35). By the time of the Uruguay Round, the opposition to concessions to LDCs, particularly with regard to import restrictions on the ground of adverse balance of payments, had reached its peak (Watkins, 1992: 40). The backward countries were expected to 'graduate out' of infant industry and balance of payment protection arguments (Hindley, 1987).

Reciprocity, fair trade and infant industry argument

The principle of non-discrimination implicit in the MFN clause, was eventually overshadowed by the principle of reciprocity. Reciprocity was demanded on each and every issue. Any access given to tropical products in rich country markets was to be matched by further access of rich country economic operators in LDC markets. GATT was increasingly seen as a forum for bargaining where a country or a group of countries had to give something to get something. This was repeatedly stressed during the eighth round of GATT negotiations: if the United States was to agree on the dismantling of MFA or a reduction in agricultural subsidy, the LDCs were expected to open up their markets to services, or safeguards could be dispensed with by the rich countries if the poor ones were willing to do without article XVIII (Low, 1995: 29–30). Similarly, the principle of free trade, that more trade was better for everyone concerned, was increasingly replaced by the principle of 'fair trade', a subjective concept which can be applied for discriminatory action against a trading partner (Low, 1995: 27–28).

The theory of comparative advantage was also implicit in the GATT economic philosophy. A country was supposed to be guided by this principle while identifying possible export areas. Its natural endowments indicated its relative advantages in producing and exporting in certain items. A country was expected to specialise in these, while importing others at a cheaper price from the rest of the world. On this principle, an LDC was, generally speaking, expected to specialise in producing and exporting in agricultural goods, while importing industrial goods from its richer counterparts. However, such a theory binds export possibilities to the existing static, historically given resource base, and thus, also to a low level of development. Further, it limits diversification of trade and makes a country vulnerable to fluctuations in global terms of trade. Taking a dynamic view of comparative advantage, it is possible for a country, by way of investment in capital- and knowledge-intensive infrastructure, to create its own comparative advantage (see Chapter 6).

However, as the East Asian experience shows, a dynamic view of comparative advantage presupposes some import substitution and protection from foreign predators in the early stages of development, and an active interventionist state capable of executing such policies. This was a major argument of the Singer–Prebisch thesis, popular in the 1960s in Latin America and Asia. But even the formal neo-classical trade theory allows for the 'infant industry' argument, where protection is seen as a temporary, time-bound measure, with the long-term objective of strengthening domestic production (and also of export) capabilities. High subsidisation of technologically advanced domestic industries can be justified on the ground that such capital costs cannot be fully recouped by firms that incur them and that the absence of government support would lead to sub-optimal solutions (Low, 1995: 146). In the GATT circle, however, the tendency was not to take the 'infant industry argument' seriously.

The peripheral role of the LDCs

From its inception, GATT negotiations had a pro-rich country bias, despite the apparent democratic form of the organisation. Unlike the World Bank or IMF, G7 countries did not enjoy majority voting power in GATT, but the decisions involved consensus where the countries with larger economies, measured by GDP, and hence, having a larger market, had a more decisive voice (Watkins, 1992: 36). The combined GDP of LDCs being less than that for the United States and the European Community, their numerical majority meant very little when it came to decision-making (Hopkins, 1993: 144). The United States, EC and Japan were the three major players, with the SOE group (smaller open economies and EFTA countries), as a possible fourth, and GATT, for all practical purposes, was a forum for negotiations among them. The poor countries operated in the periphery, seldom consulted until the rich ones had completed negotiations amongst themselves. As one commentator pointed out: 'Whatever the skills of negotiations from the South, for the most part they are like extras on the GATT stage: the show can't go on without them, but nobody is remotely interested in what they have to say' (Watkins, 1992: 37).

One major reason for the poor performance of the LDCs in the negotiations, apart from their weak economic power, was the lack of specialised staff and advice. In the 1990 Brussels meeting during the Uruguay Round of negotiations, Carla Hills, US Trade Representative, brought 400 advisors, a number that exceeded the combined strength of all the Sub-Saharan African and Latin American trade missions put together. Alongside these 400, a powerful group of 200 corporate giants, including American Express, Citibank and IBM, lent their own staff to the US delegation. On intellectual property rights (IPR), a coalition of agro-chemical conglomerates—led by Pfizer, Monsanto and Du Pont—was active, while the support of the Cargill Corporation was very much in evidence on grain negotiations. There was no way the LDCs could match this formidable rich country combination of governments and corporate giants (Watkins, 1992: 37–38).

The weak bargaining position of the LDCs was ruthlessly demonstrated during the Uruguay Round, which continued from 1986 to 1993. Between 1986 and 1991, for five years, the LDCs showed a certain sense of purpose and unity by resisting the introduction of services and IPR in the negotiations. But after the collapse of the Soviet Union in 1991, they seemed to have lost the will to fight the single superpower left on the world stage. There was little resistance from the LDCs to the Dunkel draft proposed in December 1991. If the discussion on the Dunkel draft dragged on for another two years, that was largely because of serious disagreements between North America and Europe. The LDCs, having no role to play, greeted the proposal with resignation, as a fait accompli, and as being reflective of the distribution of global negotiating power, and meekly signed on the dotted line (Watkins, 1992: 131–32).

Unlike USA, Japan, the European Union or the Cairns Group of agriculturally advanced rich and middle-income countries, the LDCs seldom functioned as a group with a unity of purpose or devoted much effort or time to coalition building or lobbying. Uncertainty, combined with lack of organisation and research skills, and absence of political commitment eroded whatever bargaining power they could have gathered collectively. They had no proposal of their own and merely reacted to those of others. They were not consulted or taken into confidence by the major players and were often given drafts on the day of the meeting. Though 70 out of 108 countries in the GATT negotiations were the less developed ones, they had no voice and expressed their views, on the few occasions they did, 'within a framework scripted by the major industrialized states' (Hopkins, 1993: 143–49).

A major difficulty was that the LDCs were far from a homogeneous group. The rich countries preferred to do business with a small number of more advanced LDCs that were likely to benefit sufficiently from cooperating with the West, while the others were looked down upon as 'backward' and as 'free riders', who sought concessions but had nothing to give in return. Two yardsticks were usually deployed to mark out the privileged, advanced ones from the rest: their share in world trade and their absolute size. Brazil, Hong Kong, Indonesia, Israel, South Korea, Malaysia, Mexico, the Philippines, Thailand and Yugoslavia were preferred as substantial exporters; while Argentina, Egypt, India, Nigeria and Turkey were also treated well as their markets were large (Hoekman, 1993b: 477).

Among the LDCs there were major differences on specific issues, e.g., agricultural sudsidies. Some were net food importers, who were keen to obtain food at the lowest possible price from the world market, no matter what the source was or how the price was fixed (Hoekman, 1993b: 478). They were, naturally, the least interested in maintaining subsidies that served the interests of the producers in countries like India. While G15 countries led by India and Brazil had one kind of strategy, another group of 20 LDCs threw in their lot with the West.

Changing international political perspective

The severe erosion in the bargaining position of the LDCs also arose from the weakening of the socialist block from the 1980s, and then from the demise in 1991 of the Soviet Union, which acted as the countervailing force and as an alternative power centre in international trade from the mid-1950s for about three decades. The latter helped the LDCs with cheap and subsidised credit, barter trade arrangements that left no deficit, turnkey industrial projects without equity participation, a large market for non-traditional exports and supply of critical articles like oil and military hardware at competitive prices. More important, it provided the LDCs with an option and vastly improved their bargaining position vis-à-vis the West.

The improved bargaining position was reflected also in the formation of the movement of the non-aligned countries. Beginning with the 1955 Bandung conference of Afro–Asian countries, a series of conferences of non-aligned countries was held. Their rank swelled in the 1960s and the 1970s, when most countries of Africa became independent and joined them, and in response to their insistence, the UNCTAD was set up as an agency dealing with the relationship between trade and development. From the 1970s the Western countries began losing votes in the UN fora. Towards the end of the 1970s, the exasperated US government withdrew from two UN agencies, threatened not to pay its dues and even asked the UN to remove its headquarters from New York.

In the oil crisis of 1973, the LDCs saw an opportunity for turning the terms of trade in their favour through the collective action of groups of primary producers and by asserting their role in world trade. The historic sixth special session of the UN General Assembly, held from 9 April to 2 May 1974, unanimously adopted a programme of action for the establishment of a New International Economic Order (NIEO). Towards the end of the year, in the 29th session of the UN General Assembly, the Charter of Economic Rights and Duties of States of 1974 was adopted which asserted the right of every country to control its own resources and to regulate and exercise authority over foreign investment. The Lima Declaration sought the location of 25 per cent of industrial output in the LDCs by the end of the century (Tinbergen et al., 1976; UNIDO, 1975; UNCTAD, 1994b: 136–37). The United Nations Commission on Transnational Corporations drafted a code of conduct for MNCs that covered a wide range of subjects, from respect for national sovereignty and laws to transfer pricing and nationalisation. Subsequently, a declaration (The Set of Multilaterally Agreed Equitable Principles and Rules for the Control of Restrictive Business Practices) was issued that recommended to MNCs that a set of guidelines be observed (UNCTAD, 1994b: 136–37).

In the past also, the LDCs had insisted on their own sovereign rights to take whatever actions they felt necessary in terms of local laws. The Havana Charter, finalised in 1947–48, while admitting that international investment could be of great value, also recognised the right of a member 'to take any appropriate safeguards necessary to ensure that foreign investment is not used as a basis for interference in internal affairs or national politics' and also 'to determine whether and to what extent and upon what terms it will allow foreign investment' (UNCTAD, 1994b: 136). The 1962 UN resolution on Permanent Sovereignty over Natural Resources recognised the inalienable rights of the sovereign states to dispose of their natural resources in accordance with their national interest. But these very important resolutions were hardly noticed as the LDCs were not collectively that strong in those days. The 1970s, following the oil crisis, presented an altogether different international political and economic environment.

The momentum generated by the developments of the 1970s, including the NIEO resolution, could not be maintained by the non-aligned countries in the 1980s. A major reason was, perhaps, the debt crisis discussed in Chapter 3, and the consequent role played by structural adjustment in their economic life. Changes within the Soviet Union—particularly its economic problems, and the emergence of Gorbachev as its leader—also played their part. The new leadership assigned more importance to a closer relationship with the West in order to avoid nuclear catastrophe and virtually ignored the non-aligned movement. The G77 countries, so active as a group in the 1970s, broke up, though later attempts were made to revive it in truncated form, as G15. This was the background against which the Western countries turned protectionist in the 1980s and then, after the demise of the Soviet Union, established a new, multilateral trade regime under WTO.

Trade restrictions in the West

During the 1980s the developing countries 'lowered their tariffs much more than their industrialized trading partners' (ECLAC, 1994: 44). The trade restrictions imposed by the developed countries took a variety of forms. Here, we are mainly dealing with safeguards, anti-dumping legislations and countervailing duties, VERs, the MFA, Super 301, and voluntary import enhancement. In the concluding part, we shall examine the role of the multinational corporations.

Safeguards

From the early days of GATT, the rich countries freely used its 'safeguard' provisions (given in article XIX of GATT) to keep third world exports out of the way. Safeguards denote government action against imports that are deemed to harm the importing country's economy. Such actions are supposed to be of a temporary nature, to help the economy adjust to the new imports, and can take various forms such as tariffs, quantitative restrictions, etc. Further, such actions are supposed to be taken only against 'unfair' trade; but unfairness being difficult to define, it is usually inferred from the damage caused. The complaining party only has to show that, as a result of 'unforeseen developments', (*a*) import of a certain product is increasing, and (*b*) as a consequence, the domestic producers have been seriously injured, or threatened with serious injury. If these can be proved, the party concerned can seek escape from GATT obligations (UNCTAD, 1994b: 41; Jackson, 1993a: 183–91).

Up to May 1993, safeguard actions had been invoked 151 times, mostly (136 times) by the rich countries. Only for 15 of these—Chile (3), South Africa (4), Nigeria (1), Peru (1), Rhodesia (1), Israel (1), Czech–Slovak Federal Republic (1) and Hungary (3)—countries other than the rich ones made use of this article XIX. Among the rich countries, Australia used it 38 times, US 27 times, Canada 22 times and EC 21 times. Forty-three of these had been against agriculture and food products, and 27 against textiles and clothing, the two areas which have been kept out of safeguard provisions in the Marakesh agreement, and have been covered by separate agreements. One-third of these had been invoked since the Tokyo Round—of which the highest, 18, was by EC (13 of them on processed foodstuff), and 4 by USA (on preserved mushrooms, motorcycles, porcelain-on-steel cookware, steel) (UNCTAD, 1994b: 59–60, Tables 4–5; Schott, 1994: 94). In the US Trade Act safeguards figure as Section 201, which is almost as famous or notorious as Section 301.

From the 1950s, several unsuccessful attempts had been made by the Western countries to incorporate selectivity in the safeguard provisions, mainly to apply them against the Japanese imports. When this failed, the former tried to introduce the concept of 'market disruption' for selective action against a particular source, if (*a*) serious damage had been caused (or was going to be caused) by a sharp rise (or potential rise) of imports of a product from that source, and (*b*) if these products were offered at prices that were substantially below those for similar goods of comparable quality prevailing in the importing country market. When this also failed, the concept of 'market disruption' was introduced to bring MFA into existence. In recent years, the tendency among the industrialised countries is to take recourse to VER and anti-dumping suits rather than the safeguard provisions, in order to avoid the discipline of article XIX (UNCTAD, 1994b: 42–44).

The 1994 Marakesh Agreement on safeguards appears to have introduced selectivity, albeit, through the back door, in terms of what it describes as 'quota modulations' (article 5: 2 [b]). Under this, when a global import quota has been imposed by the importing country, shares are allocated to various members in such a way that it would be less for countries contributing more to global injury. However, such provisions cannot be used against LDCs responsible for less than 3 per cent of imports (or less than 9 per cent, collectively) (UNCTAD, 1994b: 48–50).

Anti-dumping measures and countervailing duties

A country suffering from dumping, an unfair trade practice (article VI of GATT), is permitted to impose countervailing duties on that imported product to offset the impact of dumping. Like safeguards, this provision too has been extensively used by the rich countries in order to keep poor country exports out. This measure has served, to quote an UNCTAD 1994 document: 'As tools of protection of the elite' (UNCTAD, 1994b: 87). To quote a Fund–Bank document: 'Antidumping has increasingly become the cutting edge of restrictive trade policy. It is the pressure valve of the system' (Development Committee, 1994: 77). To quote yet another, an ECLAC document: 'It should be noted that the industrial countries interpret these mechanisms very differently and allow themselves considerable latitude in applying them, often in breach of both the letter and the spirit of GATT arrangements, and with clearly protectionist motives' (ECLAC, 1994: 133). Often filing of anti-dumping suits against a foreign country product has been a prelude to make that country agree—by harassing, creating uncertainty, demoralising and 'softening up'—to some other protectionist measure such as VER or to raise the prices of the product, or to come to some price-fixing arrangement (UNCTAD, 1994b: 65, 88; Low, 1995: 78–86).

An example of the use of these provisions with the objective of restricting imports is provided by steel, an industry dominated by the United States until recently, but, over time, facing serious competition from Japan and other East Asian countries. While in 1950, the United States imported only 1 per cent of its requirement, by 1983 the figure rose to 20 per cent. Failing to compete in the world market, and even to protect their own domestic market, in 1966, the US producers sought import quota on steel, and also filed many anti-dumping petitions. Fearing control, Japanese and European exporters agreed to restrict exports during 1969–74. Again, following a slump in demand in 1975, the US steel producers filed import relief petitions under Section 201 of the 1974 trade legislation, seeking safeguards, and then forced Japan to conclude an export restraint agreement. In 1978, what is known as Trigger Price Mechanism (TPM), was launched. It established a set of trigger prices based on the production costs of the most efficient producer (Japan) such that any imports entering the US below these prices would automatically provoke a self-initiated, accelerated anti-dumping investigation. More or less the same story was repeated in the case of automobiles and semiconductors, new industries at the frontier of technology (Low, 1995: 101–6, 118–24).

In the Marakesh agreement, an attempt has been made to define dumping in terms of prices of the product ruling in the domestic market of the exporting country, where the amount of the product sold is no less than 5 per cent of the amount exported to the importing country alleging dumping. In applying the 5 per cent rule, domestic sales below cost of production are overlooked. Where such exported product has no domestic market, the agreement works out ways of constructing a domestic value, but which, by all accounts, is a highly complicated calculation procedure. Equally difficult are procedures for calculating injury and threat of injury. The agreement, however, provides that if the margin of dumping is less than 2 per cent of the export price, or if the amount imported from this source is less than 3 per cent of the total import of like products (and 7 per cent collectively from all sources), and if the injury is negligible, no anti-dumping measure is warranted (UNCTAD, 1994b: 73–80). The new agreement also contains a 'sunset' clause (article 11.3) which says that any anti-dumping duty would be normally valid up to five years, and cannot be continued beyond that period unless 'continuation or recurrence of dumping and injury' is proved (UNCTAD, 1994b: 83).

Voluntary export restraint (VER)

Voluntary Export Restraint is the core of new protectionism in the West (Low, 1995: 76). Western countries prefer VER to import restrictions, because these are quick to impose or remove and help to maintain the 'mythology of free trade' (Bhagwati, 1991: 171). In this arrangement, a fiction is maintained that a country is on its own restricting exports of a particular product to another country. In practice, there is nothing voluntary about these arrangements. The arm of the exporting countries is twisted in a variety of ways to make the agreement look voluntary. VER is one of several 'grey area measures', including Orderly Marketing Arrangements (OMA), whose legality is in doubt, but which are difficult to identify as GATT-inconsistent measures.

In 1989, the GATT secretariat listed 236 VER agreements. Rearranging the list by countries forcing such 'voluntary' arrangements, EC is found to be responsible for 127 such agreements, US for 67, Japan for 12, Canada for 12, Sweden for 6, Australia for 4, Norway, Poland and Finland for 3 each, and Switzerland and Austria for 1 each. About 10 per cent of the world trade and a good part of the trade by East Asian countries is covered by VERs: 49 of these operate against Japan and 33 against South Korea, and the remaining East Asian countries account for a bulk of 52 such VERs directed against LDCs. VER is the preferred instrument of protection for declining, uncompetitive industries and agriculture in the West. Of 236 VERs in the world today, 60 cover food and agricultural products, 50 cover steel and steel products, 27 cover electronic products, 21 cover non-MFA textile and clothing items, 17 cover automobiles and road transport equipment, 16 cover footwear, 13 cover machine tools and 32 cover others (Low, 1995: 77–78).

It is interesting to recall how VERs came to be born. In the early 1980s the US government was under pressure from the automobile industry to impose quota restrictions against Japanese cars, but President Reagan, while sympathetic to their cause, was hesitant because such policy did not correspond with his own public rhetoric on free trade. As described in the autobiography of President Reagan, in an effort to break the impasse, Vice-President George Bush suggested, 'We're all for free enterprise, but would any of us find fault if Japan announced without any request from us that they were going to *voluntarily* reduce their export of autos to America?' (italics by Reagan). The President liked the idea, so much so that he immediately sent a message to the Foreign Minister of Japan, saying that pressure was building up in favour of import control and added, 'I don't know whether I would be able to stop them . . . . But I think if you *voluntarily* set a limit on your automobile exports to this country, it would probably head off the bills pending in Congress and there wouldn't be any mandatory quota' (italics by Reagan). This says everything about the voluntary character of such agreements, that were later extended to many other products and directed also against other East Asian countries (Development Committee, 1994: 75; Low, 1995: 112–16).

The 1994 Marakesh agreement seeks to eliminate VER. Under it, countries commit not to 'seek, take or maintain any voluntary export restraints, orderly marketing arrangements or any other similar measures on the export or the import side' (article 11: 1b). It also proposes to phase out existing gray areas within four years. However, it remains to be seen whether this provision would be given effect. There is a fear that VERs may go underground, and take the form of unwritten market sharing arrangements among private firms. Or, its formal demise may give rise to a growing number of anti-dumping suits or countervailing duties (UNCTAD, 1994b: 63).

Multi-fibre agreement (MFA)

The MFA came into being as a panic reaction against Japan's entry into GATT. A short-term agreement on international trading in textiles (in 1961), was followed by a longer-term agreement until 1974, and then replaced by Arrangement Regarding International Trade in Textiles (in short, the Multi-Fibre Agreement or MFA). This agreement is renewed after every three, four or five years. MFA IV covered 41 countries (taking the European Economic Community as one unit) and thousands of products and imposed quota limits on exports from individual countries. In all these agreements, the exporting countries (all except Japan are LDCs) have been bound by quota restrictions in the importing (all developed) countries. The agreements are made bilaterally, or on terms that are fixed unilaterally, specifying quantities of textiles and clothes to be imported, and then reported to the Textile Surveillance Body (TSB). Initially working on cotton textiles, MFA now covers synthetics, silk blends, vegetable fibres, practically all types of fibre excepting one or two (UNCTAD, 1994b: 107–8).

One of its declared objectives at the time of inception was to restrain low cost production from market disruption. Shorn of rhetoric, the simple objective was not to allow countries with abundant labour to enjoy their comparative advantage, and to permit autonomous industrial adjustment in the developed countries, that is, of replacement of dying and non-viable ones by more dynamic and modern ones, in order to save jobs and the ruining of backward areas (UNCTAD, 1994b: 110; Jackson, 1993a: 226; Low, 1995: 108–9). Over time, with increasing capital deployment in order to raise productivity and to economise on prevailing high wages, employment has sharply declined in these industries in the West, and, in this situation, 'MFA is increasingly becoming a regime for protecting machines rather than jobs' (UNCTAD, 1994b: 109). In each round of agree- ment the coverage has been more wide-ranging in terms of products, while becoming more restrictive in terms of quotas. A major consequence of MFA has been to reduce the share of the LDCs in the rich country markets. For example, their share in the UK textile market has declined from 32 per cent in 1974 to 25 per cent in 1993, while the share of EC has increased from 36 per cent to 53 per cent (Watkins, 1992: 49–51).

The Marakesh agreement provides for the liquidation of MFA, as a major concession to the LDCs. With its liquidation it is expected that the high-wage rich countries would move away from the production of textiles and apparels, and the market, including those in the rich countries, would be gradually taken over by the less developed ones. However, the withdrawal of MFA is backloaded (Development Committee, 1994: 75). The phasing out would take place in four distinct phases. There would be an immediate removal of quotas on products that accounted for at least 16 per cent of imports. At the end of the first phase (1995–97), another 17 per cent of imports would be so covered, and another 18 per cent at the end of the second phase (1998–2001). Thus, only 51 per cent would be covered in seven years, while another 49 per cent only in the last phase (2002–4) (UNCTAD, 1994b: 117–18). Further, within the format for the liquidation of MFA, the member countries maintain substantial discretionary power in structuring their quota liberalisation, in terms of categories of products, etc. The provision of 'specific transitional safeguards' permitted in the Uruguay accord, and drafted on the lines of the market disruption argument in the old agreement, will allow new quantitative restrictions to be imposed, as the old agreement is phased out. These would also be applicable against non-MFA members. As one recent study shows, monitoring the integration process during the 10-year period is not going to be easy (Trela, 1975: 55). Though article 9 of the agreement on textiles categorically states that MFA would not be renewed, there is a fear that 'since the most sensitive items will be the last to be liberalized, one can expect tremendous political pressure for an extension of quotas, and/or the imposition of import safeguards, as the transition period draws to an end' (Schott, 1994: 56–57; UNCTAD, 1994b: 127).

The rich countries are already taking elaborate safeguard measures to contain the surge of imports following liberalisation, and undoubtedly some of the exporting countries will be facing anti-dumping suits and will then be coerced to enter into agreements on VERs (Schott, 1994: 57). One impact of the removal of output restrictions would be tariffication. Though there would be some cuts, a substantial amount of tariff will remain even after the Uruguay reform (Schott, 1994: 58). World export of textiles increased from $96 billion in 1980 to $248 billion in 1992, accounting for 7 per cent of global merchandise (Schott, 1994: 55). One estimate shows that the removal of MFA restrictions by industrial countries would lead to a welfare gain of $15 billion, half of which would accrue to poor countries (Trela and Whaller, 1990, quoted in Low, 1995: 110).

Super 301

What is known as Super 301 is actually section 301 of the US Trade Act; the adjective super is commonly added to indicate its power and importance. Section 301 gives the President the broad authority to retaliate against other countries for 'unreasonable and unjustifiable' trade practices affecting the commercial interests of the United States. Here 'unreasonable' is defined to include acts, policies, or practices that might not be in violation of or inconsistent with the international legal rights of the United States, but which in any case are deemed to be unfair or inequitable. 'Unreasonable' practices may include denial of fair and equitable market opportunities, opportunities to establish an enterprise, or adequate protection of IPR. Persistent denial of workers' rights, export targeting and toleration by foreign governments of anti-competitive behaviour among firms that adversely affected US farms—these are also defined as 'unreasonable actions' (Low, 1995: 56). 'Unjustifiable' is an act, policy or practice that is in violation of, or inconsistent with, the international legal rights of the United States. Such violations may include the denial of MFN, national treatment, the right of establishment, and IPR (Low, 1995: 61).

The articles under this section empower the United States Trade Representative (USTR) to issue notices to countries accused of unfair trade against US exports. The issue of notice is usually followed up by detailed discussion with the officials of the country concerned with the objective of removing unfair trade practices. Between 1975 and 1990, 77 such notices were issued, and retaliatory action was taken in eight cases: three against EC, two against Japan, and one each against Canada, Brazil and Argentina. EC was provoked to take counter-retaliatory measures in two out of three cases and Brazil moved to court which led to the withdrawal of US sanction. The other 69 cases were either dropped or led to a trade liberalising settlement (Low, 1995: 89–91).

If consultations fail, after 150 days, USTR is expected to begin formal GATT dispute settlement procedures, if appropriate. The time limit for retaliatory action is between 30 and 180 days (Low, 1995: 63). If the country on the hit list agrees to end the offending practices within three years, by permitting incremental US exports over this period, then the action would be dropped. USTR has to give annual reports on the progress with 301 cases to the Congress. Retaliatory action is mandatory in case of 'unjustifiable' practices, the exceptions being as follows: (*a*) the practice was not GATT-inconsistent, (*b*) the foreign country was eliminating the practice, (*c*) the foreign country offered compensation, (*d*) the adverse impact of retaliation on the US economy would outweigh benefits, and (*e*) retaliation would cause serious harm to the national security of the United States. USTR retained discretionary authority to retaliate with respect to 'unreasonable' or 'discriminatory' pratices that burden or restrict the commerce of the United States (Low, 1995: 63–64).

In 1989, five practices and three countries were mentioned: quantitative import restrictions by Brazil, government procurement of satellites and supercomputers by Japan, technical standards of forestry in Japan, and export performance requirements and protection of the insurance market in India. However, no retaliatory action was taken against India because investment and services were being discussed under the Uruguay Round. In 1990, the only country named under Super 301 was India—for alleged barriers to foreign investment and to foreign participation in the Indian insurance market. In April 1991, India, China and Thailand were put under Super 301 as priority countries, while Australia and EC were put on the priority watch list. However, not a single case went up to retaliation stage under Bush (Low, 1995: 92–95). In April 1992, US named India, Thailand, China and Taiwan for investigations under 301 (Development Committee, 1992: 93).

In all these cases, whatever the United States had done was unilateral. There was no question of mutuality or reciprocity, or of some country putting the United States on their hit list. The notices under Super 301 took the form of summons in criminal proceedings and the entire procedure of investigations by the United States smacked of a trial of another country for violation of trade norms. As Hudec pointed out:

> Foreign reactions have been sharpened by irritation over the self-righteous tone of the new law. The detailed procedures are structured as a series of public investigations and decisions which makes them appear to be "trade crimes" trials. Foreign governments have bristled at having their policies "tried" in this manner and have gone out of their way to ridicule the quasi-judicial appearance of these procedures. Section 301 proceedings, they note, are a totally one-sided affair in which the United States plays both prosecutor and judge, in which the defendants are tried in absentia, and in which the Congress has ordained certain guilty verdict in advance, particularly with regard to Japan (Hudec [1990] reproduced in Low, 1995: 90).

The East Asian countries have been relatively more vulnerable to the Super 301 retaliatory trade measures.

There is also something called 'Special 301', which relates to IPR and is covered by section 1303 of the trade legislation. It requires USTR to identify foreign countries that 'deny adequate and effective protection of intellectual property rights, or deny fair and equitable market access to US persons that rely upon intellectual property protection'. The legislation conveys the impression that the protection of IPR is vital to maintain the competitiveness of the United States in the world market (Low, 1995: 64–65).

With the setting up of a multilateral trade organisation, WTO, it has been asked whether a unilateral action such as Super 301 has outlived its utility from the point of view of the United States. However, in the years since the establishment of WTO, Super 301 has not ceased to work. During the Uruguay Round negotiations, USA had insisted that 301 would stay, to allow private parties a right to complaint and to handle non-GATT issues (Low, 1995: 230).

Voluntary import enhancement (VIE)

One of the objectives of the Super 301 notices to Japan was to force that country to discuss the issue of market access. Therefore, it was followed by what came to be known as negotiations on Structural Impediments Initiative (SII) (Low, 1995: 92). This particular policy has been described by Bhagwati as Voluntary Import Enhancement (VIE), where a country agrees to open up its economy to another, and the agreement specifies the extent of such access. Here the word 'voluntary', as in the case of VER, is safely within quotes (Bhagwati, 1991: 179). In the 1985 Market Oriented Sector Sensitive (MOSS) talks, specific market access issues were taken up, such as telecommunications, electronics, medical equipment and pharmaceuticals, forestry products, and transportation machinery and auto parts. In the 1989 SII talks, saving and investment, land use policy, pricing mechanisms, domestic distribution systems, anti-trust policy, and *keiretsu* relationships were the issues (Low, 1995: 99–100).

Another way in which the United States wished to obtain both greater market access and a lowering of their bilateral trade deficit, then running at $50 billion, was by forcing the Japanese to overvalue their currency and, thus, to make their goods relatively dearer. The 1985 Plaza Accord of G7 countries led to an appreciation in the value of the yen and a corresponding depreciation in the value of the dollar. The idea of a North American Free Trade Association (NAFTA) was mooted in the same year, again with the same objective of finding a larger market for US goods. In the same year, the US filed an 'anti-dumping suit' against Japanese semiconductors, which was withdrawn after one year, on the understanding that Japan would allow US companies a 20 per cent share in the Japanese market within five years. Still, in 1988, based on the allegations of the US companies, the US government imposed a 100 per cent punitive tariff on selected Japanese electronics imports, such as laptops and desktop computers, colour TVs and power hand tools. Though eventually capitulating under US pressure, the government of Japan maintained that a predetermined share of US companies in the Japanese semiconductor industry was uncalled for, and that the market share of a company should be the outcome of competition (Okuda, 1996: 176–78).

In this particular case, Japan, rather than being an unfair trading country, was simply a more dynamic and forcefully competitive economy with very high saving and investment rates. Though Japan continued to negotiate then, and also afterwards, and even conceded many of the US demands, the exchanges were often acrimonious and left the Japanese side with a bitter taste in the mouth. Looking at the issue from the other side of the fence, Tsurumi commented: 'In Japan, the image of the United States as a fat, lazy, incessant nag that blames Japan for its own problems has steadily been gaining ground' (Tsurumi 1989–90, quoted in Low, 1995: 98–99). While the United States accused Japan of not consuming enough, Japan charged that the US did not save enough. They wanted taxes to be raised in US to bridge budget deficit, and also emphasis on export promotion, corporate competitiveness, workforce training and education to improve the functioning of the US corporate sector.

However, one interesting consequence of these pressures and restrictions, and the consequent increase in the wages and values of Japanese exports, was the shift of a considerable amount of Japanese investment to low wage Southeast Asian countries, which operated under the Original Equipment Manufacture (OEM) arrangement, and was instrumental in changing the industrial landscape of that region (see Chapters 3 and 7).

The Uruguay round

We have already noted that the negotiations under the last, the Uruguay Round, continued longer than in any other round in the past. A major reason for this was the introduction of a fairly substantial list of new issues that the rich countries wanted to discuss for the first time in GATT; IPR, services, and investment among others. Besides, this round of GATT negotiations produced several new institutional arrangements regarding dispute settlement and trade policy review mechanism and proposed a new, multilateral trade organisation. Further, drastic trade liberalisation was proposed in the case of textiles, agriculture and government procurement, while several trade rules such as anti-dumping, subsidies, countervailing measures and safeguards came under discussion.

As we have already noted, the two years of discussion on the Dunkel draft (1991–93) was an exclusively rich country matter. The dispute was mainly between Western Europe and the United States on the question of agricultural subsidy. Both the United States and the Cairns group demanded elimination of subsidies, while the European countries, particularly France, stuck to the Common Agricultural Programme (CAP). Several rounds of discussion, including the Blair House accord of November 1992, G7 meetings and meetings of the Quad group (USA, EU, Japan and Canada) failed to reconcile their differences. The agreement was brought about just before midnight on 15 December 1993, the deadline declared by the United States Congress, in the fear that, in case the GATT agreement collapsed, the United States would walk away and align itself more closely with the Asia Pacific Economic Cooperation (APEC), which accounted for half of the world's GDP and 40 per cent of world exports (Schott, 1994: 6–7). By then the United States had also launched NAFTA (12 August 1992) as an insurance against the failure of the GATT negotiations.

The GATT agreement, based on the draft prepared by Dunkel, has a number of important features, apart from its volume and the range of issues discussed. For instance, signing on the dotted line makes a country liable for the entire agreement; there being no escape clause, e.g., as in the Treaty of Rome. A member cannot say that while it broadly agrees with the text, it is opting out of such and such clause(s). Another is the detailed and time-bound manner in which most of the provisions have been drafted. The maximum time span for the implementation is 10 years—which is split up into periods of three, three and four years. The agreement specifies what a country is expected to achieve at the end of each of these sub-periods. The agreement also specifies a machinery for dispute settlement and also for multilateral action against countries violating the agreement.

General agreement on trade in services (GATS)

There were several reasons why the Western countries were pushing the case of services for negotiations under the eighth round so hard. First, since the second world war there has been a significant change in the character of their economies, in terms of contributions of various sectors to GDP. Services now accounted for around two-thirds of both GDP and employment, while manufacturing and agriculture played a minor role (Hoekman and Stern, 1993, Tables 14.1 and 14.2: 18–19). The rich countries were, therefore, keen to take advantage of the role the services played in their own economies by extending their service activities to other countries. Second, in international trade, services were growing much faster, at 15 per cent, than trade in merchandise, at 9.8 per cent, during 1982–92. By 1992, world export of commercial services was valued at about $1 trillion, accounting for more than one-fifth of world exports in goods and services. In the same year, the US firms exported $162 billion worth of services and imported $108 billion worth (Schott, 1994: 99). G7 countries account for 52 per cent of world exports for services, and the East Asian NICs another 6 per cent, while the rest comes mainly from other rich countries (ECLAC, 1994: 75).

In 1980, the United States began a public relations campaign to build a consensus on this issue, suitably aided by extensive research. The 1988 Omnibus Trade and Competitiveness Act allowed USTR to apply sanctions against countries indulging in discrimination against US services (UNCTAD, 1994b: 145–46). The negotiations on services were launched, in 1986, at the ministerial level, and, after seven years of negotiation, the resistance of the LDCs was broken. The Marakesh agreement contains three elements—basic obligations that apply to all the parties, specificities relating to individual sectors along with exemptions, and schedules of specific commitments, the last two being detailed in annexes to the agreement (UNCTAD, 1994b: 150–51).

In the Marakesh agreement, the General Agreement on Trade in Services (GATS) defines trade in services in terms of four modes of delivery: (*a*) cross border supply of a service; (*b*) movement of the consumer to the country of the supplier; (*c*) movement of the supplier to the country of the consumer; and (*d*) temporary movement of natural persons employed by the supplier to the country of the consumer (UNCTAD, 1994b: 153–54). However, the definition of services and its distinction from goods has never been an easy exercise. There is still confusion as to what 'trade in services' entails, e.g., would this include social security? According to Stern and Hoekman, two criteria may be used: (*a*) services cannot be stored, produced and consumed simultaneously; and (*b*) services tend to be intangible. Services can be complementary to or a substitute of trade in goods, or be unrelated to goods. Because of their non-storability and intangibility, in order to be tradable, services have to be applied to or embodied in objects, as information flow or persons. Available means of transportation must then be employed to move the objects, persons or information from country to country—for the trade to occur. Thus, international transaction in services is more complex than that in goods (Hoekman and Stern, 1993: 393–94).

While calling for a free flow of services, GATS recognises a country's right to impose domestic regulations relating to qualification requirements and procedures, technical standards, and licensing requirements. GATS generally accepts the MFN principle, and does not include the national treatment obligation, excepting those sectors that are listed in a country's schedule of commitments (article XVII). Emergency safeguards also exist, but by July 1998, these are supposed to be negotiated and settled. These can be called for on balance of payment grounds, to deal with concentration of ownership and market domination, for protecting infant industries and for correcting structural problems.

The agreement permits restrictions on international transfers and payments for balance of payment purposes, but only as a temporary measure to be phased out progressively (article X). Article XIII of GATS specifically excludes government procurement of services from MFN, market access and national treatment obligations. Members may also take exemption from their GATS obligations to protect public order or human, animal, plant health or life, to ensure compliance with laws and regulations, and for national security reasons, provided the exceptions are applied in a non-discriminatory way (Schott, 1994: 104).

The main implication of introducing services has been that it opens up the entire economy of a country to the foreign economic agents. Services include practically everything that was not earlier included under industry or agriculture, from transport, communications, and computers to schools, hospitals and groceries. At the same time, the foreign private companies may not be interested in offering those services that are of vital importance to the economy and the people but are not attractive as business propositions, e.g., crop insurance or power transmission in thinly populated areas. However, article IV, dealing with 'increasing participation of developing countries' permits the latter to seek reciprocal concession in sectors of export interest to them in exchange for liberalisation in their service sectors. Article XIX: 2 provides that the process of liberalisation will take account of national policy objectives and the levels of development of individual countries. Unlike TRIMs, it is possible to impose conditions on foreign service suppliers, e.g., on technology or use of local inputs, or insistence on joint ventures. Access to information, including computer reservation systems (CRSs) can be one of the major conditions (UNCTAD, 1994b: 155–56).

To the extent GATS accepts that 'movement of persons' constitutes trade in services, it keeps open the possibility of demand for changes in immigration laws in rich countries for easing the movement of labourers from the LDCs. As UNCTAD (1994b) observes: 'There still remain some asymmetries between the treatment of labour and capital'. The agreement permits a member to impose measures for regulating the entry of natural persons. It says, more specifically, in the annexe, that, as distinct from a person temporarily moving across the border for providing a service, it will not apply to measures affecting natural persons seeking access to employment, citizenship, or residence on a permanent basis (UNCTAD, 1994b: 154, 173–74).

As expected, the Western countries are mainly interested in accessing markets in banking, insurance, telecommunications, information technology, civil aviation and the like for their companies. On the other hand, there are understandable apprehensions about their roles in the LDCs. While the rich countries are primarily interested in liberalisation, the host country interest lies in prudential regulation of these spheres. In recent years, particularly in India, foreign banks and telecommunication companies have been found to be associated with major scandals. Some of these involve issues of national security, for instance, telecommunications. The annexe on financial services included in GATS, based on proposals submitted by several LDCs, attempts to address some of these issues. However, domestic regulations (including denial of access) are subject to recourse to dispute settlement by the country exporting such services (UNCTAD, 1994b: 177–80).

Trade-related investment measures (TRIMs)

The agreement on trade-related investment measures aims at ending discriminatory policies against foreign companies, which are considered to be trade-distorting and constraining. This came about as the culmination of the repeated attempts by the developed countries, ever since the conclusion of the second world war, to establish an international investment regime that favoured MNCs domiciled in their own countries (UNCTAD, 1994b: 136).

The main thrust of the final TRIMs agreement is against 'local content requirements', that ask the foreign companies to use a certain number or percentage of local manpower or material, to transfer technology, to seek trade-balancing (linking exports to import of inputs) or foreign exchange balancing requirements, or involve measures against monopoly pricing or monopsonist hiring practices. Similarly, it is against product-mandating requirement that a firm supplies to some specific markets, licencing requirements, remittance limitations, local equity requirements, and so on. In other words, this agreement debars national governments from imposing rules and regulations on MNCs for protecting or promoting domestic industries, personnel, foreign exchange and other resources or exports or for controlling their abuse of market power. However, the agreement allows exemptions on a number of grounds, such as balance of payments safeguards, promoting development objectives, preserving national security and health (Maskus and Eby, 1993). Export performance requirements remain permissible (UNCTAD, 1994b: 143).

Taking TRIMs together with GATS, these measures take away the powers of the national governments to regulate activities of the foreign economic agents. One major post-Marakesh development is an attempt made in the 1997 WTO ministerial meeting at Singapore, to introduce global investment and competition policy regimes.

Non-agricultural subsidies and countervailing measures

Going by the logic of the market economy, subsidies that aim to change the composition of industrial output are trade distorting as they influence relative prices. What is not known is that even the rich Western countries provide enormous subsidies to their industries. For example, in Germany, the percentage of subsidies to the manufacturing sector rose eightfold during 1974–84, and subsidies to shipbuilding and steel, as a percentage of total industrial subsidies, rose from 23 per cent in 1977 to 50 per cent in 1983. In UK, such subsidy was doubled between 1977 and 1981. Such subsidies are usually defended by the Western countries on the following grounds: (*a*) to help the local companies establish control over high technology industries enjoying economics of scale, by keeping the foreign competitors out; (*b*) where subsidies reduce final user costs because of external or linkage economics, and so expand social welfare (e.g., in steel, petrochemical, machine tools or semiconductors); (*c*) for the defence of the country, e.g., as food security is used to justify agricultural protection and intervention; and (*d*) to help the traditional industries survive competition from low-price (mostly LDC) exports, e.g., in the case of clothing, textile, shipbuilding, steel, footwear, also on the ground that such declining industries are often concentrated in regions with few alternative employment opportunities (Development Committee, 1987b: 1–9). Concorde and civil aviation in general and channel tunnel are some of the recent examples of activities receiving heavy subsidies in operation besides the amounts spent on research and development.

The Uruguay Round subsidies agreement makes a distinction between three types of subsidies. First are the prohibited ones, those which are export-promoting or favour domestic against imported goods (article 3). These are to be eliminated within the prescribed time limits. Second are those described as non-actionable subsidies, that are not prohibited as such, but are actionable if they cause injury to the domestic industry of another signatory or seriously prejudice their interest. If subsidies cover operating losses (except one-time ones) or provide debt forgiveness or grants for debt repayment or if the total ad valorem subsidisation of a product exceeds 5 per cent of the recipient's annual sale of that product, or 15 per cent of the total invested fund, these are presumed to be prejudicial to the domestic industries of other countries (article 6). The provisions on non-actionable subsidies are subject to review after five years. The agreement appeals to members to desist from causing adverse effects to interests of other members. Then there are permitted neutral subsidies, which are non-selective and are not directed specifically to some enterprises or industries (article 2).

Then there are others, which are not neutral and are specific in their impact, but are still tolerated: e.g., those on industrial research, pre-competition development activities, and those providing assistance to disadvantaged areas (article 8). These exemptions are also rigorously defined: R&D subsidy should not exceed 75 per cent of the certain specified costs of industrial research and that on pre-competitive development, the cost should not exceed 50 per cent; regional aids can be given only to those areas where the income per capita is less than 85 per cent; or the unemployment average is more than 110 per cent of national average; and safe harbour, that is, to support environmental infrastructure and pollution control investments, are one-time and non-recurring ones (article 9).

Countries with less than $1,000 per capita GDP, including India and other South Asian countries, are, however, exempted from the prohibition on subsidies that are contingent on export performance (article 27). In this case, if a country reached a share of at least 3.25 per cent in world trade in a particular product for two consecutive years, it would be required to phase out its subsidies in two years (eight years for the LDCs) (UNCTAD, 1994b: 93–98; Schott, 1994: 86–92). Subsidies aiming at helping privatisation within a specified period are exempted from countervailing actions (UNCTAD, 1994b: 98).

In case of non-compliance by a member, some specific remedies have been suggested. The issue can be raised with the Dispute Settlement Board (DSB) of WTO, if no agreement is reached within 30 days. A permanent group of five experts (PGE) will also be available for consultation (article 7). The panel established by DSB will be required to give its report within 90 days. On receipt of the report, DSB would get another 30 days to make a decision, unless an appeal has been referred to the Appellate Body. For the actionable subsidies, the issue can be raised with DSB after 60 days, the report of experts would be submitted within 120 days and DSB would take a decision within another 60 days. Countervailing measures can be sought when imports cause material injury to domestic industries. But in such cases, if the overall level of subsidies on that product does not exceed 2 per cent of its value, or the volume of the subsidised import represents less than 4 per cent of the total imports of the like product in the importing country, the investigation for imposing countervailing measures will be terminated. But even where the share of import is less than 4 per cent for a single country, if the total import from all developing countries collectively accounts for more than 9 per cent of total import of the like members in the importing country, then the countervailing action is permitted.

However, three major areas have been excluded from most of these rules on subsidies—agriculture, for which a separate agreement was made, civil aviation and the multilateral steel agreement. The discussions on the last two were not completed when the Marakesh agreement was signed (UNCTAD, 1994b: 103–4).

International patent regime (IPR)

The most serious for the LDCs are, of course, the implications of the GATT agreement on TRIPs which establishes an international patent regime and expects the member countries to amend their own patent laws in conformity with the latter within a given time frame. While the developed countries have been asked to change their patent laws within one year of the Marakesh agreement of 1994, the LDCs have been given five years, and, in case of pharmaceuticals and some other activities, 10 years. The least developed countries have been allowed 11 years to change their laws. This measure at once closes the option of liberally using foreign technologies and applying 'reverse engineering techniques' for adapting technologies available elsewhere for indigenous industrial development.

Apart from taking away the option of using foreign technologies as liberally as the East Asians, and effectively closing the option that was available to industrialising countries so far, the new patent regime contains several highly restrictive conditions. One of these extends patent rights to 20 years (from seven to 14 years in case of the Indian patent law), though, given the very high rate of obsolescence of the modern technologies in today's world, a downward revision to five-seven years would, probably, have been more in order (Lesser, 1991: 15–16). This longer period would allow the rich countries to enjoy the high economic rent of their patented technologies for a very long time. Further, it will virtually rule out indigenous development of technologies in the backward countries and will keep these perpetually dependent on the rich countries for technologies. To quote a joint Fund–Bank staff paper: 'Countries with less immediate scope for attracting high-technology investment or exporting intellectual property tend to regard TRIPs as a mechanism for transferring economic rents to technologically advanced countries' (Development Committee, 1994: 77).

Another controversial issue has been the decision to terminate the distinction between product and process. Article 28 extends to the product, protection enjoyed by the process, if that product has been obtained directly by that process. Thus, the poor countries are denied the option to acquire a 'process' by paying royalty and then to produce the 'product' at a cheap cost by using local materials and manpower. The industry to be hurt most by this condition is the pharmaceutical industry which, in India, supplies life-saving drugs at a fraction of the cost in the rich countries, by using processes with low cost inputs. As the UN ECLAC concludes: 'The rules on intellectual property are a particular cause of concern, since they may raise the prices of medicines and other patented products in the short run, but may also limit access to new technologies in the longer term' (ECLAC, 1994: 44).

Some have raised the question whether IPR is a 'trade' issue to be covered by GATT negotiations. Until recently the World Intellectual Property Rights Organisation (WIPRO), established in 1974 following a World Intellectual Property Convention in 1967, was the agency to look after such issues (Lesser, 1991: 10–11). The main argument for including it in the GATT agenda was that protection of IPR would enhance trade. By granting and enforcing patent rights internationally, it was argued, owners of patents would no longer be forced to keep details of their inventions secret, since such details would form a part of their patent application, and thus, the knowledge itself would be disseminated more freely

(Deardorff, 1993b: 436–37). The other side is that patents create monopoly and massive economic rent and erect barriers to dissemination of knowledge.

Unless patents are judiciously bound by time and space, there is every likelihood of the gains from incentive for innovation through patents to be negated by the restriction on the flow of knowledge. Since most such patents originate in the rich countries, these restrictions widen global inequality between the rich and the poor countries and deny the poor countries the opportunity to move along the learning curve (Deardorff, 1993a: 145). Vaitsos sees patents as a 'defensive strategy' adopted by rich country corporate interests: ' . . . (the patent) is to preserve markets that were once captured through exports and are subsequently threatened by competitors and/or by the import-substituting strategies of the host countries. In this context, patents, far from providing a stimulus to foreign investment, appear to be a critical factor in blocking investments' (Vaitsos, 1972: 77). Nadal sees patents as a 'powerful instrument to achieve control over markets, even without direct investment' (Nadal, 1977: 229).

The main rationale behind TRIPs is that, by protecting his rights for 20 years, it gives the inventor an incentive to invent. Otherwise, in a world where R&D is becoming increasingly costly, commercial life cycles of products are becoming increasingly shorter, and immediate copying has been made easier by technological innovations, the inventor would fail to recover his costs and earn a profit. An IPR regime, by making the patent owner feel relieved that he would get his price, is likely to ease transfer of technology to an LDC, and to even make him invest more. On the other hand, from the point of view of the LDCs, apart from raising the cost of technology and their level of dependence on the developed countries, fear is being expressed that IPR would actually obstruct the flow of technology, if those holding patent rights do not do enough to produce or give licences to others for work. Compulsory licencing, provided for in the Marakesh agreement, can partly mitigate this problem. Under this agreement, generally, one would expect to get authorisation from the patent owner on reasonable terms and conditions before getting a licence. But if this does not materialise within a given time period, then a compulsory licence may be issued and the patent owner can be paid an adequate remuneration by the authorities, taking into account the economic value of the licence.

Still another controversial provision (in article 34) is to reverse the burden of proof; it is for the defendant to prove that an identical product has been produced by a process other than the patented one. No less controversial is the issue of pipeline protection, for pharmaceuticals, which asks the countries that are not giving immediate effect to patent protection, to receive applications for patents from the date of enforcement of the WTO agreement. These applications will be examined after 10 years, when such patent laws come into effect, but will give the applicant a certain position in the queue. Similarly, Exclusive Marketing Rights (EMR) have been given for products, patented in some other country, to the patent-owning company, in other member countries, for five years.

A major issue concerns patent rights on seed varieties. Under the agreement, plant varieties are protected in three ways—by patents, a *sui generis* system, or a combination of the two. In general, the issue of IPR in relation to living matters is still in its infancy, which is why article 27: 3(b) calls for a review after four years, that is, one year before the five-year period for the LDCs expires. Generally speaking, the agreement excludes naturally occurring and traditional breeding methods, but permits patentability in cases of cell manipulation or transfer of genes. As for the biological material existing in nature, while the developed countries would like to make them patentable in some form, the LDCs take the view that biological material existing in nature cannot be taken as 'invention' and thus made patentable.

The Earth Summit of 1992 gave a call for enhancing biodiversity, but the new patent regime is likely to have the opposite effect. Ever since the conclusion of the Marakesh agreement there is a mad rush from the large multinational firms, to collect germ plasms of wild plant varieties in the LDCs and then to patent them. The most talked about has been the patenting of the *neem* tree, which is a part of Indian folk culture and whose medicinal and other properties have been known to the Indian people from time immemorial. Since 1985 over a dozen US and Japanese companies have taken out patents on formulae for *neem*-based solutions and emulsions, and one of them has set up a plant in India for exporting processed *neem* seeds. The irony of such patenting is that *neem* products, processed by the foreign companies, would now have to be purchased by Indians who are used to getting it free in nature (Shiva and Holla-Bhar, 1993; Blaikie and Jeanrenaud, 1996: 29–30).

While the demand for a global patent regime arose from the fear of widespread poaching of rich country innovations, inventions and technology by the poorer ones, the biosphere of the latter is now being plundered by the rich country corporate interests under the new regime.

One way of handling this problem is to echo the proposal of The International Undertaking on Plant Genetic Resources, an FAO initiative, that all germplasm be recognised as a public resource and a part of the heritage of mankind. This way, at the minimum, the poor countries would be able to retain some control over their own plants and other forms of life (Lesser, 1991: 64). Another way would be to legislate on the plant breeders' rights (PRB), for which a time period of five years has been allowed by the Marakesh agreement.

Much depends on the political will of the government of the country concerned. While conforming to the 1994 Marakesh agreement and recasting the domestic patent law in line with the international patent regime, there is some room for manoeuvre by making skilful use of some of the articles of the agreement. Virtually all patent laws exclude mere ideas or theories; patents are intended to apply to the embodiment of those ideas. The national laws can be so drafted that the flow of ideas is not obstructed (Lesser, 1991: 28). Further, under articles 27.2 and 27.3 of the Marakesh agreement, the countries may deny patent protection for reasons of morality or for protecting human, animal or plant life or for protecting the environment. Protection can be denied for certain inventions such as those which involve 'diagnostic, therapeutic and surgical methods for the treatment of humans and animals, and plants and animals (other than micro-organisms) and biological processes (other than microbiological processes) for their production' (UNCTAD, 1994b: 189; Schott, 1994: 118).

As for other types of intellectual property, copyrights would normally follow the Berne Convention for the Protection of Literary and Artistic Works (as revised in 1971). Computer programmes are also included in it. Trade marks more or less follow the Paris Convention. Trade secrets are also handled by the Paris Convention.

Dispute settlement

A major distinguishing feature of WTO is the procedure laid down for settling disputes amongst its members, as elaborated in the Dispute Settlement Understanding (DSU). One objective of such dispute settlement procedure was to replace unilateral retaliations by multilateral actions. It was expected that the establishment of WTO would obviate the need for United States to rectify its grievances through unilateral actions such as Super 301, which was always in gross violation of GATT norms. However, as we have seen repeatedly over the past two years, that has not been the case. Super 301 hit lists continue to be prepared alongside sanctions by WTO.

Another reason for setting up an elaborate dispute settlement procedure was to account for the expected sharp increase in the number of disputes in view of the much wider coverage of the world economy. In case of a dispute, a party can seek consultation, to which reply should be given within 10 days, and consultations should be entered into within 30 days (articles 4:1–4:6). If the dispute has not been settled within 60 days, at the instance of the complaining party, a panel for dispute settlement will be set up, based on names recommended by the WTO secretariat to disputing parties, which is expected to give a report in nine months. The panel report is automatically approved unless appealed against; if challenged, it is to be decided upon and adopted within 60 days. Panel rulings are subject to review by a new, standing Appellate Body, which will decide within 60–90 days. From start to end the dispute process is not expected to take more than 20 months (UNCTAD, 1994b: 206–14; Schott, 1994: 126).

If the panel recommendation is not implemented by the offending party within a reasonable time period, the party suffering damage can suspend its obligations to the offending party and retaliate, unless DSB decides against it by consensus. Twenty days are given for a request for retaliation, 30 days for authorising such a request, and 60 days for final arbitration. Cross-sector retaliation is possible, though it should normally try to be specific to that sector under article 22.3 (UNCTAD, 1994b: 214; Schott, 1994: 127–29).

It is not clear whether the decision of a panel for dispute settlement is binding on the United States. To quote Schott:

> However, it can still choose to ignore its findings, because panel rulings are not self-executing in US law. In other words, if WTO decisions require changes in US law, new legislation would need to be enacted to bring US practice into compliance. The WTO can not compel the United States to pass such legislation. However, inaction could result in the United States being in violation of its international obligations . . . .Countries whose trade is adversely affected by the US violation would have the right to retaliate. However, most countries simply do not present the United States with a credible threat of retaliation; the US market is too important for them to risk escalating the trade dispute. But it would cut confidence in trade rules and would reduce the moral position of USA. In sum, the WTO can reprimand but not severely punish violations by major trade powers. When they regard it as necessary, big countries can still abuse the system (Schott, 1994: 129–30).

The implications of the dispute settlement procedure in WTO for Section 301 of the United States Trade Act are far from clear. To quote Schott: 'Section 301 of US Trade Act of 1974, as amended, is designed to promote the enforcement of US rights under international trade agreements, and to coerce foreign countries into eliminating unfair trade practices that adversely affect US trading interests.' Sometimes action under Super 301 is consistent with GATT, at other times it is not covered by the GATT discipline. Under WTO, the US is required to win its case before DSB previous to taking action. 'However, the claims of European and other negotiators that the Uruguay Round accord deranged Section 301 are grossly exaggerated. They can take unilateral action in cases not covered by WTO. The new procedure conforms to US law in terms of time limits' (Schott, 1994: 126–33).

WTO

The WTO turns GATT from a trade accord into a membership organisation. It establishes a legal framework that ties together various trade pacts that have been negotiated under GATT auspices. It signifies little extra for countries like the United States, but forces the LDCs to comply with GATT obligations that they were able to avoid under various concessions. WTO incorporates TRIMs,

TRIPs, GATS, the dispute settlement mechanism and trade policy review mechanisms (TPRM). In addition, it contains four plurilateral agreements—the civil aircraft agreement, the government procurement agreement, and the meat and dairy arrangements—that bind only their signatories.

WTO does not permit 'grandfather rights' relating to laws passed before 1947 that were exempted from the GATT discipline. Only waivers that are permitted by the WTO agreement (annex 1A), such as the US–Canada Auto Pact, the Caribbean Basin Economic Recovery Act and the Andean Trade Preference Act need to be terminated within two years after WTO comes into force unless extended.

Members must deposit their schedules of commitment within two years of joining WTO, commitments to be counted from the date of the beginning of WTO. Members may withdraw by giving six months' notice. Members may invoke 'non-application', as a one-time measure at the time a new member is taken: US may apply it against China.

We have already noted that, in terms of voting rights, WTO follows more or less the United Nations pattern of 'one country one vote', but to minimise what is known in WTO parlance as the 'tyranny of the majority', it provides the minority with sufficient power to block rules on most issues, e.g., for waiver of an obligation, a three-fourths majority is needed. Amendments generally require two-thirds majority. However, if amendments alter the rights and obligations of the members, they would apply only to the countries that accept it. In fact, the tendency is for the Quad group (USA, Canada, Japan and EC) to decide issues first and then to bring them before WTO (Schott, 1994: 133–39).

Labour standards

While environmental standards will be taken up in Chapter 5, here we will deal only with labour standards. One of the most controversial issues has been the attempt to influence the flow of trade in terms of the pattern of labour use. Rich countries tend to take the view that the LDCs are enjoying a differential advantage over their richer counterparts in terms of cheap labour cost. To rectify this, the rich countries are proposing uniform and standardised labour market behaviour, including conformity in terms of wages paid and the conditions under which the workmen operate. The opposition of the LDCs stems from their view that, given the state of their economy, their workers cannot expect a wage or working conditions that are comparable with those in the rich countries. There is a strong feeling that this is less a concern for the plight of workers than for reducing the competitiveness of the poor country exports. Some would go even further and add that the only advantage that the LDCs, bereft of capital, technology and management resources, enjoy is in terms of their relative wages, without which they would lose whatever small share of the world market they still hold. Nor would it be possible to raise only wages without a corresponding rise in GDP.

The second labour issue relates to the international flow of labour. If, under structural adjustment and the GATT agreement, the mobility of capital and technology, as also of goods and services is assured, then why should labour—a major input of production—not be equally mobile across international frontiers? Like commodities and capital, labour too should flow, from the labour-surplus areas, to markets where the demand for labour exceeds its supply. If the MNCs are to enjoy 'national treatment' in all countries, why should not the labour power, irrespective of its source, enjoy the same non-discriminatory treatment vis-à-vis local labour? The fact is that, in an era when the rich countries have been strongly articulating their demand for free movement of goods, services, capital and what not, there is a clearly visible reticence to extend mobility to labour power. On the contrary, the immigration laws have been considerably tightened in the past two decades to contain flow of labour power from the LDCs. Obviously, a concept that is good, both philosophically and economically, for capital and commodities, is not as good when it comes to poor country labour exports.

Another fallacy is that, alongside the demand for better labour standards in poor countries, the rich country MNCs have been demanding the dilution of labour laws that protect their interests, e.g., minimum wages, job security against lay-offs and closures, better working conditions and compensations in case of injuries, provident funds and trade union rights. Here the argument is that such legislations make the movement of wages rigid and do not allow the labour market to adjust to the demand and supply forces. Further, such legislations discourage foreign investment while poor countries need more FDI in factories and industries. One ILO document concludes, 'The overriding tendency [of the World Bank] has been to criticize existing labour laws and regulations, whenever they may raise the cost of labour and otherwise impede the freer operation of market forces' (Plant, 1994: 57). Such a view looks at the problem only from the side of management, as if production is only undertaken by management, ignoring the contribution of the workforce and the sufferings, uncertainties and poverty they undergo to keep the wheels of industry moving.

On the contrary, it is a moot question whether such a purely market-oriented approach towards labour can ever succeed. Japan's industries offer lifetime jobs to their employees and their promotions are guided more by seniority than by efficiency, and yet this country has managed to sustain a very high rate of growth of industry over many decades. Those preferring the Japanese way would claim that the security enjoyed by their workforce has strengthened their bond with the management and has made them more loyal to the enterprise than they would have been otherwise. Flexitime workers paid by the hour may be more successful in equating demand with supply, but are unlikely to produce a result that is better than Japan's. A study on Zimbabwe shows that 'real consumption wages' are quite flexible, while a World Bank study, based on 12 countries, disputes the view that wages are rigid in LDCs. Both studies conclude that labour market wage constraints are not real constraints to growth (Horton et al., 1991; Kanyenze, 1996: 69–70).

One major issue that is seldom discussed, is the distorting impact of MNC management salaries on the overall wage and salary structure in a country. In many cases, MNCs are offering a salary level that is many times the existing one for senior administrators and business personnel in a given country. To protect their own management staff from poaching by MNCs, the local firms are often being forced to pay salaries that are completely out of tune with the salaries of the lower level of staff. In some countries the ratio between the highest salary for the management and the lowest for those working on the shopfloor is as high as 100:1. This is leading to serious unrest in the workforce and is operating as a negative incentive for the majority of the workers.

Agricultural issues

The agricultural policies of the United States and Europe

For many decades, agriculture has been under heavy protection in the developed countries, with astronomical levels of subsidy and import control measures. The main rationale behind this being a concern for national security. However, the degree of protection and the level of subsidisation seem to have gone beyond control. These countries, enjoying no comparative advantage in food production whatsoever, now not only produce enough food to meet their own national consumption needs, but also produce a very large surplus that needs to be exported or given away in the form of a food grant under PL480 (Public Law 480 of the United States). As a consequence, a totally non-viable economic activity has been catapulted, by way of state support, to become a major export item, in fact dominating the world market in wheat and several other items. In other words, a policy that began as one of import substitution in a sensitive area has succeeded in creating for the United States and Western Europe, a comparative advantage that they do not possess naturally

It is interesting to recall that one of the major opposition groups in the United States against the proposed ITO in the later 1940s, was the agricultural lobby, which has been used to protection from 1935, and feared that such state support would wither away under multilateral control (Cohn, 1993: 21). When the GATT system became operational (in 1955) the United States pressurised the other countries to allow it to continue with a highly prolectionist policy for agriculture, i,e., to waive the normal GATT rules (Low, 1995: 24). In later years, when food surplus became a regular feature, food diplomacy, mainly involving food supply under PL480 to deficient countries facing famine, became a major plank of the US foreign policy (Cohn, 1993: 22). Protection was given in other forms too, by nearly all the rich countries, to keep poor country agricultural exports away. We have already noted that a very large proportion of VERs covered food and agricultural products (Low, 1995: 77). Along with subsidies, a ridiculously large agricultural administration has come into being in the United States: there is now one bureaucrat for every five farmers and the budget of the US Department of Agriculture exceeds the net income of all farmers (Atkin, 1995: 26–28; Folmer et al., 1995).

While US agricultural subsidies have a long history dating from the 1930s, the Common Agricultural Policy (CAP) of the EC was initiated in 1962, at the conclusion of the Dillon Round of GATT negotiations. Under CAP, high support prices were maintained for major crops, as a variable levy system was imposed that ensured that foreign agricultural goods would always be dearer than their local counterparts. Further, export subsidies (referred to as export refunds or restitution) were given to agricultural producers to dispose of surplus. During the Kennedy Round of GATT negotiations (1964–67) EC refused to make CAP a subject for negotiation on the ground that it was an essential element to bind its members together (Cohn, 1993: 25).

Over time, agricultural subsidies have increased significantly, accounting for 60–70 per cent of the common fund of EC (Moyer and Josling, 1990: 23; Atkin, 1995: 26–28). EC budgetary support for agriculture rose from 4.7 billion ECU out of the 6.2 billion ECU overall budget in 1975, to 46.3 billion ECU out of the 58.4 billion ECU budget of EC in 1991 (Atkin, 1993: 85). While, in 1970, EC was primarily importing agricultural goods, and exporting only a few items, by 1980 it was self-sufficient. By 1986 its agricultural exports—cereals, beef, sugar, and dairy products—actually surpassed those from the USA (ibid., 1993: 196). In other words, these massive subsidies have transformed this essentially food deficit region into one exporting more than anyone else.

With this high level of subsidies, OECD countries (taking EC, USA and others together) account for 80 per cent of total world cereal trade, more than 55 per cent of which is sold to LDCs (OECD, 1993: 13). By way of this subsidy, the OECD countries have raised their share of world trade in beef: from 40 per cent to 62 per cent during 1980–84, while that of the LDCs has fallen from 52 per cent to 27 per cent. For sugar, over the same period, the share of OECD rose from 17 per cent to 28 per cent, and correspondingly, that of the LDCs declined from 73 per cent to 67 per cent. While EC was deficient in sugar production until recently, now these subsidies and other support measures have made it the largest sugar exporter—of 4m tons (Watkins, 1992: 61). It is estimated that a reduction of 30 per cent in average levels of protection in OECD countries would produce a gain of $195 billion for the world economy, which is greater than the entire income of Sub-Saharan Africa. Of this $195 billion, about $90 billion would accrue to LDCs, an amount that is twice the official development assistance per year to these countries. Complete abolition of protection would entail a global welfare gain of $475 billion according to this estimate (Atkin, 1993: 117). These subsidies have kept world prices at a level that is 8–17 per cent lower than would have been the case otherwise (Atkin, 1995: 50).

Change in US attitude towards agricultural subsidy

How the US opposition to GATT's consideration of agriculture, over the first seven rounds, changed and the US policy made a 180-degree turn during negotiations on the eighth, is a question that deserves examination. Perhaps the decisive factor was the very scale of subsidy that the country had to offer when the US budget was showing enormous deficits, thereby seriously threatening the macro-economic balance. According to one calculation, even in 1989, the United States government provided farm subsidy to the turn of $32 billion, while the corresponding figures were $53 billion for the EC and $33 billion for Japan (Hillman, 1994: 46). The total amount of subsidy annually given by OECD countries to their agricultural producers reached a figure of $240 billion (Watkins, 1992: 70). One OECD study in the early 1990s estimated production subsidy equivalents (in percentage of producer prices) in 1991 at 66 per cent for Japan, 49 per cent for EC, and 30 per cent for the United States (Development Committee, 1992: 94). This level of subsidies proved too high even for an economic giant like the United States. Chronic budget and balance of payment deficits led the United States to look for a solution with lower levels of subsidies for its own agriculture; and it was, therefore, in its own interest to make the rest of the world conform to its policies.

Further, with the emergence of EC as a major competitor in the global wheat market, the US share was declining. In the case of wheat, it declined from its peak of 45 per cent in 1980–81 to 29.6 per cent in 1985–86. This led to a war on subsidies between Europe and the United States, and in 1985, the latter launched an Export Enhancement Programme (EEP) to regain lost market (Cohn, 1993: 27–30). In 1986, the US agricultural exports slumped to $26 billion, but the government handout to farmers, at $30 billion, exceeded export earnings. To protect its share, a further substantial increase of subsidies was warranted, but that could only further destabilise macro-economic management. Besides, there was no guarantee that such subsidies were capable of restoring the previous share or even of protecting the existing one. The subsidy war with Europe was increasingly going out of control. One alternative actively promoted by the US government was to induce its farmers to leave the land fallow in exchange of subsidy; thus the farmers were paid not to produce. 'It was in this atmosphere that the United States led the way towards the Uruguay Round and in the process proposed a new departure to negotiations: namely, the inclusion of domestic subsidies and import quota restrictions on the agenda, along with all other non-tariff agricultural trade barriers' (Hillman, 1994: 32–33, 46).

Uruguay round negotiations and the Marakesh agreement

In the eighth round of GATT negotiations on agriculture, the LDCs, 70 out of 108 and accounting for half of the world food imports, had no role to play, nor was any attempt made to form coalitions to counter the propaganda for ending all subsidies and protection. The Cairns Group, a group of 14 middle-income and rich countries—Argentina, Australia, Brazil, Canada, Chile, Colombia, Fiji, Hungary, Indonesia, Malaysia, New Zealand, the Philippines, Thailand and Uruguay—with large agricultural production and close links with the rich countries, and accounting for one-tenth of world GDP and manufacturing output, 30 per cent share in world agricultural exports and a strong bargaining power vis-à-vis the rich countries, made a much bigger impact than the much larger group of LDCs (Typres, 1994: 89). Nor did the LDCs try to form an alliance with Japan, a rich country that was opposed to agricultural liberalisation. All this despite the fact that an UNCTAD model showed that full OECD liberalisation would lead to net loss of foreign exchange and also net welfare loss for the LDCs. A study by USDA's Economic Research Service showed, for them, a net foreign exchange loss of $4.5 billion but a welfare gain of $2–3 billion, only if all the countries liberalised. Only the study by Anderson and Tyer showed the possibility of a gain by LDCs, if only the OECD countries liberalised, to the extent of a net welfare gain of $11.5 billion in 1995, and if all the countries liberalised, to the extent of $56.3 billion (Hopkins, 1993: 143–49).

However, US did not propose complete elimination of producer subsidy in the Uruguay Round discussions; it wanted only that part of the subsidy which was tied to output-increasing incentives to go.

Through this agreement, it was expected that the Western governments would no longer have to engage themselves in subsidy wars, the US producers would gain from all-round subsidy reductions, their competitiveness would be enhanced, and they would not be exposed to large market shocks, while the US safety regulations in relation to internal food supply would not change (Hillman, 1994: 51).

As it turned out, agricultural subsidies became a highly divisive issue in the last lap of the Uruguay Round, dividing Europe (and Japan) from the United States. EC, particularly France, was alarmed that such a policy shift might completely undermine CAP. Japan too was opposed to it as it valued its own food security highly and was unwilling to depend on the world market for meeting its needs (Hoekman and Cremoux, 1993: 299; Watkins, 1992: 121). Eventually, under their pressure, agricultural subsidies were exempted from articles 3, 5, 6, and 7 in the subsidies agreement and a separate agreement on agriculture was worked out (UNCTAD, 1994b: 99).

In this agreement on agriculture, under reduction commitments, the members were expected to reduce their budgetary outlay on agricultural subsidies, from 1986–90 levels, by 36 per cent and their volume by 21 per cent, over a period of six years. For the LDCs, a 24 per cent cut in value and 14 per cent in volume in 10 equal annual instalments was ordained. The Aggregate Measure of Support (AMS), which is calculated in value terms as a global measure and not specific to products, is expected to be reduced by 20 per cent in six years, at an aggregate level, allowing flexibility in shifting support between products. No new export subsidy on products not subsidised before was permitted. Further, a de minimis provision allows the countries to exclude from AMS calculation, any support that does not exceed 5 per cent of the value of production of that commodity, and, for non-product-specific support, where it does not exceed 5 per cent of the value of the country's total agricultural production. For the LDCs de minimis level is 10 per cent, and specified agricultural input subsidies are excluded from AMS (UNCTAD, 1994b: 98–102). However, given that subsidy levels were already high in the United States and Europe, even after such reductions the actual subsidy given to their agriculturists would remain high, compared with those in the less developed countries (UNCTAD, 1994b: 101).

Surprisingly, the direct payments under production limiting programmes, such as US deficiency payments and EU compensation payments to their agriculturists, were exempted, as also a long list of other subsidy programmes, on the ground that, according to GATT, these have no or minimal trade distorting effects on production. To avoid the GATT trap, under the MacSharry Plan, EC had already delinked support to farmers from output, and based it on area sown in a past reference period. Farms with more than 40 acres of cereals were asked to remove 15 per cent of their land from production to qualify for compensation. Compensation was given according to a sliding scale—bigger farms receiving less per hectare than the smaller ones. All these measures, according to GATT dispensation, removed trade-distorting effects of these subsidies (Watkins, 1992: 122).

What is not widely known is that the Marakesh agreement also allows import control for some specific purposes, e.g., sanitary and phytosanitary measures in order to 'protect human, animal or plant life or health'. It has been left to the country concerned to work out its own acceptable level of risk, but the controls are to be used on a non-discriminatory basis. The EU ban on hormone-fed beef from USA was based on this provision (Schott, 1994: 52–53). This provision was also applied by both EU and US against some third world exports.

Adverse terms of trade effect

No study has come forth to predict the terms of trade implications of such a scramble for rich country markets (following the collapse of the protectionist regimes in the United States and Europe) for poor country primary product exports. The study by Rafter and Singer shows that Sub-Saharan African countries pay 20 per cent more for imports, because of insufficient bulk and market knowledge. Such a situation can be partly mitigated by an alert state, through exchange of information with other LDCs, and by way of a regional procurement agency working with a wider database. However, such regional cooperation is frowned upon as it stands in the way of global integration (Rafter and Singer, 1996: 198–99). For several decades now the global terms of trade have been unfavourable to agricultural exports. Most studies, mainly undertaken by the World Bank, IMF and UNCTAD, indicate not only how terms of trade have been moving against primary exports, but the fearful prospect of the trend persisting until the end of the first decade of the next century. The index of real commodity prices fell by half between 1980 and 1993, and, according to Lewis T. Preston, President of the World Bank:

> Today the real prices of many non-oil commodities are the lowest they have been since 1945; in many cases prices are so low that they do not cover production costs. For 1993, the transfer in purchasing power from the developing to the developed countries due to the fall in non-oil commodity prices between 1980 and 1993, was about $100 billion—more than double the net aid flows to developing countries in 1993 (Development Committee, 1994: 8).

Not only that the negative terms of trade effect outweighed the positive effect of aid inflow, they also accounted for a massive loss of up to 7 per cent of GNP in case of the LDCs. The document predicted that during the next 10 years, commodity prices would increase slightly faster than those of manufactured goods, but, after that, the long-term declining trend would again assert itself (ibid., 1994).

The share of food in world trade has declined from 21.4 per cent in 1962 to 9.5 per cent in 1992; and of non-food agriculture from 10.2 per cent to 2.1 per cent. Over the same period, the share of metals and minerals has slided from 7.7 per cent to 2.4 per cent, of fuels from 11.4 per cent to 4.3 per cent, but of manufacture has greatly increased from 49.2 per cent to 81.6 per cent. Even in the case of the LDCs, the share of food in their exports has declined from 37.3 per cent to 12.1 per cent. Over the past two decades, 'the volume of world trade in manufactures has increased twice as fast as the volume of primary commodities . . . for each percentage point of increase in world output, trade in manufacturing went up 2 per cent, while trade in primary products rose only 0.6 per cent' (ECLAC, 1994: 39).

There is a hope, in many LDCs, that, at the conclusion of the 10-year period following the establishment of WTO in 1995, as the subsidies given to agriculture in the USA and Europe are reduced, their own agricultural export opportunities would expand. Had only a few countries been making such calculations, there could have been a reasonable chance of these expectations being fulfilled.

The fact is that practically all the LDCs have been generously rendered this advice by the World Bank and all of them are making preparations for the day when the partial withdrawal of subsidies would open up huge rich country markets for them. As a consequence, the familiar 'fallacy of composition' has come to play. In this situation, more production and export of agricultural commodities, in-line with their static comparative advantage, by all the poor countries of the world together, is likely to pull down their prices even further, and harm them collectively. There is every likelihood that this secular tendency towards further decline in terms of trade—because of technical and other changes that have reduced the intensity of the use of minerals, metals, and agricultural products in the developed countries—would now be reinforced by the scramble for rich country agricultural markets in the first decade of the 21st century. Thus, whatever gains the LDCs would make in terms of volume is likely to be overweighed by their losses in value terms. During the 1980s, the volume of agricultural exports increased by 2.3 per cent while their value increased by only 1.4 per cent a year (ECLAC, 1994: 38, 69–70). On the other hand, whatever the rich countries would lose in terms of loss of agricultural exports would be more than made up by their saving in terms of subsidies and the cheapening of the cost of industrial production because of low prices of agricultural imports.

A major shortcoming in the Fund–Bank policies is the assumption that only the governments of these countries are responsible for the failings of these economies. Such policies do not consider adequately the constraints within the world trade structure that inhibit growth of their exports. As one econometric exercise shows, terms of trade and weather produce better results on GDP growth than Fund–Bank policy or finance (Mosley et al., 1991: 208–17). Such decline in terms of trade cannot be explained by the demand factors alone; the collapse of international stabilisation schemes for some major commodities, partly induced by Fund–Bank hostility towards marketing boards, have contributed in no small measure to price volatility (Development Committee, 1994: 53–60).

The goal of self-reliance vs food security via trade

Several policy issues arise for the LDCs, following the Marakesh agreement. One is whether the goal of self-sufficiency in food production should be discarded in favour of 'food security through trade'. The latter rests on the dubious assumption that world trade is free, that anybody can buy anything from the world market provided he has the means. Further, such a view fails to take account of the strategic importance of food in a war or cold war situation, when supply, though available in the world market, might not reach a particular destination. Or, of a situation where, dependence on another country for food might force the country to yield on other vital trade, military or foreign policy matters at a high economic or political cost to the country.

That such fears are not merely theoretical has been amply illustrated, again and again, over the past five decades. In the early 1990s, India's request for US wheat imports was denied because a few months earlier India had sent a shipload of paddy to starving Cuba (Mukherjee, 1994: 164–65). We have already noted that food diplomacy had been, admittedly, a major component of US diplomacy during the cold war years (Webb and Krasner, 1989; Frankel et al., 1979: 2–3). In India's case, devaluation of 1966 was not wanted by anyone, including the Finance Minister, but could not be resisted because of its dependence on PL480 food support for 15 per cent of its food requirement at that time.

Japan, a country that can buy anything from anywhere at any cost, is continuing with high subsidy for domestic rice production, because, despite its economic power, it finds the alternative of dependence on foreign sources for food alarming from political and military standpoints (Hoekman & Cremoux, 1993: 299). In 1988, the Japanese Diet passed a resolution confirming self-sufficiency in rice as a policy objective. Its rice imports amount to only 50,000 tons compared with the domestic demand of 10 million tons a year. Japan is unwilling to replace quantitative control over rice imports by tariffs in conformity with GATT principles because tariffication alone would not give the country the necessary control it desires against food imports (Hemmi, 1994: 149–55). We have already noted that both USA and EC began giving agricultural subsidies for security reasons.

No less serious is the question: How are food-deficit countries going to find food? Very few countries in the world are surplus food producers or exporters. USA, Canada, Western Europe, Australia and Argentina are practically the only countries with wheat surplus for export in the world (Atkin, 1995: 74). Thailand and Vietnam are among those few with rice surplus. If, after the 10-year period, the rich countries retreat from the world market in food exports, there is likely to be a shortfall in world food production and exports. Further, the world grain trade is dominated by large buyers like China or Russia, who, in some years, are capable of mopping up the entire surplus food production in the world.

Impact of withdrawal of subsidies

So far we have discussed the issue of subsidies from one particular angle; how the reduction of agricultural subsidies in the United States and the EC is going to affect agricultural exports in the LDCs. Let us now examine it from another angle: How is the withdrawal of internal subsidies going to affect agricultural production and even generation of surplus for exports in the LDCs?

Generally speaking, subsidy withdrawal leads to a reduction in agricultural production. In India's case, agriculture performed very badly during 1991–97, despite the very unusual favourable occurrence of eight successive good monsoons, a significant increase in the flow of capital to agriculture via cooperatives, substantially higher support prices and a highly supportive adjustment programme, mainly because of (*a*) a drastic curtailment in public investment in agricultural infrastructure, and (*b*) an increase in the prices of potassic and phosphatic fertilisers, following subsidy reduction, with a consequent disproportionate increase in the consumption of nitrogenous fertilisers (Dasgupta, 1997b).

GATT opposition to subsidies is based on the view that a project or economic activity should cover its costs and provide returns within a given time frame. A broad social cost-benefit analysis, recognising the linkages of the projects with the rest of the economy and taking a long time horizon into account, would go beyond such a time-bound and project-bound framework. A subsidy can be treated as an investment for creating viability at a future date, or even as a measure that protects the interests of the future generation or of the environment. We will have occasion to adequately deal with this issue in the next chapter.

Changes in land use and cropping patterns in response to world prices

There is also the related question of whether to adjust to a country's cropping pattern in line with 'world prices'. Those taking the Fund–Bank view argue, on the basis of the comparison of Indian prices with the cost, insurance and freight (c.i.f.) prices of various crops imported from outside the country, that India should refrain from seeking self-sufficiency in oilseeds, and should instead concentrate on wheat and a few other items (Pursell and Gulati, 1995; David, 1985: 64). Such an argument is based on two false premises. First, that the c.i.f. price is a valid 'world price' that has emerged from interaction of forces of demand and supply, and is objective enough for the government to take it as the basis for our own cropping decisions. This, we have already noted, is patently false. Second, that it is possible to switch the use of land from oilseeds to wheat without any difficulty, oblivious to agro-climatic and infrastructure constraints that would not permit such a switch. Most of the land under oilseeds gets little irrigation water and is unsuitable for crops requiring a large quantity of water.

Further, world prices, both absolute and relative, do not exhibit enough stability to base domestic cropping decisions on them. Unlike crops responding to subsistence or domestic commercial needs, those supplying to the world market have always been vulnerable to fluctuations in global demand and supply, collusion by oligopolistic buyers and manipulation of auction prices by vertically integrated MNCs involved in production as well as processing and marketing. Had Keynes' ideas about commodity buffer stocks operated by an international trade agency been accepted, there could have been some hope of price stabilisation at the global level. In this situation, relative profitability of one crop over another changes from year to year.

No less significant, both production and export of these crops and products are controlled by MNCs operating in many countries, who may have their own, global reasons to push more or less of exports from a particular source, or to produce more or less from a particular source. As it has been repeatedly found, in cases ranging from crude oil to prawn farming, MNCs, for their own perfectly valid reasons, seek low-cost sources of production and would have no hesitation in abandoning a higher-cost source if that optimises their profits at the global level. In this situation, a country relying on one or two major crops or products for exports, and enjoying healthy export earnings based on these for many years, may be left high and dry by such locational shifts of MNC operations.

One possible way out is to follow the East Asian example of offering a wide range of export goods, so that even if the global market for one collapses, there would be several others to fall back upon. This also raises the broader issue, whether a country should go only by historically and naturally given comparative advantages, or should adopt a more dynamic concept of actually creating a desirable comparative advantage by making suitable investment in industrial infrastructure (see Chapter 6).

The changing land use pattern, motivated by profit, with adverse environmental implications, is becoming a universal phenomenon. The replacement of traditional forests (with diverse plants supporting a wide variety of animals and birds) with eucalyptus, has been a major issue with environmentalists for over two decades. While eucalyptus is a paying activity, as far as the firm owning the plantation is concerned, it does not permit undergrowth and lower order vegetation that in turn could support many different species and grazing. The takeover of rural wastelands by industrial enterprises is displacing people who had been surviving on these for generations. The fact that the supposed wastelands are also useful to some people who need to be rehabilitated does not always dawn on the policy-makers. The standardised commercial crops promoted by these firms do not allow much room for biodiversity. Aquaculture farms producing prawn for exports create another wide range of land use and environmental problems (to be discussed in Chapter 5).

In general, increasing commercialisation of agriculture within a country is a major consequence of export orientation promoted by global economic integration. While such a drive towards increasing production of commercial crops is unavoidable, and even justifiable on a number of grounds subject to fulfilment of domestic food needs and price stability considerations discussed earlier, several major consequences of such a process are changes in labour use and production relations. One, the growing concentration of land and farming in the hands of the larger holdings that are capable of making necessary investments in agricultural machinery and other inputs. Two, the consequent growing proletarianisation of small agriculturists who, unable to compete with their large counterparts, are selling or leasing out their land and moving to other occupations. Three, the phenomenon of growing landlessness, along with the increasing casualisation of the workforce. In certain situations, as in West Bengal (India) such inherent tendencies of commercialisation have been greatly neutralised by institutional reform, mainly land reform, cooperativisation, and the devolution of power to elected local rural bodies at grass-root levels, but that is an exception (Dasgupta, 1997b).

There is also a fourth consequence, of changing production relations. Farmers working on contract with MNCs are no longer independent producers. They operate on the basis of input packages supplied by the latter and in accordance with specifications laid down by the company. They produce under their supervision, and deliver their entire product to the company. Both the prices of inputs the company supplies, and the prices of outputs the farmer delivers, are fixed by the company. Though operating on their own lands, the contract farmers in effect work as labourers for them. In addition, in many cases, the companies manage their own farms, on lands purchased or leased by them, with hired labourers.

The changing landscape of the world food industry

Lastly, let us examine some of the major changes that are now taking place in the world food industry which have serious implications for the future of agriculture as we know it today and for relations of production involving the producer, the owner, the land and the ultimate consumers. Agriculture today serves two main functions—as a source of food and as a source of raw material for the industries. It is also the biggest employer of people, accounting for 60–80 per cent of employment in the LDCs.

In the rich countries of today its role as an employer is steadily declining. In the United States, agriculture accounts for about 3–4 per cent of the working population, but the food industry accounts for twice as many. While, traditionally, food industry was taken as an appendage of agricultural activities, the tendency in the rich countries today is for the former to take over as the major partner. Further, while in the LDCs there is a clear and recognisable link between agricultural output and the food eaten—e.g., rice, cabbage, potato and so on—this link is becoming weaker as the multinational agri-business firms are producing synthetic or 'fabricated' foods (Goodman, 1991: 37) such as hamburgers, margarine, or Coca Cola, and are creating tastes for these through vigorous advertisement campaigns. 'The new foods they bought were often the inventions of corporate "kitchens" rather than culturally transmitted recipes, and they were intimately linked to the use of new appliances that permitted weekly shopping, long storage, and new ways of preparing meals for families whose gender and age relations were radically restructured' (Friedman, 1995: 24). Folk knowledge about food preparations and the link between agriculture and the dish served are being replaced by the researched knowledge of experts (Friedman, 1995: 22).

For this new food industry agriculture is only one of several major inputs. Chemical industry is increasingly replacing agriculture as the principal source, while the hydrocarbon industry is another (Goodman, 1991: 37). Inputs of the food industry can potentially be derived from a much wider range of materials: food and non-food crops and even from non-renewable resources. Biotechnology now enables the food industry to use biomass, and not specific crops, to produce a particular food item of their choice that also fulfils nutritional specifications—protein, calorie, cholesterol, saturated and polyunsaturated fats and fibre content—and other conditions, and is relatively cheap. Genetic engineering can convert biomass into food, fuel and chemicals (Goodman, 1991: 48, 55). The new processing techniques break down field crops into generic intermediate food ingredients (carbohydrates, proteins, fats) for use in downstream manufacturing. 'Product fractionalism can be seen as a reduction process which transforms field crops into chemical constituents to serve as "building blocks" in the production of industrially constituted food products' (Goodman, 1991: 37–38).

Now, truly industrial food products can be manufactured to replace the original agricultural products using biocatalytic fermentation. Biotechnologies thus open the way for the food industry to join the wider trend away from agricultural inputs, breaking the close identification with specific crops (Goodman, 1991: 38). Research also goes into making that food item tasty, while advertisements attempt to create a preference for such food items by making it a part of the mass culture. Moreover, such production is flexible and subject to 'design change' in line with current fashion (Goodman, 1991: 45).

ICI and Rank–Hovis–McDougall have produced a protein-rich ingredient, Myco-protein, a micro-fungus whose textural properties can be used to imitate meat, poultry or fish protein. Myco-protein is produced by the continuous fermentation of a micro-fungus on a glucose substrate, usually obtained from wheat or corn starch, although any carbohydrate can do. Biotechnology can now transform cheap carbohydrates into high grade proteins. Further Myco-protein has a doubling time of only five hours in contrast with the lengthy conversion of vegetable protein into animal protein in livestock production. Myco-protein is increasingly emerging as a substitute for the livestock industry (Goodman, 1991: 47). High Fruitcose Corn Syrup (HFCS), made of maize starch transformed by enzymes, has ousted sugar from soft drink production, resulting in a sharp decline in US sugar imports, nearly by half, between 1970 and 1987. Single cell proteins (SCPs), made from fuel oil, are another possible replacement for both sweeteners and protein animal feed (Barrat Brown and Tiffen, 1994: 53; Friedman, 1991: 76).

In this environment, the established agriculture–food relationship has come under serious threat. This development,

> definitely disrupted the primordial connection between, on one side, the land and labor that cultivates plants and rears animals, and, on the other side, the human activities that acquire, transform, prepare, serve, and share meals in daily life and on festive and ritual occasions. Instead of selling products to be consumed after minimal transformation, farmers became suppliers of raw materials to industries (Friedman, 1995: 22).

'Land and labor are increasingly disembedded from the social relations in which food is produced and consumed' (Friedman, 1995: 29). 'Modern biotechnologies threaten the continued organization of the food system around the reproduction of specific crops and production systems' (Goodman, 1991: 38).

Alongside this development is the tendency to concentrate production in the hands of the multinationals that are capable of conducting research on biotechnology, e.g., ICI, Heinz, Ciba–Geigy, Sandoz, Shell, Sinclair are among the major players in the field. While on the one hand crop agri-processing firms are moving into chemicals, chemical and even petroleum companies are moving into agri-chemicals. The tendency for the source of profit to shift from agricultural production and trade to manufacturing, distribution and food services, and for increased commodification of food and industrialisation of agriculture noticed since World War II with the growth of agro-food corporations, is being strongly reinforced by these new developments (Friedman, 1995: 22).

In this situation, more than ever before, farmers would no longer directly supply their products to the consumers. The relationship between the farmer and the consumer would be mediated by the multinational food firm, which will buy agricultural crops and biomass, combine these with chemicals and hydrocarbons, reduce all these inputs into their nuclear constituents, and then, through their sophisticated high-tech processing biotechnology, would produce new food items that would be healthy and nutritionally balanced. Thus the traditional division of agricultural and industrial products would disappear and would be replaced by a system where the agri-food sector would become central to world capital accumulation (Friedman, 1991: 65). The locus of food production would also shift to the rich countries where genetic engineering would be feasible. Generic sweeteners now account for 40 per cent of consumption in the United States (Friedman, 1991: 76). 'As the preparation of meals moves from kitchen to factory . . . crops change from final consumer goods to industrial raw materials . . . . What is wanted is not sugar, but sweeteners; not flour or cornstarch, but thickeners; not palm oil or butter, but fats; not beef or cod, but proteins' (Friedman, 1991: 74).

The multinational corporations (MNCs)

In view of our frequent references to the MNCs and their deeds and misdeeds in this book, it is high time that we attempt to define this particular breed of firms, differentiate them from others, and summarise the major implications of their activities for world trade in particular and world economy in general.

MNCs: Main features

A general description of MNCs would be that these are: (*a*) large, (*b*) vertically integrated, (*c*) firms whose area of operation covers many countries where their numerous subsidiaries and affiliates are located, and (*d*) which operate in oligopolistic markets (Dasgupta, 1974; Penrose, 1967).

Their vastness can be measured by their turnover, assets, manpower (in particular the very highly skilled layer), R&D expenditure and control over technology. The figures of annual sales for the larger ones amongst these exceed the GDP of a vast majority of LDCs, and for the top ones the turnover is not far from the GDP figure for India, a country of 950 million people. In 1980, the 380 biggest MNCs accounted for $1,000 billion in foreign sales (Development Committee, 1985a: 14–15). Their size and enormous economic power give them a decisive advantage when bargaining with the governments of the LDCs. In the case of the smaller countries, very often MNCs, operating in the domestic market and specialising in one or two crops, account for around 80 per cent of exports, GDP and employment. Given their economic clout, these companies also wield considerable political power, and not too infrequently play a role in the making and breaking of governments. Their colossal R&D investment makes it possible for them to operate at the frontiers of technology and human habitation, in remote, inaccessible areas such as the deep sea, tundra, deserts and dense tropical forests.

Their vertically integrated character implies their participation in all the major activities connected with this field. In the case of the mineral companies, this begins with exploration, development and production, and stretches to transport, refining and marketing. Similarly, in case of the agri-business firms, their activities range from production in the field to sales to ultimate consumers. Vertical integration, providing both forward and backward linkages within a corporate framework, enables a company to plan its operations better, to ensure supplies at various stages and to avoid wastage. This also makes it extremely difficult for a new competitor to enter the market by spreading its activities to all the areas at once. Those specialising in one or two areas would be forced to depend on the established vertically integrated ones for other activities, e.g., an exclusively refining company would have to find ways of transporting the crude and marketing, and thus becoming, in effect, an appendage of the established ones, or would otherwise be forced out of the market.

Their multinational character imparts a great deal of flexibility to their operations. Their control over both production and consumption in many areas makes it possible to blend material from diverse sources to exactly match the demand pattern in a particular place. At the same time, their interests become identified with the interests of their countries of domicile in foreign diplomacy and economic policy matters. This helps them in negotiations with the LDC governments, in clinching deals, and even in resisting attempts to restrict their activities or to expropriate their property. Whether fighting oil nationalisation in Iran in 1949, or the expropriation of mining and telecommunications in Peru or Chile in the 1970s, or, on more mundane matters such as obtaining a specified share of the Japanese market in a given product in the 1980s, they can count on the support of their own governments.

Their oligopolistic character makes it necessary for them to come to some understanding with fellow oligopolists, in order to avoid costly price wars that can easily spread to all the markets in the world. Such understanding—in the past, taking the form of a written contract that specified standardised price formulae and market sharing arrangements, that are illegal now in most countries—is reached, tacitly, more in social clubs over drinks than in board rooms, and in terms of compliance with an informal code. Their interlocking interests are reflected in joint ventures for production and distribution, in long-term supply agreements, and in localised swapping arrangements aimed at minimisation of transport costs. The oligopolistic rivalry generally takes the form of non-price competition, including under-the-counter discounts. While the attitude towards fellow oligopolists is cooperative, given their size and power, their smaller competitors are treated harshly and beaten to submission: either they are eliminated through ruthless competition or incorporated within their framework.

Implications for LDCs: Possible areas of conflict

From the point of view of the host LDC governments, their method of functioning has a number of important implications. First, there is an inherent conflict between the global profit-maximising objective of an MNC and the national objectives of a host country. For understandable reasons, an MNC would choose, between several alternatives, the low-cost sources for production, while the host governments would be primarily interested in mineral development within their territories. An MNC, while not developing a particular concession, might be keen to hold on to it in order to keep the competitors out, but it would be in the interest of the host government not to allow such under-utilisation or even to foster competition by inviting others to take over (Brandt, 1980: 187–200; Dasgupta, 1974).

The MNCs decide what to produce and how to produce, where to sell and at what price. In this unequal relationship, not only the tiny countries but even the large ones often find themselves without the data to counter the MNC viewpoint, and therefore, turn out to be no match for these corporate giants in negotiations. The MNCs may deny the host governments vital information that might have improved the latter's bargaining position, and may even punish a host government for adopting a hostile attitude by not producing or exporting enough from that source. It may even induce its own government to impose an embargo on the trade of the country should the host government retaliate by nationalising. Various proposals, for greater transparency in their negotiations with LDC governments, for making them follow a code of conduct, for monitoring their activities by UN and for exchange of information among the LDC governments for effective bargaining, have not gone very far, largely because of lack of enthusiasm, sometimes direct antagonism, on the part of the rich country governments (FitzGerald, 1979: 13–17).

Second, a great deal of what passes as international trade is, from the point of view of an MNC, given its multinational character, an intra-company affair, a transfer between two affiliates located in two different countries. Towards the end of the 1970s, such intra-firm, but international trade accounted for about 30 per cent of total world trade. As for the United States, intra-firm MNC transactions contributed to half of its manufactured goods exports, and about 45 per cent of total imports, and, in the case of imports of minerals, it accounted for shares of 70–80 per cent (FitzGerald, 1979: 11). Further, 27 per cent of Mexican exports and 42 per cent of imports to and from United States were intra-firm operations of US companies. For Brazil, 14 per cent of exports to US in 1990 were intra-firm (ECLAC, 1994: 55). These companies are also involved in a great deal of trade amongst themselves: by the early 1980s trade between the 350 largest Trans-national Corporations (TNCs) amounted to an estimated 40 per cent of global trade. MNCs also dominate technology flows, most of which remain confined within the corporate framework: for the US four-fifths of technology receipts are intra-firm and over 90 per cent for Germany (Stewart, 1993: 4). A handful of MNCs (say, six to 10), account for 60–70 per cent of the world production of leading minerals, such as bauxite, copper, iron ore, nickel, and zinc, and also major agricultural exports such as tea, coffee or banana.

The prices at which goods are transferred between affiliates of the same company, located in different countries, have no bearing on the amounts demanded or supplied, as both are decided for their affiliates by the headquarters of the parent corporation. The buying affiliate cannot refuse buying because the price is too high, nor can the selling affiliate refuse to close the transaction on the ground that prices are too low. These intra-company but international trade transactions are not responsive to price changes, do not result from bargaining at arm's length, yet these constitute a massive proportion of the world trade. Such prices, known as accounting, or transfer or book-keeping prices in the literature, are determined to maximise global profit and, more specifically, to minimise tax burden by taking into account taxation rates on various activities in different countries. The important point to note is that given their multinational and vertically integrated characters, they can locate their profit, through such book-keeping prices, in any activity and in any country, in-line with their tax-minimising objective, without prejudicing production or trade (Penrose, 1967). On the other hand, such prices, arising not from demand–supply interactions but from internal considerations of an MNC, have an important bearing on foreign exchange earnings, and reserves of individual countries and on terms of trade in general.

A third implication is environmental. The operations of MNCs, guided by global considerations of profit maximisation, often come into conflict with the long-term interests of the country, particularly in terms of rational and optimal utilisation of resources and the interests of the future generation. We have noted that their operation might give rise to under-utilisation of local resources. An opposite example, of over-utilisation, is that of Venezuela, whose oil resources were virtually exhausted when the world oil prices were low, to meet the insatiable US demand for oil, and now very little of its oil is left to take advantage of the current high prices.

Generally speaking, to the MNCs, the LDCs are not their preferred alternatives for industrial location. They would rather sell their goods than invest in industries in these countries. In 1980–81, at the time of the launching of structural adjustment, out of $94.9 billion of FDI, 73 per cent was devoted to the developed countries, 14 per cent to the LDCs of the western hemisphere (mainly Brazil and Mexico), 2.4 per cent went to the OPEC countries and only 1.9 per cent to Africa, while, of the remaining 8.3 per cent going to Asia, half went to Singapore, Hong Kong,

Malaysia and the Philippines, ignoring 0.3 per cent that was unreported (Development Committee, 1985a: 16). Their investment in the LDCs is usually connected with the possibilities of capturing domestic markets, mainly in partnership with some local companies, or with the need to comply with national requirements, or to evade environment control measures in the developed countries by locating the polluting ones. Otherwise, they prefer a few selected countries, such as those in East and Southeast Asia or in Latin America. With the tightening of environmental measures in the rich countries, there is a tendency to locate polluting industries in the poor countries, where environmental legislation is non-existent or is not properly implemented, e.g., as exemplified in the Bhopal gas tragedy (OECD, 1992b: 202).

In the context of the recent drive towards globalisation, it is instructive to make reference to a highly important OECD document which, among other things, also discusses globalisation and its impact on the LDCs. It says:

> Globalisation represents a new phase in the process of internationalisation and the spread of international production. It refers to a set of emerging conditions in which value and wealth are increasingly being produced and distributed within worldwide corporate networks. Large multinational firms operating in concentrated supply structures are at the hub of these conditions.

It then goes on to add:

> As a result, in a growing number of industries in manufacturing and services, the prevailing form of supply structure is world oligopoly . . . . As a result of the convergence of computer, communication and control technology, it has now become feasible for MNEs to install captive intra-corporate world-wide information networks, through which management can link production marketing and R&D facilities around the world. Although many MNEs still locate their strategic R&D near their corporate headquarters, networks offer such firms new opportunities for the internationalisation of R&D, as well as for international sourcing of technological resources (OECD, 1992b: 209).

As for the consequences, this document states categorically that:

> The first concerns the marginalisation of developing countries within the globalisation process. The second concerns concentration as a world process and whether a global competition policy is needed and how it might be implemented. The third relates to the problems posed by support given by governments to firms engaged in global competition and the need for new rules and codes of behaviour. The fourth relates to standards and norms in a context of rapid and pervasive technological change, corporate concentration and globalisation (OECD, 1992b: 209).

MNCs: Pros and cons

The main arguments in favour of MNC operations are as follows: they take risks, they bring capital, they bring technology, they promote exports and, in general, they help to make the local economy global, outward-oriented and modern. Let us examine these in turn.

As for their risk-bearing role, there is indeed a considerable amount of truth in this view. At the same time, the world is replete with cases where the initial risk has been taken by a smaller company, which has made the discovery or invention, but then, lacking capital and other resources, has sold the deposit, technology or whatever it is, to an MNC, which has then developed it and amassed huge profits. This is as much true of oil deposits in Iran or North Africa as of Microsoft.

As for bringing capital, while this is true about the initial investment, in most cases, in later years, there is a tendency to reinvest a part of the profit earned in the country concerned, while the larger part of the profit is remitted. The MNCs also exhibit a remarkable capacity to mobilise domestic resources, often in partnership with local firms (Development Committee, 1985a: 14–15).

As for technology, as our chapters on East and Southeast Asia (Chapters 6 and 7) demonstrate, MNCs are, generally speaking, shy about technology transfer, are cautious about any dissemination that would give away their competitive advantage, and are unwilling to train local staff as they are scared of poaching. In fact, this issue of lack of technology transfer from MNC sources has been raised repeatedly in many international fora, and has given rise to concepts such as Technical Cooperation among Developing Countries (TCDC) and South–South cooperation.

As for export promotion, there is no doubt that MNCs, with extensive links all over the world, can and do play an important role in this. But this role is subject to the point made earlier regarding the possible conflict between their global objectives and the national objectives of a country. While locating their activities in a small country, their main objective is usually production for exports, otherwise they would not be interested. However, when locating their activities in a large country like India, Brazil or China, the principal objective is to capture the domestic market, and even to enjoy the fruits of import substitution. In the case of Pepsi in India in the late 1960s, while they agreed to export a certain proportion as a condition for obtaining a licence, they began dragging their feet afterwards, and eventually agreed to export things other than what they produced, such as tea.

As for making the countries providing unlimited access to their operation modern and efficient, this has not happened in the vast majority of such countries, including Pakistan, Congo and Haiti.

Taking everything into account, there can never be a level playing field in the competition between the resource-rich MNCs, with worldwide connections, supported by BWIs and the governments of their countries of domicile, and the local companies. Apart from anything else, the MNCs, having access to low interest developed country credit markets, always enjoy an advantage of 4–17 per cent in terms of interest alone (UNDP, 1992, Human Development Report 1992, Table 4.2; quoted in Stewart, 1993: 3). Another major advantage lies in their immensely superior economic power and capability to project their goods and to capture markets by making full use of the television screen and other media, and even by deploying an army of world beauties crowned with various awards. Their proficiency in packaging and product differentiation aided by technology, and their R&D capability, help to maintain their distance from local rivals. Their entry into domestic economies is usually followed by a spate of takeovers and mergers after some token resistance.

Keeping all these in mind, there have been repeated demands in the past, from the LDCs, for keeping the MNCs in leash. The demand for the NIEO in 1974 was mainly prompted by the fear of MNC domination of world economy, as also several other resolutions of the 1970s. It was mainly the fear of the multinationals that often induced the governments to seek import substituting industrialisation led by the public sector. UNCTAD was formed in 1964 mainly because of the feeling among the LDCs that they had no influence over the world trade system, and the issues of trade should be linked with their concern for development. It was at their instance that a body, under the auspices of the United Nations, was formed to monitor the activities of the MNCs, to bring about some transparency in their mode of fixing prices and taking other decisions and to help the host countries with information and legal interpretations when negotiating with MNCs. However, such a body could have no role to play in a world dominated by structural adjustment, and so was closed down in the early 1990s (Stewart, 1993: 20).

A major consequence of structural adjustment and also of the Marakesh agreement has been to make these MNCs free from the controls and regulations of the host governments and to widen their access to the markets that were hitherto closed. By eliminating 'local content requirements' and by insisting on 'national treatment', the conflict between the global objectives of the MNCs and the national objectives of the host governments has now been resolved in the former's favour, while the reduction of subsidies and the establishment of a global patent regime would help them to more effectively penetrate the local economy and to maintain their superiority over local producers for a long time to come.

Conclusions

Linking the discussion on the global trade regime in this chapter with the one on structural adjustment in the previous one, our discussion shows that the World Bank, IMF and WTO, the holy trinity of the contemporary world economy, share a common economic philosophy on trade issues. They project the image of world trade as one where prices are determined by forces of demand and supply, and these can be taken as the objective ones for deciding what to and what not to produce and export. We conclude that world trade is far from free and competitive and the prices ruling in the world market are trade-distorting, and therefore, cannot be taken as bases for deciding on goods in which a country enjoys a comparative advantage. Distortions are principally due to two factors: massive subsidies and protection given by the rich countries to their own production and exports, and the fact that a large proportion of what passes as international trade is intra-company transfer by MNCs at book-keeping prices that have no bearing on demand and supply for the goods in question.

We then discuss various forms of trade distortion practised by the rich countries themselves—such as VERs, VIEs, MFA, and the blatant use of GATT safeguards, anti-dumping legislations and countervailing duties and Super 301, the last being a unilateral action undertaken by the United States to force a country to open its markets to the MNCs from the West. While the Western countries have been asking the poor countries to desist from erecting non-tariff barriers, they themselves have been strengthening these during the 1980s to keep the LDC exports out. Similarly, while theoretically the Western countries are opposed to subsidies, in practice they operate an elaborate system of subsidies. In case of agriculture, their astronomical subsidies, initially motivated by a concern for security, have transformed industrial countries with no comparative advantage in food production into main food exporters. These also reveal some other features of their double-speak: (*a*) that countries should conform to their own naturally and historically given comparative advantage, and (*b*) that countries should not seek self-reliance for security or other reasons; they should instead seek security via trade.

Coming to GATT, we show how some of the laudable principles have been subtly changed to create grounds for protectionist measures in the West, e.g., from free trade to fair trade, and from non-discrimination to reciprocity. The extent to which US has played a much more than proportionate role in its round by round decisions, is partly revealed by the names given to various rounds, some after prominent US personalities taking initiatives in negotiations. Alongside, the LDCs, bereft of extensive research help, money power and ability to give something to get something, have tended to play a peripheral role. Though some concessions had been given to them in the earlier rounds, to counter Soviet trade offensive, in the last two rounds they have been advised to grow out of these. At the same time, exemptions have been given from

GATT provisions to domestic agricultural systems to suit US and European interests, while within regional economic groupings—such as EC, NAFTA or ASEAN—discrimination in favour of their own members was allowed. The GATT-inconsistency of MFA was never in doubt, still it was allowed to operate in order to protect the dying textile industry in the rich countries.

We have discussed in detail the specific features of the Marakesh agreement, which followed the eighth, the Uruguay Round of negotiations, particularly those on investment, services, patents and subsidies, all of which would have the effect of opening up the markets of the LDCs and of integrating them more closely with the global economy. The powers hitherto exercised by the governments to regulate foreign investment, in terms of local content requirements, were taken away. But such mobility across the border was not permitted to labour, one of the three critical factors of production, and one of the two mobile ones amongst those, and the concerned governments (the rich ones in this context) were permitted to continue with regulations in this sphere in their national interest. This asymmetry in the treatment of capital and labour was noted by UNCTAD and some other UN agencies. We noted that the main impact of the establishment of the global patent regime would be to perpetuate the technological dependence on the rich countries. In agriculture, while a large part of the agricultural subsidies in US and Europe have been found to be neutral and non-trade distorting, and, therefore, permitted, the reduction contemplated in other subsidies, of 36 per cent in six years, would still retain a high level of subsidy after 10 years. On the other hand, curtailment of agricultural subsidies in the LDCs, by no means anywhere near those given by the rich countries in scale, is likely to affect agricultural production and income distribution in rural areas, as the experience of India during 1991–97 shows.

After a period of resistance, the LDCs gave in to rich country demands, as they lacked cohesion and a common sense of purpose to put up a challenge to the US–EC hegemony. A major factor was the demise of the Soviet Union which demoralised them and made a dent in their bargaining power. Though the LDCs are being offered two large carrots—of markets in textiles and food in the rich countries—there is every likelihood of the fallacy of composition operating. As nearly all the LDCs would be chasing these markets, there is the possibility of a glut in global production in relation to the market opportunity to be created, which in turn is likely to further depress world prices in primary goods. As for textiles, a lion's share of that market is likely to be cornered by the East and Southeast Asians (Development Committee, 1992: 96–97). This brings to the fore issues relating to comparative advantage and terms of trade: whether, given the adverse movement in terms of trade, the LDCs can gain much by producing these for exports, and whether a more dynamic view of comparative advantage a la East Asian countries, should be taken, of trying out a more diverse pattern of industrial production and exports under the leadership of an interventionist state.

This chapter also considers what prompted the United States to oppose the formation of ITO in the later 1940s and then to promote WTO in the 1990s. An explanation is given in terms of the changed international political landscape since 1991 and the opportunity it created for the United States to play a hegemonistic role as the single superpower in the world. To the question whether now unilateral sanctions in the form of Super 301 would be replaced by multilateral sanctions through WTO, there cannot be any definite reply, since the United States is continuing to use the Super 301 option.

Lastly, the chapter discussed MNCs, their main features and role, and the implications of these for the LDCs. It concludes that the inherent conflict between the global objectives of the MNCs and the national objectives of the host governments has now been resolved, in the Marakesh agreement, in favour of the MNCs by ruling out local content requirements and other forms of state regulation.

five

Environment and structural adjustment

Introduction

In this chapter we will attempt to link our discussion on structural adjustment and the world trade system with the concern for the protection of the global and national environment. More specifically, we will ask: first, at the national level, whether the adjustment package, discussed and analysed in the previous chapters, would hasten environmental degradation or whether it is indeed possible to preserve and even improve the environment by way of a rational price system and a corresponding set of property rights. Second, whether it is possible to extend this analysis to the global level, with a corresponding price–tax structure along with clearly demarcated property rights. In particular, we will ask whether the concern for environment and the rights of the future generation would imply any change in the conventional cost–benefit analysis. Finally, what kind of global regime would be environment friendly, and whether the WTO-led one would be the answer.

We begin with the neo-classical marginalist analysis of Pigou and examine the objections raised against conventional project analysis when environmental considerations are taken into account. Then we examine the implications of SAPs for environment, particularly whether appropriate pricing, identification of private property rights and a tax-subsidy system can take care of the environment. Next, we deal with the environmental implications of the commercialisation of agriculture and changes in the land use pattern. Our analysis is then extended to global commons, and we ask whether the market-based remedies would help in solving environmental problems at this level. This is followed by an examination of the implications of the new global trade regime for the environment. Finally, we look into the environment–development relationship, including the Brundtland Commission's report.

Environment and traditional cost-benefit analysis

Pigou: Polluter pays

Pigou, in his discourse on welfare economics, makes a distinction between two types of costs, with reference to his famous smoke-chimney case (Pigou, 1920). For the factory responsible for pollution, the damage it causes is 'external' to itself, and therefore, it pays nothing and its private cost is zero, while the chimney imposes a social cost on the community living nearby, in terms of the incidence of diseases and cleanliness. For Pigou, the problem, essentially, was how to bridge the gap between these two sets of costs—social and private—and his solution was to force the factory to 'internalise' the social cost, by way of a tax or a fine that would be equivalent to the social cost of the chimney to the community.

A corollary of this 'polluter pays' principle was a 'compensation principle', that those suffering from air pollution, emitted by the smoke-chimney, would be fully compensated with the proceeds of such a tax. Therefore, in the case of a particular pollution, the task of an authority or a society, seen in this perspective, was to identify the polluting agent and those who were at the receiving end of such an environment-degrading practice; to assess the damage, to make the offending party pay and then to compensate those hurt by its action from the fund so secured.

In the 1970s, with the environment campaign in full swing, several doubts were expressed about the Pigovian solution, of taxing the polluter and compensating the victim. First, how can one establish a cause–effect relationship and identify an agent responsible for damage and degradation when environmental degradation tends to get diffused over space? For instance, how would one tax those responsible for deforestation in the foothills of the Himalayas for the flood caused in south Bengal more than one thousand miles away? Even more difficult are cases where a high dosage of pesticide or some other pollutant is carried by water over a long distance and harms non-target organism, including the fish population and mother's milk, over a very large area.

Similarly, the same problem arises when environmental degradation, never much at a time, accumulates and assumes an alarming proportion after many decades or even centuries. For instance, how would one pin down those responsible for deforestation in Sahel areas, or for the hole in the ozone layer over Antarctica? Such a task of identification of offenders and estimation of damage attributable to each, is compounded when degradation in a particular time-space is the joint product of activities of many agents over varying lengths of time.

A broader criticism would be that the marginalist solution of the Pigovian type does not apply to damages, or potential damages, on a massive scale, e.g., the 'outer limit' cases such as nuclear catastrophe, global warming inundating a large part of the globe, genetic engineering getting out of control, ozone layer depletion making the globe unfit for human habitation, and so on (Mathews, 1976). Granting that the tax-compensation solution can work in many areas at a micro level, the neo-classical framework for policy analysis breaks down when confronting macro issues on such a scale.

More important issues arise in relation to traditional time-bound and project-bound cost-benefit analysis, which is limited to a small set of identifiable items of benefit and cost. Such an analysis, it is contended, would not normally take account of the consequences of a project for the rest of the economy or society, or for future generations. At the discount rates usually applied to future earnings for deriving their present value, any earning beyond a period of, say 15 years, is nearly as good as zero. This is the time horizon beyond which a private company is unlikely to look while calculating the profitability of an enterprise. Given his time preference for the present earnings and costs over the future ones, why should a private agent bother, while making investment decisions, about an environment impact that would not influence the present value of his future earnings and costs? In this situation, how can one make the present generation pay for the environment problems it creates for the future generations (Dasgupta et al., 1977)?

The consensus in the 1970s was that the initiative for protecting environment had to come from the public authorities by way of regulations and controls, as prices and markets were not giving out right signals for protecting the environment. However, the important distinction made by Pigou between social and private costs and benefits was preserved, and the search was for appropriate social cost-benefit analyses. Once environmental costs were added, the outcome and conclusion of many of the old-style cost-benefit analyses underwent drastic changes. In the case of energy, while many of the projections undertaken in the 1970s predicted that, by the 1980s, among various sources, the largest share would come from nuclear energy, its cost figures proved to be considerably less attractive once the entire array of environmental costs was taken into account, such as the following: the costs of (*a*) providing health protection to employees and neighbouring areas, (*b*) safe methods of waste disposal guarding many generations until the level of radiation became harmless, and (*c*) protection against stealing of nuclear material or possible terrorist raids. Further, while in volume, nuclear waste was not that large, accounting for only 1 per cent of toxic waste, more important was the qualitative difference it made in terms of its impact on human tissues (OECD, 1996a: 12–15).

Similarly, while the Tennessee Valley Authority (TVA) became a model of river valley development in the 1950s, by the 1970s the environmentalists had added a long list of missing items to their cost, which made many of the river valley projects unsustainable and even dangerous. These included: loss of fertile land, destruction of human settlements including historical relics and the cost of resettlement of the evicted, dangers of flooding and increased salinity of soil, rise in malaria and other water-borne diseases, loss of fish, snail and other eatables, particularly the migratory varieties, and so on.

Even after adding these cost items, the question would always remain whether all the relevant cost components had been added. Given the concepts of interdependence and ecological balance, even one missing component might make all the difference between viability and disaster. Thus, availability and reliability of information became a major issue of the environment debate. In cases where information, based on exclusive research, was the monopoly of a private enterprise, it was not always in its self-interest to divulge these and thereby to bring disaster onto itself; as the behaviour of many enterprises during the debate on CFC and greenhouse gases (GHG) revealed. In cases where the information was under the monopoly of the sensitive departments such as Defence, there would be no guarantee that such information, often prejudicial to these departments and their activities, would be forthcoming, e.g., the impact of the emission of jet fuel on the ozone layer, or of weather modification or biological weapon programmes. Information was viewed as a scarce and privileged commodity in most instances and uncertainty was too vast to be handled by traditional accounting methods. The World Bank admitted in a major document that 'uncertainty is an inherent part of the environmental problem' (World Bank, WDR, 1992: 37).

Once the concept of ecological balance sank deeper into popular consciousness, showing how interdependence can make a particular ecosystem viable, and how even a small change in one component of the system can push the entire ecosystem out of balance and make it unsustainable, measurement of each and every important item of benefits and costs became a major task in place of casual computations to make the project acceptable to decision-makers. On the positive side, it showed, in the case of the forest ecosystem, how a not-so-fertile land can sustain an enormous amount of biomass in the form of a tropical rain forest, as the droppings of birds, dry leaves and decaying animals continuously enrich the soil, while the forest itself protects the soil from invading wind and water. In this situation, the forest acts as a vast reservoir that releases water slowly and regularly throughout the year, making springs and rivers perennial. On the negative side, the virtuous cycles of nature can easily turn into vicious ones, as deforestation begins, making forces of wind and water stronger, and initiating a process that, beginning with the removal of the cover of green biomass, eventually ends by removing top soil and exposing bare rocks.

A related question was whether and how a conventional cost-benefit analysis can protect critical non-renewable scarce resources such as petroleum and other hydrocarbons. Here the process of degradation is irreversible, excepting in terms of very long geological time periods. But even in case of biological matters which are reckoned as renewable by conventional definition, exhaustion and degradation beyond a critical threshold might make the process irreversible, as is the case with many species that are on the verge of extinction. The answer that emerged was that conventional cost-benefit would not do, the issues were too vast to be handled incrementally, while institutional solutions should be sought, with the state and various public authorities playing an important role in devising and implementing regulations.

One solution that suggested itself was to simulate nature itself. Left on its own, the environment is capable of rectifying a great deal of abuse. The important thing is to allow nature some respite from human intervention from time to time and not to allow degradation to reach a level that would make such a self-correcting system unworkable. Leaving the land fallow from time to time will allow it to recover its fertility while helping to limit the dependent pest population. Another approach is to rely more on biological options, as against chemical remedies, for rectifying environmental degradation. While the former is clean and virtually without side effects, the latter, while solving one problem might give rise to others, e.g., cats vs pesticides for eradicating rats. The concept of zero waste in nature points out that in nature there is no place for waste; everything is useful to some element or another. In contrast, pollution is largely man-made, e.g., that arising from the use of those hydrocarbons which are not part of nature's cycle. A solution that simulates nature is to recycle waste, that is, to turn what is conventionally a waste into something useful.

While state regulation was a preferred alternative to the interplay of market forces, on the premise that the private agents on their own were unwilling to adopt measures that would reduce their profitability though welfare-augmenting for the society as a whole, another solution that emerged was to induce popular participation in the development process. Application of global rules to specific local, ecological conditions was to be the responsibility of grass-root level community organisations—perhaps elected ones, and at various levels, from villages to towns and municipalities—operating with a large measure of autonomy and not dominated by oligarchical economic interests (Vivian, 1991; Barraclough and Ghimire, 1990: 22–24).

The case for the decentralisation of decision-making, thus, emerged as another offshoot of the debate. A small community, close to nature, taking account of the specific conditions of local ecology was likely to make better decisions on land use, crops, seed varieties, technologies and institutions than would the do-gooding administrators operating at higher levels and imposing standardised development formats out of tune with local soil, water, forest conditions and human capabilities. Of course, this preference did not take away anything from the fact that the small, local communities were better at making only a particular class of decisions, or that the interests of various localities using a common resource—river or forest—might be in conflict with one another, requiring a higher authority to reconcile and settle them. Further, 'small', 'local' are relative terms, which help to emphasise the need for a multilevel approach to development issues.

Broader institutional issues also came to the fore, e.g., poverty, unemployment, measurement of GNP and quality of life. Poverty forces people to undertake environment degrading activities for survival, e.g., destruction of forests by poor tribals working as employees of timber merchants, over-use of marginal land by poor farmers that hastens the process of desertification, or the occupation of high-valued urban land in central business districts by squatters. At the other end of the income scale, inequality facilitates an energy-intensive and polluting lifestyle with cars, chemical fibres and aerosols. The environment would be safer, other things remaining the same, in a more equal society, and therefore, the environmental campaign had an egalitarian focus, apart from the democratic and participatory one mentioned above. Further, while the Club of Rome viewed growth as a constraint on environment, the structuralist economists adopted environment as a major objective of development. A simple quantitative measure of development, such as GNP per capita, was not acceptable to them, while in their multidimensional concept of development with its emphasis on quality of life, the environment was treated as a key socio-economic indicator (Dasgupta et al., 1977).

Structural adjustment: Delayed response, but no harm done

The decade of the 1980s belonged to the World Bank. But was the World Bank interested in environment? It was not, at least not until the very end of the decade. The fact is that the word 'environment' appeared quite frequently in Fund–Bank literature, but in a general sense (e.g., business environment, investment environment, political environment, external environment, policy environment, and so on) and not in the sense of natural (or even social) environment, as we understand the term in this chapter. In the conditionalities these two agencies imposed on the countries receiving their support, environmental issues were conspicuous by their absence until the very end of the decade.

The Brundtland report commissioned by the United Nations pleaded with the World Bank to take environmental implications of their projects into account (WCED, 1987: 18). This pleading, in a sense, recognised the primacy of the World Bank even in the field of environment, despite there being a specialised UN agency—UNEP—solely concerned with this task. In April 1987, a meeting of Fund–Bank luminaries first discussed the environment formally (Development Committee, 1987a: 1–23). The next meeting of the Development Committee went into some further details and urged the integration of environmental concerns in national planning and Fund–Bank lending programmes (Development Committee, 1988a: 1). It was only at the very end of the decade, in 1989, that for the first time, a structural adjustment loan, given to Ghana, suggested an environmental action plan for land management, control of soil degradation and forest conservation.

A World Bank document admitted that, 'Most adjustment programs have not specifically addressed environmental issues until recently' (Webb and Shariff, 1992: 80–81). The year 1989 witnessed a spate of World Bank publications on environment, all more or less repeating the same arguments in varying contexts (Ahmed et al., 1989; World Bank, 1990b). But in that same year only seven out of 34 adjustment operations contained some environmental conditions such as those relating to the pricing of energy, fertiliser and water (Webb and Shariff, 1992: 80). It was not, however, until 1992, that the World Bank, in its World Development Report, presented its more complete and coherent view on environment (World Bank, WDR, 1992).

In all these documents, while admitting that the World Bank had arrived somewhat late on the scene, the Bank asserted that this did not in any way prejudice the outcome of their lending programmes. As a meeting of the Development Committee in 1989 pointed out:

> Adjustment lending has not, until recently, paid explicit attention to environmental issues. But it does not follow that the

> consequences of this omission have necessarily been adverse. Indeed, in many cases good economics is good for the environment; long term economic and social justice can often be well served by short term adjustment policies (Development Committee, 1989: 23).

The World Bank argued that the emphasis on growth and on getting the prices right in their conditionalities applied equally strongly to environmental issues. A 1989 study by the World Bank found no evidence of association between adjustment lending and environmental degradation (Development Committee, 1989: 24). There was no sense of guilt as, according to the World Bank, no harm was done to the environment by its disregard of it until then (ibid., 1989: 23). The countries that had adopted the 'correct' policies and had moved on the growth path had also been the ones to perform better on environment. 'The self-interested decisions of private owners will produce more desirable environmental outcomes than will open access', the World Bank declared (World Bank, WDR, 1992: 69).

Pricing of natural resources

While the World Bank was silent on environment, a number of independent scholars, basing themselves on the economic philosophy underlying structural adjustment, projected a market-oriented package of solutions to rectify environmental abuses. Three types of remedies for environmental degradation emerged from this Bank-inspired environment literature; prices of resources arising from free market operations, establishment of clearly identifiable property rights in natural resources, and suitable taxes and subsidies.

It was argued that one of the best ways of protecting natural assets (like land, water or forest) from abuses and excessive use, was to allow their prices to reflect their scarcity values. As an example, the under-pricing of agricultural output undermines the capacity of the farmers to invest in a variety of environmentally useful activities, such as terracing, levelling, and drainage. Similarly, generous subsidies given to agricultural inputs—fertilisers, pesticides, agricultural machinery and irrigation water—encourage their wastage and over-use at high environmental costs. The Bank, however, admitted that not everything about environment should be left to the free play of market prices; the protection of village commons was mentioned as a special case where public intervention was considered desirable (Development Committee, 1987a: 22).

Establishment of private property rights: The Coase theorem

The second was the view that many of the abuses of the national resources could have been avoided with clearly identifiable private property rights over them, particularly in the case of village commons. Coase argued that in a world with established property rights, perfect access to information and without transaction cost, it would be possible for the parties concerned to negotiate the bundle of legal rights on property to evolve a solution that would do away with externality and the divergence between private and social costs. In this situation, it was not important to decide who was the polluter and how much was the extent of environmental damage. It was equally possible, e.g., in the case of those affected by the smoke-chimney, to pay the factory enough to make it worthwhile for it to move elsewhere or to incorporate machineries that would eliminate smoke or would reduce it to a tolerable level.

What was important was to carry out, through bargaining, a rearrangement of property rights that was optimal and thus acceptable to all the parties concerned. In cases where transaction costs were not zero, the important issue for the parties concerned was whether the expected gain from rearrangement of property rights would exceed such a cost. Some among the followers of Coase would even go to the extent of handing over rivers, national parks, marshes, forests, fallow land, everything that is now in public domain, to private interests, on the argument that once privatised, these would be well looked after (Coase, 1988; Eckerseley, 1996: 15). Further, automobile emission can be more effectively handled by privatising highways and making people pay according to the levels of congestion and emission (Coase, 1988). Anderson and Leal argued that technology was converting what was earlier considered as public goods into private ones, e.g., satellite tracking of migratory birds or radio collars for wild animals (Eckerseley, 1996: 15–16).

In view of the influence that the ideas of Coase (whose original article was published in as far back as 1960) carry, let us examine his thesis in detail. He argues, 'If the right to perform certain actions can be bought and sold, they will tend to be acquired by those for whom they are most valuable either for production or enjoyment'. Even those who are unwilling to use property in a particular way, can still buy the right and then not use it that way. 'The right to emit smoke at a given site can be used to stop smoke being emitted from that site [by not exercising the right and not transferring it to some one else who will]'. Again,

> If the cattle-raiser had to pay to the crop-farmer the value of the damage caused by his cattle, he would obviously include this in his costs. But if the cattle-raisers were not liable for damage, the crop-farmer would be willing to pay [up to] the value of the damage to induce the cattle-raiser to stop it, so that for the cattle-raiser to continue his operations and bring about this crop damage would mean foregoing this sum, which would therefore become a cost of continuing to raise cattle. The damage imposes the same cost on the cattle-raiser in both situations (Coase, 1988: 12–13).

Critical of Pigou for recommending state intervention in order to bridge the gap between private and social cost, he argues that in a perfectly competitive situation, private and social costs would be equal (Coase, 1988: 13).

Coase argued that in all cases rearrangements brought about through negotiations and bargaining were better than state-induced policy changes. Rearrangement of rights would take place if the cost of rearrangement is less than the value of production that follows. Coase is unwilling to accept that offenders should be asked to pay: 'If factors of production are thought of as rights, it becomes easier to understand that the right to do something which has a harmful effect (such as the creation of smoke, noise, smells, etc.) is also a factor of production' (Coase, 1988: 155). Further, 'If there is a tax based on damage, it would also be desirable to tax those whose presence imposes costs on the firms responsible for the harmful effects' (Coase, 1988: 181).

In all these cases the 'rationality' of individual or community behaviour would guarantee its success; 'rationality' being defined in an Olsonian sense, as the pursuit of self-interest. Pejorative expressions like 'polluters' do not appear in this scheme of things. Environment is taken as a commodity for buying and selling at a price. A community can buy up another which is engaged in actions that are harmful to itself, e.g., those living downstream of a river paying those upstream not to use up all the water.

Taxes and tradable emission permits

The third strand of the structural adjustment theorists on environment was to assign an important role to tax and subsidies in order to control environmental abuses. Environmental subsidies, as an instrument of public policy, have been used quite frequently in the past in the developed countries, e.g., to help farmers pay the cost of conservation as in USA; and to promote waste recycling, to reduce water pollution and to encourage research in Europe (OECD, 1996b: 77; de Castro, 1994: 30–31). The Bank view on taxes was more in line with the Pigovian approach—of identifying polluters and making them pay—and in contrast with a policy that favoured government regulations. Usually, environment legislations, forcing firms to adopt environmental protecting technology and other measures, have been applied more harshly against newcomers, and have, therefore, impeded new investment (OECD, 1992b: 193). As someone observed: 'Regulations have proved to be legally or practically unenforceable and socially rejected, technically impossible to monitor and generally with too low fines to constitute a deterrent and change behaviour' (de Castro, 1994: 20). In such situations, the question was how to turn the power of the market into an ally, supportive of government endeavour in this area. The 'polluter pays' principle, has been ratified by OECD, the Rio conference of 1992 and many other conferences, organisations and treaties.

In its search for measures that make the polluter pay (but within a market-framework) and give the former a choice, the United States government has come up with a novel idea—of traded emission permits. In these, the idea is to fix, for an area, a ceiling on, say, the emission of carbon dioxide, and then to distribute tradable permits to potential emitters of this gas whose values add up to that ceiling figure. A permit holder has the incentive to economise on the emission and to sell the remaining permitted amount of pollution to another potential user. To many, this idea of selling pollution and making money out of it is repugnant to their sense of morality. However, a positive feature of this scheme is that it forces the adherence of a limit on the level of pollution, while having enough flexibility to induce further economy on the use of pollutants by the participating firms. The US authorities claim that this scheme has enabled them to dispense with an elaborate machinery for raising the same amount in taxes. In Singapore also, auctionable permits are issued for the consumption of ozone-depleting substances (de Castro, 1994: 33).

A critical analysis: Can price work everywhere?

It was inevitable that in the 1980s, in a Fund–Bank dominated world, the role of the markets and prices would become the central issue in the environment debate. The dispute was not on whether prices would not help in environment management, but on whether prices alone can do it without institutional back-up, on how important allocation through prices was vis-à-vis allocations determined by institutional arrangements and whether prices would play a supplement role to regulations or would be the pivot in such a policy.

To put the record straight, the use of pricing of resources for environmental management figured prominently in the debate before the World Bank found an interest in this area. 'Resource accounting', including 'energy accounting' or 'water accounting' was a recurrent theme in the environmental discussion of the 1970s. Such resource accounting was to replace or run parallel to accounting in money units. If water was the critical scarce resource in agriculture, what mattered was water expenditure per unit of agricultural output. Such a policy was to favour cultivation of crops that economised on water use, e.g., a shift away from paddy towards crops with lower water intensity such as wheat or oilseeds. Similarly, if energy was the critical input in a production system, the efficiency of a production unit could be measured by the relationship between energy input and the resulting output. The lower the energy input per unit of output, the more efficient the factory or firm was (Dasgupta et al., 1977: 53–54).

Furthermore, the concern for rational and optimal utilisation of natural resources in the 1970s debate on NIEO, as discussed in Chapter 4, was not devoid of a price content. Even earlier, in the early 1960s, when Professor Maurice Adelman of MIT was making a firm prediction that if the market forces were allowed to operate freely, by the early 1970s, oil would be sold at 'one dollar per barrel', no one raised the issue with him whether such price would reflect the scarcity value of oil. During the late 1960s, oil was selling at $2.80 per barrel, nearly the same nominal price and a much lower real price compared with that two decades earlier. No one was surprised by Adelman's conclusions, nor was anyone in the West, including the World Bank, worried that oil was getting only a fraction of its scarcity value. What Adelman meant by a 'free market price' was one fixed by the 'seven sisters', a cartel of the seven largest vertically integrated and horizontally collaborating oil companies (Dasgupta, 1974).

When OPEC forced an upward revision in oil prices in 1973, one of their powerful arguments was that they were trying to catapult price to a level that reflected the scarcity value of a commodity as precious and non-renewable as oil. Further, to counter the 'market price' determined by the cartel of the oil producing companies—the 'seven sisters'—they had no option but to form a cartel of their own. The question remains whether the price revision, fully justifiable in terms of oil's scarcity value, and forced by OPEC and aided by the events that followed the US support for Israel during the fourth Arab–Israeli war, would ever have happened autonomously through the interaction of world market prices.

The World Bank is right when it says that the true value of natural resources is not usually paid for because these are treated as free goods, and argues that 'the most pressing environmental problems are associated with resources that are regenerative but are undervalued and are therefore in danger of exhaustion' (World Bank, 1992: 33). With no price constraint, a farmer uses more water than is necessary, fallow land is overgrazed, and the stock of groundwater is depleted by a rate of exploitation that exceeds the rate of recharge. Subsidies account for the difference between what a user pays and what the scarcity value of the asset is. Subsidies induce farmers to use more water, fertiliser or pesticides than are necessary, thus polluting water and killing many non-target organisms. Resource conservation is facilitated when a farmer-user is forced to pay its right price or to forego its use.

There is a great deal of truth in these arguments. On the other hand, if the implication of such arguments is to go for full cost recovery through prices in each and every case, that would be taking things a bit too far. As a more recent World Bank document indicates, 'In theory, price is the ideal mechanism for allocating resources. In practice, it is never easy to design appropriate price mechanisms for natural resources, each of which presents different difficulties' (World Bank, 1992: 144). Such resource pricing, beyond a point, may even push the poor farmers out of land and induce them to migrate, leading to socially undesirable concentration of land-ownership and/or control. Would this even be desirable on environmental grounds if, those relegated to landlessness now, and desperate to survive, forcibly occupy marginal land or forest land that is not fit for cultivation? Would a better policy not be to allow some price increase within their means, to maintain subsidies even if at a somewhat lower level, to improve their productive and earning capacities in the initial phase, and then, step by step, to raise prices to eventually equate them with their scarcity values? While prices are important, an obsession with them might put the social balance out of gear and make the application of price regime inoperative. The important point here is, whether any policy of resource pricing can be sustained over a long period without popular support and participation in its implementation, environment being so easy to abuse and policing by any type of authority being so difficult in a poor country rural society.

The Coasian world of free bargaining

Coming to the Coasian model, of settling disputes through bargaining among private agents, without the involvement of the state, it can work only under extremely stringent assumptions, such as the existence of a fully developed market, full access to information by all the parties, low transaction costs and absence of 'free riders', assumptions that are unlikely to be fulfilled in the LDC context. One cannot visualise how such bargaining can be completed to the satisfaction of all the parties concerned in a country like India, and in the case of a river like the Ganga which runs for more than 1,000 miles and crosses national frontiers, with billions of uneducated rural private agents in action (P. Dasgupta, 1991: 34). When, for example, disputes involving several states of India, and between India and Bangladesh, for a proper allocation of its water are becoming so difficult to resolve, it is mindboggling to assume that leaving everything to the market and the agents would make it easier to find a solution.

Further, even assuming that such bargaining is going to work, and a satisfactory solution will be found that achieves optimality taking into account the self-interest of all the individuals concerned, there is no logical certainty that such a solution would necessarily be 'optimal' in the interest of the environment in general. All this, apart from the fact that this act of balancing of conflicting interests of those engaged in bargaining may not favour others excluded from such bargaining but affected by its outcome, including the future generations (Helm, 1991: 9–11).

Taking land, forest or river, from public to private ownership does not create property rights—it only transfers such rights (Helm, 1991: 16). There is no a priori reason to suppose, unless one is a die-hard World Bank protagonist, that such transfer would automatically imply a better management of resources. As is known from the so-called case of 'prisoners' dilemma', even while the individuals concerned are self-interested, they can end up, in a bargaining situation, opting for a solution that is neither in their individual interest nor, collectively, in the interests of all those engaged in bargaining (Olson, 1982: 1–2; Johnston, 1996: 132–37; Helm, 1991: 12).

Nevertheless, one can find cases where there is indeed some merit in privatisation. The question is whether such prescription is applicable everywhere. The tree-*pattas*, that is, the leasing out of individual trees in a forest to individual members or families of a community, allowing them to utilise its products while maintaining the tree itself, along with some monetary incentives that arise over time as the tree survives, has worked in many areas of India. But such a policy works best in the case of trees located within or not far from the villages, and its effectiveness declines with distance. What about the trees located deep inside the forests? We are back to the participatory system of decision-making, with some ground rules that are monitored by higher authorities (Jacobs, 1996: 53).

Many tribal communities with communal land tenure system are getting the worst of the two worlds they straddle—neither is their communal system like what it was in the old days with social checks against the tyranny of the chief, nor can they derive the benefits of bank credit for investment on land as they have no title to prove their rights to land. The communal system is no longer working in isolation, and is indeed being swamped by the much stronger money economy from all sides. While the traditional communal system allowed for long periods of fallow—from 10 to 25 years—and annual rotations among members, such practices have ceased with land scarcity. Whereas in the traditional society there were taboos against the felling of some types of trees, particularly in some seasons, such values no longer exist; the emotional bond that kept man and the environment together in the traditional societies is no more. In this case, one can argue, communal land tenure is hardly capable of protecting the environment or even guaranteeing the survival of the forest people, and there is a case for exploring other types of arrangements of property rights.

But property rights alone, and even with well-functioning price systems, cannot protect the environment without some regulations and control and without some social/institutional arrangements. The fact is that a great deal of property in the countryside of the LDCs is already in private hands backed by documentation of such rights; but that has not afforded protection against abuse. The rationality of a tubewell-owning peasant makes him draw as much water as possible for his own farm and also, if possible, for his neighbours without tubewells to whom he sells water. When every tubewell owner, propelled by self-interest, exploits a common underground reservoir this way, there is every likelihood that the rate of withdrawal of water would exceed the rate of recharge by way of rainfall and seepage, and thus, the stock of water in the reservoir will decline and the water-table will drop sharply. This is a common problem of irrigated agriculture where land is privatised but the water is shared.

Here, a neo-classical solution can be to base water rates on actual use, and, if that is not possible, to measure directly, or as a proxy, to charge him on a progressive scale for the use of electricity. If the power tariff is decided at the national, state, regional or some such level, such standardised tariff, while discouraging excessive use of water, may or may not correspond with some other objectives, such as the optimum use of water for maximising agricultural production. Reservoirs vary widely in size in the amount of water they hoard, as also in terms of their rate of recharge. A standarised power tariff may, therefore, lead to over- or under-utilisation of water in the case of a particular groundwater reservoir. Fixing tariff individually for a tubewell or for a cluster of tubewells in a locality, though theoretically possible, can be very costly and a nightmare for the administrators, unless the authority for such a decision is vested in a local community organisation of beneficiaries. The latter too, cannot be guided by prices and self-interest alone. We are back to the case for promoting environmental awareness, social values that can often be in conflict with self-interest, and social participation in decision-making.

One can point to a wide range of environmental problems where neither market and prices nor localised communities can be of much help in devising optimum utilisation of resources. Going back to the example given earlier, of deforestation in the Himalayan slopes causing floods several thousand miles away in south Bengal, neither individual nor community self-interest of those responsible for deforestation would make them follow policies that would save the environment in south Bengal. The World Bank also admits that, in case of logging, though private property would make the logger evaluate his present and future benefits, it gives 'no incentive to take into account the costs of deforestation to those living outside the forests—for example, increased soil erosion and loss of biodiversity. In such cases additional environmental controls are often needed' (World Bank, WDR, 1992: 70).

As for the tax-subsidy system, it can and does work, as we have noted, but not everywhere. A joint committee of experts, set up by OECD, has listed 18 environmental indicators for this purpose of applying the 'polluter pays' principle, but to develop a single indicator out of so many has not been easy. As one study concludes: 'It is hard to estimate the imputed price of the environmental goods' (Ito, 1996: 11). No less difficult is to motivate the polluter to pay. Apart from the difficulty of identifying polluters and victims in a specific situation, it was found that if the demand for the product concerned was fairly inelastic, more often than not it was the consumer, and not the polluter, who paid for pollution (de Castro, 1994: 20). The attempt in the United States to recover the cost of cleaning up from past polluters has failed, though much has been spent on litigation. Direct tax policies appear to work better with large companies, such as power utilities and mining companies (World Bank, 1992: 77). Coming to the tradable emission permits, this system is still in its infancy, confined as it is to some areas in the United States and Singapore, and has not spread to other areas, nor even to the countries of Europe. Besides, it makes a heavy demand on administration which the LDCs are unlikely to be able to meet (World Bank, WDR, 1992: 75).

The command system rules

The fact is that, on balance, even the developed countries rely more on command systems for environmental control than on prices (Williams, 1993: 24). Indeed, a stringent set of rules and regulations, harshly administered by the government, can be the basis on which a system of resource pricing can thrive. The successes achieved by the developed countries in recent years in cleaning their environment, have been no less due to the introduction and strict enforcement of environmental legislation and regulations, backed by the increasingly vocal political–environmental lobby. The vote-catching performance of the 'green parties', and the incorporation of the 'green items' in the manifestoes of the major European parties, shows that many otherwise 'rational, self-interested, price-responsive' citizens are capable of rising above immediate bread and butter issues and even to look beyond their own lifetime (Irvine and Ponton, 1988).

Inter-generational issues

The failure of market-based policies is most evident when dealing with long-term issues. In its voluminous writings on environment in recent years, the World Bank has failed to come to grips with this. Broadly, the issue is, how would one generation assess and make room for the environmental needs of the future generations? The two generations are not like two bargaining groups in a market that would haggle, argue, negotiate, fight and then come to some settlement. There is no one now to effectively represent the future generations apart from the present generation itself (Helm, 1991: 14). The question is whether a 'rational' self-regarding present generation would be willing to refrain from activities that would add to its own satisfaction at the cost of what would be available for the future generation. If it does, whether its action would still be regarded as 'rational' in the sense in which neo-classical economics understands the term, is a matter of dispute.

If the question of the welfare of the future generations is not an issue, the 'rational' current generation, of the Coasian or Olsonian type, will apply its own time preference to discount future earnings and costs. The higher the discount rate the lower is the time horizon within which the economic agent operates. A lowering of the discount rate, by widening the time horizon, makes leaving something for the future more sensible in economic terms. Making use of this argument, some authors put forward the view that the appropriate discount rate for environmental accounting should be zero. All that the World Bank says, while violently disagreeing with such a view, is that a lower rate of return will be wasteful and will involve loss of welfare and income that could have been devoted to environment.

It is clear that the analytical tools at the disposal of the Bank will not permit it to find a satisfactory solution to the inter-generational problems; as it would not be possible to incorporate these within the standard framework of cost-benefit analysis. The Bank nearly admitted defeat when it said that in such decision-making based on the discounted present value of future earnings and costs relating to a project, environmental concern might be taken as implicit World Bank, WDR, 1992: 32). As a recent OECD document concluded: 'In the case of natural resources and the environment, however, market forces typically fail to account for even the present value of such assets, let alone their future values.' It sought a mechanism that would permit integration of the present and future values into current period decision-making (Runge and Jones, 1996: 7–23).

Risks and uncertainties

Equally perceptible is the failure of market-based prescriptions in handling risks and uncertainties. Environment degradation, according to one OECD document, threatens 'accepted notions of aggregate equilibrium and smooth adjustment, by introducing massive uncertainties and risks, including that of irreversibilities' (OECD, 1992b: 191). On this ground, the document bluntly adds, environment should be treated as a public good that cannot be handled by the market. So far, despite a significant amount of contributions on this subject, cost calculations on environmental losses appear to be still in their infancy. Hardly any country has attempted to incorporate loss of stock of natural resources in its national accounts; an attempt on Mexico has revealed a 7 per cent reduction in NNP when such loss has been accounted for, and another 7 per cent for maintaining the environment for the future (World Bank, WDR, 1992: 33).

Indeed, only a handful of countries have attempted a detailed listing of flora and fauna and assessment of their natural capital, as distinct from man-made capital. The former is identified as one that cannot be substituted by man-made capital (OECD, 1992b: 191; Kinrade, 1996: 92–93). One view is that environmental values are not merely reflected in their use and exchange in the market; no less important is their intrinsic value, something that cannot be easily priced (OECD, 1992a: 7–9). The study also puts forward a concept of option value, that the individuals are willing to pay in order to retain the option of future use of an environmental asset (P. Dasgupta, 1995: 176; Pearce et al., 1989: 61; OECD, 1992a: 7).

Most studies admit that environmental costs are extremely difficult to measure or to estimate attendant uncertainties. How can one measure acid rain, control the movement of flies or stop the neighbour from over-exploiting a common resource? Control against high health risk products is justified under the Basle Convention, but how does one define 'high health risk' that would be acceptable to all (Sorsa, 1992: 23)? Information is scarce and often biased in favour of underestimation of the damage inflicted by human action. Those in possession of information are often also those responsible for such degradation. A military establishment is, for understandable reasons, austere with information on emissions from jet aircraft or on cloud seeding. Only a handful would know about the full global environmental cost of tugging chunks of polar icebergs to West Asian deserts—for supplying sweet water to this water scarce area for drinking and irrigation purposes—if it is ever attempted and if such damage can ever be fully worked out in advance.

Corporate structure and its implications for environment

Another study by OECD explains market failure in dealing with the environment in terms of the market structure—particularly the role of the oligopolists. 'Much environmental investment would be profitable but is not undertaken for reasons that seem to involve market structure, corporate cultures and investment time horizons, given the present price signals and rates of reward to environmental friendly measures by firms'. It then adds, 'Many firms have demonstrated considerable reluctance to change the character of their core production process for environment purposes', as the bureaucracies in those firms are mainly interested in 'compliance solutions'. Automobile firms are unwilling to carry out emission control at the manufacturing stage, and rather than modifying engine technologies they prefer to add catalytic converters to their tail-pipes (OECD, 1992b: 192).

Further, these major companies tend to evade issues when confronted with very serious environmental problems. For a long time Du Pont claimed lack of scientific evidence and did nothing when the initial scientific research indicated an association between CFC and the depletion of the ozone layer. Though in 1972 Mario Molina and Sherry Rowland made the chilling discovery that the concentration of CFCs in the atmosphere was equal to its production, and that chlorine broke ozone into ordinary oxygen, Du Pont, the giant corporation producing CFC, with an annual turnover of $8 billion in 1974 and a workforce of 200,000, vigorously opposed the finding and argued: 'We may be about to extrapolate an unproven speculation, one open to serious question, into conclusions and laws that could disrupt our economy and indeed our way of life.' Further, though the Government of US banned CFCs in aerosol sprays in 1978, under Reagan, in 1982, the world CFC production regained its 1974 level, and exceeded that in 1983 and 1984. Thanks to the pressure from UNEP and countries like Canada, Finland, Sweden and Norway, who formed the Toronto group that urged a worldwide ban on CFC, to massive public boycott of aerosols, and to a second major piece of research in 1987 by Molina that provided the conclusive evidence of the discovery of a hole in the layer above Antarctica, the Montreal Protocol was established in that year. The Protocol agreed to freeze production and consumption in 1990 at the 1986 level, to carry out a 20 per cent reduction in 1994, and a further reduction of 30 per cent in 1999 (Gijswijt, 1996: 55–69; OECD, 1992b: 202). Thus, it needed the conclusive evidence of the discovery of a hole in the layer above Antarctica and the Montreal Protocol to make Du Pont agree to suspend production. Similarly, in the 1980s, Dow Chemicals changed the process that released dioxine into waterways only when they were subjected to law suits and public pressure. The great tragedy of Bhopal occurred because Union Carbide made the most of the lax environmental control and legislation in India to maximise profit (OECD, 1992b: 202). Another study points to the patron–client relationship between the corporate interests and the regulatory authority as a major explanation for the failure of state intervention in many cases (Eckerseley, 1996: 18).

Commercialisation of agriculture and land use changes

With their emphasis on market-orientation, SAPs have hastened the secular process of commercialisation in agriculture in the LDCs. Even in remote areas, subsistence farming is being phased out and, responding to relative prices, farmers are producing what they can best produce on the land they operate, subject to the availability of funding and inputs. Land use and cropping patterns are changing as agriculture, like industry, is being motivated by profit. There is no dearth of literature to confirm such price responsiveness of the agriculturists in the LDCs. Even in Europe, higher land prices lead to conversion of land into high value uses as opposed to those like conservation, wildlife and landscaping (Folmer et al., 1995: 52). The question is: To what extent is such market-orientation helping the cause of environment?

Implications of commercialisation of agriculture

According to one observer, in contrast with subsistence field crops like rice, wheat or maize, export crops—such as tea, coffee or cocoa—usually provide good green cover to the soil (P. Dasgupta, 1995: 162). But the SAP has now removed that traditional distinction between food and commercial crops. If the trade is free and global, what prevents a food crop from being exported, and an agricultural item that was hitherto classified as 'commercial crop', from being imported if the proceeds from the former can pay for the latter?

The environmental consequences of such intense commercialisation and intensification of agriculture are yet to be fully studied. We have already referred to the drop in the water-table in the areas with heavy groundwater irrigation. No less serious is the continued loss of soil fertility, as the land is continuously cultivated without a break. Even in the United States, despite a very high level of application of soil nutrients, land productivity is declining, as also in the two Punjabs of India and Pakistan. Though the environmental dangers of pesticides and fertilisers are still comparatively low in the LDCs, and the benefits at the margin are considerably higher, at their low levels of application, over time they are predictably following the route of developed country agriculture. Deforestation is being attributed to commercialisation of agriculture in a number of studies. One estimate by FAO in the 1980s attributed 70 per cent of recent disappearance of closed forests in Africa, 50 per cent in tropical Africa and 35 per cent in Latin America to conversion to agricultural uses, mainly prompted by plantations and cattle ranches (Barraclough and Ghimire, 1990: 15–16). In Thailand and other parts of Southeast Asia rapid commercial development has led to large-scale deforestation (Chapter 7).

We have already noted some other environmental issues in Chapter 4. The standardised commercial crops promoted by agri-business firms do not allow much room for biodiversity. On the other hand, the sheer quantity of biomaterial the medicinal business interests require is leading to a depletion of forest species, coral reef and wetlands. Further, biotechnologies, together with the IPR regime, are accelerating genetic erosion by inducing breeding of certain selected varieties (Blaikie and Jeanrenaud, 1996: 28–30).

Modern pest management is a new area in the LDCs. Its complexity is still unknown and, goaded by the agri-business farms selling pesticides, the farmers tend to use much more than is good for their crops. There have been cases where intense targeting and virtual elimination of a particular pest have severely disrupted the food chain, and have encouraged sudden, uncontrolled growth of second-order pests for whom pesticides are not readily available. In the case of two prosperous cotton-growing districts in the state of Andhra Pradesh in south India, in 1988, such a phenomenon reduced harvest to one-tenth of the usual average, turned a prosperous community into destitutes and led to 28 suicides.

The case of shrimp farming in coastal areas

It is now being increasingly asked whether the full price of export crops is properly reflected in the export earnings and whether environmental costs, in particular, are not being ignored or excluded. The issue has been highlighted by the debate on shrimp farming in coastal areas. The growth in shrimp farming has been induced by the high demand for seafood in United States and Japan. In response to this high demand, the so-called 'blue revolution' in marine fisheries began in the 1950s, mainly in South and Southeast Asia, and in countries such as Taiwan, Thailand, Indonesia, Vietnam and China. However, the growth leveled off in the 1980s, as practically every fishing region of the world became over-exploited. This led to attempts to produce shrimp in a controlled environment, in enclosures built near the sea where tides flowing in and out of the enclosure provided facilities for the stocking of shrimp and feed and water exchange. By now shrimp pond farming has become a major agricultural export activity in many poor countries (Skladany and Harris, 1995: 169–71).

While, given the world market demand, shrimp pond farming is highly profitable, the demand can be volatile and the spread of disease can easily turn a profitable venture into a loss-making one. The total demand is for about one million metric tons, of which half is accounted for by Japan and the United States, one-fifth by the European Community, and another 30 per cent by the rest of the world. In Ecuador, such farming has emerged as the second leading export item after oil, largely because of the proximity of the US market. But the experience is a mixed one in several other exporting countries.

Until two decades ago, these coastal areas were considered as wasteland with little economic potential and with virtually no formal property titles. This, apart from their heavy capital need, made the entry of the multinationals easier. The need for high stocking densities, frequent water exchanges, mechanical aeration, high feed levels, skilled labour and scientific management, apart from a high level of capital investment, had made large, vertically integrated multinational firms such as Mitsubishi, BP–Aquastar, Charoen Pokphand and Ralston Purina, powerful players who are controlling all phases of the industry. These firms are developing new commodity forms such as analogs (moulded mixtures of shrimp and fish, known as *surimi* in Japan), breaded shrimp, and shrimp cocktails. These companies are operating on the basis of contracts with growers. Companies are providing growers with auxiliary services—seed stock, formulated feeds, extension information and marketing outlets and are offering a guaranteed price for a standardised produce output. The control of the industry lies with the big firms through post-harvest activities and contract (Skladany and Harris, 1995: 175–80).

A major environmental objection to the functioning of these firms is the way these are transforming multi-user public coastal land into single-purpose private property. There are often reports from many places of coercion to evict coastal residents. In Ecuador, there are reports of bribes to government officials to get allocation of 'free' coastal land for pond cultivation at $10,000 per 100 hectares. Often, government officials, bank loan officers and businessmen, form partnerships to speed up the process of obtaining a concession. These firms interfere with Coastal Zone Management (CZM) in various ways (Skladany and Harris, 1995: 182; Barraclough and Finger–Stich, 1966: 28). Mangroves are destroyed to make room for them and irreversible ecological changes are brought about in an environmentally sensitive area where the sea meets the land (Skladany and Harris, 1995: 183). Further, while traditionally mangroves have been treated as common property resources, their privatisation for shrimp farming denies traditional users their customary rights. Local people lose a major source of firewood, construction material, nursery bed for fish and protection from storms and floods as mangroves disappear (Barraclough and Finger–Stich, 1996: 32).

Shrimp farming is associated with a high risk of self-pollution. Modified water circulation systems associated with shrimp cultivation alter wild fish and crustacean habitats, and increase the risk of diseases spreading from ponds to the wild. Further, clearing of coastal areas for shrimp production makes them vulnerable to floods. The sedimentation of estuaries has adverse impacts on coral reefs and mangroves, which function as nursery beds for numerous fish species. Unknown diseases also spread to the local human population (Barraclough and Finger–Stich, 1996: 26; Shiva and Karir, 1997: 10). If the experience of China and Taiwan is any guide, shrimp farming can only be sustained for a couple of decades before diseases associated with self-pollution bring production down to a non-viable level (Barraclough and Finger–Stich, 1996: 51). Each hectare of shrimp pond produces tons of undigested feed and faecal waste, and discharges ammonia, nitrites and nitrates (Barraclough and Finger–Stich, 1996: 25).

Another implication is the salinisation of fresh water sources. Discharge of pond water turns adjacent paddy land into a saline area which is no longer suitable for rice cultivation. But when demand conditions change, or the ponds are infested with disease, or cheaper supply sources are found, and in response, the multinationals relocate their activities, the abandoned land can no longer be brought back to paddy cultivation, at least not for a century or so. This is akin to the 'slash and burn' method of shifting cultivation. When Taiwan's industry was decimated by disease and land subsidence in 1987, the capital moved to other areas. Similarly, Taiwanese investment to Thailand was diverted to Central America when production there leveled off. The industry operates in 'boom and bust' cycles. 'The industry is not accountable and seeks short-term gains by sidestepping issues of long term environmental degradation and social justice' (Skladany and Harris, 1995: 182–83; Muir and Roberts, 1982). The heavy demand for fresh water—an average of 33 cubic metres of fresh water for every ton of shrimp produced—deprives other activities of water and increases the risk of contamination of fresh water sources with saline water (Barraclough and Finger–Stich, 1996: 25). In many cases uneducated and unknowing farmers become drawn to prawn fishing, at the cost of their paddy land, because of the high immediate returns that do not compensate for the irreversible environmental degradation that shrimp fishing brings about.

A third environmental consequence is the destruction of non-target marine products when fishing in the sea or collecting spawns, that come along with shrimp, as these are not commercially attractive. When calculating profit, such environmental costs—of getting 'more and more of less and less'—are seldom taken into account (Shiva and Karir, 1997: 2). Such commercialised fishing activities are undertaken without customary safeguards (e.g., the practice not to allow fishing of *hilsa*, a delicious sea fish that breeds in river water in Bangladesh and West Bengal, during certain seasons) and cause severe depletion of stock. One way of handling this issue is to raise the cost of shrimp pond farming by introducing a steep environmental tax that takes into account all these, including many irreversible, changes.

The global commons and global governance

Extension of market-centred remedies to global commons

In the discussion in and around the 1992 Rio Earth Summit, a serious attempt was made to extend the principle of 'polluter pays' to the global level. A carbon tax was proposed, which a country would pay to some global authority, that would be proportionate to its level of emission of GHGs. However, this proposal became immediately controversial. The rich countries disputed the evidence linking GHGs to global warming. Further, they argued that assessment and verification of both the extent of damage done and the level of emission would be extremely difficult (Development Committee, 1990b: 77).

Similarly, discussion on an international tradable permit in emissions, including a system of global offsets if an equal amount of emission was reduced elsewhere, could not make much headway (de Castro, 1994: 40–41). The proposal for a clearing house fund, under which a country would subsidise environment-promoting activities in other countries to protect its own environment, could not work in the case of European acid rain (Development Committee, 1990b: 77). The 1985 Helsinki Protocol, to limit acid rain to 70 per cent of the 1980 level by 1993, ran into heavy weather as half the European countries, mainly victims, signed, while the other half, those responsible for it, refused to sign. Here, the Coasian solution of one party interested in avoiding damage paying to the other for avoiding such damage could not work, because the former—mostly poorer central European countries—were not able to pay what the latter was likely to ask for (World Bank, 1992: 155).

Support for some other proposals for global taxation, based on the capacity to pay, for generating a global environment fund large enough to make a significant impact—equivalent to 0.1 per cent of a country's GNP, that could have raised about $18 billion annually—was not forthcoming from the rich countries. Proposal for levies on each country's trade, e.g., a 1 per cent tax on imports by developed countries from tropical areas characterised by high biodiversity, was equally cold-shouldered. In this proposal, it was further suggested that its proceeds could be recycled back to its countries of origin to subsidise environment-friendly activities. The same fate awaited a proposal for diversion from some other development funds, e.g., 3 per cent of International Development Assistance (IDA) loans, to build one on environment. There was no consensus on any of these proposals. Therefore, no global environment authority endowed with requisite authority, prestige and funding was formed (Development Committee, 1990b: 77).

Self-interested nations and their property rights

A major issue in the debate on environment has always been the conflicting position on the issue of national sovereignty, particularly when handling issues relating to the management of global commons, such as space, oceans and seas, and Antarctica. Many saw in these issues the need for global integration. 'Our concern for environment is global and indivisible' was a slogan repeatedly heard in the 1970s, but what did that actually imply? At a lower level of globalisation, this involved strengthening international cooperation through agencies such as the World Meteorological Organisation (WMO), World Health Organisation (WHO) or even Food and Agriculture Organisation (FAO), monitoring weather change and the spread of locusts or diseases across country boundaries. The establishment of the United Nations Environment Programme (UNEP) with its headquarters in Nairobi, in 1973, following the recommendation of the 1972 Stockholm Conference, also helped to monitor environmental indicators at the global level and to coordinate governmental responses.

The main issue was whether the concern for globalisation, for protecting the environment, would be allowed to go as far as the subordination of national sovereignty to some supra-national authority. Or whether the countries would agree to qualify their sovereign rights to permit collective, global action, even against the opposition of a concerned state, on major global environmental issues—such as the depletion of the Amazonian rain forests, or the automobile-centred environment degrading lifestyle in the West. A system of global taxation for funding environmental protection was also seen by many as a first step towards the setting up of a world government with wide powers on such issues. As the Brundtland report concluded: 'Traditional forms of national sovereignty raise particular problems in managing "global commons" and their shared ecosystems—the oceans, outer space, and Antarctica'

(WCED, 1987: 18). However, there was no evidence that any country was willing to sacrifice its sovereignty in the interest of global environment. Nor was it realistic to expect such an attitude on the part of the nation states when such supra-national authority was likely to be under the domination of one or two superpowers or a coalition of major nuclear-powered states.

There was, in fact, a move in the opposite direction. The Stockholm Conference of 1972 explicitly recognised the sovereign right of a country to exploit its own resources pursuant to their own environmental policies. As we have noted, there was a deep suspicion about the role and functioning of the MNCs in their mode of utilisation of natural resources. It was recognised that often the global objectives of profit maximisation of the MNCs came in conflict with the national environmental objectives of a nation state.

The Coasian solution would, in fact, build on this perception of self-interest on the part of these nation states and would envisage (*a*) privatisation of the global commons, as far as possible, and (*b*) extensive bargaining among nation states to reach optimal solutions. Taking 'individual' as equivalent to 'country' at the international level, it can be said that whatever of the commons could be 'privatised' has already been. Countries fight to protect every inch of their own territory and to grab more from others, if they can. The Law of the Sea took 10 years to negotiate, and another decade has gone by without its being put into effect. The only part of it that has been implemented with much enthusiasm has been the provision extending the right to national economic exploitation of the sea to an area 200 miles from the coast (World Bank, WDR, 1992: 154). National sovereignty is now projected vertically into the space up to the limit governed by the most powerful surface-to-air missile within the territory.

Not that the Coasian solution of bargaining has not been tried. Bargaining for settling international boundary disputes is quite common and as old as history in inter-country relations; and there have been cases of settling territorial arguments in exchange of money, e.g., the sale of Alaska by the Russians to USA, or has been in the form of a gift in exchange of other favours, e.g., the sale of Bombay island to Britain by the Portuguese. Generally speaking, the countries act as much in their self-interest as the 'rational' individual of the neo-classical mould would. But what has that done to the environment? In some cases it is indeed true that the individual countries, taking an enlightened view of their own self-interest, have made international cooperation work, e.g., postal and telecommunication services or WMO. In other cases, adopting a narrow, time-bound, selfish view of the issues, they have brought attempted cooperating ventures to a standstill. Looking around the globe one can make out a long list of outstanding issues that have not been resolved through negotiations and bargains for decades, either by polluters voluntarily paying or by the victim bribing the polluter, or even by occasional war and superpower interventions.

The Rio earth summit: The issue of global governance

The most spectacular environmental event of the 1990s (so far) was the Earth Summit, the popular label under which the United Nations conference on environment and development, held in Rio de Janeiro, from 3 to 14 June 1992, was projected. This was the second United Nations conference on environment, exactly two decades after the Stockholm one, and was the most representative world conference ever with 172 countries attending; 115 of which attended at the level of the head of state or government. It was indeed an 'Earth Summit' (Development Committee, 1992: 101). This was also a forum for bargaining, in the Coasian sense, between different environmental interests, e.g., would USA agree to a system of global taxation based on emission levels for various polluting gases in exchange for a guarantee by Brazil to protect its rain forests from destruction? Should not the rich countries mainly responsible for global warming compensate Bangladesh, the country to lose most from global inundation that might result from the consequent melting of the polar ice cap? Or would Bangladesh be able to afford the money, in a Coasian manner, to pay the industrialised countries not to industralise to the point where the ice cap would melt?

However, despite public rhetoric to the contrary, the conference did not succeed in reconciling contrasting environmental perceptions and attitudes of different types of governments on biodiversity and global commons. In particular, the gap between the rich and the poor countries, in their understanding of the issues and as regards how to protect global environment, was insurmountable. The former, for instance, stressed on the need to protect tropical forests, but the issue was, who will pay Brazil or Malaysia for the loss of timber trade? Would this come from some international fund collected in one of the many ways suggested above? Would this entail a sacrifice on the part of the rich countries in the form of reducing energy-intensive consumption and changing lifestyle, particularly by restraining the growth and the intensity of the use of automobiles? How would one assess the loss of forests in the rich countries in the past and its implications for the environment today? These issues have been posed, but no consensus has been reached. Everyone is united in the cause of protecting environment, but no one is willing to foot the bill. It seems that every country is waiting to see what the others would do, and, if possible, to enjoy a free ride.

The issue of global warming

The decade of the 1990s specifically dealt with two major pollution problems, for which action at the global level was called for: global warming and the depletion of the ozone layer.

The four main greenhouse gases (GHGs) are carbon dioxide, methane, CFC and nitrous oxides. Most of the additional carbon dioxide has been generated by hydrocarbons and deforestation in recent years, while nitrous oxide is released by the oceans and the soil. Biomass burning and the use of fertilisers also play a role in nitrous oxide production that has not been quantified. CFC and nitrous oxide are more damaging than the other two. While the industrialised countries are mainly responsible for these three types of GHGs, the largest source of methane in the atmosphere are natural wetlands, rice paddies and livestock, mostly located in India, China and other countries of Asia (World Bank, WDR, 1992: 61).

Two types of issues arise. First, it is now being asked whether the forecasts made in the previous decade—that sea levels would rise by eight metres—were not unduly alarming and unrelated to scientific evidence. Fresh evidence shows that the global sea level has risen by only 10 centimetres over the past 100 years and would rise by another 65 centimetres (or 30 centimetres, according to another study) by the end of the 21st century. The melting of the ice cap, because of global warming, may only rise sea level by 0.5 metre over the next 50 years. However, the scientific community also concurs that even these conclusions are far from conclusive; one is transgressing into an unknown territory, and all the possible implications of the melting of the polar ice cap have not been examined (Beckerman, 1991; 65; OECD, 1992b: 196).

Second, whatever the magnitude, how would the impact of such warming be spread over the globe? Some countries, such as those in the temperate zones, may even benefit from the resulting climatic change, improvement of agriculture and less need for water because of higher carbon dioxide level, while some others, like Bangladesh, may be devastated. The cost of sea defence would be only 0.43 per cent of GNP in case of the United States, while it would be incalculable and far beyond the means of Bangladesh (Beckerman, 1991: 63–66; World Bank, WDR, 1992: 160).

On balance, taking the world as a whole, it is unclear whether the overall impact would be positive or negative and whether those gaining would be able to compensate those, like Bangladesh, for the loss they would sustain. In any case, research indicates the possibility that all the nations will not be equally interested in fighting off global warming. Paradoxically, those responsible for global warming—accounting for 11 per cent of the world population and responsible for more than 90 per cent of global industrial carbon dioxide emission—are and more capable of withstanding its impact. That is, the rich industrialised countries located in the temperate zone would be the least affected by its consequences, while those likely to suffer most, the poor ones located in the tropics, contribute the least to global warming (Development Committee, 1989: 35).

In this situation, no global consensus is likely. Those who would be keen to establish global control are weaker than those who are not, and a straightforward bargaining is not going to produce, given this unequal relationship, any meaningful compromise. Research results are also manipulable. At one stage an attempt was made to put damage done by industrial activities in the West on an equal footing with the methane emission from the paddy fields of India and China, though the Indian scientists have contested such findings and have come out with figures that are incomparably lower.

Depletion of the ozone layer

Just the opposite conclusion holds in the case of the depletion of the ozone layer, which is likely to affect the temperate areas and the light-skin people more than the other areas/people. The ozone layer helps to shield the earth from the direct impact of solar radiation. Its depletion, because of direct exposure to ultraviolet rays, may cause the incidence of cancer to rise. One possible impact is a 25 per cent increase in non-melanoma cancers, that is 300,000 additional cases a year, and another 1.7 million additional cases of cataract a year. Another, perhaps most frightening: it can also suppress the immune system of people of all colours. It is possible that some plants would adapt to changed solar radiation levels, but many others would perish (World Bank, WDR, 1992: 63).

Until the discovery of the relationship between CFC and ozone depletion, CFCs were taken as among the most useful compounds developed by human beings. Non-toxic and stable, these do not burn and react with other substances or corrode materials. With low thermal conductivity, these were useful as excellent insulators and were good solvents for cleaning metals, apart from being inexpensive. CFCs were used extensively in refrigerators, freezers, air conditioners, coolers, etc., until hell broke lose in 1987. The possible negative impact of CFCs on the ozone layer was under research investigation from 1974, but it was not until 1987 that the connection was conclusively established that a 'hole' has been created in the ozone layer above Antarctica (Meadows et al., 1992: 142–57). Depletion of half the layer has taken place in Antarctica over the 1980s, and 5–10 per cent depletion in the middle or high latitudes (World Bank, WDR, 1992: 63).

From 1950 to 1975, CFC production grew at 7–10 per cent a year. By 1980, the world was manufacturing one million tons of CFCs annually. An average North American was using 2 pounds a year, compared with a mere 0.03 kg a year by an Indian or a Chinese (Meadows et al., 1992: 145–52).

The Montreal Protocol of 1987 proposed the phasing out of CFCs. According to present calculations, with various safeguards in place, the recovery of the ozone layer will begin after 2000, and will reach the level of the 1970s only by the middle of the next century. Under the Protocol, the developed countries have agreed to phase out CFCs by 2000 AD. The LDCs have been allowed controlled increase in CFC consumption up to 1996; after which their consumption will freeze, and, by 2010, will be phased out. Nevertheless, the chlorine concentration in the atmosphere is unlikely to reach the pre-CFC level before the middle of the next century (World Bank, WDR, 1992: 61–63). The signing and implementation of the Montreal Protocol on CFCs has proved to be easier because the polluter countries, products and companies are small in number, while, for the same reason—because of the sheer number of those involved in polluting the atmosphere—the control of greenhouse gases is proving so difficult (World Bank, WDR, 1992: 158).

Why international cooperation on environment is so difficult?

Time has come to recognise that 'self-interest'—at individual, community or national level—is itself the main hurdle towards developing an 'indivisible and global concern' for environment. There are other hurdles too. Difficulties arise because of the very nature of the major global environmental problems. If 'cloud seeding' can bring welcome rain, the technology that can achieve it can also make rain stop somewhere else. Genetic engineering has as much potential to develop as a great friend of the agriculturist as of the giant military-industrial complexes producing biological weapons. The declared intention of the peaceful use of nuclear power may be a ruse to hide the real intention of attaining nuclear weapon capability. The conquest of space, a great human achievement, may serve the military purpose of effectively directing missiles to the desired target. The fact is that the sponsors for a great deal of global environmental research are defence establishments unwilling to share their research results with others or to go beyond their brief and do something that would bring benefit to mankind as a whole.

Second, the unequal distribution of military power among nations is also a major factor inhibiting international cooperation. The superpowers are unwilling to submit to a higher international environment authority as they wish to perpetuate their domination. The smaller countries are scared of any international arrangement that takes away a part of their sovereignty, because of the fear that any supra-national authority formed for this purpose would come under the domination of the superpower or a group of powerful countries.

Third, as it was repeatedly stressed by the Brundtland report, the unequal distribution of economic power also hinders international cooperation for protecting the environment. The fear and suspicion of the LDCs is reinforced by the G7 domination of the

World Bank (with about half the voting rights), the agency that is now responsible for both development and environment in the LDCs.

Trade and environment

The environmental argument for protection

In the 1970s, the LDCs expected to gain from growing environmental awareness by way of an increased world preference for natural products. The growing concern about the exhaustion of oil and minerals was expected to stimulate the world demand for agricultural raw materials, as opposed to those for the synthetics and other chemicals. Further, inspired by the success of OPEC in case of oil, and the formation of several groups of primary producers of commodities such as coffee, cocoa, copper, bauxite and jute, there was also the expectation that the terms of trade would now move in favour of primary producers in general. Both led to further discussion on issues such as how international trade was being conducted, who controlled the outcome, and how the gains were distributed between nations. The environment debate, thus, evolved to a point where it overlapped with the demands for an NIEO, for a higher share of industrial production, for a closer monitoring of the MNC activities and for a greater role of the LDCs in global trade.

We have already noted that this expectation has not materialised; the terms of trade have not favoured the primary products. In the previous chapter we have discussed reasons for such adverse relative prices. Another explanation for this is the way environmental awareness has been manipulated by the rich country industrial interests and has been turned against poor country products. One major demand of the former—in the name of ending 'unfair competition' or opposing eco-dumping—has been to impose the high and costly environmental standards of the rich countries on their poor counterparts, and in the absence of non-compliance, to extract the difference between the two standards from the primary producers by way of tariffs and other measures. As UNCTAD has found, the concern about eco-dumping by poor countries is exaggerated and their cost effects are small (UNCTAD, 1994b:

234). The alliance formed by the industry and labour in the United States against cheaper Mexican imports under NAFTA also deployed environmental arguments to justify their call for protection (Low, 1995: 31). As one observer noted, 'If implicit subsidies were to become a source of unfair trade, the practice could open a door for abuse for all kinds of purposes; differences in social benefits, wages etc.' (Sorsa, 1992: 18).

In many instances the rich country purchasers are imposing environmental specifications and are monitoring production processes in the third world countries through their own visiting inspectors. In such cases, the primary producers, and not the purchasers from the rich countries, are paying the cost of environmental protection. The impact of banning the export of timber from natural forests would be to further bring down its internal prices, leading to even more excessive internal consumption (Sorsa, 1992: 4; de Castro, 1994: 47). While one can justify imposition of, say, limits on emission in imported cars, as Low observes: 'Problems arise when a country uses the threat of trade restrictions to impose its own views about acceptable environmental standards or appropriate production and process methods upon another country, where the restrictions have nothing to do with the enforcement of standards set domestically for domestic producers' (Low, 1995: 33).

In another category of cases, the specified environmental standards fixed in a rich country are largely based on the technical advice rendered by their own industrial interests, which are often designed to keep third world exports away. Producers in LDCs often find it difficult to qualify for the eco-label, and when they do, the adjustments they are required to make often do not have any bearing on the environment (UNCTAD, 1994b: 234). These specified environmental standards often make no sense but make the third world exports costlier (Jha et al., 1993: 7–10). For instance, costly turtle-saving appliances are being forced on Indian coastal fishing boats even in those parts where turtles are non-existent. In many cases, the line between non-tariff protection and a genuine environment policy has become very thin (Sorsa, 1992: 9; de Castro, 1994: 50). Taking all these into account, UNCTAD has urged the participation of LDC producers in the process through which technical criteria and threshold levels for the award of eco-labelling are determined (UNCTAD, 1994b: 234–35).

Extensive eco-labelling, to influence environment-friendly consumption and to deny markets to those guilty of degrading practices, has affected forest timber export, while being biased in favour of MNC-controlled plantations. The cost of application for such eco-labelling is very high by poor country standards, while the technical requirements are not widely known (Jha et al., 1993: 11). In many of these cases, such environmental measures favour domestic producers in rich countries, and thus amount to a violation of GATT provisions on 'national treatment requirement' (Sorsa, 1992: 17).

To what extent the LDCs are capable of internalising environmental costs, in accordance with the polluter pays principle, is also a function of terms of trade, and the market access they enjoy in the developed countries. This will provide them with funding to give environmental support to their domestic industries. At the same time, if they can manage to internalise the environmental cost and then get it reflected in the prices they charge for their products, and can still retain their market in the developed countries, this is going to do good both for their trade and development and environment. However, internalising of environment costs entails a very high capital cost, though the running cost tends to be low (UNCTAD, 1994b: 233–34).

Taking global pollution in general, the awareness created by the environmental campaign of the 1970s and the 1980s and the resulting legislation and regulations, has brought a massive 'environment industry' into being with a global market of $200 billion, which is expected to reach a figure of $300 billion by the end of the century. The environment industry mainly occupies itself with water and effluent treatment, waste management, air quality control and noise pollution among others, and spends about $10 billion a year, 80 per cent of which is by the private sector, in R&D. All these measures have substantially reduced emission of carbon dioxide and sulphur dioxide from end-of-pipe pollution control technologies. The progress has been less impressive in controlling nitrogen oxide emission (OECD, 1992b: 187–99). However, for the LDCs, internalising external cost would imply making purchases from this industry, which is exclusively controlled by the industrialised countries.

The Marakesh agreement and environment

Concerns have been expressed about the implications of the new Marakesh–WTO patent regime on the use of genetic material. Apart from the higher costs of patented agricultural technologies, fear has been expressed that these might narrow the genetic base, raise the high risk of genetic uniformity or inhibit access to germplasm. There is also the fear of the plundering of the biosphere of the LDCs by multinational agri-business firms and patenting it, thus virtually excluding countries which had been using these plants and species for their use excepting by way of paying a high price.

Generally speaking, GATT was not directly involved with environment, excepting for a provision that permitted governments to impose trade controls to 'protect human, animal or plant life or health' or for the protection of environment, under the Agreement on the Technical Barriers to Trade. This agreement expects all the countries to conform to international standards. Another agreement on Application of Sanitary and Phytosanitary Measures, allows measures to protect human or animal life within the territory of the importing country (UNCTAD, 1994b: 230–31). Both these measures have been taken advantage of by the rich countries and have enabled them to use the environment argument to keep the LDC exports out.

One World Bank document claimed that, to the extent expanded growth of trade would raise its income level, it would give a country the capacity to spend more on environmental protection (Sorsa, 1992: 1). Some others took the view that WTO, sharing the same economic philosophy with the World Bank and IMF, would merely reinforce the structural adjustment and its attendant environmental consequences. More concretely, outward-oriented policies, involving extracting and processing industries, generate a great deal of waste. In Thailand, as the industry's share in GDP grew to become its two-thirds along with export drive, the generation of hazardous waste reached a level of 1.9 million tons a year, and would increase fourfold by the turn of the century (Repetto, 1995: 187). Further, the protectionist trade policies of the developed countries, by impeding third world labour-intensive manufacturing exports in various forms, and, therefore, also their linked downstream processing industries, is forcing them to fall back upon natural resource-based export commodities, with all their environmental consequences (Repetto, 1995: 192).

Environment and development

The relationship between environment and development is being debated since the early 1970s. Following Pigou, for several decades, nothing new or substantial was added to the literature on social and economic aspects of environment. Then, in the 1960s, several important publications (Carson, 1983; Ehrlich, 1971; Commoner, 1972; Ecologist, 1972) and one major disaster—the spilling of 12,000 tons of oil from a tanker named Torry Canyon that caused extensive damage to marine life (Weale, 1992: 10)—awakened public interest in environment. Boulding was one of the first leading economists to raise the issue of depletion of natural resources during the 1960s. He described the naive assumption that the earth's resource base was 'a limitlessly exploitable frontier' as 'cowboy economics'. But the credit for putting environment on the international agenda should go to the Club of Rome and its alarming 1972 report, aptly named The Limits to Growth, about the long-term adverse implications of economic growth on the earth's fragile environment (Meadows et al., 1972; McCutcheon, 1979).

Formed in 1968 at a meeting of experts—on a wide range of subjects from genetics to economics—convened by the chairman of the Fiat company, the first report of the Club of Rome, published in 1971, pointed to the danger of rapid exhaustion of nearly all critical natural resources within 100 years, unless demographic and industrial growth were contained in time. Further, they warned, pollution would grow exponentially along with industrial growth, and would seriously interfere with human living and working conditions. Both the debilitating exhaustion of critical resources and crippling pollution together would make industrialisation at the existing rate unsustainable, they argued, and advocated for some strong and decisive action before the day of reckoning had arrived and brought the world to a standstill. Their specific alternative proposal was for a controlled and orderly transition from growth to global equilibrium. Zero-growth was the message the report delivered. Though in a later publication the authors disagreed that they were prophets of doom, and claimed that the report also contained a message of promise, the publication made the impact it did because of the alarming picture it painted (Meadows et al., 1992: xiii).

Not everyone agreed with the Club of Rome. Even as early as in the mid-1970s, a group of Latin American scientists and social scientists held the view that, with suitable technology, it would be possible to extract from the crust of the earth enough of scarce resources to make the industries and the economies grow at the current rate for a very long time to come (Herrera et al., 1976). It was pointed out by others that, over time, the production-reserve ratio for most natural resources had remained more or less static. Potential shortages, reflected in higher prices, induce the development of new technologies and discoveries, or of substitutes as effective as fibre optics in place of copper in telecommunications. Further, for most scarce resources, compared with the proved reserves so far, thousands of times more are available in sea-water, air and inside the earth's crust. Production from these sources is a matter of price and technology, while: 'The debate about whether the world is running out of renewable resources is as old as economics' (World Bank, WDR, 1992: 37; Beckerman, 1991: 52–83). Many also rejected the postulated negative relationship between growth and environment. They contended that growth was necessary to develop the capability to fight pollution and also to find scarce resources in hitherto unexplored areas such as deep sea, the polar ice cap, hot desert, mountains and other difficult terrain (World Bank, WDR, 1992: 37).

The third world perspective: Stockholm and Founex

Though most environmentalist writings of the period were mainly concerned with the environment-degrading activities of the industralised countries, the LDCs saw in the slogan of zero growth a ploy (an imperialist conspiracy, to some) to keep them backward forever. A certain amount of pollution was acceptable to them, if that was the price to pay for industrialisation, employment and income. If pollution was threatening the human race, they argued, it was for the developed countries—with energy-intensive lifestyles and pollution-generating industries—to take corrective measures.

The level of pollution was not as alarming in the LDCs as it was in the developed countries, they contended (Dasgupta et al., 1977: 5–6).

The World Conference on Human Environment, held at Stockholm in 1972, discussed many of these issues, but the support from the poor countries for the cause of environment was anything but enthusiastic (United Nations, 1972). To enlist their support for the cause of environment, a compromise had to be worked out. In the Founex report, prepared by another group of experts working and living together for weeks in a Swiss village motel near Geneva, a distinction was made between two types of environmental problems—natural and social. The former was considered as the primary concern of the rich countries while the latter was that of the poor ones. One of its major formulations—poverty is pollution—later became quite popular with some of the leaders of the LDCs, who projected it as their own original idea (United Nations, 1971).

Though the compromise that was sought was achieved at Founex, it came by fudging the issue, because what the Founex report meant by 'social environment' was very close to the development literature of the time, with its emphasis on development with redistribution and social justice. 'Poverty is pollution' was a good slogan and was certainly relevant in a broader context, but it hardly helped to deepen one's understanding of the main environmental issues (certainly those concerning the 'natural environment') and their implications for development. It was equally wrong to state that natural environment was not a matter of serious concern to the LDCs. Exhaustion of natural resources including top soil, pollution in the cities, severe congestion in metropolises far exceeding their carrying capacity; one can multiply examples where concern for environment applied as much to them as to their rich counterparts.

The debate also had a technological dimension. It was asked: which technologies were environmentally sound? Was it proper to continue importing through MNCs large-scale, capital- and energy-intensive technologies developed with the economy and society of the West in mind? Was it not necessary that a technology should be in tune with the host country's own environment, economy, and society? In due course, a consensus seemed to have emerged among environmentalists, a la Schumaker, that an 'appropriate technology' was small-scale, with low capital and energy intensity, used more of local materials, manpower and know-how, was easy to maintain locally, and blended more easily with the local landscape and folk culture (Dasgupta et al., 1977: 61–62). There were, of course, even in those heydays of appropriate technology, others who were sceptical and took this as another ploy to keep the backward countries technologically backward and to limit their development options.

By the end of the 1970s environment had become a major item on the global agenda. This was the first 'propagandist' phase of a movement where, more important than logic, rationality or scientific evidence, was the expression of emotions and concerns. The movement had given rise to political parties committed to 'green' manifestoes, and other major parties, driven by political compulsion, had begun taking note of their slogans and demands. By then most of the sceptics in the third world had revised their initial attitude and had identified several priority areas of environmental concern in the poor countries. One major positive contribution of the debate was to bring people closer to nature, along with the governments and the media. The ordinary people began taking more interest in flora and fauna, in natural phenomena like earthquakes, tornadoes and volcanic eruptions, and, in general, in laws of nature.

A negative aspect was, perhaps, the tendency in a great deal of the literature of the time to put man on the dock as the enemy of environment. 'People are pollution' as someone once said in a serious book on environment (Ehrlich, 1971). One elaborate study on soil erosion in Sahel countries of that period once suggested the establishment of extensive ranches as a solution, but the main worry for the authors was what to do with the nomads. Such an attitude was wrong for two very clear reasons. First, the fact that nature's agents, such as volcanoes or earthquakes, or even wind and water, are many times more powerful and are, and have always been, responsible for more profound changes in environment—both quantitative and qualitative—than human action. Two, what is and what is not 'environmental degradation' is, after all, a matter of human judgement. We care about the possible extinction of whales and seals, but would be unlikely to mourn the extinction of mosquitoes and flies (Dasgupta, 1978).

Brundtland report: Sustainable development

Many of the issues intensely debated in the 1970s receded to the background towards the end of that decade, as the debt crisis, worsening terms of trade, and the difficulties the governments of the LDCs faced in balancing budgets and external accounts got precedence. The 1980s was the decade of structural adjustment and stabilisation sponsored by the World Bank and IMF.

The most important document on environment in the 1980s was the report of the United Nations Commission on Environment and Development, which was set up in 1983. Chaired by Gro Harlem Brundtland, the Prime Minister of Norway, its report was published in 1987. The main contribution of the report was, perhaps, its advocacy of sustained development, that met the needs of the present without compromising the ability of the future generations to meet their own needs (WCED, 1987: 43). As one World Bank document put it: 'Sustainable development is development that lasts' (World Bank, WDR, 1992: 32). This generation was expected to leave the natural resources for the next generation as it had received these itself.

'Sustained development', according to the Brundtland report, was not compatible with social and economic injustice—within and between countries (WCED, 1987: 51). Eradication of poverty was a precondition for sustaining development, as also of inequality between nations (WCED, 1987: 3). Brundtland was speaking in the language of the 1970s, that clearly contrasted with many of the World Bank specifications of structural adjustment, e.g., its advocacy of self-reliance, land reform and food security (WCED, 1987: 12). There was some reference to prices and incentives here and there, but the emphasis was on institutions, particularly the need to recast international economic relations:

> If economic power and the benefits of trade were more equally distributed, common interests would be generally recognized . . . . The search for common interest would be less difficult if all development and environment problems had solutions that would leave everyone better off. This is seldom the case, and there are usually winners and losers. Many problems arise from inequalities in access to resources (WCED, 1987: 48).

In another study, Brundtland urged the countries in the West to change their consumption habits and the lifestyle of their citizens to allow for sustainable and equitable development (Brundtland, 1993: 17). The report mentioned depressed commodity prices, intolerable debt burden, declining flows of development finance, and protectionism in the developed countries as some of the factors that had contributed to environmental degradation in the poor countries (Brundtland, 1993: 6).

The decade also witnessed a shift in the debate, mainly initiated by UNEP and UNDP, towards more specific global issues on which international cooperation was vital; depletion of the ozone layer, the greenhouse effect, international water resources and biodiversity being the most important among these. Following one of the major recommendations of the Brundtland Commission, UNEP established a World Resource Institute (WRI). The latter, in its report of 1989, asked for an international environmental facility for preparing and financing conservation projects that eventually led to the setting up of a Global Environment Facility in the following year with the World Bank and UNDP as partners (Development Committee, 1990b: 64).

Under UNEP initiative a Declaration of Environmental Policies and Procedures Related to Economic Development, was issued in 1980 and a Committee of International Development Institutes on Environment (CIDIE) was formed (Williams, 1993: 14). A wide range of institutions and agencies were set up or strengthened to make the UNEP's task of monitoring environmental changes easier, including the Global Environment Monitoring Systems (GEMs), Global Resource Information Database (GRID), International Registry of Potentially Toxic Chemicals (IRPTC), Global Atmosphere Watch in collaboration with WMO, WHO on water pollution, and FAO and UNESCO on natural resources, INFOTERRA, a world-wide referral system for gathering information with 140 national country points, START (System for Analysis, Research and Training on Global Change) being developed by International Geosphere-Biosphere programme of the International Council for Scientific Unions (ICSU) to organise studies in 13 main ecosystems (Williams, 1993: 10–11).

The Montreal Protocol to phase out CFCs was signed in 1987. The Vienna Convention of 1988 made recommendations for protecting the ozone layer and limiting greenhouse emissions, while the Noordwijk Conference on Atmospheric Pollution and Climatic Change was held just outside the decade, in 1990. In the same year the Inter-government Panel on Climatic Change (IPCC) gave an interim report, followed by the second World Climate Conference in November (Development Committee, 1990b: 60–62). However, to go beyond meetings and decisions, UNDP and UNEP, as also the newly established World Resource Institute (WRI), felt the need for funding (Development Committee, 1990b: 60). The WRI report suggested an expenditure of the order of $20–50 billion per year, over the next decade, to attend to the four priority areas indicated above. For phasing out CFCs alone, it calculated, around $200–700 million per year would be needed (Development Committee, 1990b: 67). But where would the fund come from? Therefore, in due course, the global leadership on environment issues too passed into the hands of the World Bank which, as we have already noted, set up a Global Environment Facility (GEF) with the support of UNDP and UNEP.

Conclusions

At the outset, we have examined the difficulties of applying the Pigovian remedy of making the polluter pay and then compensating the victim in many situations where environmental impact is diffused over time and space and the cause–effect relationship is further confused by the joint contribution of many agents at a single point of time and space. We also noted why the traditional time-bound, project-bound, cost-benefit analysis would not work once interdependence with the bigger economy and society and the interests of future generations were taken into account. Rather than relying on market forces for correcting environment abuses, a great deal of the environment literature in those early days looked at various institutional solutions.

Then we examined the implications of structural adjustment of environment, particularly the use of prices, property rights and taxes, including emission trading permits, along with bargaining between parties involved in an environmental dispute. We concluded that, while all these are useful in many situations, these cannot be universally applied. World market prices did not reflect the scarcity value of oil, a critical non-renewable resource, until the cartel action by the oil-producing countries. Bargaining cannot be effective in rationalising resource use excepting in the case of small communities using localised common resources. Trade emission permits are still in a state of infancy and would involve administrative capabilities that the LDCs lack. All these market-based solutions flounder when information is scarce, imperfect and is in the control of the same agencies who are responsible for degradation. These also fail to protect the interests of future generations that cannot participate in bargaining. Even in the market-oriented developed countries of today, the command system rules when it comes to environment issues.

Following this we showed how commercialisation and export orientation have given rise to serious environmental problems in agriculture, particularly with reference to the shrimp-farming industry while in the next part we critically examined the attempts to apply the market-oriented solutions to the problem of preservation of global commons. Self-interest of nations, unequal distribution of economic and political power, disinformation and contrasting perception of environmental problems are cited as main factors in the way of global environmental control. We then showed how the environment standard is being used as an argument to keep the third world exports away from the rich country markets. Finally, we traced the evolution of ideas on the relationship between environment and development over the past three decades, particularly how the LDCs have come to accept environment as an issue that concerns them too.

six

The East Asian development experience

Introduction

These days East Asia looms quite large in the development literature. This is not surprising. Even excluding Japan, this region has done remarkably well economically, during the five decades since the ending of the second world war. The four countries of East Asia, described variously as four tigers, Newly Industrialised Countries (NICs), and High Performing Asian Economies (HPAEs)—South Korea, Taiwan, Hong Kong and Singapore—accounted for 10.1 per cent manufactured exports of the world in 1994 with only 1.35 per cent of the world's population. Their rate of growth of GDP, sustained for decades, is around 7–8 per cent per year. Two of these—Hong Kong and Singapore—are now listed among the most developed countries of the world in the annual World Development Report of the World Bank, while the other two are near the top of the middle-income level countries. With a population size that is nearly one-twentieth of India's, two of these four have 50 per cent bigger economies than India, as measured by GDP, while for the other two—no more than dots on the map of the world and with incomparably tiny populations—the GDP figures are only between half and one-third that of India (World Bank, WDR, 1996: Table 1). In terms of the value of merchandise exports, all four are miles ahead of India—Hong Kong exporting six times more and Singapore three-and-a-half times more, while the other two export around four times more (ibid., 1996: Table

12). By 1993, South Korea alone was exporting more than the whole of Africa put together (Little et al., 1993: 13).

This remarkable record is too consistent to be dismissed as an accident (Fishlow and Gwin, 1994: 1). While East Asia has emerged as a showpiece of success, India has failed. The failure is all the more significant because, five decades ago, when India became independent, there was hardly much to choose between them (if Japan was excluded from the list). Even in 1970, India was ahead of these countries in terms of GDP and exports. In terms of natural resources, the size of the internal market and the availability of skilled manpower, India had always been miles ahead of them. For instance, while in 1993, 57 per cent of land area in India was under crop cultivation, the third highest in the world, the comparative figures for South Korea and China were 21 and 10 per cent respectively (ibid., 1994: Table 9). Naturally, the question arises how a region, as backward as India to begin with, could develop at such breathtaking speed to be recognised as an industrialised one, while India, with immense natural endowment and a large semi-continental market base, remains in a state of never-ending economic crisis and at the bottom of the league of nations in terms of per capita GDP and other economic and social indicators of development (ibid., 1994: Table 1).

East Asia evokes interest also because of the way its growth is popularly explained. It was claimed in the past that while most LDCs isolated themselves with a high curtain of protectionism, East Asia's economy was open and allowed free trade including the participation of multinationals. Here the state took a back seat and allowed the market to decide how much to produce, how to allocate resources and at what prices, and thus, avoided wastage of resources and opportunities associated with public ownership and state intervention. They were unabashedly capitalist, and shunned socialist rhetoric (Mosley et al., 1991, Vol. 1: 12).

In recent years, with more in-depth research and better understanding of these economies and the respective roles of the state and the market therein, this particular view has been revised in the knowledgeable circles, even by the World Bank. The East Asians themselves have articulated their perception of their own development process which is in striking contrast with the policy prescriptions emanating from the World Bank and IMF. There is no doubt any more that these were highly interventionist states and their governments still account for a great deal of control and ownership in the economy. On the other hand, the World Bank and others have recently come out with an interesting array of explanations of their high and sustained growth, described as the 'East Asian miracle' in one of their major publications, which emphasise the specificity of this model of development and its constraints that make it non-replicable for other countries.

The main objective of this chapter is to identify and explain, as far as possible, the factors that account for their high and sustained growth. We will take account of the role the state played through its strategy of import-substituting industrialisation, for achieving self-reliance, and for diversifying the economy. We will show that the process of liberalisation started only after these countries had attained a high level of growth and a strong, highly competitive economy that could take on the mightiest of the world in their own countries. We will then examine how, rather than being an alternative, import substitution complemented the country's venture into the world market and its search for export items that were in line with comparative advantage 'dynamically created' through its industrialisation strategy. Other explanations will take account of land reform, repressive measures with regard to organised labour, use of the nationalised banks to direct credit towards selected industries, investments in education and health, solid macroeconomic management and foreign assistance in various forms. In the latter part of this book we will have occasion to examine, in the light of the observations made in the World Bank publication, *The East Asian Miracle*, whether and to what extent, the East Asian experience is replicable.

This chapter focuses on only three out of the five East Asian countries—Japan, South Korea and Taiwan. The two island countries, Singapore and Hong Kong, will be covered only intermittently (but more fully in the following chapter), largely because, given their limited land mass and internal market, self-reliance could never be a state economic goal in their case. The coverage of Japan is brief, mainly because of the existence of a huge literature on this country; very little, if anything, remains to be said on the course it followed ever since the Commodore Perry's cannon shells shook them out of isolation in the 1850s. Though brief, Japan has not been excluded for one very simple and important reason: the 'four tigers' have tended to follow the path that has taken Japan from the ashes following the second world war to the pinnacle of world economic power. We will discuss in this study, the 'flying geese' model that links the East Asian Miracle with Japan—as a model, as a major source of investment and marketing, and as tutor under the so-called Original Equipment Manufacture (OEM) technical-marketing arrangements.

We begin with a brief summary of the development experiences in Japan, Taiwan and Korea in substituting imports and promoting exports and in redefining the concept of comparative advantage by giving it a dynamic form. Then we review their policy experiences in relation to land, labour and credit markets are explored, followed by an evaluation of the role of human capital formulation and other social issues in East Asian development. Then comes a critical examination of the World Bank view on the East Asian miracle. Finally, we consider another controversial issue—that the key to East Asia's success has been the authoritarian character of its regimes.

The interventionist state: Import substitution, state controls and export promotion

The goal of self-reliant indigenous capitalist development

Whatever the misconception about the nature of East Asian development until a decade or two ago, by now it is accepted, even by the World Bank, that in these countries the state played a very active and interventionist role in their course of development (Taylor, 1995: 40; Chen, 1979; World Bank, 1993). A number of major studies have come out over the past five–six years, including those by Amsden and Wade, that have enlightened us about the comparative roles of the state and the market in their development. Governments of that region, as also some leading scholars from these countries, also seem to take the view that the East Asian experience violates most of the economic commandments of the World Bank and IMF theology. Japan, by far the tallest amongst these, was so keen to demonstrate that the East Asians had traversed a divergent path from that prompted by the Fund–Bank twins that it funded the massive World Bank project on the East Asian miracle, at a cost of $1.2 billion (Wade, 1996: 18).

Here comes the paradox. At a formal level, these governments have always been in favour of free trade and market-based economics, while the practice has been different. These governments were amongst the closest to the Western camp led by the United States during the cold war years (Bagchi, 1987: 35), and yet, they appear to have been more effective in defying, though subtly and surreptitiously, the economic dictates of the World Bank than some of the non-aligned countries, e.g., India. While making most of the dependency relationship in their favour—in terms of foreign aid received or trade opportunities created—the East Asian countries had always been pushing for policies that made them economically less dependent. Very often, such efforts were concealed by the public rhetoric in praise of the market, free trade and globalisation, to appease their political mentors. In practice, the progress towards liberalisation and globalisation had been deliberately slow, and only as little as they could get away with without causing a serious breakdown in their relationship with the West.

The West, on its side, tolerated a certain amount of autonomous economic development as their political–military loyalty was not in question. And that 'certain amount', not much at a time, continued to cumulate. Nor did the United States wish to 'ride hard' on the allies who were taken as major outposts of the Western defence system (Wade, 1990: 84). Over the past 50 years several major wars had been fought by proxy—in Vietnam and Korea, in particular—and East and Southeast Asia together had been seen by them as a major nerve centre of the cold war. This dialectics of international diplomacy explains both the amount of resources lavished by the United States and its allies in the West on East Asia, and the simultaneous autonomous economic development of the region, eventually making them a major competitor of the West in the world market (World Bank, 1993: 80).

State-directed development

The drive towards self-reliance took several forms—establishment of major, heavy industries under state ownership, state direction of credit and subsidies through state-owned banks, restrictions on foreign investment in various forms and inducements given to industries oriented towards exports being among these. Import substitution was a major goal; anything that could be produced within the borders and thus obviated the need to import those goods was welcome. Nascent industries were carefully protected from foreign predators. In general, MNCs, apart from facing high tariff walls and quota restrictions for the goods they wanted to export to the region, were shackled with too many rules and 'local content requirements' to make their investment in East Asia attractive.

In most cases, the state direction was mainly through rules and regulations that delineated 'permitted' and 'no go' areas. Indigenous industries selected for promotion were generously supported by subsidies, tax concessions and sponsorships outside the country. Publicly-owned banks used their power to allocate credit, often with subsidised interest rates, to push the economy in the state-desired direction. Imports of machinery and inputs for selected import-substituting industries were arranged quickly and with lesser duties.

Public sector led in the strategic areas, such as banks, shipyards, automobiles and steel plants. State-owned companies occupied the majority of the top 10 positions among companies with the largest turnover. Taking it in its entirety, public sector has played and still plays a very important role in the economy of these countries, more than it ever did in India. In Taiwan, even in 1980, public sector accounted for 13.5 per cent of GDP at factor cost and 32.4 per cent of gross fixed capital formation, half of the country's investment and 13 per cent of the workforce (Wade, 1990: 173–79). Of the 10 largest enterprises in the country, seven were in the public sector. But, unlike the Indian public enterprises, they made profits and made a 10 per cent contribution to government revenue (Wade, 1990: 178, 180). Even as late as in 1987, seven out of the 20 largest firms were state-owned (Hobday, 1995: 97). However, the importance of the public sector was generally under-played in government pronouncements, in order not to invite the wrath of the American patrons (Wade, 1990: 182). Even the most recent development plan, covering the 1991–96 period, projects a staggering expenditure of 330 billion US dollars in public sector projects (World Bank, 1993: 134).

In South Korea too, heavy industries, mostly under public ownership, increased their share in industrial output from 40 per cent in 1971 to 56 per cent in 1980, and paved the ground for the production and export of modern durable consumer goods that now compete fiercely in the world market (Amsden, 1989: 152). Public sector accounted for 7 to 9 per cent of GDP and 40 per cent of investment during 1963–79, and most of these enterprises were engaged in various types of industrial infrastructure (Kwan S. Kim, 1995: 92). Even in 1972, 12 of the 16 biggest industrial enterprises in South Korea were in the public sector, as also 20 out of the biggest 50 (Wade, 1990: 178). Apart from its size, public sector in South Korea contains some of the most efficient industrial enterprises in the world, such as the POSCO steel plant.

Restrictions on foreign investment

In these countries industrialisation took place despite strong World Bank opposition to major industries, such as steel plants, shipyards or nuclear reactors. These governments took the view that there was no alternative to import substitution and controls of various types. To quote Odagiri and Goto:

> The restriction on imports and foreign direct investment into Japan was probably the most important policy until the early 1960s. Restricting the growing Japanese market, already the second largest in the capitalist economy in the later 1960s, to Japanese firms who were competing intensively among themselves, gave a strong incentive to invest in plants, equipment, and R&D. In addition, because post-War Japan's Peace Constitution meant that the military was no longer a significant customer to businesses, industries such as automobiles, which had been helped by military procurement before the war but was still in its infancy relative to American and European producers, might have been wiped out were the market made open to foreign competition (Odagiri and Goto, quoted in Rodrik, 1994: 39).

In Japan, foreign participation in a company was limited to 50 per cent, while remittances were not permitted until 1963. In a sense, Japan's control of direct foreign investment was more stringent than that applied by the other East Asian economies in later years (Wade, 1990: 150). The 'local content requirement' was rigorous, sometimes running up to 90 per cent of licenced parts over a period of five years (Singh, 1994: 23; Nafziger, 1995: 54–55).

In contrast, in Taiwan, foreign equity participation could go up to 100 per cent, and the out-remittances were allowed without restriction, but the foreign companies were not welcome everywhere and were subjected to local content requirements and many other rules. The local content requirements were 90 per cent in case of motorcycles, 80 per cent for switch exchangers and 50 per cent for coloured television sets. The government preferred export-oriented foreign firms that did not compete with local industries—electronics, metal products and machinery and chemicals—but not those working in agriculture, forestry, paper and paper products, food processing, banking, construction or transport (Brautigam, 1995: 171). The process of liberalisation that began in the 1970s was gradual and slow. It was not until 1981 that interest rates were liberalised and not until 1983 that capital market was liberalised (Brautigam, 1995: 169). One of the leading industries in Taiwan—electronics—was given full protection by way of import restrictions until recently (Hobday, 1995: 97).

As in Japan, in South Korea too, foreign ownership was restricted to 50 per cent and subjected to many regulations. To quote Kim:

> Foreign operations would be allowed so long as it conformed to the national interests perceived by the government . . . . As such, despite the appearance of a fairly liberal environment for investment, foreign firms were subject to a high degree of restrictions and interference by the government. In general, except for special cases of investment in the strategic sectors of the economy, foreign firms could not compete on equal terms with local firms on the domestic market.

The foreign firms were, of course, welcome in export-oriented industries where the area of conflict with local firms was narrow. However, beginning in the 1980s, with the introduction of SAP, many of the restrictions have been removed by now (Kwan S. Kim, 1995: 111–12).

Selective industrialisation: Heavy industries and state subsidies

Along with selected credit, the state provided subsidies through the publicly-owned banking system and an array of fiscal concessions, e.g., tax holidays, accelerated depreciation, duty free import of capital goods, to selected industries. In many cases such preferential financing was hidden to foreign eyes, to avoid suspicion; nominal high formal taxes coexisted with such selective exceptions (Wade, 1990: 170). Though the licensing system was absent, some regulations remained for importing technology, limiting over-expansion and curbing concentration of economic power (Hoggard, 1994: 95; Wade 1990: 185).

The United States or the World Bank never liked the preference of these governments for large scale, capital-intensive, knowledge-intensive, import-substituting industries, often under public ownership. Some times they exercised their veto—for instance, to block steel plants, airlines or nuclear reactors in Taiwan in the early years—but more often than not, their expression of displeasure did not go beyond words of advice, since, as we have already noted, taking economics and politics together, the subservient Taiwanese regime was helpful to US interests (Wade, 1990: 83). Nor did the World Bank opposition prevent Taiwan from developing heavy and chemical industries (Ho, 1981: 118). The Third Plan, covering the years from 1961 to 1964, took the view that 'heavy industry holds the key to industrialization' (Wade, 1990: 87). In the 1960s, in eight out of 12 heavy industries, imports as a proportion of total domestic supply declined. Imports were high in commodities like oil, iron and steel and aluminium which the country did not produce (Wade, 1990: 125).

In the case of South Korea too, in 1960, the World Bank frowned at the idea of a steel plant, that too under public ownership and saw it as 'a premature proposition without economic feasibility'. South Korea, having no iron mine and with a smaller market than India, was not considered suitable for domestic steel production. Yet confounding the critics, POSCO, the giant state-owned steel firm, founded in 1968 and beginning production in 1973, has emerged as among the best and most efficient in the world, whose expertise is sought even by US Steel for the training of its managers (Amsden, 1989: 291; Wade, 1990: 319). Its cost of production of steel is by far the lowest in the world, even after adding the costs of various state subsidies (Amsden, 1989: 295). Its ownership was thrust upon the state as foreign firms were not interested, nor were the domestic *chaebols* willing to take the risk of a costly venture with a long gestation period, a virtual repetition of the Indian experience (Amsden, 1989: 282). It is somewhat ironical that the World Bank, an agency that did everything to prevent the state-owned South Korean steel industry from being born, praised POSCO as 'arguably the world's most efficient producer of steel' in a document published in 1987 (World Bank, 1987: 45).

The same story was repeated in the case of shipbuilding which, despite Western opposition, was launched by Hyundai in 1973, with strong state support, and later other private companies, such as Daewoo and Samsung, joined in. Within 10 years, South Korea became the largest shipbuilder in the world. The guiding principle in that industry—complete self-reliance—is expressed in the form of a slogan: 'Our own ship, our own engines, our own designs' (Amsden, 1989: 269–90).

Similarly, despite World Bank opposition to the domestic automobile industry, on the grounds that it would fail to compete in the world market (Dailami, 1991: 300), the state-owned Korean automobile industry made its beginning in 1962, aided by a 200 per cent tariff on foreign cars and generous concessions on import of parts and taxes. Later, foreign partners such as Toyota were permitted, but they were subjected to 50 per cent domestic content requirement. By 1988, Hyundai was producing 650,000 cars a year, most of them for exports (Wade, 1990: 309).

The setting up of heavy and chemical industries (HCIs), from 1973, also faced similar rough weather and from the same direction—the World Bank—but eventually, proved to be a plus factor in promoting downstream industrialisation and export of manufactured goods (Singh, 1994: 19). In 1973, heavy industries accounted for 40.5 per cent of industrial output and 13.7 per cent of exports; within a decade, in 1983, the figures had become 59.3 per cent and 54.3 per cent respectively (Gokarn, 1995: 27). Not everyone is, of course, in agreement with the view that HCIs helped South Korean industrialisation. Yoo takes the view that these led to macroeconomic instability, adverse trade balance and harmed import of capital goods for export industries. But the fact remains that HCIs widened and deepened the technological and industrial base of the country (Yoo quoted in Gokarn, 1995: 33–35). While even in 1985, textile was the leading export item, six HCIs were in the top 10 along with textiles—ships (2), steel producers (4), machinery (6), synthetic resins (8), autos (9) and electrical goods (10). Electronics (3), footwear (5) and fish (7) were the others among the top 10. In other words, the top 10, as a group, was dominated by HCIs (Gokarn, 1995: 28). The promotion of a linked set of industries in tandem, through subsidised credit allocations and consistent technology acquisition was the underpinning of the rapid and wide-ranging diversification of South Korean export (ibid., 1995: 32). Apart from widening the spectrum of product-mix, this policy 'provided domestic producers with an excellent ground for practising scale economics, which enabled economic growth to be sustained. The government's active risk sharing with private firms significantly contributed to the successful implementation of these policies' (Joon–Kyung Kim et al., 1995: 194).

The state and the private sector

The relationship of the state with the indigenous private sector was one of partnership. State intervention was nowhere at the cost of the private sector. The state was by no means market-unfriendly. Nowhere did the public sector supplant the private sector. The government stepped in wherever the private sector was not capable of doing alone what was clearly in its own collective interest. Here, the state perceived and represented the collective interest of the private firms. In many instances the state broke new grounds, but then formed partnerships with the private sector or allowed independent private sector entry into the industry, say, steel. In some instances, the state acted as a kind of umpire between feuding corporate interest groups, and perhaps reluctantly, took over the commanding heights of the economy so as not to allow one firm to dominate the others. The state promoted private sector undertakings, but the latter were expected to conform to the rules laid down by the government, again in their own collective interest—that is, in the interest of indigenous capitalist development. According to Amsden, the process of development in East Asia was 'market-augmenting' rather than 'market-conforming' (Amsden, 1989: 131). At the same time, it cannot be said that the state only acted to rectify 'market failure'.

In many instances the state promoted industrial conglomerates and cartels, but then arranged contests amongst the firms—for credit, foreign exchange or licence—in order to keep them trim and their edges sharp. But even in such situations, competition was not allowed to degenerate into cut-throat oligopolistic price wars that could ruin all the contesting parties. The state expected these industries to eventually compete in the world market without state support, but even after the period of probation was over and the firm was left on its own, in case of a sudden fall in world demand for its goods, the state was very much there to step in and to provide a cushion if that was needed (Singh, 1994: 29–30). The market thrived, and the forces of demand and supply were by no means ignored, but both the visible and the invisible helping hands of the state were also there to rectify market imperfections, to arrange things in a way that could have been the outcome had the market been perfect and foolproof. But the state was also there to create conditions that helped the firms to go beyond the static framework of comparative advantage. In some cases, state subsidies, e.g., for interest rates, were indicative of its preference for certain activities, and led to increased private sector participation in these (World Bank, 1993: 16).

After having achieved recognition as newly industrialised states and as serious competitors for numerous consumer durables and other goods in the world market, in recent years there has been a tendency to move away from control, state regulation, protection and import substitution. The economic and political basis for progress towards liberalisation and globalisation has been the confidence that they can now take on the economic might of the best in the West without protection or any other kind of state support (Amsden, 1988: 165). That does not mean, however, that by now everything has been handed over to the market. The governments of both South Korea and Taiwan have encouraged the formation of cartels—in textiles, rubber, steel, mushroom, and so on—to survive foreign competition (Amsden, 1988: 166). As repeated threats of the United States to initiate Super 301-prescribed retaliatory measures against Japan and some of the other countries show, the latter are still reluctant to discard national self-reliance by way of import substitution as a major policy.

On the other hand, their success in the world export market has driven the United States and the Western European countries towards extensive protectionism. The relationship has turned topsy turvy, with the East Asians fiercely competing everywhere in the world and the West inventing excuses to keep them away from their own territories by erecting non-tariff barriers. The conditions that prompted protectionism and import substitution in the past no longer exist. Still the fear of foreign domination persists as the repeated United States complaint regarding denial of access to some parts of East Asian markets testifies (Wade, 1990: 148).

Patterns of industrialisation

The pattern of industrial development was far from uniform in these countries. In Taiwan, mainly a large number of relatively small companies were in action. In the early 1990s, the small enterprises accounted for 90 per cent of enterprises and 60 per cent of export value in Taiwan (World Bank, 1993: 161–62). While most of the large firms were state-owned, the government relied on the small, private sector units for the growth of the most modern and most dynamic of them all, the electronics industry. The seventh largest computer goods manufacturer in the world in 1990, Taiwan worked with 700 hardware manufacturers and 300 software manufacturers, accounting for 83 per cent of the 'motherboards' and the largest number of mouses, monitors, image scanners and keyboards produced in the world (Hobday, 1995: 101). 'Taiwan's success in electronics relies on the speed, skill and agility of hundreds of local entrepreneurs, rather than the scale and financial power of the *chaebol*' (Hobday, 1995: 132). Local firms overtook MNCs in domestic production in the 1980s, but foreign firms provided technology through joint ventures in electronics, as also in bicycles and footwear among others.

In contrast, in South Korea, large corporate giants, *chaebols*, emerged and took over control with state support. The combined sales of the top 10 *chaebols* equalled 15.1 per cent of GNP in 1974 and 57.6 per cent in 1984 (Gokran, 1995: 35). *Chaebols*, the major vertically integrated business houses of South Korea, each with 15–20 affiliated units, while competing against one another, also colluded to keep foreign competition at bay and to manipulate the state machinery in their favour. They borrowed at home and abroad, brought in high technology, diversified the industries and gave South Korean industrialisation a certain continuity (Amsden, 1989: 151). Hyundai, Samsung and Daewoo are the leading *chaebol* groups that have spread their network throughout the world. The government patronised the large conglomerates, encouraged mergers between firms, regulated the entry and exit of firms according to world demand conditions and technological requirements, and restricted foreign direct investment inflows tightly to promote national interest. However, as in Taiwan, government support was conditional on performance; firms not performing were left to fend for themselves (Stein, 1995c: 12; Singh, 1994: 30–31).

However, their main policy thrust was along the lines indicated above. It is possible to periodise their industrial progress, and different scholars have come out with different types of periodisation. Still, some common features can be noted. They began their journey with textiles, household appliances and other labour-intensive light industries as their base. In the second stage, they moved to capital- and knowledge-intensive industries such as steel, shipbuilding, petrochemicals and synthetic rubber, to provide a basis for further industrialisation by way of forward linkages. In these countries, as also in Japan, the share of textiles in value added in industrial production, in exports and in the number of workers deployed, declined steadily as wages increased. In the fourth stage, export orientation, always pronounced despite a policy of import substitution, became more pronounced, as assembly-based, skill- and R&D-intensive consumer durables—electronics, computers and so on—and industrial machinery made their appearance.

Another pattern, known as the 'flying geese' model was also in evidence. First developed by A. Kaname in the 1930s and then by K. Akamatsu in 1956, under this model, Japan developed first, and as wages and other costs rose, production facilities were relocated to East Asia. Later, as the Plaza Accord of 1985 and the Louvre Accord of 1986 were signed by the G7 countries to rectify US trade imbalances, and the exchange rate of yen was further appreciated vis-à-vis the dollar, Japan, in order to retain its market share, reduced production costs and further relocated production to low-wage economies. Thailand benefited from this and 'became a production base for Japan, receiving raw materials and equipment and then producing finished goods for export to Japan and other countries' (Development Committee, 1993a: 92). Further, as US consumers turned to imports from newly industrialised countries (NICs), such as Taiwan and Korea, further US pressure came on the latter, to adjust and strengthen their currencies, which forced them also to invest more in low-wage Southeast Asian countries, including Thailand (ibid., 1993: 93). This progression from Japan to East Asia and then to Southeast Asia, took on the form of an inverted 'V', as the economies of Pacific Asia began to fly together, led by Japan. During 1986–88 the overall Japanese investment exceeded the cumulative value of FDI in the previous three-and-a-half decades (1951–85), and while most went to North America and other developed countries, a significant share went to East Asia too (Little et al., 1993: 13; Hobday, 1995: 20).

While not necessarily subscribing to the particular sequencing underlying the 'flying geese' model, other scholars have pointed to the 'neighbourhood effect' (Wade, 1994: 66) and the convergence of growth in the region (Fukuda and Toya, 1995: 259). As Easterly pointed out: 'What may be unusual about the Four's success is that they were all in the same region.' He urged more attention to economic geography, and to the fact that the growth pattern looked like growth radiating from a pole—Japan first, followed by the four tigers, and then by China and the Southern tier countries (Easterly, 1995: 283). A more recent study, based on data for East and Southeast Asian countries, confirms their synchronised development in tune with the flying geese model (Agarwal et al., 1996: 2.20–2.23).

Technology transfer and adaptation

Being 'latecomers' in the industrial field had both positive and negative implications for the East Asian economies. The negative implication was the obvious one, that their enterprises had to compete with much bigger, more established and significantly more technologically competent firms operating at the global level. The positive side was that the East Asians did not have to go through a lengthy process of product development; they could begin at the mature, standardised end of the product life cycle. By then the inefficient and small units had already been pushed out through the evolutionary process. What was paramount at this mature, standardised stage was the minimisation of cost, and here the East Asians, with lower wages and operational costs and with a highly skilled workforce, had an advantage over many competitors.

In the beginning, the East Asians specialised in simple assembly skills and developed production capabilities for churning out standardised products. Over time, they moved incrementally, to improve upon quality and the speed of operation. An interesting feature of technology absorption at this stage was what is known as 'reverse engineering of products'. The engineers and technicians began with the end-product and worked back to find the components, their interrelationships, and the technologies. This way they upgraded their own technological awareness and capabilities without much risk. Up to this stage, the local companies were largely dependent on foreign buyers and the relationship was of the patron–client type. Later, these companies developed full production skills and product design capability and undertook process innovations as they moved out of the bounds of their country markets and began infiltrating into the foreign ones. Ultimately, research and development (R&D) came to occupy an increasing share of their investment, R&D became increasingly linked with the assessment of long-term marketing needs, capabilities for innovation and product design developed and new products were launched. This full process took a considerable time to be completed, with inter-country variations in experiences. On the whole, the pattern of their experience in this field was very similar (Wortzel and Wortzel, 1981).

This evolution of technological competence and capability was associated with various successive stages of market development. In the early stages, cheaper labour was deployed for assembling and then selling to buyers for distribution. With 'reverse engineering' was associated a move towards higher quality production in response to foreign buyer demand. As production skills and design capacities developed, the companies attempted to reach foreign markets on their own account and with their own designs. In the next stage the companies, by now ready with a range of products, tried to popularise their own brands by undertaking a vigorous sales campaign. In the last stage, emphasis was on direct marketing through their own independent channels and wide advertising and in-house market research (Wortzel and Wortzel, 1981).

Hobday has listed the following channels of technology transfer: (*a*) FDI, (*b*) joint ventures, (*c*) licensing, (*d*) Original Equipment

Manufacture (OEM), (*e*) Own-design and manufacture (ODM), (*f*) sub-contracting, (*g*) foreign and local buyers, (*h*) informal means (overseas training, hiring, returnees), (*i*) overseas acquisitions/equity investments, and (*j*) strategic partnership for technology (Hobday, 1995: 35)

Of these, OEM and ODM played a major role in technology adaptation and upgradation, eventually leading to independent designing and development of technology. We will discuss both in some detail below, after disposing of some of the other conventional channels as briefly as possible. As for (*a*), we have already taken note of East Asian sensitivity about this particular source. Joint ventures were relatively more welcome, though they seem to have played a modest role in technology transfer. Licensing implies a somewhat higher capacity to absorb and apply technology. Under various licensing arrangements, the local enterprises sold goods to major Japanese buyers—e.g., Mitsubishi, Mitsui, Marubeni–Ida, Nichimen—who, in turn, sold them to the markets in the United States. This arrangement certainly involved the local suppliers in producing things according to foreign technical specifications, but what contributed most to East Asian technological upliftment, at least in the early stages, was the OEM arrangement (Hobday, 1995: 37).

OEM, a specific form of sub-contracting, evolved out of the joint operations of foreign buyers and East Asian suppliers and became the most important channel for export marketing in the 1980s. Under OEM, the local enterprises produced largely under the technical guidance of, and according to the order placed by, foreign partners. The latter was involved in the selection of capital equipment and in the training of managers, engineers and technicians, and offered advice on various things. Though the relationship was tightly controlled and resembled a patron–client one, this was an important step in the technological ladder. ODM was a stage forward, under which the local supplier did everything according to a general design layout supplied by the buyer, and the goods were sold under the latter's brand name (Hobday, 1995: 37).

Taking South Korea's electronic industry as an illustration, it began with the production of transistor radios in 1958, under the domination of MNCs. In the 1960s, the major players included Motorola, Signatics and Fairchild. Even in 1972, eight foreign firms accounted for 54 per cent of electronic exports from South Korea. The foreign firms were not interested in transferring technology, imported most of their inputs and imparted little of their technical know-how to the South Koreans (Hobday, 1995: 57–58, 65). In the next phase, joint ventures with Japanese firms, e.g., Samsung–Sanyo, Toshiba–Goldstar, became more common and accounted for 15 per cent of foreign participation in the 1970s (Hobday, 1995: 59). OEM supplanted joint ventures and opened up new areas of production, particularly in computers, consumer electronics and microwave ovens. Under this arrangement, the foreign buyers supplied key components, material design and capital goods, and around three-fourths of these were imported. Needless to add, the foreign buyers captured most of the post-manufacture value added, and sold these goods under their own brand names. Yet, the overall impact was a highly positive one: 'OEM was a harsh industrial training school for South Korean firms who learnt their skills from Japanese and American TNCs . . . . Invariably, production had to be of the highest quality at the lowest price' (ibid., 1995: 67). In 1988, OEM accounted for 60 to 70 per cent of electronic exports.

In the 1980s, the *chaebols* took off and sought more independence from their patrons. First, there was a switch from OEM to ODM, under which they were doing practically everything, but for the fact that the production was based on a general layout design supplied by the foreign patron and the goods were sold under the patron's brand name. In the next stage, their marketing strategy was to rely more on their own brand names. They had always the fear at the back of their mind that the Japanese patrons under OEM arrangement would eventually turn off the supply of capital equipment and components as the former became more competitive. Further, there was always the risk of the Japanese trying out new, low-cost areas for OEM arrangements. This strategy worked, and by the early 1990s, several of them had established themselves as leading firms at the global level, occupying fifth (Samsung), 12th (Goldstar–Electron) and 13th position (Hyundai) in dynamic random access memories (DRAM) production (Hobday, 1995: 60, 69), their aggregate exports amounting to $106 billion in 1992 (ibid., 1995: 71). Where the South Korean experience contrasts with the Taiwan one, is in the failure of the latter 'to break through OEM/ODM, and float their own brands' (Hobday, 1995: 133).

There can be no doubt that the scale of the South Korean operation, through *chaebols*, was decisive in making the necessary jump to own brands.

No less important, but seldom discussed, was the part played by the absence of an international patent regime of the type imposed since the conclusion of the eighth round of GATT negotiations in April 1994 at Marakesh, in encouraging technology adaptation in the East Asian countries. Almost all had none or loosely composed patent or copyright laws and 'it is impossible to calculate how much of Taiwan's early growth was fueled by the learning that went on while trying to reproduce products protected elsewhere in the world'. In the early 1980s, the US Trade Representative's office accused Taiwan of being responsible for 60 per cent of counterfeit and pirated items in the world market (Brautigam, 1995: 170). Whether one can describe what East Asians did as 'piracy' is, however, a matter of opinion, since they were guided by their own laws or absence of laws, until the recent GATT decisions on IPR. The point to make here is that, at a time when these countries were fast becoming industrialised, there was no global restriction on copying technology of another country (Hoggard, 1994: 107).

Import substitution, export orientation and a dynamic concept of comparative advantage

While import substitution was a major policy goal, it was never counterpoised against export promotion in the East Asian countries. In Taiwan, industries with export potential were given preferential treatment, so that, on the basis of the experience gained in the domestic market, they could launch themselves into the foreign markets (de Melo, 1992: 223). In fact, these two strategies—import substitution and export promotion—were taken as complementary. A protected industry, with a secure access to the domestic market, was expected to eventually grow out of such a protective shield and compete in the world market on its own. During the period of protection, the privileged firm was expected to make regular and noticeable progress towards reducing the price-distance between their products and internationally traded prices. Further, such protection was not free-ended, but strictly time-bound and its continuation was dependent on satisfactory performance. Protection was withdrawn for those firms which were failing to raise their quality and efficiency and to reduce their costs within a given time period. No firm was under any illusion that state favour was there for ever—they had to earn it by performance and that too only for a given time period. 'Even those in the protected domestic markets knew that sooner or later their time to export would come' (World Bank, 1993: 22). The export-push brought knowledge and technology into the country and made export performance the yardstick for continuing government support, something that, according to the World Bank, mitigated their violation of World Bank fundamentals (ibid., 1993: 23).

While exporting, the East Asians—mostly countries with limited natural resource endowments—refused to subscribe to a static concept of comparative advantage. Japan was the first to break away from the so-called 'natural path' of comparative advantage that would have consigned it to the production of textile and other light industries for ever. In its effort to move away from the low income–low productivity–few export goods trap, Japan opted for a calculated but high-risk path of building heavy and chemical industries against stiff opposition from the World Bank (Shinohara, 1982).

Following its concept of 'dynamic comparative advantage', Japan wanted to create an industrial infrastructure that would, in the long run, provide the base for the development of a dazzling array of durable consumer goods with a high income-elastic demand in the developed countries. Thus, rather than reconciling itself to historically and naturally determined comparative advantage in textiles and other light industries, Japan deliberately decided to *create* its own comparative advantage. This decision, criticised by many as economically non-viable within a narrow time horizon, was fully justified by its success in later years when a wide range of export-oriented industries surfaced and competed with the West on all fronts.

This is how OECD, in its 1972 study on Japan, concurred with such a view:

> The MITI decided to establish in Japan industries which require intensive employment of capital and technology, industries that are in consideration of comparative costs of production should be the most inappropriate for Japan, industries such as steel, oil-refining, industrial machinery of all sorts, and electronics . . . . From a short run, static viewpoint, encouragement of such

> industries would seem to conflict with economic rationalism. But, from a long range viewpoint, these are precisely the industries where income elasticity of demand is high, technological progress is rapid, and labor productivity rises fast. It was clear that without these industries it would be difficult to employ a population of 100 million and raise the standard of living to European or American level with light industries. Whether right or wrong, Japan had to have these heavy and chemical industries (OECD, 1972: 15).

It is inconceivable that without such an extensive industrial infrastructure, Japan's industry would still have grown by nearly 13 per cent per year between 1953 and 1973, its GNP by nearly 10 per cent and its share in world export of manufactures by 10 per cent (Singh, 1994: 15). Nor can it be claimed that a radical transformation of the composition of trade—the displacement of primary products by industrial goods and of textiles by heavier industrial articles (Table 6.1)—would have been achievable were things left entirely to the market forces. To quote Gold:

> Virtually all empirical findings of comparative advantage represent no more than ex-post facto rationalisation of past trade patterns . . . . Moreover, even the demonstrable comparative advantage prevailing in a given period has frequently been undermined and even reversed thereafter through determined efforts to advance technologies, shift input requirements, alter transport costs and develop new markets . . . . The very identification of current comparative disadvantages often represents the first step in developing means of overcoming them (Gold, 1979: 311–12).

Further, this tremendous growth in exports was not delinked from the internal market. There is no direct route to the export market. A firm usually first tries out its goods in the domestic market and, only after gaining experience and accumulating capacity to invest would venture into the export market, if possible. Even in the case of Japan, 'trade has constituted only a relatively small share of Japan's GNP: the expansion of domestic markets was far more important for growth' (Fishlow and Gwin, 1994: 10). On the other hand, the fact that the East Asians have a long list of

Table 6.1
East Asian countries: Foreign trade indicators

Variable	*Year*	*Japan*	*South Korea*	*Taiwan*	*Hong Kong*	*Singapore*
Exports ($m)	1980	130000	17500	12682	19800	19400
	1994	397000	96000		151395	96800
Annual percentage growth rate in exports	1970–80	9.2	22.7			9.9
	1980–90	5.0	13.7		15.4	12.1
	1991–94	0.4	7.4		15.3	16.1
Share of primary commodity in exports (%)	1970	7	24		5	70
	1993	3	7		7	20
Share of textiles in exports (%)	1970	13	41		44	6
	1993	2	19			4
Imports ($m)	1980	141000	22300	11033	13452	13049
	1994	275000	102348		138658	85234
Gross international reserve ($m)	1970	4876	610		627	1012
	1980	38919	3607			
	1994	135145	15809			
Total external debt ($m)	1980		29480			
	1994		54542			
Debt service as percentage of exports	1980		20.3			
	1993		7.0			

Source: World Bank, WDR, of various years up to 1996.

items to sell in the export market has an important economic implication: they are unlikely to face devastation of the kind that is caused to economies dependent on one or two export items when the world supply–demand conditions suddenly become adverse and export earnings slump, giving rise to serious balance of payment difficulties. This is one of the major reasons why, unlike most countries in Latin America, Africa and Asia, the East Asians—except for a short period in the early 1980s by South Korea—never had to seek SALs from the World Bank or stabilisation support from the IMF, and thus, could avoid their conditionalities.

Limited trade liberalisation

It follows from what we have said so far on import substitution and export promotion drives, that trade in East Asia was rigorously controlled by the government, mainly to keep the potential competitors to domestic industries out. In Korea, 'the trade regime was far from liberal, with both tariffs and quantitative restrictions in place, although in the eighties the government relaxed these barriers. Exchange rate policy was oriented to maintaining the external competitiveness of Korean exports' (Stevens and Solimano, 1992: 123). However, as in Taiwan, the rhetoric was always that of free enterprise. To quote Amsden: 'If industrial expansion succeeds, success is typically interpreted as being a validation of market principles, and the institutions financially supporting them. If it fails, failure is seen as a result of the violation of market principles, perpetrated by perverse institutions' (Amsden, 1989: 139).

Though trade liberalisation was carried out in a number of phases, even in 1970, out of 1,312 basic items of import, 524 were restricted and 73 were banned altogether (Mosley et al., 1991: 353–54). Though liberalisation was taken up more seriously in the late 1970s, in both 1978 and 1982, the rate of effective protection was 49 per cent (Wade, 1990: 19). Even the protagonists of liberalisation, such as the President of the Korean Development Institute, are not sure, between liberalisation and good economic performance, which one was the cause and which one was the effect (Corbo et al., 1987: 9).

In Taiwan, though exports surged since the 1950s 'the trade regime was a model of controls, high and variable tariff protection, quantitative restrictions and administrative allocations' (Brautigam, 1995: 165). In public, the government frequently promised trade liberalisation, to appease the Americans, but that was seldom carried out—both tariff and non-tariff barriers were retained at high levels throughout the 1960s. Even by 1984, half of the imports, in value terms, faced restrictions (Wade, 1990: 131). Internal economy was no less subjected to controls and price regulations. According to one estimate, in 1966 about 40 per cent of the total economic transactions in South Korea were subjected to price control (Kwan S. Kim, 1995: 92).

Generally speaking, trade liberalisation, as also liberalisation in other spheres, followed attainment of a high level and rate of growth. The growth itself was achieved in a regulated environment. One of the ironies of the East Asian experience is that, while in the early days of their development they frantically tried to protect their industries in numerous ways from foreign competition, in recent years, the tables have been turned, and now they are at the receiving end of protectionism in the Western countries. We have seen in Chapter 4 how such protectionism has been manifested in various forms, e.g., the MFA, the VER, VIE, and Super 301 provisions in the US trade legislation.

We have also noted earlier that one interesting consequence of these pressures and restrictions, and the consequent increase in the wages and values of Japanese exports, was the shift of a considerable amount of Japanese investment to low-wage Southeast Asian countries, which operated under OEM arrangement, and which was instrumental in changing the industrial landscape of that region (Chapter 7).

Land, labour, credit, foreign aid and debt

Land reform and agricultural development

In all the three East Asian countries with a substantial agricultural sector—Japan, Taiwan and Korea—land reform was rigorously implemented and parasitic landlordism was uprooted prior to industrial take-off. Large landholdings were replaced by vastly more efficient and modern but tiny ones which the tillers themselves owned/operated with family labour. The limitations of scale have not worked against productivity, and indeed, despite a low cultivated land–man ratio, production per unit of land in East Asia is amongst the highest in the world and agriculture is highly diversified and market-oriented. The modernisation of agriculture, following land reform, has gone hand in hand with a sharp decline in the proportion of population dependent on agriculture as also in agriculture's contribution to GDP, along with a significant increase in urban-industrial population (Table 6.2).

Land reform contributed to industrialisation in a variety of ways. First, it destroyed land monopoly and the attendant socio-economic inequalities. Aided by the state, the beneficiaries of land distribution seized the opportunity with both hands, introduced new technologies and cropping practices and formed cooperatives that mitigated their weakness as smallholders (World Bank, 1993: 161). Second, by helping to modernise agriculture, land reform was also instrumental in creating an agricultural surplus that made the transfer of workforce from agriculture to industry and from rural to urban areas, feasible. The increasing agricultural productivity and output, paradoxically, but in line with international experience, helped to reduce the share of agriculture in GDP and among the working population and also the share of the rural in total population. Third, it also contributed to the state fund by way of land tax, and the indirect rice tax, where rice was exchanged at a low price with state-distributed over-priced fertilisers. However, the state also took care to build rural infrastructure in the form of roads, bridges, irrigation, power, sanitation, etc. (World Bank, 1993: 33). Fourth, by diffusing and widening the rural purchasing power, it provided the industries with a reasonably large domestic market. Modern, efficient agriculture accompanying industrialisation–urbanisation meant that the rural–urban disparity, in terms of wages and levels and living, was reduced.

In the case of Japan, the first round of land reform was carried out during the Meiji Restoration in 1868, but the second round took place under US occupation at the end of the second world war (Nafziger, 1995: 70–75). In the case of Taiwan, the first round of land reform took place under the Japanese colonial regime, while the second round was conducted by the mainland Chinese,

Table 6.2
East Asian countries: Growth, investment and saving

Variable	*Year*	*Japan*	*South Korea*	*Taiwan*	*Hong Kong*	*Singapore*
GNP per capita (US$)	1980	7280	1160	1400	3040	3290
	1994	34630	8260	–	21650	22500
Annual GDP growth rate (%)	1970–80	4.3	10.1	–	9.2	8.3
	1980–93	4.0	9.1		6.5	6.9
	1985–94	3.2	7.8		5.3	6.1
Gross domestic investment (% of GDP)	1960	34	11	20	19	11
	1970	39	24	–	21	39
	1978	31	32	26	26	36
	1994	30	38	–	31	32
Gross domestic savings (% of GDP)	1960	34	1	13	1	3
	1970	40	15	–	25	18
	1978	32	28	33	15	27
	1994	32	39	–	33	51
Inflation rate	1960–70	4.8	17.5	4.1	2.3	1.1
	1970–80	8.5	19.5	–	9.2	5.9
	1980–93	1.5	6.3	–	7.9	2.5
	1985–94	1.3	6.8	–	9.0	3.9
Proportion of agriculture in GDP	1960	40	28	4	4	
	1970	6	25	–	2	2
	1978	5	24	10	2	2
	1994	2	7	–	0	0
Proportion of agricultural labour force	1960	33	66	56	8	8
	1978	13	41	37	3	2
	1990	7	18		1	0

Table 6.2 (Continued)

Proportion of urban population	1960	62	28	58	89	100
	1970	71	41	–	88	100
	1980	78	55	77	90	100
	1994	78	80		95	100
Energy consumption p/c (kg in coal equivalent)	1960	1171	258	583	468	372
	1978	3825	1359	2202	1657	2461
Energy consumption p/c (in oil equivalents)	1970	2654	495	–	973	3863
	1980	2972	1087	–	1117	2651
	1994	3825	1936	–	2280	6556
Fertiliser consumption in agriculture (100 gm/hectare)	1979/80	4777	3857	–	–	5375
	1990/91	4654	4601	–	–	56000

Source: Same as Table 6.1.
p/c: per capita
– : not available

who landed in the island after the communist revolution in 1949 (Amsden, 1988: 145; Brautigam, 1995: 132; Wade, 1990: 73). In the case of South Korea too, the first round of land reform was conducted by the Japanese, though the second one was undertaken by the South Koreans themselves to neutralise the favourable impact of land reform in the communist North Korea (Amsden, 1989: 27–38).

Colonial or occupation forces had their own reasons for carrying out land reform, but whatever their motive, it helped East Asian development. The success of land reform in East Asia, in contrast with its failure in most LDCs, has been attributed by Hayami to the erosion of the power and confidence of the ruling elite by war and occupation. Other factors listed by Hayami are the existence of good land records and a disciplined bureaucracy, the active role of the tenant organisations and the negligible number of agricultural labourers in those countries (Hayami, 1991: 170).

The agricultural development that followed land reform was not an outcome of the interaction of market forces. To quote T.H. Lee, who later became the Vice President of Taiwan:

> The price mechanism was not considered as an incentive for adopting new technology and increasing agricultural output. Government allocation of chemical fertilizers, pesticides, irrigation water, funds and subsidy compensated for the price mechanism. Government collection of rice, sugar and other important products in addition to the unfavorable terms of trade resulted in a tremendous net capital outflow from agriculture (quoted in Stein, 1995b: 45).

To quote Amsden: 'In sum, agriculture in Taiwan gave industrial capital a labor force, a surplus, and foreign exchange' (Amsden, 1988: 163). While land reform was followed by net transfer of resources out of agriculture by way of land and/or rice taxes, its negative influence was mitigated by a more equal distribution of resources in the rural areas. Both the state and the landless gained at the cost of the erstwhile landowners, who were compensated with bonds in various enterprises and were encouraged to become industrialists. In fact Fei and Ranis were among the first to point to the role of agricultural surplus in setting off the process of development in Taiwan and South Korea (Ranis and Fei, 1963). In later years, the adverse terms of trade were corrected and the flow was reversed as the industry took off and more was invested in building rural infrastructure.

As this brief account shows, in East Asia, rather than correcting 'urban bias', removing price control and encouraging agricultural exports, and offering free market prices to agricultural producers in line with NPE prescription, the state policy favoured a significant transfer of rural surplus to urban/industrial activities, by way of taxes and under-pricing of agricultural produce, subsidised urban consumers, and used the state apparatus for activities that could have been undertaken by the private sector, such as distribution of fertiliser. If such a policy did not lead to strong peasant resistance, that was largely because of its success in the ending of landlordism and monopoly, the redistribution of land to the landless, recognition of the rights of the tenants and the drive towards agricultural modernisation.

Labour policy

We have noted that one of the principal objectives of land reform was to modernise agriculture and to ensure a regular and assured supply of food at a cheap price, in order to maintain wages and inflation at low levels. A complementary objective was to control the organised labour movement and unrest and to restrain wages. Struggles of working people for higher wages and/or an equitable share of national income were brought down with a heavy hand. To quote the World Bank study on *The East Asian Miracle*, in almost all the East Asian countries (except Hong Kong), and in the most Southeast Asian countries the 'governments restructured the labor sector to suppress radical activity in an effort to ensure political stability . . . . Labor movements in Indonesia and Thailand, while not subject to systematic restructuring, were nonetheless routinely suppressed at the first sign of radicalism' (World Bank, 1993: 164–65).

Where permitted, the labour unions were mostly controlled by the ruling party or the management, and had no independent voice. In Korea, Taiwan, and Singapore, government-sponsored labour organisations were promoted in order to dominate and control the movement of workers (Agarwal et al., 1996: 3.46–3.48;

Hoggard, 1994: 98). Even now, unions are usually not allowed in the public sector. In the private sector, the tendency is to allow only one union to operate in an enterprise, no 'undesirable' union is permitted, and the union is expected to work in harmony with the management. The unions are not permitted association with opposition political parties, though they tend to maintain close relations with the ruling party. In Japan too, the management was far from friendly to the trade unions, particularly the left-wing variety, but their harshness was partly mitigated by the norm of lifetime employment for a bulk of employees within a paternalistic social-administrative corporate framework (Bagchi, 1987: 44–47).

Labour legislations were non-existent, or weak or were diluted in order to encourage private, including foreign, investment. Formation of industry-wide unions was prohibited, enterprise unions were encouraged, while the government gave bureaucracy and business a strong voice in dispute settlement. The management had the unrestricted right of hiring and firing. In recent years, South Korea has witnessed a surge in trade union militancy despite various restrictions and coercive measures. The number of working days lost, increased from a mere 12,000 in 1982 to a staggering 3,258,000 in 1991. Taking population size into account, this figure is much higher than India's, at 26,428,000 in that year. South Korean experience in recent years is, however, an aberration if one takes the totality of the East Asian experience over a long period (1958–92) into account (Agarwal et al., 1996, Table 3.28: 3A.22).

One major objective behind this ruthless suppression was to keep wages low. However, after this policy of wage repression had succeeded in promoting production and achieving a higher level of GNP, the government took a more relaxed attitude towards wages, helped by the switch-over to more capital-intensive and less labour-intensive industrial strategies (Hoggard, 1994: 96). In the case of Singapore, where the major aim of labour policy was to retain high level of MNC investment in the island and not to allow these to be diverted to neighbouring low-wage countries such as Indonesia, Thailand or Malaysia (Lim, 1995: 223) this switch was packaged under 'wage correction policy' after 1972, by when full employment had been secured and the main thrust was favouring capital-intensive industries (Lim, 1995: 215). In the case of South Korea, during 1969–77, real wage increases kept ahead of labour productivity increases, perhaps to compensate for low wages in the previous period (Gokran, 1995: 25). In Taiwan, the switch came in 1968 when Taiwan became a labour-scarce economy and wages were substantially increased (Stein, 1995b: 46).

Wages, even when allowed to grow, lagged behind labour productivity increases and the share of labour in national income was deliberately brought down to make room for profit, accumulation and investment. In the case of South Korea, the share of labour in manufacturing value added, declined from 36.6 per cent in 1959 to 23 per cent in 1975 (Kwan S. Kim, 1995: 117). Though the share increased in 1978 to 27.10 per cent and in 1980 to 29.30 per cent, it has been declining steadily since then, reaching 26.90 per cent in 1992 (Agarwal et al., 1996, Table 3.27: 3A.21).

A major emphasis in the labour policy of these governments, along with its repressive nature, was on raising labour productivity through training and introducing modern management methods. The quality of labour power had always been a major area of concern, helped by the realisation of nearly universal literacy by the 1970s.

Bank and credit policy

In Japan, as also in South Korea and Taiwan, publicly owned banks were one of the main instruments of state control over industry and other economic activities. Beginning in 1872, when the first state-owned bank was established in Japan, during the course of its development, the financial sector was strictly controlled by the state (Nafziger, 1995: 66). For most of the time in the course of their development, publicly owned banks handled the lion's share of deposits and credits, the privately owned ones making only a marginal contribution. In the case of Taiwan, even in 1980, four non-government banks accounted for only 5 per cent of the deposits (Wade, 1990: 61–62). Even five years after the 1985 decree on nationalisation, 75 per cent of bank loans in Taiwan continued to be state-directed (Brautigam, 1995: 162; Wade, 1990: 161–67). Even today, in almost all the East and Southeast Asian countries, the largest five (sometimes three) banks are state-owned, and account for 50 to 75 per cent of the total bank deposits (Agarwal et al., 1996: 3.24).

Like other sectors of the economy, the banking sector too has been subjected to liberalisation in recent years, particularly since 1980, but despite this, the governments maintain a very high degree of control over the banking sector. In South Korea, the government undertook disinvestment in state-owned banks by selling a majority of shares to the public, but it still retains control through its appointment 'of the bank chairman, various laws and regulations, and the past tradition in banks of unquestioningly following the government's directions' (Agarwal et al., 1996: 3.25). In 1989, Taiwan permitted entry of privately owned banks, including the foreign-owned ones, but fixed the maximum permitted equity holding in order to discourage concentration of private banking power in foreign hands (ibid., 1996: 3.26). In all these countries, banks were required to maintain cash reserve ratios that far exceeded the developed country norms, even exceeding India's in case of some of these countries. For instance, Taiwan's ratio of actual reserves held by banks to total bank deposits, at times as high as 30–37 per cent during 1964–93, was always higher than the corresponding yearly figures for India. South Korea's ratio was higher than India's during 1964–78, and even in 1993 it was as high as 11 per cent, compared to India's 16 per cent and the developed country average of 1.1 per cent (Agarwal et al., 1996, Table 3.20: 3A.14). All these countries (except South Korea) also maintain high liquidity requirements—that a bank will have to invest a certain amount of its total deposits in government or government-approved securities, at a lower-than-market interest rate (of around 10–20 per cent) which is high, though relatively lower than the corresponding Indian figures (Agarwal et al., 1996: 3.27–3.28).

The vast majority of firms in East Asia relied on banks for credit support as the other financial institutions were not so developed. The 'curb' banks or street banks charged a much higher interest rate, and thus access to bank credit was seen by firms as a privilege. Through banks the state mobilised saving and directed lending towards desired areas. The foreign banks were marginalised and were subjected to stringent conditions, such as daily reporting of all transactions to Central Bank, limits to lending and access to local deposits. In all these countries, in recent years, the share of non-bank financial institutions in the total deposits is growing; in the case of South Korea, the latter's share grew from a mere 8.6 per cent in 1972 and 34 per cent in 1980, to 47.6 per cent in 1985, and then exceeded the share of the banks and became 54.2 per cent in 1990 (Gokarn, 1995: 41). While the interest rates of the non-bank financial institutions were lower earlier, in recent years there is a tendency towards convergence (Gokarn, 1995: 42).

Investment was encouraged by undertaking what the World Bank's study of *The East Asian Miracle* described as 'financial repression', that is, by keeping interest rates deliberately lower than the one at which the market would have been cleared. Such financial repression did not affect saving as savings are not responsive to marginal changes in positive real interest rates, but encouraged more demand for credit than would have been the case were only the market to rule. The excess demand for credit allowed the government to ration it through the banking system to desired industries and activities, mainly those with a high return, especially exports. This financial repression, a clear deviation from the neoclassical model, did not inhibit growth in these countries, according to the World Bank study (World Bank, 1993: 17). The fact that the government, in most cases, owned the institutions offering investment funds and gave guaranteed credit or guaranteed the financial viability of a firm in various ways meant that the government was bearing a large proportion of private sector investment risk (ibid., 1993: 18). The state never sat back and watched as an enterprise collapsed, as a neutral referee in a free contest where some would win and some would lose; the East Asian society expected the state to extend its helping hand and to undertake attendant risks.

Even the World Bank admits, in *The East Asian Miracle*, that

> recent assessments of the directed-credit programs in Japan and Korea provide microeconomic evidence that directed-credit program in these economies increased investment, promoted new activities and borrowers, and were directed at firms with high potential for technological spill over. Thus, these performance-based directed-credit mechanisms appear to have improved credit allocation, especially during the early stages of ıapid growth (World Bank, 1993: 20).

Directed credit policy with subsidised interest rates (up to 75 per cent), coupled with export quotas and high prices in domestic market free from foreign competition (Stein, 1995c: 14; Amsden, 1989: 144), had always been a major policy instrument of South

Korea. Even in 1990, 47.5 per cent of the total bank loan was given to the priority sector, a figure much higher than India's at 40.7 per cent. In contrast, Taiwan had scaled down its priority sector lending from 21.4 per cent in 1975 to a mere 1.6 per cent in 1988 (Agarwal et al., 1996, Table 3.22: 3A.16). On the other hand, interest rate subsidies in cases of priority lending, peaking at 36 per cent in 1970 and reduced to 4.5 per cent in 1980, have been eliminated in South Korea since 1982. Taiwan's interest rate subsidies, never as high as South Korea's, and peaking in 1965 at 6.54 per cent, have been scaled down to 1.37 per cent in 1988. In all these countries liberalisation of the financial sector has led to increasing deregulation of interest rates, but except for South Korea, the deregulation has not been completed yet.

Macro-economic management

Efficient macro-economic management by the East Asian countries has been repeatedly cited by the World Bank as a major reason for the economic success of the East Asian countries. Therefore, it is important to examine this issue in depth.

The gross domestic investment, as a ratio of GDP, was low to start with and even by 1960, for all the countries except Japan, it was lower than 20 per cent. But even this low investment was higher than the gross domestic saving rate that was abysmally low; and to bridge the difference, these countries had to rely heavily on foreign aid in the early years of the development process. These figures seriously question the idea that institutions and policies that encouraged saving and investment led to growth. Rather, causation appears to be the other way round; high growth creating a situation where consumption could not catch up with income and left a hefty sum as saving that could be invested. In three decades, the figures have undergone a radical transformation, saving rates passing one-third of the GDP mark.

Further, the saving rate is consistently higher than investment, the surplus going the Western way and helping the economy of the United States to survive with heavy deficits in its book (Table 6.2). Perhaps the role of the state-owned banks and of various state institutions (including provident fund and other forced savings) in encouraging both saving and intervention should not be overlooked. According to the World Bank, the welfare costs of making the consumers save more than they wanted were surpassed by the benefits as 'savings, forced or not, generated high pay offs based on consistently high rates of return to investments' (World Bank, 1993: 16).

A recent study shows that in the East Asian countries, the two major explanations for high saving are (*a*) a high rate of growth of GDP and (*b*) a lower dependency ratio because of successful demographic transition. Interest rates and other financial variables were not found to be determining influences on saving (Agarwal et al., 1996: 3.14–3.17). As for investment, here again a high rate of growth of GDP was a major influence, along with availability of domestic credit (itself a function of domestic saving). More important, from the point of view of our analysis, availability of domestic credit had been more important than FDI, the latter being statistically significant only in Thailand and Malaysia, while it also contributed substantially to capital formation in Singapore. Interest rates, however, had no significant bearing on the investment ratio (Agarwal et al., 1996: 3.17–3.21).

Generally speaking, the East Asian countries have been successful in controlling inflation, which also helped to keep the real interest rates positive and thus, to promote saving (World Bank, 1993: 16). But the picture was not uniform. A notable and persistent failure can be recorded in the case of South Korea; until 1980, and for the entire period from 1961 to 1991, its average inflation rate was 12.2 per cent but that did not come in the way of its high growth rate. Even though the rate of inflation declined after 1979–81, this has not affected growth either way (Gokran, 1995: 24–26). In *The East Asian Miracle*, this high inflation rate is not taken as a sin by the World Bank. Citing Dornbusch and Fisher, it says that 'inflation below 20 per cent . . . can be maintained for long periods without generating macroeconomic instability' (World Bank, 1993: 110), a generous view that is not likely to become fashionable with its mission in India.

Further, the claim by the World Bank that the task of controlling inflation was greatly facilitated by the ability of these governments to keep government expenditure in control, is probably partly true, but even here generalisation is difficult. Comprehensive data on fiscal and budget deficits for all the high performing Asian economies (HPAEs) were not available even to the World Bank, and whatever was given did not reveal much of consistency—

compare the 'public sector' deficit of 1.89 per cent for South Korea with that of 10.80 per cent for Malaysia (World Bank, 1993: 109).

Perhaps Stein is right when he says that 'growth is compatible with a wide variety of inflation rates' (Stein, 1995c: 15). Brazil's growth was at its highest in the 1960s and the 1970s when the rate of inflation was, to say the least, astronomical, exceeding a few hundred per cent a year. As Stein shows, between 1970/72 and 1986/88 Malaysia's per capita GDP grew by half when its M2/GDP ratio trebled, while in the case of Thailand, South Korea and Taiwan, the relevant figures were two-thirds and double; treble and one-quarter; treble and two-and-a-half times, respectively. Further, South Korea, with a tight money policy and an impressive growth rate, failed to contain inflation—while Malaysia, with a high money supply and low interest rate, could (World Bank, 1993; Stein, 1995c: 14–15).

A recent study shows that the governments in East and Southeast Asia scrupulously maintained current account surpluses, which spared the pain of borrowing in order to keep the administration ticking. Most governments have succeeded in increasing, over time, the share of capital expenditure in GDP during 1973–90, but for Malaysia and Thailand during the late 1980s. In all cases, the governments showed willingness to cut expenditure in order to balance their books whenever facing a crisis or emergency situation, e.g., in the case of Indonesia, when world oil prices dropped in 1982, during the recession in Singapore in 1985, or during the high inflation in South Korea in 1980, or during the crisis facing Malaysia following a drop in world prices of primary products in the mid-1980s (Agarwal et al., 1996: 3.6–3.12).

Foreign trade and debt

This region has always received much more than its share of financial flows from the international agencies and the corporate sector. According to one World Bank estimate, in 1993, the net total resource flow (including official development assistance, other official flows and private sector flows) to the developing countries reached an all-time high of $169 billion, a 12 per cent increase, but the major beneficiaries were East Asia, Pacific and Latin America, while Sub-Saharan Africa and South Asia received a small share (Development Committee, 1994: 9). Similarly, most of the gains from expanded trade, following the eighth round of GATT negotiations, among the countries outside Europe and America, is likely to accrue to East Asia because of its highly diversified trade pattern. Foreign trade surpluses have helped these countries to accumulate and maintain stable foreign exchange reserves (Table 6.2).

Generally speaking, East Asian countries avoided borrowing from the World Bank and IMF, the only exception being South Korea during 1980–85, following the second oil crisis. Unlike Taiwan, which recovered from the oil crisis of 1973 without much damage, South Koreans faced a heavy deficit in foreign account (of $5.3 billion in 1980) and a steep rise in prices (29 per cent in 1980) and were, thus, forced to draw on one IMF standby loan and two World Bank SALs in the early 1980s. The two SALs paid for 13 per cent of their external finance needs during 1982–83 (Dailami, 1991: 386, 390, 402). The conditionalities made them deregulate the interest rates, to move away from directed credit allocation and to take up import liberalisation more vigorously (Dailami, 1991: 397–98).

However, they got over the crisis soon, and by 1987, they acquired a healthy surplus in foreign account of $13 billion, outstanding debt was cut significantly, inflation was brought down to a figure of 7 per cent, and the external assistance from the World Bank and IMF was discontinued. While in 1984 the latter's foreign debt was the fourth highest in the world and in 1985 it accounted for 52.5 per cent of GNP and 142.4 per cent of exports, by 1991, thanks to high growth, and particularly high export growth, the corresponding figures came down to 15 and 45.2 per cent respectively (Dailami, 1991: 114).

These countries have been generally more successful than other LDCs in maintaining the stability of exchange rates, by pegging their currencies to the US dollar and by resorting to devaluation whenever higher currency value came in the way of higher exports. The exchange rates of their currencies have maintained flexibility, permitting movements in both directions, thus avoiding appreciation in their values. Further, as the case of South Korea shows, they have been more adaptable to external shocks. Success in this area has also given the governments of these countries a certain measure of independence in formulating economic policies over the past four decades.

Human capital formation: Social and cultural factors

Education

Better education and health levels have been important preconditions for development in East Asia. At the same time, the high growth rate has expanded the capacity of the state to invest in human capital and thus, to improve health and literacy levels. By 1960, Japan was more or less a fully literate society, and the others—except Taiwan with 54 per cent—exceeded 70 per cent literacy figures. By the early 1980s, all these countries became virtually fully literate societies, but for a handful of old illiterates, and by the mid-1970s, all the children of school-going age were in schools.

What is remarkable is not only the current figures but the fact that these societies had taken up education as a high priority area many decades ago and have sustained their effort through many twists and turns in their history. In the case of Japan, ever since the Meiji Restoration of 1868, compulsory schooling of children and universal literacy had been a high priority item on the agenda. This stock of knowledge and skill proved helpful for this country with a very limited supply of mineral resources and with all its factories and towns in ruins at the conclusion of the second world war. In the other East Asian countries also, the literacy level, even before the take-off, was quite respectable by the standards of other backward countries. In Taiwan, even by 1940, almost 60 per cent children were attending primary schools (Wade, 1990: 74) and the literacy rate was 27 per cent (Brautigam, 1995: 149). All these countries spend around 15–20 per cent of the central budget on education, a very high figure indeed. In the case of South Korea, education's share in the budget was raised from 2.5 per cent in 1951 to 22 per cent in 1987 (Hobday, 1995: 54).

While land reform freed ordinary men and women from feudal control, values and attitudes and provided a surplus for industrialisation, the steady and high investment in education led to the formation of a skilled workforce that was capable of absorbing the best of world technology and then producing their own in later years. Today, the performance of East Asian children at the international level, on the basis of internationally standardised tests on cognitive skills, surpasses those of even the pupils of very high income countries (World Bank, 1993: 45); even in countries like USA and UK, the descendants of East Asian migrants consistently do better in schools than their indigenous counterparts. However, while this impressive record in the field of education has undoubtedly helped to step up economic growth, it is no less true that high economic growth has made it possible for these economies to spend more on education and health. As the economy is growing rapidly, even the same percentage figure of expenditure on education implies a much higher input in absolute terms (World Bank, 1993: 193).

No less significant a lesson for the other third world countries is the priority the East Asian countries accorded to primary and secondary education in the government budget, while leaving most of the tertiary education to be covered by private sources. This policy, along with some other factors, helped to make the economy and society more equitable (World Bank, 1993: 200).

Rodrik found, in his econometric exercises, that compulsory schooling and less of inequality in terms of landholdings and income were two powerful explanations for the success of the East Asian experience. In his first regression exercise, the investment ratio and gini-coefficient for land (negatively) emerged as two major and significant explanatory variables, but when, in the second stage, investment ratio was dropped, primary school enrolment became significant. Then, taking investment as a dependent variable, he found primary enrolment in 1960 and the negative of the gini-coefficient for land as the two most significant explanatory variables. He also found, taking population growth as a dependent variable, that it is negatively associated with primary enrolment and per capita GDP in 1960 and positively with the gini-coefficient for land. R-square, measuring the proportion of variation explained by the variables included in the exercise, was, generally speaking, between 0.46 and 0.67 in these exercises (Rodrik, 1994: 20–21). Rodrik concluded that the World Bank downplayed the role of equity and education and low fertility–mortality rates as preconditions for growth in East Asia (Rodrik, 1994: 16).

Health

As for health, the death rate came down to around 7–8 per cent in all the East Asian countries by 1960, except South Korea which, with a 13 per cent figure, took a few more years to even out with the other East Asian countries. The sudden fall in death rate, with a not-so-sharp fall in the birth rate, initially led to a demographic growth rate of around 2–3 per cent, but eventually, the birth rate too came down to reduce the demographic growth to around 1 per cent. The demographic transition that took Europe nearly two centuries, was accomplished in East Asia within three decades (World Bank, 1993: 38). The average life expectancy is pushing towards 80, a very high figure by world standards, while, with a calorie level of around 2,800 per day, the East Asians are, generally speaking, quite healthy. From the mid-1970s, all these countries have brought down their death rate to single digit figures, while infant mortality figures are among the lowest in the world (Table 6.3). Nearly the entire population has access to safe drinking water (Table 6.4).

A more equitable distribution of gains

A major advantage these societies started with, over other less developed counterparts, was that disparities and inequalities were not as oppressive as they had been in countries in Latin America and South Asia. Further, the second world war, Japanese colonial domination, and in the case of Japan, domination by Allied forces immediately after the war with all its devastation, proved to be great levellers. Land reform in the post-war years abolished landlordism, while equal opportunities for education and access to healthcare also contributed to the egalitarian base. So, despite military and authoritarian rules, the healthy rate of economic growth was more shared in these societies than has been usually the case with most LDCs. Thus, contrary to the general experience—as documented and analysed by Simon Kuznets—of increasing inequality as the growth process is started, the East Asians have been remarkably successful in keeping inequality low while growing (World Bank, 1993: 29–32; Table 4).

Cultural aspects: The Chinese connection

Some of the studies on the East Asian experience offer, at least as a part-explanation of their success, explanations based on their cultural traits and value systems. They underline that the vast

Table 6.3
East Asian countries: Demographic indicators

Variable	*Year*	*Japan*	*South Korea*	*Taiwan*	*Hong Kong*	*Singapore*
Population (m)	1980	117.0	36.6	17.1	4.6	5.6
	1994	125.0	44.5		6.1	2.9
Population (average growth)	1970–80	1.1	1.8		2.5	1.5
	1980–90	0.6	1.2		1.2	1.7
	1990–94	0.3	0.9		1.3	2.0
Life expectancy at birth	1980	76	63	72	72	70
	1994	79	71		78	75
Crude birth rate	1960	18	41	39	35	38
	1970	19	30		21	23
	1978	15	21	21	19	17
	1993	10	16		11	16
Crude death rate	1960	8	13	7	7	8
	1970	7	10		5	5
	1978	6	8	5	6	6
	1993	8	6		6	6
Infant mortality rate	1960	31	62	90	42	31
	1970	14	46		19	21
	1978	10	37	47	12	12
	1993	4	11		7	6

Source: Same as Table 6.1.

Table 6.4

East Asian countries: Social indicators

Variable	*Year*	*Japan*	*South Korea*	*Taiwan*	*Hong Kong*	*Singapore*
Adult literacy rate	1960	98	71	54	70	
	1975	99	93	82	90	75
	1990	100	96	–	100	100
Proportion enrolled in primary	1960	103	94	95	87	111
	1970	99	103	–	117	105
	1977	100	111	100	119	110
	1992	102	105	–	108	107
Population having access to safe drinking water (%)	1970		58			100
	1980		75		100	100
	1990	96	93		100	100
Daily calorie supply p/c	1977	2949	2785	2805	2883	3074
	1990	–	–	–	–	–
Central govt expr on education (% of total expenditure)	1980		17.1			14.6
	1993		16.8			22.3
Central govt expr on health (% of total expenditure)	1980		1.2			7
	1993		1			6.1
Central govt expr on defence (% of total expenditure)	1980	–	34.3	–	–	25.2
	1993	–	20.1	–	–	24.5
Percentage share of household income by lowest 20% households	1970s	7.9	5.7	8.7		
	1980s	8.7	7.4	–	5.4	5.1
Percentage share of household income by highest 10% households	1970s	27.2	27.5	24.7		
	1980s	22.4	27.6		31.3	33.5

Source: World Bank, WDR, 1980 and 1993.

p/c: per capita

– : not available

majority of population in all these countries—but for South Korea—are ethnic Chinese, subscribe to Confucian values that favour respect for education, order and self-discipline and are linked through extended families in wide financial networks that cut across international frontiers and extend even to countries such as Indonesia, Thailand and Malaysia with substantial Chinese business communities (Redding and Tam, 1995: 183). There are others who, while not entirely ruling out cultural factors as explanations, question the degree of importance that can be attached to such explanations as opposed to others discussed in this chapter.

A major criticism of this cultural hypothesis is the fact that in the Confucian scheme of things, those engaged in business and mercantile activities are ascribed very low ranks, after the scholar, farmer and artisan (Redding and Tam, 1995: 183). Clearly, such low esteem of mercantile activities in the Confucian value system did not deter the East Asian pursuit for money. Further, the current myth of 'hardworking East Asians' is in striking contrast with the observations made by the Western scholars and writers in the past, ridiculing the East Asians for low work ethics and indolent habits (Kwan S. Kim, 1995: 130–31). Confucian ethics, now seen as a positive element, was supposed to be a factor inhibiting work culture. Hoselitz observed in 1952 that 'the Western apparatus of . . . production remained an . . . indigestible element in Southeast Asia . . . the economic strategy for a vigorous resurgence (was) lacking' (Easterly, 1995: 278). (In this observation, 'Southeast Asia' also included East Asia.)

Chenery and Strout predicted that over the period 1962–76, India and Pakistan would have a higher per capita income than Taiwan or Korea. Rosenstein–Rodan predicted that Sri Lanka would do better than Hong Kong or Singapore. The World Bank Economic Report of 1957 was more optimistic about growth prospects in Burma and the Philippines than in East Asia. A World Bank report of 1967 predicted more than 7 per cent growth rate in cases of seven African countries, all of which actually had a negative growth rate during 1970–88. One can give numerous examples of low opinion and expectations about the East Asian economy in the past. The fact is that the spectacular rise of East Asia was never predicted (Easterly, 1995: 278–79).

Perhaps, more important than the common Confucian values was the relative cultural and ethnic homogeneity of their population that helped communication and dissemination of information on success stories, lowered transaction costs and avoided unnecessary conflicts (Kwan S. Kim, 1995: 131). According to one view, while South Korea was mainly influenced by Japan in its method of functioning and in the role played by the conglomerate structure in the economy, the other three tigers were influenced by the 'Chinese style, characterized by autocratic patriarchal management, fast response to changing market niches and overseas family connections'. The more traditional overseas Chinese businesses rely heavily on personal connections some times called *guanxi*. There are families whose male head may be residing in Hong Kong or Taiwan, one son in the Mainland China, another in the USA. Around 80 per cent of Hong Kong's Chinese have relations in Guangdong and there are about 55 million overseas Chinese in the world of whom 51 million live in neighbouring countries of Asia. The 'GNP' of overseas Asian Chinese is $450 billion, which is 25 per cent more than that of China in 1990. In that year there were 7.2 million people of Chinese origin in Indonesia, 5.8 million in Thailand and 5.2 million in Malaysia, and in each of these countries they constituted a major segment of the business community. In Indonesia, the ethnic Chinese, 4 per cent of the population, control 17 of the 25 largest business groups (Hobday, 1995: 21–23).

In recent years, particularly since China opened its doors to foreign investment in 1978, the economic relationship between the East Asian countries and China has become stronger. In 1992, the total trade of China, through Hong Kong and Taiwan, amounted to $10 billion, and by 1991, Taiwan had invested $3.4 billion in the mainland (Hobday, 1995: 13). As labour costs are rising, there is a tendency in Hong Kong and Taiwan to move their factories into the mainland where workers can be employed at a lower wage. By 1992, three million Chinese in the Guangdong province of China worked in factories located in the mainland but controlled from Hong Kong, while 70,000 workers from the mainland were actually working in Hong Kong itself (Hobday, 1995: 170). Between 1979 and 1990, Hong Kong accounted for 58.5 per cent of cumulative foreign investment in China (Kwok, 1995: 77). In the case of the industrially advanced Guangdong province of South China, Hong Kong accounted for 90 per cent of FDI and for the major share of remittance, though reliable estimates on it are not available (ibid., 1995: 86).

As for Taiwan, China freed imports from this island from tariff in 1980, but because of political opposition in Taiwan, most of the trade had to be routed through Hong Kong and Macao. In the early years, enterprises trading with China maintained a low profile and were engaged mainly in short-term transactions. The reversal of the Taiwanese official policy in 1988 helped to bring about a dramatic increase in the flow of trade in both directions and also a massive Taiwanese investment in building factories—mainly electronics and textiles—in the mainland. While Guangdong is the area of special attention as far as Hong Kong is concerned, Xiamen, a commercial port located in the Fujian province of China, across a narrow strait, plays the same role vis-à-vis Taiwan (Wei and Zhu, 1995: 113–19; Chiu, 1995: 146–49). In 1986–92, Taiwan invested $8.9 billion in China compared to $13.5 billion in the ASEAN countries (Chiu, 1995: 149). Nor was South Korea, another neighbour of China, left behind in this scramble for the Chinese market and cheap skilled manpower; in 1992 South Korean exports to China amounted to $4.49 billion and imports to $3.73 billion (Si Joong Kim, 1995: 199).

The East Asian experience—The World Bank view

The East Asian miracle

There can be no dispute about the wide divergence between the Fund–Bank prescriptions outlined above and our own account of the development experience of the East Asian countries. While under the Fund–Bank format, the state had hardly any role to play in the sphere of economics, in the latter, the state led development. While the former disapproved of controls, public ownership, and directed credit, these played important roles in the East Asian industrialisation process. While the Fund–Bank package allowed for free flow of capital and commodities from outside, the East Asians were choosy about which foreign enterprise was or was not to be allowed in; the entry of foreign companies was not permitted if that was likely to undermine local industries. Those allowed in had to conform to rigid local content requirements.

Despite this clear violation of Fund–Bank norms, the East Asians seem to have done exceedingly well, thus confounding the argument that such distorting activities would have an adverse impact on development. For a long time, these deviations were ignored by the World Bank, and in fact, a misleading image of East Asia was projected as a paragon of free market virtues. The success of East Asia was explained in terms of its compliance with Fund–Bank fundamentals. The East Asian countries, particularly the Japanese, were not happy about it because, in their perception they followed an altogether different path. Eventually, a Japanese-funded research project, resulted in a high profile World Bank publication: *The East Asian Miracle*.

Some frank admissions

This study contains many observations and statements that one would not normally expect in a World Bank publication. It contains a clear admission that in East Asia the state, rather than taking a backseat, has been unhesitatingly and unbashedly interventionist. To quote from the document:

> In most of these economies, in one form or another, the government intervened—systematically and through multiple channels—to foster development, and in some cases the development of specific industries. Policy interventions took many forms: targeting and subsidizing credit to selected industries, keeping deposit rates low and maintaining ceilings on borrowing rates to increase profit and retained earnings, protecting domestic import substitutes, subsidizing declining industries, establishing and financially supporting government banks, making public investments in applied research, establishing firm and industry-specific export targets, developing export marketing institutions, and sharing information widely between public and private sectors. Some industries were promoted, while others were not (World Bank, 1993: 5–6).

This study also agrees that not only was the state interventionist, such intervention in economic matters had not inhibited growth and had, indeed, led to 'higher and more equal growth than otherwise would have occurred' though 'these interventions violate the dictum of establishing for the private sector a level playing field' (World Bank, 1993: 6). Further, in some other parts of the study, it admits that the neo-classical paradigm is too rigid, while the East Asians managed a high level of accumulation, efficient allocation and rapid technological catch-up by a judicious and flexible mix of state-led and market-led policies (ibid., 1993: 10). In another part, the study admits that there are multiple paths to growth, and the ability of these East Asian countries in trying out purposeful but varying mixes of policies and instruments has been a major explanation of their success (ibid., 1993: 87). To those familiar with the Fund–Bank publications and theology, all this would come as a big, perhaps also a pleasant, surprise. To quote Fishlow and Gwin, the study

> represents an important acknowledgement by the World Bank, that industrial policy, involving systematic government intervention in the market over extended periods of time, played a role in the rapid economic growth of the East Asian region. That experience clearly challenges the teachings of neoclassical economic theory and the prevailing policy wisdom advanced by the Bank itself and by its industrial-country member governments, except Japan (Fishlow and Gwin, 1994: 2).

Still, in another part, the study admits that the Adam Smithian 'invisible hand' does not hold even in the industrialised countries, and indeed major European firms cooperate with one another for sharing information and for rectifying other market imperfections. Such market imperfections are an important reason why in most countries equity markets tend to be weak and credit is rationed, not necessarily in favour of the highest bidder who may not be the safest. 'As a result, capital is allocated by a screening and evaluation process that is quite different from the anonymity that characterises resource allocation in an idealized market' (Fishlow and Gwin, 1994: 91). Indivisibilities and externalities of various kinds can also justify intervention in market allocation. However, even when the state is intervening, the social cost of such intervention can be minimised by the state simulating a competitive environment and arranging contests for access to licence, credit and foreign exchange and by imposing export performance for measuring success (ibid., 1994: 93–102).

Success in getting the basics right

However, having made these very important points, which appeared to indicate a reversal of thinking in the World Bank regarding the respective roles of the state and the market, *The East Asian Miracle* adds a massive number of 'if's and 'but's to make that late acknowledgement of the role of the state in economic development somewhat dubious. While state intervention was important, more important, according to the report, were the successes of the East Asian countries with macro-economic management and in 'getting the basics right' (World Bank, 1993: 5).

The basics represented six specific policies: (*a*) maintaining macro-economic stability, (*b*) maintaining an effective and secure financial system, (*c*) limiting price distortions, (*d*) investing highly in human capital, (*e*) opening the economy to foreign technology, and (*f*) promoting agricultural productivity and not taxing it too much (World Bank, 1993: 89). On the other hand, the interventionist policies, according to the report, were of four types: (*a*) export push, (*b*) financial repression, (*c*) directed credit and (*d*) selective promotion. Of these four, the study concludes that (*d*) did not work, (*b*) and (*c*) worked but were risky for other LDCs, while (*a*) was the one that had been the most successful combination of fundamentals and policy interventions (ibid., 1993: 24, 88).

The Bank study is most dismissive about the contribution of (*d*), that is, the policy of selective industrial promotion. It states, rather unconvincingly, that 'We find very little evidence that industrial policies have affected either the sectoral structure of industry or rates of productivity change. Indeed, industrial structures in Japan, Korea and Taiwan, China, have evolved during the past thirty years as we would expect given factor-based comparative advantage and changing factor endowments' (World Bank, 1993: 21).

Not a replicable model: Need efficient and impartial referees

Further, the World Bank study made the point that the East Asian experience was not replicable and the LDCs would be ill-advised to follow that model. To quote the report: 'The prerequisites for success were so rigorous that policymakers seeking to follow similar paths in other developing economies have often met with failure'

(World Bank, 1993: 6). The 'prerequisites' were mainly the development of an institutional mechanism—especially an efficient and impartial bureaucracy—that 'allowed them to establish clear performance criteria for selective intervention and to monitor performance. Intervention has taken place in an unusually disciplined and performance-based manner'. The second prerequisite was to keep the cost of intervention low in terms of subsidies and resulting fiscal deficits, and not to allow price distortions arising from selective intervention to get out of control (ibid., 1993: 7).

In other words, the World Bank is not saying, at least in this study, that state intervention in the economy is bad per se, but that such intervention, to be successful, requires an efficient and disciplined functioning of the regulatory authority. In order to make selective policy work, particularly in making allocations efficient by encouraging contests between firms—for credit or foreign exchange—within such selective framework, strong and impartial referees in the form of high quality civil servants is an essential prerequisite (World Bank, 1993: 11).

Macro-economic stability and human capital formation as major explanations

Coming to macro-economic stability, which (along with prudent financial management and control of inflation) ranks highest among World Bank explanations for high and sustained growth in East Asia, it is clear that these countries managed their financial system well and kept inflation at a relatively low level. But, as we have already pointed out, this is not consistently the case, and South Korea, with quite a high inflation rate, managed a very high growth rate. Nor is the claim—that low levels of government expenditure, and the corresponding low levels of deficit, kept inflation low—substantiated from the data given in *The East Asian Miracle*, as we have already noted above.

As for high saving and investment ratios, these were quite low to start with, but became high as the GDP grew at a fast rate. The line of causation was not what was suggested by the World Bank; it worked the other way round. This is apart from the fact that in promoting saving as well as investment, the state-owned banks played a major role (see above). Further, even if it is accepted for the sake of argument, that maintaining macro-economic stability was the key to East Asian success, one wonders why a government that is so good in this very difficult area would not be equally competent in running industries or formulating industrial policies.

The attribution of a large measure of credit to human capital formation by the World Bank report would not be disputed, but here too the role of the state was decisive. Similarly, success in raising agricultural productivity can be closely related to effective implementation of land reform measures, another plus point for the state. And if the state was open to the introduction of foreign technology, that was largely done by way of government agencies as the MNCs were kept in leash. Thus, while all the six 'basics', pointed out by the report played a certain role in the development process, adherence to such 'basics' went beyond neo-classical paradigm and involved an activist and interventionist state.

Coming to the four interventionist policies listed by the report, it ranks financial repression and directed credit as successful policies, but with the rejoinder that its implementation is risky and conditional on various prerequisites mentioned above. Export push was reckoned as the most successful among the four, but, as we have noted already, the global political context in which this was carried out is not replicable in today's world. The main thrust of the report was to demonstrate that the fourth, state's selective industrial growth strategy, mainly directed towards high-tech capital-intensive industries, did not work, while industries enjoying comparative advantage in terms of factor endowments (that is, those with high labour intensity) came out better.

Selective promotion of industries

To judge whether factor endowments or selective strategy produced better results, the report carried out a test: If factor endowments predominated, as a causal force in structural change, growth in sectoral shares of value added should have been negatively correlated with sectoral wages and value added per worker, whereas the opposite should have been the case if government policies predominated. The report compared the figures from the East Asian countries with Holis Chenery's inter-industrial pattern, and found that two industries stood out: metal, electronics and machinery, and textile and garments. The World Bank took the view that the persistence of the second was an indication that the effort of the government to move into capital-intensive industries had been largely ineffective. The general conclusion of the report was that, in terms of total factor productivity (TFP), there was no substantial difference between promoted and non-promoted industries and it was high TFP growth that led to growth in manufacturing, including non-promoted and labour-intensive industries.

This particular statistical exercise on TFP has been disputed on definitional and methodological grounds. Singh (1994) takes the view that the TFP model 'works with full employment of resources and perfect competition, none of which obtain in the real world'. The greater openness of the economies during the 1980s has not led to an increase in TFP, but actually a universal fall in nine out of 10 world regions according to the World Development Report of 1991; the one where TFP showed an increase was, incredibly, South Asia (Singh, 1994: 10). Wade has pointed out that Chenery cross-country norms used by the exercise included interventionist states like India, and, therefore, these norms do not provide clear and unambiguous criteria for judging the success or otherwise of market-based policies. For some countries, achievement of cross-country norm itself should be taken as a success, since without state intervention that was probably not realisable (Wade, 1994: 58). Further, the 'infant industry argument' in support of protection for indigenous industries involves comparison between countries for the same industry, while the World Bank exercise unfairly compared the performance of promoted and non-promoted industries in the same country.

'More generally, the measurement of TFP depends critically on assumptions about production functions, the choice of output measure (value added versus gross output), the use of capital stock versus flows of capital services, the quality of inputs, cyclical smoothing, the time period studied, and so on. Different assumptions yield radically different results' (Wade, 1994: 60). A study using a non-Cob Douglas Production Function incorporating an assumption of imperfect markets and non-economic returns to scale, finds the coefficient for TFP growth negative (Wade, 1994: 61). Rodrik contends that 'the factor proportion theory has no implication for the correlation between growth rates and factor intensities across industries' (Rodrik, 1994: 30).

Issues regarding how the impact of the industrial policy would be assessed have been raised. The externalities created by such policy may not show up in growth in two-digit sectors, but may be revealed in possible links between textiles and textile machinery, automobiles and machine tools, chemicals and plant engineering and raw materials and chemical processing. Further, the modest financial repression, a policy reckoned as a success by the World Bank, was an integral part of the industrial policy. Again, selective industrial strategy not only decided on allocation but also helped the industries concerned to accumulate (Wade, 1994: 62–63). In any case, the main issue which the World Bank document did not address was whether without selective policies the countries concerned could have succeeded in achieving what they did achieve in the cases of the promoted industries. Lastly, no less important is the institutional context, highlighted among others by Wade and Amsden, within which these interventionist policies were implemented in East Asia. Their intervention was mediated through a complex web of social and administrative relationship with the individual enterprises and industries, and never routinised and uniformly applied.

Others have raised the question whether there was room for generalisation based on the TFP-related study. While in Korea and Taiwan there was not much difference in TFP figures between promoted and non-promoted industries, there was a substantial difference in Japan (Wade, 1994: 60). The comparison of South Korea in 1970 with 1985 has been questioned when in fact the development process began in right earnest only in 1975 (ibid., 1994: 63). Rodrik raises doubts about the use of the David Dollar index of openness by the report in its statistical analysis, because it puts Japan, South Korea and Taiwan a long way behind India in terms of 'openness' (Rodrik, 1994: 36). Rodrik also questioned the use of export performance as the measure of efficiency in a country, in preference to some of the other indicators such as output, employment or net foreign exchange use (Rodrik, 1994: 40). Some have argued that, if a country has performed well in terms of export promotion, according to this report, how can it be faulted on the ground that selective policies forming an important basis of such an export push were wrong? There is clearly some lack of consistency in such an argument.

Since one major target of criticism of *The East Asian Miracle* is the highly promoted HCIs, it is instructive to look at the experience of these industries in South Korea. The criticism focuses on macroeconomic imbalances that resulted from the HCI drive, leading to budget deficits, inflation and a high level of indebtedness in the early 1980s. Such criticism, rather unfairly, does not isolate the role of the oil crisis of the 1970s in putting the macro-economy of South Korea, an oil importing country, out of gear and attributes the blame almost entirely on selective state intervention.

The main objective of the TFP exercise was to show that the government patronage in favour of some selected industries did not work. Industries in which a country enjoyed comparative advantage (i.e., the labour intensive ones in this case) did better than others not enjoying such comparative advantage (e.g., the capital-intensive ones). The traditional labour intensive textile sector, for instance, did better than the government-backed capital-intensive HCI sector in terms of production performance. However, as a recent study shows, the HCI drive was never at the cost of traditional exports which continued to enjoy the incentives given earlier and performed as well as in the past during the period of the HCI drive. But the single biggest contribution of the HCI drive has been to provide a domestic industrial infrastructure of intermediate goods for capital- and knowledge-intensive finished goods such as consumer durables and to *create* a dynamic comparative advantage in these when competing in the world market. While in the short run, the protection given to HCI made domestic production of some exports, depending on imports that were substituted by HCI, more costly than it would have been otherwise, in the long run the exports gained from such domestic infrastructure of capital goods that supplied intermediate goods at internationally competitive prices without protection. It was a question of choice between short- and long-term interests. In the case of *chaebols*, deeply entrenched in textiles and other export oriented industries and then vigorously participating in HCI, the cost of the HCI drive was easily internalised. Eventually, HCI created the basis for phasing out labour-intensive industries such as textiles, and opting for industries on the frontier of technology (Agarwal et al., 1996: 4.8–4.20).

In any case, the report left the main question unanswered: What explains the high growth rate in East Asia? If the growth rate would have been the same even without state intervention then, one wonders, why countries with relatively open economies such as the Philippines, Pakistan and Bangladesh failed to grow. On the other hand, the argument that the Southeast Asian countries enjoyed fast growth without such direct promotion does not hold, because of the 'neighbourhood effect' of East Asia on them (Wade, 1994: 66). As we shall see in the following chapter, there is a clear and direct link between growth in East Asia and the subsequent growth in Southeast Asia.

The authoritarian character of the regimes

The East Asian countries and their development experience have been used frequently to justify NPE, though differently over time. We have noted that in the early days of structural adjustment, East (and Southeast) Asia was projected as a shining example of economic liberalism, of what can be done in a free trade economy with minimal government controls and regulations, in order to contain rent-seeking. Afterwards, when the high level of state intervention in the East Asian economies entered their consciousness, some of the other attributes of East Asian development were highlighted—such as its authoritarian character, its repressive policy towards organised unions and the presence of an insulated bureaucrat–technocrat elite. In place of economic liberalism, East Asia became a show-piece of political authoritarianism that kept rent-seeking in leash.

Leaving aside Japan and Malaysia, which are democratic states with regularly held parliamentary elections, all the other states in East and Southeast Asia are unmistakably authoritarian in character. Japan too was an authoritarian state when it made the transition from backwardness to development, while in Malaysia, politics is based on ethnicity—the majority Malays maintaining their domination over other ethnic groups who constitute nearly half of the population. Hong Kong is still under colonial domination. Singapore, led by Lee Quan Yew and his Peoples' Action Party, had been one of the most ruthless authoritarian regimes brooking no opposition, while South Korea has lived from the beginning through a succession of military juntas. In Indonesia, the regime of General Suharto came to power in 1965 through a bloodbath that killed more than 600,000 communists and Thailand, like South Korea, tends to move from one type of military rule to another. Thus, out of seven countries, four are definitely under authoritarian rule, one is under colonial domination, and only two are countries adhering to parliamentary democratic norms.

Deepak Lal, an ardent advocate of the rule by the market forces, is brutally frank and candid when he calls for 'a courageous, ruthless and perhaps undemocratic government . . . to ride roughshod over special interest groups' (Lal, 1983: 33). Wade puts the same message across, but somewhat mildly, when he states: 'To do selective industrial policy well on the scale done in East Asia probably does require a strong, fairly authoritarian state' (Wade, 1994: 76). Several others appear to concur, taking into account a variety of implications of such a state for the economy. Hoggard takes the view that the authoritarian state, by repressing trade unions, helped to keep the wages and inflation low and labour productivity high (Hoggard, 1994: 84), and thus, helped enterprises with a healthy profit and reinvestment fund.

There are some others who may not be prepared to go the whole way with the NPE, but would apply arguments that would amount to, in the present day LDC context, an argument for a less-than-democratic state for a successful transition from backwardness to industrialisation. To them the Myrdalian concepts of 'hard' and 'soft' states come handy. In the 'hard' states, laws and government directions are meant to be followed, while in the 'soft' ones, despite proliferation of legislations, rules and orders, there is little correspondence between these and the reality at the ground level. In the latter, rules can be bent or violated with impunity by those capable of bribing or having access to those in power, while in the 'hard' states, the cost of violating regulations and controls is high. In the world of today, authoritarian states like Singapore are the real hard ones among the LDCs, while India, with all its parliamentary institutions and regular elections, is universally recognised as a 'soft state'. Some take the view that the very concept of 'soft state' is an indication that the development economists of the 1960s did not entirely believe in the benevolence of the state (Toye, 1991: 113).

How come the East Asian states are 'hard' while the South Asian states and those in Africa are not? Wade attempts to explain the difference in terms of social dislocations, serious military threats and support from the international state system, all of which, according to him, led to concentration of social control in the hands of the state in East Asia (Wade, 1990: 37). There can be no doubt that, compared with the countries of South Asia, Africa or Latin America, these states have demonstrated their capacity to translate into action the policies they espouse. One of the most spectacular aspects has been their ability and willingness to trim and/or, if necessary, to chop off, state support to firms or sectors that fail to live up to the expectations of the state in terms of their export performance. But factors that have led to the emergence of a 'hard state' in East Asia cannot simply be those enumerated by Wade. On the basis of these, many countries in Africa and Latin America should have made the transition from 'soft' to 'hard'.

Mitigating factors

The possible negative political impact of authoritarianism on the masses, in the East Asian context, according to NPE, was mitigated in two ways. First, by maintaining a close relationship with the private sector. Even while playing the role of protector or umpire, as the case might be, they devised rules that helped, even with the state as the leader, to approximate free market conditions. Even while operating within the confines of a controlled economy the state wanted the allocation of goods and resources and their prices to closely resemble what could have emerged from free interaction of market forces. One novel way of getting this done was by way of organising 'contests' among the privately owned companies, and sometimes between state-owned and privately-owned companies, for the allocation of foreign exchange, for quotas of market allocation in a foreign country or even for loans at subsidised interest rates. In this way the state found a way of maintaining a balance between 'securing the confidence of the private sector and capitulating to its demands. This finding is at the heart of the discussion of "contests" and implies that, in wooing the private sector, it is crucial for the government to maintain its autonomy as well' (Hoggard, 1994: 83). This way, Hoggard argues, the 'rent-seeking behaviour' of the bureaucracy was also kept in check (ibid., 1994: 82). 'Deliberation councils' that maintained dialogue between the state and the private sector also played a role in keeping the state policies in line with the private sector interests (Rodrik, 1994: 43).

However, deliberation councils in some form are not unknown in other LDCs. Nor should the organisation of contests convey the impression that the state was always neutral between contesting parties. In numerous instances the state was unabashedly partisan and pushed those it favoured against others with, perhaps, equal or better claim for state support. Nor was the role of the state confined to 'picking the winners'. More than picking the winners, the state in East Asia was more concerned with the task of 'fostering winners' by identifying key industries with future potential for growth and exports for support (Wade, 1994: 70).

Second, this heavy-handed authoritarianism of the state, according to NPE, was made bearable by 'shared growth'. While the large domestic firms, such as *chaebols* in South Korea, prospered, the booming economy made it possible for the state to significantly improve the conditions of life of the common masses too. The universalisation of literacy, land reform, and the widespread opportunities for improving one's knowledge and skill at the expense of the state, gave everyone a chance to better his standing in the society. Despite repression of the working class movement, after an initial period of misery, real wages surged (though still remaining behind GDP and labour productivity increase for most of the time). Subsidisation of housing, done more extensively in Hong Kong and Singapore than in other countries, also helped to eradicate poverty. All these points gave the repressive regimes the 'legitimacy' they were looking for to keep opposition within limits. In some cases such regimes appealed to parochial and ethnic sentiments to gather support for their policies, e.g., the 'sons of the soil' policy in favour of the majority Malay communities in Malaysia (*bhumiputra*) or Indonesia (*pribhumi*), in the allocation of jobs, subsidies and other types of state support, as opposed to the Chinese communities (Hoggard, 1994: 92).

The role of crisis in legitimising repression and pain of adjustment

The role of crisis in creating opportunities for structural reform was more typical of the Southeast Asian countries which were more faithful to Fund–Bank ideology than the East Asian ones. In Indonesia, stabilisation followed the accession to power, after the massacre of 1966 by the Suharto regime, which put the blame for very high inflation and low living standards on the previous Sukarno regime. Later, when in the mid-1970s, money from oil revenue began flowing in, again import substitution was pushed forward by a group of engineers and a large number of state enterprises were brought into being. Subsequent decline in oil prices again created a crisis situation, which brought back the proponents of structural reform to state favour (Hoggard, 1994: 89). In Thailand also, the economic shock of the early 1980s, following a rapid hike in imported oil prices, led to the introduction of stabilisation and structural reform under the Fund–Bank framework, but the enthusiasm for such reform waned in the late 1980s, particularly in relation to the textile industry, only to be reinforced by the military takeover of 1991 (Sahasakul, 1991: 106–9; Hoggard, 1994: 90).

The role of the bureaucrats and technocrats

The success of the East Asian countries is, to a great extent, attributed in the NPE literature to the presence of a far-sighted and competent civil service that was capable of taking balanced and long-term decisions that were not hindered by narrowly focused political interests. They were also lauded for continuing the wise, upright and honest Confucian bureaucratic traditions in the region.

The prominent role attributed to the bureaucrats in East Asian development has been criticised on a number of counts. First, had the presence of an elitist civil service been an important condition for success, the Indian economic story, with a powerful and talented Indian Administrative Service cadre, selected through competitive examinations at an early age, and succeeding the colonial Indian Civil Service with a reputation for competence, would have been an altogether different one.

Nor has the bureaucracy been impartial and only working with standardised impersonal rules in order to avoid rent-seeking. In East Asia, as Rodrik argues, in place of 'simple, uniform rules' many of the state interventions had been specific to firms, complex and non-uniform. Further, bureaucrats, endowed with enormous discretionary power, have often changed rules in favour of their chosen enterprises (Rodrik, 1994: 44). Corruption and bribery are not uncommon in East Asia, though these may not be as widespread as in India (Rodrik, 1994: 43). Only recently, two former South Korean Presidents have been punished by the court for making money for themselves and stories of rampant corruption have led to a virtual collapse of the ruling party of Japan for many years. However, one may argue that in East Asia, corruption, though no less in magnitude and seriousness than in many other countries, is concentrated at the top (Rodrik, 1994: 46). The point to make is that rent-seeking in various forms had been quite extensive even in these East Asian countries despite this presumption about bureaucracy. In fact, authoritarian regimes are likely to be more corrupt as there is no public scrutiny (Hoggard, 1996: 208).

On balance, one might suggest that the association one finds between the authoritarian character of the regime and economic success in the East Asian context is a mere coincidence. As our discussion shows, a whole variety of factors blended to produce this phenomenon, and the form of government was one among many in that multidimensional context. Had this been a determining influence, it remains un- explained why even more authoritarian regimes with a longer history, and with no less strong commitment to free enterprise, failed to develop all over the world. Perhaps, there is some truth in the hard/soft dichotomy; that the state was more committed to getting its own rules and laws implemented, and to use its coercive power as fully as possible to get this done, than had been the experience with many other LDCs.

Conclusions

In this chapter we asked the question whether the East Asian development experience conforms to the norms laid down by SAP of the World Bank. The reply that emerges from our study is that, at least the three major countries, Japan, South Korea and Taiwan, violated all the major adjustment norms, and yet managed to maintain a very high rate of growth. In fact, we argue that such violation was necessary to engineer growth in a highly competitive world dominated by MNCs of rich country origin, and to move out of a static understanding of comparative advantage that consigned these countries to agriculture and textiles.

The State played an active role in the economy, through public ownership in major industries and banks, through policies that provided subsidised credit and otherwise promoted selected industries and activities, through transfer of resources from rural areas, through a deliberate policy of keeping foreign competition out of the way in areas where the domestic industry needed a breathing space for a few years, and through encouragement given to exports.

Whether in relation to trade, industry, finance, fiscal sector or public enterprises, their experience directly contradicts World Bank policy prescriptions in those areas. The fact that these countries now possess an array of items for exports, and compete with rich country MNCs even in their own territories, and to such an extent that the latter are resorting to VERs and other highly protective measures to keep them out, bears testimony to the success of a dynamic understanding of comparative advantage. If they are now liberalising their economies, this is largely because, having attained a certain level of industrial development, they can afford to. It is not liberalisation that has brought growth; it has been the other way round (comments by Mosley in Corbo et al., 1992: 37). Correspondingly, it puts a big question mark on structural adjustment as *the* remedy for all economic ills. No less important is the fact that the governments of these East Asian countries believe that their experience does not conform to the structural adjustment model.

We have not attempted any unilinear explanation of this remarkable phenomenon. A variety of factors combined to make what East Asia is today. Land reform, high investment on education and health, and the relative cultural homogeneity were important, as also their success with macro-economic management. Overshadowing everything else was perhaps the active role of the state, in carefully nursing nascent industries, protecting these from predators, and then letting them fly away to the foreign countries when the time came. No less important, apart from the selective nature of their support—for mainly heavy and chemical industries and those with a good potential to eventually stand on their own without support—was their willingness to withdraw support when the industry concerned failed to fulfil their expectations. Unlike India, import substitution was not a timeless exercise, nor an end in itself, nor was it counterpoised against export promotion. The blessings showered on them by the Western countries in the initial years, for their political support in the cold war, in the form of access to their markets and foreign assistance also helped to bridge the gap between domestic investment and saving at a low cost.

There is a tendency in the World Bank literature to discount the role played by state intervention in East Asian growth. Though the claim of the earlier years that the experience of these countries corresponded with the free market model was later abandoned and the role of the state was recognised, even in *The East Asian*

Miracle, export orientation and 'getting the basics right' were highlighted as the major explanations for success. The impression was conveyed as if what they achieved could have been achieved without the state playing any major role in the economy. Krugman has attempted to explain East Asian growth as being based on 'expansion of inputs, rather than in growth in output per unit of input' (Krugman, 1996: 169). The growth had been achieved, according to him, by the increasing application of the stocks of human and physical capital (e.g., more employment, better skill and education, machines, buildings and roads), and not by way of raising productivity. They had been more successful in mobilising resources than in using those resources efficiently. Therefore, he concludes that, no matter what has been achieved by these countries so far, there is a limit beyond which they can go (Krugman, 1996).

The basis for his assertion is a set of papers by Alwyn Young, which purports to show that the entire growth in East Asian countries (including Japan) can be explained only in terms of inputs, and reveals no productivity growth (Young, 1994). All that one can say on such a paper is that there must be something fundamentally wrong with the concepts they use, or the methodologies they deploy or the statistical exercises they undertake, or all three put together. The poverty of Krugman is immediately exposed when his assertion that 'per capita income in Japan may never overtake that in America' turned out to be wrong even before the ink used for printing his book had dried (Krugman, 1996: 180).

We have already noted in Chapter 2 that we do not subscribe to the contention that bureaucrat–technocrats, influenced by Confucian thinking, were a determining factor. Indian bureaucracy was more reputed and more widely known for its method of recruitment, competence and so on. As for the Confucian influence on work, we have pointed out that the same notions were, until three decades ago, treated with contempt by the West for their negative attitude towards work. However, the fact that the major business component in nearly all the countries of East and Southeast Asia were (and still are) the ethnic Chinese, must have helped to reduce transaction costs and to diffuse new ideas on technology, management and trade possibilities in the vast area from mainland China to Indonesia.

As to the question whether the past East Asian experience can be replicated in the other LDCs in today's world, the answer is not easy. Even if the same policies are applied, these may not work in a vastly different international environment. The Western countries of today are more protective than they had been during the years of East Asian high growth. The global patent regime introduced by the Marakesh agreement of GATT in April 1994, and now strictly monitored by the newly founded WTO, has taken away that option of having virtually free access to intellectual properties originating outside the country. Further, the East Asian growth was synchronised, for at least a good part of the time, with growth in world production and trade (Tan, 1991: 150), while, since the mid-1980s, the growth has been slow, often negative. In addition, through technological innovations and changes in product-mix, the rich countries have by now considerably reduced their dependence on the poor country products, most of the rich country trade now being amongst themselves.

The East Asian experience also repudiates the arguments of the dependency school that integration with global capitalism would hinder development in the peripheral countries. The latter, mainly inspired by the works of Samir Amin and Andre Gundar Frank, attempted to explain every policy in an LDC in terms of the global capitalist system and its interests. Writing in the 1970s, when the world market was not as integrated as it is today, they treated all governments in LDCs as alike, as 'compradors' and as subservient to world capitalism, irrespective of their levels and patterns of development. What the experience of East Asia underlines is that, even the politically and militarily most subservient and economically most integrated regimes are not devoid of nationalist aspirations and the capability to seize the opportunity, when it comes, for indigenous capitalist development (Amsden, 1988: 143).

seven

A global overview: East and Southeast Asia, Sub-Saharan Africa, Latin America and India

Introduction

Having discussed the three main East Asian countries—Japan, Taiwan and South Korea—in Chapter 6, in this chapter we will examine, first, the two of the four tigers left out from our account so far, then, the countries of Southeast Asia, also known as the Southern Tier countries, followed by an examination of Indian, Latin American and Sub-Saharan African experiences.

In this chapter we begin with a look at Hong Kong and Singapore, both listed among the high income economies of the world by the World Development Report of the World Bank. Singapore holds the position of the 14th richest country and Hong Kong the 19th, in terms of GNP per capita. Then follows an examination of four Southeast Asian countries—Thailand, Indonesia, Malaysia and the Philippines—which are listed among the lower middle income economies, and which, like their East Asian counterparts, except for the Philippines, have also been quite consistent with high growth rates over the past two decades. Here, we will also take a close look at the Philippines, the odd country out, which was, once upon a time, reckoned as the one with the best growth potential in the region. Then follows Sub-Saharan Africa (SSA), the region that has the closest and longest association with structural adjustment, and has done the worst, becoming poorer in the process. Then, the three leading Latin American countries—Brazil, Mexico and Chile. While Chile has been recognised as one of the rare success stories with structural adjustment, Brazil is an enigma in the sense that, during 1965–80, it had, despite a very high level of inflation, one of the fastest and most consistent growth rates in the world. Neither Brazil, nor Mexico, the country which declared bankruptcy and plunged international banking into a severe crisis in 1982, and again in 1995, seem to have benefited from adjustment. Finally, we deal with the Indian experience, but rather briefly, largely because this subject merits a separate, comprehensive book.

Singapore and Hong Kong

Hong Kong and Singapore, two tiny island countries in the region, do not belong to the same league as Taiwan or South Korea, not to speak of Japan, except in terms of a very high rate of growth of GNP. The agricultural sector being small and largely irrelevant, the experience of land reform in the latter could not be replicated here. Population is almost entirely urban and the economy and livelihood dependent on industry and tertiary activities (Table 7.1). Further, internal market not being large enough to permit import-substitution on a large scale, foreign trade is the means through which scale economics can be reaped.

Like the other two of the 'four tigers', all protégés of the Western countries, these islands benefited from the two wars in Korea and Vietnam and from the continuation of cold war atmosphere surrounding China. Being small and surrounded by the sea, the main resource of these countries is their strategic location. Hence, the main concern of their rulers has been to strengthen the role of their countries as ports of entry and to specialise on two major economic activities that they could best perform under the circumstances—financial sector and highly import-intensive industrial processing for exports (e.g., electronics, computers, watches and textiles).

Table 7.1

Southeast Asian countries and India: Growth, investment and saving

Variable		*Indonesia*	*Malaysia*	*Thailand*	*The Philippines*	*India*
GNP per capita (US$)	1980	360	1090	490	510	180
	1993	740	3140	2110	850	300
Annual GDP growth rate	1970–80	7.2	7.9	7.1	6	3.4
	1980–93	5.8	6.2	8.2	1.4	5.2
Gross domestic investment	1960	8	14	16	16	17
	1970	16	22	26	21	17
	1978	20	25	27	30	24
	1993	28	33	40	24	24
Gross domestic savings	1960	8	27	14	16	14
	1970	14	27	21	22	16
	1978	22	31	22	24	20
	1993	31	38	36	16	24
Inflation rate	1960–70	–	−0.3	1.9	5.8	7.1
	1970–80	21.5	7.3	9.2	13.3	8.4
	1980–93	8.5	2.2	4.3	13.6	8.7
Proportion of agriculture in GDP	1960	54	37	40	26	50
	1970	45	29	26	30	45
	1978	31	25	27	27	40
	1993	19	–	10	22	31
Proportion of agricultural labour force	1960	75	63	84	61	74
	1978	60	50	77	48	74
	1993	–	–	–	–	–
Proportion of urban population	1960	15	25	13	30	18
	1970	17	34	13	33	20

	1980	20	29	14	36	22
	1993	33	52	19	52	26
Energy consumption p/c (kg in coal equivalent)	1960	129	242	64	147	108
	1978	278	716	327	339	176
Energy consumption p/c in oil equivalent	1971	71	436	178	222	111
	1993	321	1529	678	328	242
Fertiliser consumption in agriculture (100 gm/hectare)	1979	600	944	150	383	329
	1993	1147	1977	544	540	720

Source: World Bank, WDR, 1980 and 1993.
– : not available.
p/c: per capita

In both, saving and investment ratios have been exceedingly high, the former exceeding the latter. In the case of Singapore, the saving ratio reached an almost improbable figure of 51 per cent in 1994, leading to a surplus saving of 19 per cent over investment, while in the case of Hong Kong it was 33 per cent, a respectable figure and exceeding the saving ratio by 2 per cent (Table 7.1). In both, inflation has always been kept in leash, more spectacularly in Singapore. The structural transformation in trade and industry has brought a drastic fall in the share of primary products and textiles since 1970 (Table 7.2). As in the other East Asian countries, increasing real wage is forcing the investors to move away from textiles and other labour intensive industries (Lui and Chiu, 1996: 41). Even then, garments accounted for 19.1 per cent of establishments and 34.4 per cent of workforce in 1991, compared with 3.5 per cent and 10.9 per cent, respectively, for electronics, in case of Hong Kong (ibid., 1996: 45). These island countries have relied considerably on the skill and education of their population. Investment in human capital has, like their other two cousins, therefore, been a high priority area of the government from the very beginning. Further, trading and banking being their principal concern, the state, especially in Hong Kong, has been far less interventionist than in the other three (Mosley et al., 1991: 56).

Singapore

The irrelevance of land reform does not imply irrelevance of agriculture in Singapore. Traditionally, urban agriculture was efficient and accounted for the major share of domestic demand for meat, eggs and vegetables. However, from December 1985, the government abandoned the pursuit of self-reliance in food production, phased out the existing pig farms and opted for high-valued farming such as aquaculture, intensive layer system, pig and cattle embryo transfer research, artificial insemination, and plant biotechnology, all centring round agricultural parks covering only 2,000 hectares of land (Ufkes, 1995).

As for labour, ever since the country's independence, the government policy towards labour has been a repressive one. Labour organisations sponsored by the ruling party and the government were imposed on the working class and were taken as their sole representatives in wage and other negotiations (Hoggard,

Table 7.2
Southeast Asian countries: Foreign trade indicators

Variable		*Indonesia*	*Malaysia*	*Thailand*	*The Philippines*	*India*
Exports ($m)	1978	11643	7413	4085	3425	6614
	1993	33612	47122	36800	11089	21553
Growth in exports	1970–80	6.5	3.3	8.9	7.2	5.9
	1980–93	6.7	12.6	15.5	3.4	7.0
Share of primary commodities in exports	1970	98	93	92	93	48
	1993	47	35	28	24	25
Share of textiles in exports	1970	0	1	8	2	27
	1993	17	6	15	9	30
Imports ($m)	1978	6690	5929	5266	5143	7954
	1993	28086	45657	46058	18757	22761
Gross international reserve ($m)	1970	160	667	911	255	1023
	1993	12474	28183	25439	5934	14675
Total external debt ($m)	1980	20944	–	8297	6611	20582
	1993	89539	–	45819	23335	91781
Debt service as percentage exports	1980	13.9	6.3	18.9	26.6	9.3
	1993	31.8	7.9	18.7	24.9	28.0
Net FDI ($m)	1993	2004	4351	2400	763	273

Source: Same as Table 7.1.

1994: 98). One major motive behind this was to make Singapore attractive to the foreign firms as a place for investment and, in later years, to retain its competitiveness in the face of competition from low-wage neighbours (Hobday, 1995: 140). However, after 1972, by when full employment had been secured and the main thrust of the economic policy was favouring capital intensive industries, the government undertook a policy of 'wage correction' and raised wages. But this wage correction did not necessarily lead to relaxation of restraints on labour movements in Singapore. In fact, the labour movement continued to be tightly controlled by the ruling party, the Peoples' Action Party, through 'company unions' under its leadership. The fact that wages eventually increased in real terms—despite a steady decline of the share of wages in the national income—perhaps, made it easier for the government to continue with the cap (Lim, 1995: 211–14).

The banking sector in Singapore is dominated by two government-owned banks and three privately owned ones, though there are 35 full-licence banks in the island, 22 of which are foreign-owned. The Central Provident Fund (CPF) of government employees plays a major role in mobilising private saving. Set up in 1955 to make people save compulsorily—a sin in the eyes of the World Bank as it involves welfare loss on the part of forced savers—both employers and employees paid 25 per cent each of their salary in CPF until 1986, when these shares were reduced to 16.5 per cent and 23 per cent, respectively. Under the law, CPF is required to hold the majority of its surplus funds in long-term government securities—another sin, frowned upon as 'selective investment' by the World Bank. A part of this fund is used to buy foreign exchange reserve. In 1986, three government-owned or -controlled agencies accounted for 61.6 per cent of savings: CPF (38.9 per cent), Post Office Saving Bank (14 per cent) and Development Bank (8.7 per cent). However, foreign exchange control was liberalised in 1978. Macro-economic management is good in the sense that the rate of inflation is low, there is no foreign debt, the foreign exchange reserve is a healthy one of $30 billion, and the interest to repay internal debt is less than the return from public sector investments (Agarwal, 1995: 85–90).

The state in Singapore has always been active and interventionist. An integral part of Malaysia at the time of independence from British rule in 1957, Singapore experimented for a time with the policy of import substitution. The Economic Development Board, established in 1961, had this as its major objective to start with, and set up a number of public enterprises, and gave special incentive in several areas including housing (Stein, 1995b: 43). However, with the separation of the island from Malaysia, its hinterland, in 1963, the strategy was changed to one in favour of promotion of exports of labour-intensive manufactured goods. The government provided a wide range of fiscal benefits, financial assistance including equity participation and medium/long-term loan with low interest, and, through the state-owned Jurong Town Corporation, built standard and fully serviced factories for sale and rental. While the private sector was promoted, state-owned enterprises—numbering 450 in a small area such as Singapore even in the 1980s—also played a major complementary role and accounted for 25 per cent of GNP. The government owned 75 per cent of land and 80 per cent of the population lived in subsidised government housing in the 1980s (Stein, 1995b: 44). The state was by no means neutral between sectors or companies—state support was targeted to clearly specified areas, mainly in export industries such as petroleum refining, transport equipment and oil rigs and electronic products and components. From 1979, the direction was in favour of capital intensive high-tech industries (Lim, 1995: 206–15).

However, unlike the other two East Asian countries, participation of foreign companies was sought, and FDI grew from Singapore $778 million in 1970, to Singapore $21,490 million in 1989, a 30-fold increase in nominal terms and a 15-fold increase in real terms in less than 20 years (Lim, 1995: 217–18). MNCs prefer Singapore for a variety of reasons, apart from its strategic location: security of their investment, easy repatriation of their profits, absence of labour dispute, efficient bureaucracy, single window for them, investment incentives and low tariff, being among these (Agarwal, 1995: 67–68). Further, this was the time when the demand for electronics was booming in the world and textile and garments exports benefited from large, early MFA quotas despite competition from low cost alternatives in later years (Lim, 1995: 223). In 1992, electronics accounted for 40 per cent of both production and exports, followed by chemicals and chemical products, all controlled mainly by MNCs (Hobday, 1995: 144).

By 1990, 3,000 MNCs were operating in the island, led by Philips, General Electric and NEC and Fujitsu of Japan. In 1991,

250 electronic firms were selling goods worth $31 billion. As wages rose, the government felt the need to move their activities to adjoining areas of the neighbouring countries where wages were low—Johor (Malaysia) and Riau island (Indonesia)—on the basis of an agreement reached in 1990 between these three countries. Batam Industrial Park in Indonesia, at a distance of only 20 kilometres from Singapore, with a land base of 200 hectares and a wage level half as high as in Singapore, has emerged as a major subsidiary growth centre of the island. By 1992, 32 Singaporean corporations had invested in Batam and a government agency had invested $5 billion for infrastructure development in the triangle (Hobday, 1995: 143). Here again, one can find a parallel with the extension of production activities to mainland China in cases of South Korea, Taiwan and Hong Kong.

On the other side, from the point of view of the island economy, the MNCs take away the cream of the skilled workforce by offering high wages and salaries and thus create a wage-salary distortion in the labour market as the government and indigenous private sector try to compete with them by offering similar wages and salaries. Further, they get a preference in the credit market and tend to crowd out the local entrepreneurs. As for technologies, the MNCs tend to import those from their own countries of origin. Local employees are seldom properly trained for fear of poaching by competitors and, in case of Japanese firms, half the management staff tend to be Japanese (Agarwal, 1995: 63–68). The local firms account for only 16 per cent of total manufacturing investment (Hobday, 1995: 145), and, generally, play the role of suppliers to MNCs, owners of some of the former being the former employees of the latter (Lim, 1995: 222).

Hong Kong

In the case of Hong Kong, industrialisation was initiated by Shanghai capitalists who migrated from the mainland after the communist takeover, and specialised in textile machinery. In the 1950s, Hong Kong was known for plastic goods, toys, watches and clocks and low-grade electronics. The last-named, beginning in the late 1950s as transistor radio companies owned by the Japanese, went through several stages, as the local companies produced cassette tape recorders, calculators, electronic watches and clocks in partnership with MNCs, and then, in the 1970s, supplanted the foreign companies.

By the 1980s, Hong Kong was exporting TV games, personal computers and their peripherals, digital telephones and so on. By 1987, electronics was responsible for 22.6 per cent of manufacture and 35.2 per cent of exports, second only to textiles. In 1990, the shares of various items in exports were as follows: watches and clocks (22.4 per cent), components (27.8 per cent), computer parts (16.4 per cent), computer peripherals (6.2 per cent), radio parts (5.5 per cent), telephones (2.1 per cent), videotapes (2.5 per cent), TV (2.7 per cent), other consumer goods (12.3 per cent) (Hobday, 1995: 162–66). Backward linkages from electronics stimulated a variety of supply industries such as plastic casings, metal parts and plating, tools, printed circuit board assembly, metal working, and materials and components (Hobday, 1995: 169).

The island has additionally played the role of mainland China's window to the world. Trade in a massive volume of goods takes place between China and other countries with Hong Kong in the middle. Transactions that were fruitful for both sides but could not be undertaken because of the prevailing cold war atmosphere, were mediated through Hong Kong. We have already noted how Taiwan's trade with the mainland was mediated through Hong Kong for a number of years. Further, migrants, both legal and illegal, continued to come from the mainland, to bridge the deficit in the island between the demand for and supply of labour. With the accession of Hong Kong by China in 1997, such mediation would no longer be necessary, but Hong Kong is likely to continue with the present style of business and the level of state intervention is not likely to increase. The electronic industry has practically moved into the mainland, while maintaining R&D and marketing activities in the island (Lui and Chiu, 1996: 41–43).

About three million Chinese work for Hong Kong factories from their location in the mainland, at Guangdong (Hobday, 1995: 170). Most Hong Kong companies are small, leaving aside a few like Vtech, specialising in TV games or Kong Wah, the holding company of a group of electronic manufacturers, which annually exports goods worth around $2.5 billion (ibid., 1995: 168, 171). These companies mostly work under OEM/ODM arrangements (ibid., 1995: 173).

An additional role enjoyed by both, especially Hong Kong, is the hosting of the regional headquarters of a large number of multinational firms. One of them—Hong Kong and Shanghai Banking Corporation—holds assets that are worth well over twice the country's GNP (Wade, 1990: 331). According to a World Bank estimate, of the total market capitalisation of the emerging equity markets of $133 billion, $58 billion is accounted for by Singapore and Hong Kong. This amount is a quarter of the European figure and 10 per cent of all stock traded outside USA (Development Committee, 1985a: 28).

While among these East Asian countries the level of state intervention is the lowest in Hong Kong, it is by no means unimportant. From the mid-1950s the state has been running a rice control scheme, involving procurement from farmers, maintenance of a buffer stock based on procurement and import, and selling to consumers at a low price. As a corollary of the scheme, rice import is subjected to control. State support to industries is less industry-specific than in the others, but the allocation of government-owned land reveals its bias in favour of some projects. Lending at subsidised interest is not uncommon, while 40 per cent of population live in subsidised government housing projects (Stein, 1995b: 41–42).

The southern tier: The Southeast Asian experience

The three Southeast Asian countries becoming increasingly known for their high and steady growth in recent years—Thailand, Indonesia and Malaysia—are also known as the southern tier. The fourth country of the region—the Philippines—once a flourising area and perhaps the most advanced, and now the 'sick man' of Southeast Asia, with declining growth rate and falling exports—will be examined later (Mosley et al., 1991: 39). Unlike East Asia, all four in the region are rich in natural resources—mainly plantations, forestry and minerals, and with a high ratio of cultivable land to the total landmass.

For the three successful countries, the growth rate was far from remarkable during the 1950s and the 1960s, but the figures approximated the East Asian ones during the 1970s and the 1980s. Over the past two-and-a-half decades, Southeast Asia, once a backward, rural, agricultural area, has been transforming into an urban–industrial society, though the degree of success in that direction varies among the countries..In Thailand, the urban population is already more than half, as also in the Philippines despite its low growth rate. Even Indonesia, with a very large land area spread over 3,000 islands (some of which are not inhabited) and covered with forests, has reached an urbanisation level that is higher than India's. But more important are the other two indices—changes in the proportion of labour force engaged in agriculture and the share of agriculture in GDP. Agriculture now accounts for only 10 per cent of GDP in Malaysia and Thailand and less than 20 per cent in Indonesia (Table 7.1). A negative aspect of this rapid pace of urbanisation, combined with commercialisation and industrialisation, has been a severe decline in the forest wealth of these countries. In the case of Thailand, the intensive commercialisation, accompanying globalisation, has led to a very high rate of deforestation—of 3.3 per cent per year during the 1980s, leading to about 41 per cent decline in forest resources. Malaysia has also suffered a 22 per cent decline in forest area during the 1980s.

In all these countries, the economies are largely market-oriented, but this has not been consistently so in the past three decades. Periods of liberalisation and incentives given to foreign enterprises have been punctuated by heavy import substitution and a high level of government activity. Even now, tariff protection is quite high in some sectors, and policy-makers are divided on these issues. The natural tendency to move the East Asian way is, however, constrained by the solid economic presence of the BWIs. As the share of textiles in production and exports is declining in East Asia, it is increasing correspondingly in the southern tier. In none of these countries unlike East Asia, does land reform rank highly in the agricultural agenda. In all, banks and financial institutions are mainly in private hands, unlike East Asia. However, as in East Asia, the attitude towards an organised labour movement is repressive (Deyo, 1996: 72; World Bank, 1993: 164–65).

The demographic transition in Southeast Asia, unlike East Asia, has not been completed, as the birth rates are still high (Table 7.3). Income inequality is high too, though these societies are moving fast towards universalisation of education (Table 7.4). The success with macro-economic management is uneven. A deeper

Table 7.3
Southeast Asian countries: Demographic indicators

Variable		*Indonesia*	*Malaysia*	*Thailand*	*The Philippines*	*India*
Population (million)	1980	136	13.3	44.5	45.6	643.9
	1993	187.2	19	58.1	65	898.2
Population (average growth)	1970–80	2.3	2.4	2.7	2.5	2.2
	1980–93	1.7	2.5	1.7	2.3	2.0
Life expectancy at birth	1980	47	67	61	60	51
	1990	63	71	69	67	61
Crude birth rate	1960	47	39	46	45	43
	1970	40	36	38	39	39
	1978	37	29	32	35	35
	1993	24	28	19	30	29
Crude death rate	1960	23	9	17	15	21
	1970	18	9	10	10	16
	1978	17	6	8	9	14
	1993	8	5	6	6	8
Infant mortality rate	1960	125			98	
	1970	118	45	73	71	137
	1978	–	31	68	65	–
	1993	56	13	36	42	80

Source: Same as Table 7.1.
–: not available.

Table 7.4

Southeast Asian countries: Social indicators

Variable		*Indonesia*	*Malaysia*	*Thailand*	*The Philippines*	*India*
Adult literacy rate	1960	39	53	68	72	28
	1975	62	60	84	87	36
	1990	77	78	93	90	48
Proportion enrolled in primary	1960	71	96	83	95	61
	1970	80	87	83	108	73
	1977	86	93	83	105	80
	1992	115	93	97	109	102
Population having access to safe drinking water	1970	3	29	17	36	17
	1980	23	63	63	45	42
	1990	34	78	77	81	73
Daily calorie supply p/c	1977	2272	2610	1929	2189	2021
	1990	–	–	–	–	–
Central government expenditure on education (percentage of total expenditure)	1980	8.3	18.3	19.8	13	1.9
	1993	10	20.3	21.1	15.9	2.2
Central government expenditure on health (percentage of total expenditure)	1980	2.5	5.1	4.1	4.5	1.6
	1993	2.7	5.7	8.2	3.0	1.9
Central government expenditure on defence (percentage of total expenditure)	1980	13.5	14.8	21.7	15.7	119.8
	1993	6.2	11.8	17.2	10.6	14.5

Table 7.4 (Continued)

Variable		*Indonesia*	*Malaysia*	*Thailand*	*The Philippines*	*India*
Percentage share of household income by lowest 20 percentage households	1970s	3.3		3.7	4.5	–
	1980s	8.7	4.6	6.1	6.5	8.8
Percentage share of household income by highest 10 percentage households	1970s	39.6		53.9	26.6	
	1980s	27.9	37.9	35.3	32.1	27.1

Source: Same as Table 7.1.
– : not available.
p/c: per capita

look at the state of the economy of these 'southern tier' countries shows that these are anything but clones of East Asia, certainly not in the sense the latter cloned Japan. The East Asians were by and large free from the foreign debt trap; this malaise runs deep into the heart of the Southeast Asian economy, particularly Indonesia and Thailand.

Industrialisation since the early 1970s has taken place mainly under the OEM arrangement discussed in Chapter 6. The initiative for this has come from the large retail chains of Japan, who in turn receive their orders from the West. The demand is passed on to firms in Southeast Asia either directly or through firms from South Korea and Taiwan. The host Southeast Asian countries 'provide only the labour, land, energy, and the right to pollute the environment' (Wade, 1994: 67) and also their names as countries of origin to evade trade restrictions under MFA (ECLAC, 1994: 56; Wade, 1994: 66). In a sense this is not dissimilar to the early experiences of Taiwan and South Korea, but there is yet no indication of a qualitative jump out of the OEM arrangement. Unlike the East Asians, there has been no effort towards developing HCIs and to widen the industrial base.

Malaysia

While Southeast Asia's experience appears somewhat different from that of East Asia, nevertheless, there is some evidence that the countries of the former were greatly influenced by the latter in choosing their industrial strategies, at least initially. In case of Malaysia, as early as in 1981, Dr. Mahathir, the Prime Minister, announced a 'Look East' policy and opted for state support for certain industries and activities such as palm oil processing, wood products, rubber remilling off-states, rubber and plastic products, textile and clothing and electronic and electrical machinery. The support involved tariff and quota protection, tax holidays and investment incentives. The subsidy equivalent of such protections rose from $2.3 billion in 1979 to $4 billion in 1990, accounting for 3.7 per cent of GNP. But, as Edwards complains, there was too much of support and too little discipline and control, unlike Taiwan or Korea (Edwards, 1991: 239–44). Despite this, the heavy industries supported by the state improved their competitiveness over the 1980s (Agarwal et al., 1996: 2.15–2.17).

Many of the restrictions imposed on the economy stemmed from non-economic, ethnic considerations; to push the Malay majority (constituting 60 per cent of the population) ahead of the more dynamic Chinese (30 per cent). However, almost from the time of independence, the government was equally keen to promote exports. A reasonably large land area compared with its small population, rich in agricultural (palm oil, and rubber among others) and mineral resources (including oil), the export sector, dominated by foreign companies, was insulated from the restrictive policies in the rest of the economy, by way of free trade zones, from the late 1960s.

Its macro-economic management is among the best in the region: debts are within limits and the debt-service ratio has been maintained within single-digit figures, inflation is under check (at 3.6 per cent during 1970–92) and interest rates are positive. Its substantial crude oil production has allowed the country to avoid the crisis facing oil importing countries in the 1970s. Banks, mostly in private hands, are required to devote 25 per cent of the credit into directed (most of it again in favour of the *bhumiputras*, that is, ethnic Malays) areas (Agarwal et al., 1996: 3.30). Interest rates, under control from time to time, have been fully liberalised from 1991 (ibid., 1996: 3.33).

Indonesia

With a GDP growth rate of around 7 per cent, Indonesia, a country bracketed with the poorest in the world and holding a rank lower than India or Bangladesh until the early 1970s (Thomas and Stephens, 1994: 6), has not only gone past India by now, but has been promoted to the category of 'lower-middle-income countries' in the World Development Report (Table 7.1). A country with abject poverty only two decades ago, today has only 15 per cent of its population below absolute poverty level (ibid., 1994: 11). Until 1966, the main thrust in its economic policy, as in the East Asian countries, was in favour of self-reliance based on import-substituting industrialisation. After the coup and the bloodbath that killed about half-a-million people and brought a pro-Western military government to power, the economic policy became mainly liberal and pro-market in its orientation. A major step undertaken early under General Suharto, was to pass a law on foreign investment in 1967 which returned those enterprises which were nationalised during the previous regime to their erstwhile foreign owners. The policy of liberalisation was continued until 1971.

Between 1971 and 1981, spurred by the oil bonanza, import substitution made a return. A major objective of this period was to use oil revenue to build non-oil industries that would take care of the economy when oil eventually ran out (Simatupang, 1996: 51). Industries such as cement, synthetic fibre, fertiliser and iron and steel were given heavy protection (ibid., 1996: 62). In 1981–82, oil and gas accounted for 70 per cent of government revenue and 71 per cent of all exports (Mishra, 1995: 103–6). Investment rose from 13 per cent of GDP in 1967 to 22 per cent in 1973–81 (Simatupang, 1996: 54).

The policy changed again in the 1980s, as the world oil prices registered a significant drop: from $35 per barrel in 1981 to $9.86 in August 1986. By 1989–90, the share of oil in revenue and exports had declined to 40 per cent and 39 per cent, respectively. At the same time, inflation returned and macro-economic management came under threat. From the mid-1980s, responding to IMF pressure, import substitution was abandoned again, the Rupiah was devalued twice, the currency was linked to a crawling peg based on a basket of currencies, the capital market was deregulated, interest rate controls, sectoral credit ceilings and subsidised credit were removed, government expenditure was curtailed and foreign investors were allowed up to 95 per cent of equity (Mishra, 1995: 106–18). The tariff ceiling was lowered from 225 per cent to 60 per cent and the number of tariff levels was reduced from 25 to 11 (Simatupang, 1996: 54, 64).

Until 1988, the banking system in Indonesia was exclusively controlled by the state-owned banks, when for the first time the private banks were allowed. In 1992, the state-owned banks were converted into limited liability companies and were allowed to go public (Agarwal et al., 1996: 3.26). For a long time the banks offered highly subsidised discounting facilities, at a fixed nominal rate of interest of 12 per cent, covering about 56 per cent of all loans advanced to the private sector. Even after the banking reform, all domestic banks are required to lend 20 per cent of their portfolio to small firms and cooperatives. In the case of foreign and joint venture banks, the requirement is that at least 50 per cent of the loan would be for export oriented activities (Agarwal et al., 1996: 3.30).

While stabilisation and SAPs have brought inflation and fiscal deficit under control, one actually notices a decline in growth rates during 1980–94, compared with the preceding period of 1970–80. The debt–service ratio is still exceptionally high in Indonesia, at 31.8 per cent, though it has declined from a peak of 38 per cent in 1986, while total external debt amounted to $89.5 billion in 1993, almost as high as the Indian figure (Table 7.1). However, both investment and saving ratios—around 30 per cent—indicate significant increase in the 1980s, but one is never sure how far it is because of these Fund–Bank policies or whether it is because growth has been sustained, with all the twists and turns in policies, for a reasonably long period. At the same time, the country is undergoing a significant structural transformation as the share of agricultural–rural among earners/population has declined considerably. While agriculture accounted for more than half the GDP in 1960, by 1993, its share came down to a mere 19 per cent (Table 7.1). Further, while the share of primary products in exports declined sharply, there was a noticeable growth in the share of textiles (Table 7.2).

The industrial policy in Indonesia oscillates between import substitution and liberalisation mainly along with the vagaries of oil prices. Among the bureaucrats and technocrats there are two identifiable groups—one for self-reliance and import substitution and the other for globalisation and liberalisation. Apart from oil, and some of the industries promoted by oil revenue, we have noted above how the spread of industries in Singapore is spilling over to the neighbouring areas of Indonesia. This industrial property is giving rise to ethnic tension, because the ethnic Chinese, with a mere 3 per cent of the population, account for 70 per cent of all corporate assets. Wealth, particularly the corporate component, is highly concentrated. Two hundred conglomerates, mostly controlled by the Chinese, account for $50 billion worth of assets, that is, 35 per cent of GDP (Simatupang, 1996: 66–67).

Thailand

As in the Indonesian case, in the case of Thailand too, periods of heavy import substitution alternated with periods of open economy. But even during phases of import substitution, as in the East Asian case, export promotion remained another major policy plank. In the late 1970s, the government undertook a drive to promote heavy industries with public fund, including a major petro-chemical complex that would be based on indigenous oil and gas resources. From the 1980s, particularly following the Plaza accord, the inflow of Japanese capital has been a major factor in the industrial scene (Development Committee, 1993a: 91–92; Agarwal et al., 1996: 2.17–2.18).

The first adjustment loan, a two-year standby from IMF, was taken in 1981, coupled with some more funding under Compensatory and Contingency Financing Facility (CCFF) and buffer stock facilities, which was followed by another, bigger, standby (Sahasakul et al., 1991: 79). This was followed by a World Bank loan covering the period 1982–84. The immediate reason for taking these loans was the economic crisis precipitated by the second oil crisis of 1979, which sharply raised the inflation, deficit, debt and debt–service ratio. An additional, no less important reason was the sharp reduction in US military expenditure in the area following the conclusion of the Vietnam war in 1975 (Leeahtam, 1991: 15). The government was required to anticipate the conditionalities and to take some action towards liberalisation before negotiations with the twins could begin. In fact, about half the measures had to be implemented even before adjustment agreements were signed, as a kind of down payment (ibid., 1991: 74).

Despite all these, the twins did not always get everything their way. A great deal of Fund–Bank money was used to finance state enterprises in order to relieve them of pressure to raise service charges, and not for the projects for which funds were earmarked. Some of these projects were ongoing ones and were funded from the normal state budget, but these were also included in the applications to the World Bank and IMF, in order to secure additional resources for the state. Measures to raise petroleum prices, bus fares, and charges for electricity and water supply, were attempted only half-heartedly, as these were going to be unpopular, as also those purporting to reduce protection to domestic production (Sahasakul et al., 1991: 95–106; Leeahtam, 1991: 39–41).

None of these affected the growth in exports. In 1985–87, export growth rate averaged 18 per cent and 15.9 per cent during 1979–87. The share of manufacturing in exports increased from 28 per cent in 1979–81 to 53 per cent in 1987, and that of agriculture showed a corresponding decline from 40.2 per cent to 23.5 per cent. The growth in exports was despite restrictive policies in the West and Japan. Tapioca was put under VER in Europe, frozen seafood and maize faced quantitative restrictions in Japan and sugar in Europe. Canned food exports faced rigorous chemical tests, while industrial goods faced a variety of restrictions. Indonesia, a large market for Thailand, became self-sufficient and reduced buying of food from outside. Textiles were hit by MFA (Leeahtam, 1991: 43–44).

As in Indonesia, the share of textiles, employing 800,000 workers and accounting for 15 per cent of exports in 1992, has grown steadily. This industry is heavily protected, tariff being 30 to 100 per cent on various textiles and garment imports. Now, there is a conscious attempt to shift to high-tech industries, mainly electronics (Sen, 1995: 153). As for the banks, mostly in private hands, 40–45 per cent of the credit is directed, of which 20 per cent is to be spent in the rural sector (Agarwal et al., 1996: 3.30). Interest rate ceilings have been removed in 1990 (ibid., 1996: 3.33).

The growth rate has been on the whole steady, around 7.3 per cent during 1965–80 (Sen, 1995: 134, 142). Both investment and saving ratios increased from 14–16 per cent to 22–27 per cent between the early 1960s and the late 1970s, and then, spectacularly, jumped to 36 per cent in the case of saving and 40 per cent in the case of investment ratios in 1993, while the contribution of agriculture to GDP declined to 10 per cent. Unlike Indonesia, inflation was never a serious problem in Thailand, but it declined further during the 1980s (Table 7.1). Unlike Indonesia, Thailand has succeeded in keeping external debt and debt–service ratios low, while in the inflow of foreign capital direct foreign investment is higher than the speculative capital (Table 7.2).

As in the other two, Japanese MNCs dominate the economy. Unlike labour practices in Japan itself, where employment is usually for life, these enterprises prefer sub-contracting on a piece-rate basis, often to household (mostly female) workers, and casualisation of labour force and do not mind a high labour turnover. At the same time, unlike Singapore's experience with Japanese-owned firms, here they emphasise on labour quality by way of training, encourage multi-skilling of the workforce, job rotation and flexible labour deployment (Deyo, 1996: 73–75).

The Philippines

The Philippines, the sick man of Southeast Asia, is a puzzle. A country with a booming growth rate in the 1950s, the manufacturing output growing at a 12 per cent rate in real terms (Mosley, 1991: 39), its rate of growth was only 2.8 per cent during the 1960s and the 1970s and the slide is continuing (Table 7.1). Where the decline is mystifying is that, of the four, the Philippines has been always the closest to the West, and, in terms of a number of social and economic indicators, the most modern among the southern four. In terms of education and schooling, its record is by far the best (Table 7.4), as also, until the 1980s, in terms of the ratio of gross investment to GDP (Table 7.1), while more than half its population lives in urban areas. On the other hand, the income disparity is also very high, in fact, the highest in Southeast Asia, the top 10 per cent of households accounting for more than half of the aggregate income (Table 7.4).

This country, once a colony of the United States (1898–1946), and of Spain prior to that, where Christians account for more than 84 per cent of the population, has always been culturally and politically aligned with West. The US army, navy and air bases directly or indirectly employ 69,000 people and provide a large market. Overseeing the straits of Malacca and Sunda, through which 90 per cent of Japan's crude import from the Gulf comes, is a major strategic function that this country plays on behalf of the Western interests. Its successive governments, good or bad, have always extolled the virtues of a free market and have never been known for interventionist intentions. While in Indonesia, Thailand or Malaysia, a section of the bureaucrats and ruling elite, from time to time, attempted to push the government policy towards import substitution, such attempts have never been known in the Philippines case. Further, from the early days of structural adjustment, from 1980 in fact, the Philippines has been a regular client of the World Bank and IMF. In fact, between 1970 and 1985, this country received IMF support every year (except in 1982) and the World Bank pumped in a hefty sum of $2.779 billion during 1970–82. One would have expected no difficulty, on the part of this government, in 'owning' SAPs, because their ideas converged with those of the twins (Mosley, 1991: 41–42).

However, the relationship between the twins and the government of the Philippines was far from smooth. Very early in the SAL implementation the government insisted on public investment on 11 heavy industries, and withdrew only four under Bank pressure. In 1984, IMF forced a highly deflationary package down the throat of the government which brought down inflation and balance of payment deficit only at a high cost: GDP fell by 10 per cent, investment from 27 per cent to 16 per cent between 1983 and 1985, and unemployment rose from 7.9 per cent to 11 per cent over the same period. This, in turn, led to a reversal of tariff reform as a 10 per cent import surcharge was imposed (Mosley, 1991: 41–55). However, growth rates in GDP and exports improved after the reimposition of control in 1986 (Mosley et al., 1991: 225). Relationships improved after President Marcos was deposed, but investment remained depressed as also the flow of foreign fund (Mosley, 1991: 54–63). Despite this, a World Bank assessment of the Philippines classified it as a moderately successful country in terms of the implementation of the package (McCleary, 1991: 197).

On the whole, free economy and generous support from the World Bank and IMF have failed to generate in the Philippines the kind of growth that has been witnessed in the other three Southeast Asian countries. In time, both Malaysia and Thailand have left this country behind, while Indonesia, once ranked far below the Philippines in the World Development table, is now only six steps behind and is poised to run past the latter's faltering economy. During 1980–93, Indonesia's GDP grew at 5.8 per cent per annum, and those for Malaysia's and Thailand's at 6.2 per cent and 8.2 per cent, respectively, while the Philippines' grew at 1.4 per cent (World Bank, WDR, 1995: Table 2).

Conclusions on the southern tier

Unlike the 'northern tier' countries discussed in Chapter 6, which have, by and large, avoided the clutches of the World Bank and IMF, all the countries in the southern tier have been clients of the twins for some time or the other and have been more under their influence.

As a consequence, unlike the northern tier, here the state has not played a strong and leading role in economic development. From import substitution, a dynamic concept of comparative advantage and land reform to a spectacular trade offensive in the

West, this familiar picture of the East Asian scene is conspicuous by its absence here. The World Bank is happy that here growth has taken place without state direction and without selective industrial policies, though admitting that their capacity to administer and implement specific interventions may have been less than in Northeast Asia (World Bank, 1993: 7). Further, 'their rapid growth, moreover, has occurred in a very different international economic environment . . . ' (ibid., 1993: 7). Its report on *The East Asian Miracle* also makes a distinction between 'productivity-driven growth' in East Asia and 'investment-driven growth' in the Southeast. The World Bank affirms that, between the two, the 'initial conditions' in the Southeast were similar to those in most LDCs of today, and hence, their experience would be of greater relevance to the latter group of countries (ibid., 1993).

However, to say that these countries succeeded because of their liberal economic polices would be stretching the facts a bit too far. Had this been the case, the Philippines, rather than the other three, should have been in the foreground. Further, as our brief account suggests, these countries, in the course of their history, had seldom been the apostle of market economy. In each of these, there had been periods of state intervention, and liberalisation under the pressure of the twins following an economic crisis. In each, those in power are divided into two sections, one of which would prefer their government to go the East Asian way. Market economy, therefore, cannot be a strong explanation for their high and sustained growth over the past two-and-a-half decades. Perhaps, one should look for other explanations, and, possibly, such explanations would vary from country to country.

In the Indonesian case, as we have noted, oil was a major factor, at a time when the country could manage a high volume of oil exports at high prices, while most other countries in East and Southeast Asia were reeling under the impact of high oil prices. Oil and gas exports together accounted for 34 per cent of total exports in 1991 in Indonesia, while it produced 76 million tons of oil in 1990. Malaysia too benefited from the oil bonanza, though not to the same extent. Oil exports accounted for 15.7 per cent of the total exports in 1991, while it produced nearly 33 million tons of crude oil. Though Thailand too produces a certain amount of crude oil, it met about 10 per cent of the domestic demand in 1990. But its oil imports accounted for only 9.2 per cent of its total imports in 1991, when the comparable figure for India was 27.5 per cent. The Philippines produces a very modest amount of oil and most of the oil it needs is imported. Even in 1991, its oil imports accounted for 14.9 per cent of imports. Oil, thus, explains very clearly the difference between the Philippines and the other three countries in the region. While Thailand is also a net oil importer, its dependence of oil imports is not that high, and there were other compensating factors such as high Japanese investment (Encyclopedia Britannica, 1994: 630, 662, 692, 728).

The pressure put by the United States and other Western countries, for access in the Japanese market, later reinforced by the Plaza and Louvre accords, of 1985 and 1986, respectively, played a role in the diversion of Japanese investment towards Southeast Asia. Under these accords and the pressures by the G7 countries for access in the Japanese market, the value of yen was revised—from 260 yens per dollar to 140–50 yens per dollar—which forced a part of the Japanese capital to look for new pastures. This made Southeast Asia in general and Thailand in particular, 'a production base for Japan, receiving raw materials and equipment and then producing finished goods for export to Japan and other countries' (Development Committee, 1993a: 91–92).

Another factor was quota restrictions in the US and European markets on exports from East Asia, by way of MFA and a variety of VERs and other non-tariff barriers, discussed above. To avoid such restrictions, the East Asian capital, technology and management moved to the South, undertook production under OEM arrangement in these territories with the local labour force and then exported their products to the Western markets as products of these territories, and, hence, were not so rigorously subjected to trade restrictions in the West.

A third compulsion was to avoid higher wages in the East Asian labour markets and to make use of cheap but efficient labour in the southern tier countries. Whether one sees in it a manifestation of the 'flying geese model', discussed above, or of the neighbourhood effect, as described by some scholars, the fact is that the capital, technology and production of the northern tier spread to the southern tier, and became an important factor in the growth of its economies.

Another explanation, apart from the southern tier's proximity to East Asia, is cultural. As discussed in Chapter 6, the network of ethnic Chinese residents of these three countries, the dominant business component in their population, despite their low proportion in the population, played an important part in bringing East Asian capital to Southeast Asia (Wade, 1994: 65–68). This also explains why the growth did not spread to the Philippines where the Chinese constitute, in terms of their proportions in the population, in business or in politics, a negligible factor. Had the main thrust of development come from the United States, on the East Asian scale in terms of capital and technology, perhaps the Philippines would have been the chosen location. The Japanese, the South Koreans, as also the ethnic Chinese in Singapore, Hong Kong and Taiwan, had other priorities, and found it easier to do business with the people they knew and understood.

In this sense, the Southeast Asian development is a projection of the East Asian development. However, unlike East Asia, here the companies under foreign tutelage have failed to make the transition from OEM to ODM and then to production under their own brand name. One major reason being that, while in East Asia, from the early 1970s an effort was made to establish an industrial infrastructure, such effort is conspicuous by its absence in the southern tier. The foreign enterprises work as 'enclaves' in isolation from the rest of the economy, with few forward and backward linkages, and with labour power as the only local resource in demand. The domestic industries and firms seem to play a passive and subservient role to foreign MNCs and very little of technology transfer seems to have taken place in favour of the domestic companies. The possibilities of technology transfer are limited, as the foreign firms, fearful of poaching or industrial espionage, do not trust local personnel with sophisticated technologies.

While the East Asians, by insisting on up to 90 per cent 'local content', helped the growth of local industries, in Southeast Asia, local content requirements are low or non-existent. In case of a Japanese firm in Malaysia, though the local content requirement is 30 per cent, that too is produced by a subsidiary of a foreign firm (Wade, 1994: 67). There is no indication of any aggressive initiative to move on to the dynamic route of comparative advantage and to grow out of textiles, by sponsoring HCIs. Whereas East Asians have already carved out for themselves a chunk of global trade territory, the southern tier is still a long way from that comfortable position.

Given this pattern of industrialisation, once described by Wade as 'technologyless industrialisation', without a strong infrastructure base and linkages with the local economy, and with heavy dependence on foreign firms for nearly all the major operations, it is questionable whether the growth achieved so far is sustainable (Wade, 1994: 67–68). In fact, keeping this industrialisation and high growth would become a stupendous task, if, for a variety of reasons, the foreign firms withdraw and move to another territory. Nor would these economies survive any curtailment of the United States market by way of 'adjustment' to rectify its balance of trade deficit.

Generally speaking, the macro-economic management of the Southeast Asian countries has not been as good as that of their East Asian counterparts. Indonesia and Thailand have been burdened with heavy external debt, an alarmingly high debt–service ratio and high inflation, while the debt burden, compared with its very small population, appears to be very high also in the case of Malaysia. In 1993, their external debt amounted to $90 billion, $46 billion and (for a population of 25 million only) $23 billion respectively, all very high figures. The debt–service ratio of Indonesia, as a percentage of exports, is exceedingly high at 31.8 per cent, though the figures for others, at 18.7 per cent and 7.9 per cent, respectively, are within tolerable limits.

Sub-Saharan Africa

A vast area with diverse ecological conditions, from the semi-desert Sahel area and long grass savanna to dense tropical forests and coastal areas, Sub-Saharan Africa has always been one of the poorest regions of the world. Despite a favourable land–man ratio, agriculture is backward and the new agrarian technologies associated with high-yielding seed varieties have not reached this part of the globe (Killick, 1992b: 37). The colonial rulers introduced a variety of commercial crops, and arranged for their export to 'mother' countries through commodity boards, at fluctuating prices controlled by the colonial masters. MNCs always had a strong presence, mainly in the production and export of commercial crops and minerals.

While GDP growth declined from 6.4 per cent during 1970–74 to 2.5 per cent during 1975–79 and then to 1.3 per cent in 1980–84, foreign private capital dried up, leading to a widening current account deficit, from 2.8 per cent of GDP in 1970–74 to 6.3 per cent by 1980–84. The proportion of external debt to GDP increased from 27.4 per cent in 1980 to 92.1 per cent during 1985–91 (Muzulu, 1993: 11).

Many of the Fund–Bank conditionalities did not take into account local conditions. The winding up of marketing boards led to a decline in the quality of export crops like cocoa and coffee and to decline in foreign exchange earnings (Muzulu, 1993: 32). In most cases the choice is not between the private and public sector, but between the domestic public sector and foreign private companies, or between a weak private sector and a bureaucratic public sector. Local capitalists are too small and inexperienced to run those enterprises that are under public ownership (Berg, 1995: 92).

On balance, financial and research outflow exceeded inflow, and these poor countries became poorer under structural adjustment. Their external account was now more in balance, thanks to a severe deflationary policy, as imports were reduced to the level of meagre exports, but GDP growth rate dropped and became negative in due course. Devaluation tended to be deflationary rather than expenditure-switching, as, given low price elasticities, the import bill mounted and export earnings suffered a decline. Out of the 28 SSA countries examined, only 10 showed increases in the share of exports in GDP, and in the case of 12 it declined, while it remained unchanged in the other six (Muzulu, 1993: 59–60). Devaluation and import liberalisation has hit textile production in Zambia and vehicle production in Nigeria (ibid., 1993: 67).

It is questionable whether export-led development can work with all the primary producers in the region. 'If all the poor countries that produce beverages or fibres or oilseeds were to expand output, the argument goes, resulting falls in prices might mean lower export earnings rather than higher' (Berg, 1995: 91). Between 1980 and 1990, the prices of coffee and cocoa dropped by 70 per cent, and the real price of cotton by 28 per cent (World Bank, 1994a: 77). Between 1970 and 1985, SSA's share of world exports declined from 2.4 per cent to 1.7 per cent (World Bank, 1989: 19).

The crisis of the late 1970s hit not only the traditionally poor countries but even some of the better-off ones—such as Ivory Coast, Senegal and Ghana. The oil crisis in 1973 was a major factor, but there were other reasons too. One reason was that during most of the 1970s these countries got good prices for their principal export crop, and then were enticed by the international private banks to get even more money than they needed. Lacking democratic institutions with checks and balances, their autocratic West-supported rulers wasted the money in various ways (Killick, 1992b: 34–36). Towards the end of the decade they faced a number of calamities at the same time; the banks refused to lend more and wanted their money back, the export prices collapsed, and the interest rates on loans went up. Facing imminent collapse, these countries landed on IMF's lap, and later the World Bank also entered the scene with SALs. A part of their loans was waived and another part was rescheduled under the London and Paris Clubs; and these, plus the loans from the BWIs guaranteed that these countries never defaulted on their loans to private international banks.

Attempts to reduce fiscal deficit by curtailing public investment reduced overall investment, as private investment was not forthcoming, which in turn negatively influenced GDP growth. Between the second half of the 1970s and the early 1980s, investment ratio declined from 21 per cent to 17 per cent, and showed only a marginal improvement in the later years. In fact SSA's investment ratio was as high as South Asia's until 1980, but the difference was in the return to investment, largely because of declining productivity. Saving was low, only around 8 per cent of GDP, as the economy was not growing and poverty was mounting (World Bank, 1994a: 154–56). As a Bank document admitted: 'It is a sorry state of affairs when we know least about poverty in the region where poverty is most a problem.' But it still had no problem in concluding that adjustment-led growth had 'probably' helped the poor (ibid., 1994a: 164–65).

As the accounts given by the BWIs show, the pace of implementation of structural adjustment and stabilisation was uneven. A food riot here (e.g., Zambia, 1987) and an attempted coup there (Madagascar, 1991) were enough to unnerve the governments of these countries, to go back on conditionalities and even to scrap adjustment agreements (Foroutan, 1993: 31). Sometimes, the BWIs themselves, exasperated by the unwillingness of the host governments to carry out reform, would cancel the agreement and then wait for a more friendly government to take over the reins of the government before resuming adjustment. A major reason for the high mortality of adjustment programmes was their neglect of 'human issues', and the attempt to harshly push through the package irrespective of local sensitivity and conditions these countries were in. Lack of political stability was another, but that was in a sense exacerbated by the adjustment programme and the accompanying economic misery.

The irony of the BWI programmes was that they drew out more resources from these poor economies at a time when a more generous funding would probably have been more helpful. Or some measures that strengthened their terms of trade or stemmed the decline in real commodity prices in global trade, and, thereby, improved export earnings (Killick, 1992b: 17). In a regression analysis, carried out in an unpublished study by El Farhan, using data for 32 (out of 45) SSA countries, growth of export earning, also for import growth when it substitutes the former, emerged as the two strongest variables influencing GDP growth, while debt–servicing entered with a negative sign. Curiously, terms of trade showed no significance, though, predictably, investment ratio gave a high positive sign and the population growth had a negative one. Political instability was negatively correlated, for each of the three periods into which the overall time period was divided, but its significance disappeared when the three periods were lumped into one (Killick, 1992b: 12–17).

There is no way of knowing how the mountain of debt would ever be repaid. SSA's total debt increased from $6 billion in 1970 to $134 billion in 1988. By that period, total debt was equal to the aggregate GDP of that region, and three-and-a-half times more than annual export earnings. Debt-service obligations amounted to 47 per cent, as a percentage of export earnings (World Bank, 1989: 20–21). By 1989, 45 SSA countries together owed $147 billion. Twenty-two of them were severely indebted low-income countries and accounted for $102 billion of this amount. Excluding Nigeria, which alone was responsible for one-third of such a loan, the remaining loan of $68 billion was divided as follows: $30 billion to foreign governments, $22 billion to multilateral institutions, $7 billion to private creditors on medium- and long-term credit and $9 billion in part to private creditors in payment for short-term loans and in part in arrears. The rescheduling involved cancellation of only $4 billion out of $102 billion, though one UN report recommended liquidation of the entire loan burden (Lancaster, 1991:

22–24). As the Brundtland Commission observed, such debt burden has adverse environmental implications: 'Debt that can not be amortized forces the African countries dependent on raw materials to deplete their fragile soils, with the result that good land is turned into desert' (quoted in World Bank, 1994a: 174). A World Bank report on Africa mentioned the following quote from a report of the Conservation International: 'A heavy external debt burden clearly contributes to the economic and exploitative pressures placed upon a country's natural resource base' (World Bank, 1994a: 174).

A number of scholars, e.g., Killick and Bates, attribute to the political system and process a major explanation for this failure. What is described as 'crony capitalism', based on patronage and plunder, has led to squandering of state resources at the cost of growth and welfare of the citizenry. Petty tribalism on the one hand, and a coalition of businessmen, bureaucrats and rich farmers on the other, have dominated state politics and have not permitted broader issues of growth and development to be examined and analysed (Killick, 1992b: 34–36). Zaire under Mobutu, Uganda under Idi Amin, Nigeria and Ghana under various military rulers, are examples of such a political system at work, but these regimes were tolerated and strongly supported because of their anti-communist and anti-liberal stand, and rebellions against them were squashed with armed support, by the very same Western countries who are now moaning about their political system.

A World Bank report, while noting that the rate of growth in SSA had declined to 2.4 per cent in 1987–92, claimed that those among SSA countries which had implemented adjustment on a consistent basis showed 4 per cent growth, that is, a net 0.9 per cent growth in per capita terms. The main causes for slow recovery were domestic policies, institutional deficiencies and external environment (Development Committee, 1993b: 16–17).

However, the UN Economic Commission for Africa (ECA) had always been opposed to the adjustment programme (ECA, 1996: 243–55). In a report, written in 1989, ECA concluded: 'There is mounting evidence that stabilization and structural adjustment programs are rending the fabric of the African society. Worse still, their most severe impact is on the vulnerable groups in the society—children, women and the aged—who constitute two-thirds of the population' (ECA, 1996: 253).

As one African observer put it:

> If there was a referendum in Africa today an overwhelming majority of the people would vote against their governments having anything to do with the Bretton Woods Institutions . . . . They know too well that there has definitely been a considerable net welfare loss to them as a result of the way these two agencies have been operating in their countries during the past decade and a half . . . that far from helping it to become economically viable, these two institutions have been capitalising on, exacerbating and perpetuating Africa's crisis. Little wonder that there have been many IMF riots throughout Africa and that youth, workers and women have rebelled against structural adjustment programmes (SAP), the parade horses of the Bretton Woods Institutions (Adedaji, 1993: 2).

The 1990 Arusha Declaration on Popular Participation, following an ECA-led conference, sought radical political reform, decentralisation, fairer distribution of wealth, mass literacy, and creation of jobs as top priorities in Africa. It also called for regional and subregional cooperation, and emphasised on sovereignty. It expressed concern 'about an increasing tendency to impose conditions of a political nature by those who provide economic assistance to Africa' and deplored the heavy political and social cost of structural adjustment programmes. The declaration also reaffirmed the need to uphold human rights, the rules of law and high standards of probity and accountability in African societies (Yansane, 1996: 24–25). The Lagos Plan of Action of 1980 by OAU, sought to create an African Common Market by 2000, and worked out a two-stage plan for achieving this. However, the target of an agricultural investment of $22 billion between 1980 and 1985 was not met because the international prices of agricultural goods collapsed.

The objective of collective self-reliance, particularly in terms of food security, failed too. The United Nations Programme of Action for African Economic Recovery and Development, 1986–1990 recited the following list of internal constraints—low capacity for domestic resource mobilisation, excessive dependence on import of consumer goods and production inputs, high population growth and shortage of skilled labour. Political instability and drought were also mentioned as two other major causes. In this programme, the countries committed themselves to popular participation, reduced population growth, better domestic economic management, and a greater concern on gender-related issues. However, the goals set by the document were not realised (Yansane, 1996: 16–18).

The World Bank's *Adjustment in Africa*, published in 1994, repeated the standard Bank cliches, without seeking to understand why its programme failed. After noting that SSA's agricultural growth declined from 2 per cent a year during 1965–80 to 0.6 per cent a year during 1981–85, all that it observed was that it was time that Africa began to adjust (World Bank, 1994a: 19). In another part the report moaned that SSA countries had not diversified their exports, but again did not consider whether the Fund–Bank conditionalities had something to do with it (ibid., 1994a: 18). Poverty was explained by 'poor policies', and more specifically by overvalued exchange rate, heavy government spending, inward looking trade policy, political instability and so on. Terms of trade appeared somewhat late in the list, but then 30 per cent decline in the terms of trade of non-oil exports and 50 per cent in mineral exports were noted (ibid., 1994a: 26). In its evaluation, the Bank document concluded that of the 26 adjusting SSA countries, 15 had made advances but conditions in the other 11 had deteriorated (ibid., 1994a: 57). In its analysis 'success' was defined as conformity with Bank conditionalities, and the report was particularly unhappy with the progress achieved with the public sector.

Another Bank report, compiled by Foroutan, and based on 10 case studies, is more analytical. It blamed the priority given to political over economic logic as the main explanation for the poor outcome. The politicians were only interested in power; moving in an adhoc manner from one policy to another in order to stave off the crisis: e.g., import control to fend off foreign exchange crisis and price control to dampen inflation. They swallowed conditionalities under pressure, but the implementation was half-hearted, and 'in none of the countries did trade policies turn around during a period of relative stability and prosperity simply out of a change in economic philosophy' (Foroutan, 1993: 8–9). This was despite SAL and SECAL provisions of $6.4 billion between 1980 and 1991. The report concluded by saying: 'What the analysis did show was that the process of trade liberalisation in SSA is going to remain slow and the achievement fragile for quite some time in future' (Foroutan, 1993: 38).

Ivory Coast

Ivory Coast is an interesting example of the way things have worked in this region since the 1970s. Once regarded as a miracle in terms of economic growth, its economy is now in ruins. Its economic boom in the 1970s helped its classification as a 'middle income country' and, in terms of per capita GDP, it was ranked the second highest in SSA, while its growth rate was as high as 8 per cent. At that time it did everything right as per the World Bank norms. Its economy was as open as it could possibly be, the movements of labour and capital were unrestricted, 10 per cent of GDP was spent on education, and foreign investment was invited in a big way. There was some import substitution in 1973, but nothing compared with those in most other countries.

One major reason for its high growth turned out to be the cause of the downfall of the economy in later years. During 1975–77, world prices of two of its major export crops rocketed to very high levels: the price of coffee increased 3.6 times and of cocoa, three times. This high export income was treated as a windfall and was lavishly spent by the francophone and patrimonial regime of President Houphouet–Boigny. When the prices declined during 1979–80 by 30 per cent, there was nothing to fall back upon. In 1981 a recovery of world prices helped the economy to return to the 1975 level, but no lesson was learnt from the previous debacle and the money disappeared quickly. As a consequence, the country was put under a rigorous adjustment programme in 1981. However, there was little progress until 1983, though the conditionalities were small and weak, in view of the known pro-market stance of the government. At one stage IMF refused to release the last tranche of ESAF, as the country was facing drought and further deterioration in its terms of trade. The second SAP (1984–86) was somewhat more successful, as fiscal deficit was reduced from 11.7 per cent of GDP in 1983 to 2.4 per cent in 1986, while the Paris Club helped reschedule a part of the debt. Despite this, real per capita GDP declined by more than 20 per cent between 1981 and 1988.

However, whatever gain was recorded in this period was negated by developments in the following period. The trade liberalisation programme was scrapped and payment of interest to foreign debtors was discontinued in 1987. Fiscal deficit increased from 2.9 per cent in 1986 to 12.6 per cent in 1990. The current account deficit reached 10.5 per cent of GDP in 1990. This was followed by severe unrest. A new agreement with BWIs was made towards the end of 1989 (Azam and Morrisson, 1994: 26–69). As one observer concluded: 'After 12 years of adjustment effort and an investment of $1380 million by the World Bank in structural adjustment lending alone, Côte d'Ivoire's process of economic decline does not show many signs of reversal and her trade regime remains as distorted as ever' (Foroutan, 1993: 24).

Kenya

In this country, again an open economy with a pro-West government, with a significant nomadic population, not-so-fertile land, and a rich animal life, the first IMF standby in 1979 was cancelled in 1980 because of the failure of the government to meet conditionalities. Drought and worsening terms of trade led to an SAL and another standby from IMF in 1980, but the IMF programme was suspended because of government borrowing from the central bank to finance salary increase, food import and defence. Following two devaluations, an IMF tranche was released in 1982, with tougher conditions, including reduction of fiscal deficit from 10.6 per cent to 7.5 per cent. Another IMF standby loan was given in 1985, and the Managing Director of IMF praised Kenya 'for its effective and successful stabilization policies', but things did not go well with the Bank's adjustment loans, as negotiations for the third SAL broke down, not to be resumed until 1988. Huge repayments were made to IMF during 1986–87 though no fresh credit was given. A mini-boom in coffee prices led to relaxation of fiscal and monetary discipline, and the consequent worsening of the balance of payment position. In this way, both Bank and Fund programmes were pursued, off and on, the GDP growth rate remained at around 2.4 per cent, indicating a fall in per capita level, until external support ceased in 1991 (Levin, 1994: 3–7).

A joint IDA/IMF team (February/March 1993) found the progress unsatisfactory, following which the Shilling was floated, foreign exchange retention accounts were reintroduced and the private market in coffee and tea became more important. But the tighter monetary policy was not acted upon, and following further disagreement, the relationship with the IMF/Bank turned worse, retention accounts were abolished, the floating exchange rate was abandoned, and foreign exchange had to be sold to the central bank. Again another IMF/IDA mission went to Kenya in April 1993, as 'the government was again down on its knees' and agreed to conditionalities. Per capita GDP declined from 1.5 per cent in 1988 to −2.9 per cent in 1992. The annual average rate of growth in manufacturing declined from 6 per cent in the late 1980s to only 1.2 per cent in 1992, while gross capital formation declined from −0.9 per cent in 1989 and 3.5 per cent in 1990 to −2.9 per cent and −9.3 per cent in 1991 and 1992, respectively. Again, a new PFP has been formulated for 1994–96. The saga goes on, as Kenya struggles with the lowest level of living ever (Levin, 1994: 9–15, 30).

Ghana

Though Ghana is projected as a success story, such success is relative, that is, in comparison with some social and economic indicators for the 1970s. As we shall see below, that too is not fully true. Going further back in history, comparing the present with the period under Nkrumah, when Ghana was classified as a middle-income country, would undoubtedly give an unfavourable picture of the present under structural adjustment (Leechor, 1991: 527). As one World Bank document pointed out: 'Ghana, despite the success of its adjustment policy until recently, is still poor and its per capita income is falling' (Development Committee, 1993b: 3). If success is measured in terms of compliance with IMF–World Bank guidelines, Ghana is indeed a success story.

After an initial period of political uncertainty following the overthrowing of Nkrumah in 1966, the reins of the government fell in the hands of a military dictator, J.J. Rawlings, in 1981, who had no political base, but who managed to develop a good rapport with the BWIs and the West. In 1982, IMF moved in, to be followed by the World Bank. In the following years, Ghana's 'success' with structural adjustment was attributed to its leader, someone who stood above rent-seeking groups.

A major success was with public sector reform, one of the few in SSA, as a large number of ghost workers—15,000—were retrenched while another 12,000 were pensioned off or sacked. Regulations and controls were withdrawn, as also subsidies in a large area. Another success was with the system of auctioning of foreign exchange from 1987, following periodic devaluation, that eliminated rent-seeking. The state gold mining corporation was given to an international mining consortium for management. Thirty state-owned organisations were put up for sale, or liquidated. But institutional reform, e.g., in banking, proved to be more difficult. The cocoa marketing board could not be dismantled, despite Bank urging, because of the fear that that the quality of service would fall with privatisation. Fertiliser use declined as subsidy was reduced (Toye, 1991).

However, a comparison of Ghana's performance during 1980–91 with 1970–80, does not reveal any success story. Real GDP growth has been wiped out by population growth at 3.1 per cent population growth. The rate of growth of GNP per capita during 1980–91 has been a negative one at −0.3 per cent. The growth rate has declined from around 6 per cent during the mid-1980s to around 2.7 per cent per year towards the end of the 1980s, despite good weather and flow of foreign money. Extraction of minerals has probably gone beyond what is justified by a long-term environmentalist view. Manufacture has declined, as also food and livestock production, while the contribution of the service sector has increased from 37 per cent of GDP to 42.5 per cent. The heavy emphasis on cocoa production—70 per cent increase between 1983 and 1988—might create difficulties in future years as its world prices are dropping, apart from the fact that the gain from cocoa is far from diffused; the top 7 per cent of cocoa cultivators own half of the land cultivating cocoa (Hammond and McGowan, 1994: 79). Inflation has soared from an annual rate of 35.2 per cent during the 1970s to 40 per cent during 1980–91, despite IMF conditionality, though this is an improvement over the 122 per cent rate in 1983. Though gross domestic investment ratio showed an improvement, from 14 per cent in 1970 to 16 per cent in 1991, made possible by foreign borrowing, the gross domestic saving ratio declined from 13 to 8 per cent over this period. Similarly, imports exceeded exports by $0.5 billion a year. As a consequence, the total external debt increased from $1.4 billion in 1980 to $4.2 billion in 1991, and the debt–service ratio deteriorated from 13.1 per cent of export earnings in 1980 to 26.9 per cent in 1991 (World Bank, WDR: 1993).

The Latin American experience: Chile, Brazil and Mexico

Here we are dealing with the experiences of three Latin American countries, each of which adds something to our understanding of the adjustment process initiated by the BWIs. While Chile is a low-middle-income country, both Brazil and Mexico are upper-middle-income countries. In the case of Chile, adjustment worked better than anywhere else in the continent, while Mexico, despite massive BWI support, has faced two major crises in 1982 and 1995. Brazil, an enigma for more than one reason, has subjected itself to an adjustment process since 1980, unguided by the BWIs.

Chile

The only consistent success story in Latin America, as far as structural adjustment is concerned, Chile's success is largely in comparison with the failures during the first post-Allende period of 1974–82, when the economy operated under the advice rendered by the so-called Chicago boys, the experts educated by the Chicago academia. A comparison with the earlier periods, including the one under President Allende, variable by variable, does not reveal any clear superiority of the current figures.

The major thrust of the post-Allende militarist government, during the 1974–82 period, was towards privatisation, mainly to undo the measures taken by the Allende regime to boost the public sector. But the privatisation led to a concentration of assets in industrial and financial conglomerates with a weak capital base, many of which later collapsed. Financial liberalisation, another policy component, led to risky lending; credit was channelled to unprofitable but affiliated firms on the implicit insurance that the government would bail them out in case of trouble. Production in agriculture and industry declined; and the government's expectation, based on a faith in automatic adjustment—as taught by the Chicago boys, that everything would be sorted out by the free play of market forces—did not materialise (Moran, 1991: 468–71). When commercial lending from private international banks stopped after the Mexican crisis of 1982, the economy collapsed, GDP registered a 14 per cent fall, and, in 1983, unemployment reached a figure of 28 per cent. The country suffered a terms of trade decline of 20 per cent during 1980–82, while the debt–GDP ratio stood at 48 per cent (Moran, 1991: 472–76; Marshall et al., 1983: 314).

In response to the crisis, the government intervened in the banking sector in 1983, guaranteed deposits, subsidised credit to rescheduled peso-denominated private debts and introduced a preferential exchange rate for US dollar denominated debts. Then, in contrast with its earlier policy, boosted public investment programme, which increased by 7 per cent between 1985 and 1989, and which in turn led to a recovery in GDP by 6.3 per cent in 1984, and unemployment declined to 22 per cent (Edwards, 1991: 490). IMF and Bank support came from 1985. Compared with the regime under the 'Chicago Boys', this phase is known as one of 'pragmatic neo-liberalism'. There was also a change in the composition of capital. The new pragmatists were dominated by 'fixed asset internationalists' investing in production rather than the 'liquid asset' variety that was mainly interested in speculative capital flows, and the coalition of interests included the domestic capitalists too (Silva, 1996: 173).

A major issue was the massive external debt, and a great deal of the effort of the government and of the supporting agencies went in finding ways of reducing that burden. Two types of debt conversion were carried out. First, was the system of buy-back of external debts and their conversion into domestic debt certificates that could be sold in the domestic capital market and used in a variety of domestic transactions. The second, the debt–equity swap, available to foreign investors, permitted external debt instrument to be converted into equity investment. Both conversions were carried out at the official exchange rate. The external debt certificates were bought at a discount in the international secondary market but were recognised at near par value in Chile. In this way, $1.2 billion of debt was retired under buy-back, and another $1 billion was covered by the debt-equity swap. Such a swapping arrangement, needless to add, did not imply any new investment, nor did it reduce a country's net liability position with respect to the rest of the world. However, since these excluded interest and dividends on foreign loans, debt ratios were reduced. Though the swap increased the flow of funds mainly for re-privatisation, it was accompanied by a net fall in foreign direct private investment. Postponement of payment of debts of commercial creditors, of

$12.4 billion, falling due in 1988–91, was arranged, and an agreement was reached with creditor governments on non-repayment of principal during 1985–88 (Moran, 1991: 472–76, 478).

Repeated devaluation brought down the value of peso by 90 per cent. The country followed all the Fund–Bank guidelines on export orientation. Despite this Chile was listed by the Bank's World Development Report of 1987 only as 'moderately outward oriented'. 'Since Chile's economic growth record during the period was poor, one suspects that the authors were influenced in their classification by a desire not to spoil the "findings" of a positive relationship between outward orientation and performance', and, therefore, did not include Chile in the more successful group (Agosin, 1981: 5). By 1989–92, exports had become 32.4 per cent of GDP, by far the highest in three decades (ECLAC, 1994: 103).

GDP growth rate began picking up during 1985–87, and by 1989–92 reached a solid figure of 6 per cent per year, comparable with 6.3 per cent in 1978. Investment also increased, to 19.1 per cent, a figure higher than that for other periods excepting 1961–71, at 20.2 per cent (ECLAC, 1994: 103). By 1993, the volume of external debt had become $18 billion, but the debt–service was still high at 33.9 per cent of export earnings (World Bank, WDR, 1993: 279, 285). Even during the mid-1980s, there was apprehension whether Chile would be able to sustain growth as the economy appeared to be vulnerable. But the momentum of growth has been maintained (Moran, 1991: 485; Edwards, 1991: 493).

The burden of adjustment has fallen disproportionately on those at the lower end of the income scale, and has benefited capital against labour. Real wages declined by 13 per cent during 1982–87 and minimum wage declined by 44 per cent in real terms during 1982–87. Wages for domestic employees and construction workers declined by 25 per cent and 33 per cent, respectively, but only by 12 per cent and 13 per cent, respectively, in financial and modern sectors. Financial rehabilitation and reprivatisation favoured US dollar debtors and the wealthy, but mortality and nutrition figures were good, though health infrastructure deteriorated (Moran, 1991: 485; Edwards, 1991: 493).

Brazil

Brazil, the Latin American giant, physically almost as large as US or China, is an enigma, as far as its economy is concerned. Though limping since the 1980s, during the preceding three decades, particularly during 1955–80, Brazil's real growth averaged 8.5 per cent, a very high figure by any criterion, which was achieved by flouting all Bank norms and logic, with an inflation rate of 40 per cent (Dornbusch, 1992: 114; Stevens and Solimano, 1992: 122). Its rate of inflation, considered quite normal when maintained within 50 per cent, sometimes reached astronomical figures exceeding a few hundred percentage points, but still managed to have no negative bearing on economic growth during this period. While the question why things went wrong after 1980 is relevant, no less relevant is how the economy managed to work so well with such a high level of inflation for such a long period.

Another feature, to be noted in the context of this book, was its adoption of self-reliance based on import-substituting industrialisation as its development strategy, despite World Bank opposition, during its period of growth. An upper-middle-income country, with around $3,000 per capita GNP in 1993, with a vast natural resource base, and with a favourable land–man ratio despite a population exceeding 150 million, Brazil was taken as a country that had the required market base and technological proficiency to convert its natural resources into a wide range of industries mainly catering to the domestic market. This high growth was not affected by the policy of import substitution, and many will argue, had benefited from it. The industrial–trade policy was characterised by 'a highly restrictive import policy managed through import licenses and outright bans, which were an essential component of industrial policies, active export promotion including fiscal incentives, various lines of financing and drawbacks on imported inputs and a crawling peg which avoided overvaluation and excessive fluctuations in real exchange rate' (ECLAC, 1994: 104). Import substitution helped with the diversification of exports, unlike African countries. In 1970, Brazil's 10 main exports accounted for 68 per cent, but the figure became 37 per cent in 1991 (ECLAC, 1994: 75).

What made Brazil work despite high inflation was its method of wage–price indexation. As prices moved, the companies added predictable mark-ups to their prices, while the nominal values of wages were raised in a predetermined manner (Bacha, 1983: 334). All these increases were structured, transparent and predictable, and so did not create uncertainties or lead to perverse speculations (Dornbusch, 1992: 114). Along with GDP, industrial growth revealed high figures of 11–16 per cent (Marshall et al., 1983: 312). According to the post-1964 wage policy, once every 12 months on a specific date for a category of industries, a decision was taken on wages at the labour court. The wage hike consisted of three parts. First, it equalled 50 per cent of the cost of living in the previous two years. This was aimed at bringing the real value of wage at the time of readjustment to its average real value during the previous two years. The second part was an additional hike of 50 per cent of the inflation predicted for the coming year. The third part, wage bonus, corresponded to the yearly increase in aggregate labour productivity. These together, in theory, helped to maintain the constancy of wage share in GNP; but, in practice, inflation was underestimated in the prediction, and wages lagged behind prices. By 1973, there was a wage loss over time of 38 per cent in terms of what should have been the wages under the formula. Still, this lag could have been greater without indexation (Bacha, 1983: 324–25).

Though on several occasions Brazil went to IMF during this period of high growth to rectify temporary shortfalls, that was more as a precautionary measure or to improve its credit-worthiness. Of the eight IMF standbys, between 1965 and 1972, Brazil drew on only two (Marshall et al., 1983: 300). Inflation actually declined from 80 to 40 per cent, the country registered a balance of payment surplus in all but one year, and private capital continued to flow in, despite policies of protection and import substitution, as its policies enjoyed credibility (Marshall et al., 1983: 305–8). However, a negative feature was the regressive distribution of income and wealth. Participation in national income of the poorest 50 per cent declined from 18 per cent in 1960 to 12 per cent in 1976; for the next 30 per cent from 28 per cent to 21 per cent; while, of the richest 5 per cent, it increased from 28 per cent to 39 per cent (Marshall et al., 1983: 315).

There has been no clear analysis of the factors that led to a reversal of growth since 1980. Between 1980 and 1991, GNP per capita grew annually by only 0.5 per cent, one of the lowest. One reason could be the late effect of the oil crisis of the 1970s. Though a large producer of oil itself, producing around 30 million tons a year, its oil consumption is double that figure. Another could be the failure to maintain macro-economic balances. Both external debts and balance of trade deficits went out of control. Its $117 billion debt in 1991 was by far the highest among the countries, and the debt–service ratio, at a mindboggling figure of 63.3 per cent in 1980, climbed down to a figure of 30 per cent in 1991. The compulsion to balance the external account has succeeded to a great measure, but at a heavy cost, since 1980. Year after year now, exports far exceed imports, e.g., in 1991, exports accounted for $32 billion while imports for $23 billion, thus producing a surplus of $9 billion. This net resource outflow is also indicated by saving and investment figures. Between 1970 and 1991, gross domestic saving increased sharply from 20 per cent of GDP to 30 per cent, while gross investment declined from 21 per cent to 20 per cent (World Bank, WDR: 1993).

A series of programmes have been undertaken to rectify macro-economic imbalances. For instance, trade reform from 1985, which has produced the results indicated above. Tariff has been reduced to an average of 14 per cent by mid-1993, while export incentives have been eliminated since the mid-1980s. However, despite a tighter macro-economic control, more in line with Fund–Bank guidelines, inflation now is much higher than it was during the period of high growth—another puzzle. The average annual rate of inflation has increased from 38.6 per cent during 1970–80 to a figure nearly 10 times higher, at 327.6 per cent, during 1980–91 (World Bank, WDR, 1993: 239). High inflation seems to coexist with all kinds of growth levels. Demand constraint has not influenced the 'rhythm of inflation' while devaluation seems to fuel inflation by raising the cost of imported inputs (Bacha, 1983: 334).

The Brazilian case illustrates how little we know about the cause–effect relationships that influence macro-economic management. And, therefore, why a monolithic view of global macro-economic norms is misleading.

Mexico

This book cannot be completed without reference to Mexico, a country that shares its border with the United States and is now a part of the trade alliance led by the United States, NAFTA. More important, Mexico featured prominently during the 1982 crisis, when it declared its bankruptcy, and later in 1995, when the BWIs, along with G7, had to put together a massive package to save the country's economy.

One of the largest countries of the continent, with a population of 83 million, Mexico too is classified as an upper-middle-income country, closer to the West than to the South in terms of nearly all development indicators. Though never reaching Brazilian proportions, its inflation rates had always been high. And like the Brazilian case, paradoxically, the adjustment programme since 1982 seems to have catapulted prices to new and alarming heights—from 18.1 per cent during 1970–80 to 66.5 per cent during 1980–91, again without any valid explanation. As Nash concludes: 'Inflation, it appears, adds "noise" to relative price movements, but it does not alter the fundamental pattern of shifts in prices following changes in trade policy . . . . Inflation, therefore, should not be considered an insuperable obstacle to adjustment' (Nash, 1991: 512).

Another similarity with Brazil lies in the adoption of self-reliance based on import substituting industrialisation as the development strategy from the 1960s, again defying BWI opposition. State enterprises proliferated more than in Brazil, and public spending accounted for 45 per cent of GDP in 1982, compared with 21 per cent in 1970 (Nash, 1991: 494). The number of public enterprises increased from 100 to 1,000 during 1970–82 (Nash, 1991: 503).

Reasons for the 1982 crisis are not well-understood. Oil prices were not an explanation for the crisis. Unlike Brazil, Mexico was a net exporter of oil at the time of the crisis. By 1991, however, it had turned into a net importer. The crisis, most probably, had its origin in the late 1970s, in some major lapses in macro-economic management. Though a stabilisation programme of IMF was put into operation in 1976 and 1977, and fiscal and trade deficits and inflation were reduced, things went wrong within 3–4 years, per capita GDP failed to rise and unemployment increased. The very high share of public enterprises in the economy also created some management problems, as public deficit rose to 18 per cent of GDP in 1982. Another reason cited is the nationalisation of commercial banks and the conversion of foreign exchange accounts to peso accounts, in 1982, in order to control foreign exchange outflow, which had the opposite effect of encouraging capital flight. The very high and rising level of inflation, despite IMF intervention from the mid-1970s, perhaps eroded confidence during a critical time (Nash, 1991: 195).

The crisis in August 1982 led to suspension of foreign interest payments, followed by an agreement with IMF for a loan of $3.57 billion, on the assurance that public sector deficit would be reduced from 18 to 3.5 per cent in 1985. This was followed by a sharp reduction in public sector borrowing, imposition of more taxes and higher domestic prices of oil products and public utilities, devaluation in July 1985 by 20 per cent, and so on, but still the economy remained, by and large, protectionist. Inflation, foreign exchange loss of $500m per month, worsening balance of payment position—all these led to suspension of drawing of IMF loans by 1985. The terms of trade declined by 37.6 per cent (3 per cent of GDP) as oil prices declined, but the cost of debt-servicing was reduced by 6.1 per cent of GDP as real interest on external debt declined (Nash, 1991: 494–96).

This was followed by a comprehensive agreement with the World Bank and commercial banks, under which $12 billion of new money was pumped in, $2.3 billion was given as contingency (of which $0.5 billion was used) and $70.5 billion of external debt was rescheduled. However, unlike most other countries, the World Bank was accommodating in terms of conditionalities, and was unwilling to do anything that would have weakened the supporters of adjustment in the government (Nash, 1991: 513). Liberalisation of the trade regime was undertaken in 1986 and 1987, and administrative and fiscal reform in 1988. Public sector spending declined from 10 per cent of GDP to 5 per cent of GDP, but total public spending continued to be at 47 per cent (the 1978–81 average was 34 per cent) because of inflation and higher interests. Under the divestiture programme, of 1,000 public sector companies, 250 were sold, 395 were liquidated, 80 were merged and 30 were transferred to state governments (Nash, 1991: 500–3).

Under structural adjustment, real interest rate was pitched at a very high level, which led to a sharp fall in investment ratio by 8 per cent during 1982–89. Most of the curtailment was in public investment, and there was no compensatory increase in private investment. Particularly in agriculture, public investment dropped from $1.8 billion in 1982 to $0.5 billion in 1987 (Knudsen and Nash, 1991: 140). However, figures improved in later years, and by 1991, investment ratio reached a figure of 23 per cent, compared with 21 per cent in 1970, while the domestic saving ratio registered a slight improvement from 19 to 20 per cent. Unlike Brazil, investment exceeded saving, the difference being made up by foreign inflows, which became responsible for the 1995 crisis (Stevens and Solimano, 1992: 121; World Bank, WDR, 1993).

Unlike Brazil, imports exceeded exports by a wide margin, during the first half of the 1990s, of $9 billion dollars in 1991. The government did not seem to mind as long as private capital was flowing in. In 1991, current account deficit exceeded $13 billion and, as we have already noted, ECLAC warned Mexico and other Latin American countries not to depend too heavily on short-term speculative capital. Mexico did not heed this advice, and eventually this became the undoing of its economy in 1995 (ECLAC, 1994: 196–206).

As in 1982, management of debt became a crucial issue. In 1991, Mexico's external debt amounted to $102 billion, not far from $118 billion owed by Brazil, a much larger country (World Bank, WDR, 1993: 279). As the Mexican experience shows, trade in financial assets is not comparable with that in goods. 'Trade in financial instruments is inherently incomplete or underdeveloped insurance markets, informational costs and other distortions, ex ante and ex post valuation of financial assets may be radically different.' There may even be serious errors in subjective valuation (ECLAC, 1994: 226). To quote ECLAC:

> Latin America's external adjustment in the 1980s illustrates this point very well: much higher interest costs on the foreign debt and deterioration in the terms of trade, coupled with a severe shortage of financing, forced a massive adjustment of domestic expenditure. At the same time, resource rigidities and serious contractions in the supply of imported inputs and investment contributed to unprecedented losses of output from which many countries still have not recovered (ECLAC, 1994: 225).

The Indian experience

Here we are mainly asking the following two questions: (*a*) why, despite following a policy of import-substituting industrialisation under the leadership of an intervening state, during the pre-1991 period, India could not succeed like East Asia, and (*b*) what has been India's experience since adopting structural adjustment in 1991?

As in East Asia, in India, the activist state played a variety of economic roles. The role of the state in providing economic leadership was recognised in the industrial policy resolutions of 1948 and 1956 that, with minor variations, placed the strategic and heavy industries in the public sector, while both public and private sector were to operate side by side in another large slice of the economy (Mookherjee, 1995b: 3–9). Following these, a huge public sector came into being, mainly in capital- and knowledge-intensive industries as also in the financial sector (particularly after 1969), accounting for an investment exceeding Rs 100,000 crores. By the end of the 1980s, public sector accounted for 27.2 per cent of GDP, 9.3 per cent of gross saving and 48.1 per cent of gross investment (Mookherjee, 1995b: 18). Like the East Asian countries, this extensive public sector was private-sector friendly. The majority of public sector enterprises were new undertakings in which—given their vast capital requirements and long gestation periods—the Indian private sector was not interested. Many private sector units on the verge of winding up were also taken over to protect jobs, in nearly all cases at the instance of those companies themselves. The main exception to this being the nationalisation of 14 private banks in 1969 which was undertaken to establish the control and authority of the government over the financial sector.

The private sector was regulated, until 1991, by a system of licensing under the Industries Development and Regulation Act (IDRA) of 1951 and a Monopolies and Restrictive Trade Practices (MRTP) Act that sought to limit concentration. Substantial protection was given to indigenous industries from foreign competition in various forms—such as, up to 250 per cent ad valorem high tariffs, quotas, 40 per cent limit to foreign equity ownership in a company and various import content requirements. This strategy of self-reliance based on import-substituting industrialisation brought near self-sufficiency in a good number of industrial items, including military hardware, refineries and so on. As we have noted already, given its much wider natural resource endowments and the size of its market, like Brazil, India was in a better position than East Asia to seek self-reliance by way of an import-substitution strategy.

The main explanations for the Indian failure are as follows. First, the non-implementation of land reform excepting in three left-dominated states, largely because of the important political role the rural elite played in mobilising votes. Second, a low priority was given to the task of human development, as reflected in the budgetary allocations. While, in 1991, only 4.1 per cent of the central government expenditure went for education and health in India, the comparable figures for Singapore, Hong Kong and South Korea were 24.5 per cent, 19.3 per cent and 17.8 per cent, respectively. Third, non-implementation of land reform and class bias in access to educational and health facilities, made the society more unequal than the East Asian ones. Fourth, while the government went for import substitution in a big way, unlike the East Asians, this was not linked with an effort towards export promotion. While even in 1970 India was exporting more to OECD countries than any of the East Asian countries except Hong Kong, by 1991, India's export was of the order of $9 billion, while that for Hong Kong, Singapore and South Korea was $21 billion, $25 billion and $41 billion, respectively (World Bank, WDR, 1993: 270–71).

These were the major differences between India and East Asia. Some other explanations, given from time to time, do not carry conviction. One is about the role of the bureaucracy, the argument being that the East Asian one, imbued in Confucian work ethics, performed better. In fact, as we have already noted, the Indian Civil Service, with its method of recruitment ('catching them young' and giving them rigorous training in a variety of jobs)and mode of functioning, was recognised as the best among the colonised countries during the period under the British rule. There is no comparative study that shows that during relevant periods the East Asian bureaucracy had made a qualitative jump forward or that their counterparts in India made a qualitative jump backwards to account for such vastly different performances. A second one is that the East Asians performed better in macro-economic management. This argument cannot be a valid one up to mid-1980s. Even in 1985, India's inflation rate and fiscal deficit were low in comparison with the figures for most of the LDCs, external debt was of a manageable dimension, debt–service ratio was low, and the country was self-sufficient in food production. Though India took an IMF loan in 1981, that was mainly because of the oil crisis, and even then many thought that India had gone to the Fund prematurely. The last tranche of that loan, a substantial one, was not utilised. However, the rate of growth of the economy was slow, at around 3.5 per cent of GDP, but that is a different point.

As for cultural factors, we have already examined in the chapter on East Asia how such explanations appear in the form of a post facto analysis. The level of corruption is indeed quite high in India, but countries of East Asia—particularly Japan and South Korea—are not free from this malaise either. There may be some truth in the fact that multiplicity of languages, caste–religious differences and other measures of cultural diversity make communications more difficult and raise transaction costs. One can add that, possibly, non-implementation of land reform has loaded the bureaucracy and other spheres of life in India with feudal values. Lastly, the contrasting outcome from the same policy package is also explained in terms of the differences in the character of the governments—that while the East Asian governments, being authoritarian could impose their will more effectively, India was handicapped by a majoritarian rule. While we have discussed this question already in Chapters 2 and 6, all that we will say here is that had authoritarianism been a major explanation then, Bangladesh and Pakistan in South Asia, should have emerged as developed states.

Growth in the 1980s: Seeds of crisis

Judging by the growth rates of GDP, industrial and agricultural production, independent India had never had it so good as in the 1980s. Not only was the 'Hindu rate of growth' surpassed, it was sustained at 5.5 per cent. Industrial growth averaged 8.5 per cent and agricultural growth, at 3.5 per cent, was quite high. However, certain policy decisions taken during the period—e.g., domestic production of 'white' goods (e.g., fridge, television, video, washing machine and so on), which catered to the needs of the affluent section, with credit from private international banks—contributed both to this high growth and to the eventual crisis in 1990–91.

While earlier, foreign loan mostly came from governments of other countries or multilateral agencies, dependence on private international banks from the mid-1980s was a departure from the traditional practice. The latter, having abandoned their clients in Africa and Latin America since 1980–81, were looking for new clients with a good credit rating. Both they and the World Bank induced India to take their loans, which shot up from Rs 1 billion in the mid-1980s to Rs 26 billion in a matter of five years. By the end of that decade, foreign borrowing had reached a figure of Rs 100 billion, and the debt–service ratio had reached 30 per cent. This new source also made the task of debt management difficult, as, compared to a small number of large loans from Western countries and international institutions like the World Bank, there were now a very large number of smaller loans, which matured at different points of time throughout the year. Though oil prices declined and stabilised at a lower level and the domestic crude oil production increased substantially during the decade, as pointed out by Joshi and Little, no effort was made to adjust the yawning balance of payment gap during these years (Joshi and Little, 1995a: 34). While the macro-economic indicators were, on the whole, healthy in the mid-1980s, these turned adverse and led to the crisis in the second half of that decade.

The crisis of 1990–91

The crisis of 1990–91 was prompted by the following: (*a*) the repayment needs for the 1981 IMF loan, (*b*) the large size of the private bank loan, coupled with rising fiscal deficits, creating uncertainties about loan repayment, bringing down India's hitherto good credit rating and foreclosing opportunities for further loan from such a source, a near repeat of the African experience in the late 1970s, (*c*) the Gulf crisis of 1990, with sudden and massive escalation of oil import cost, disappearance of $2-3 billion of annual remittance from Indian workers in Kuwait, Iraq and other Gulf countries, and the heavy cost of airlifting of Indians residing in Kuwait, and (*d*) heavy speculative outflow of NRI funds held in India—up to $1 billion, within a short time—to East Asia (Joshi and Little, 1995a: 34; Agarwal et al., 1995b: 159–60). The crisis came at the end of a decade when, as we have noted, the average growth rate was 5.5 per cent (Ahluwalia, 1995: 14).

In January 1991, a small IMF loan was drawn from reserve tranche and, therefore, without conditionalities, and fresh borrowings were made from the Bank of England and Japan in exchange for physical delivery of gold by boat. But these failed to improve the balance of payment position. By June 1991, when the new government took over, India's foreign exchange reserve was enough only for two weeks of import. It is a matter of debate whether India could do with a smaller loan and a lower level of IMF conditionalities to stave off the 1991 crisis.

The new political economy of adjustment in the Indian context

The SAP was introduced in July 1991, almost immediately following the formation of a new government under Prime Minister Narasimha Rao. Without losing any time, the government applied for a loan of $2.3 billion from IMF and began fulfilling 'anticipatory conditionalities', including two successive devaluations and withdrawal of export subsidies, to smoothen the passage of the application (Agarwal et al., 1995b: 182). The budget of July 1991 fully reflected the SAP, which came to be known as the New Economic Policy (NEP).

Every political–economic step taken by the government was in accordance with the major prescriptions of the NPE, discussed in Chapter 2, as the following summary will show:

(*a*) That it is better to introduce reform following a change of regime. The new government introduced it almost immediately after coming to power.

(*b*) That the blame for the economic ills of the past should be put on the previous regime. This was done quite successfully and in a politically clever manner, never referring to the IMF loan of 1981, and the taking of large loans from private international banks for meeting elite consumption needs.

(*c*) That the people should be asked to make sacrifices, as the pain of adjustment was an unavoidable price to pay for past malfunctioning.

(*d*) That the pace of reform should be fast enough not to allow the opposition to coalesce. The pace of adjustment was terrific. By July 1991, a new trade policy and a new industrial policy had been announced, and before the year was over the Narasingham panel presented its report on financial reform. The fiscal reform, under the guidance of Raja Cheliah, was spread over two budgets, while clear goals were specified for controlling inflation and fiscal deficit. Above all, the ideology of reform was widely publicised through the print and electronic media, through seminars and conferences, by way of massive and high quality advertisements, and by street-corner hoardings exhorting the people to buy shares. However, some take the opposite view: that the government was in fact moving at a 'gradualist' pace, and was not running on the fast track (Ahluwalia, 1995: 13). There are still others who, while rejecting the 'big bang' approach, would not accept gradualism on the ground that it is not consistent with the 'political economy of reform' (Joshi and Little, 1995b: 63).

(*e*) That the potential gainers from reform should be politically organised against the potential losers. Conforming to NPE, food procurement prices were revised upwards, the agri-food industry entered Indian agriculture with full force to create new production relations and the trading community and stock market brokers were mobilised in support. The campaign against potential losers—such as urban dwellers, workers and bureaucrats—was not actively pursued because of political compulsions. Labour market reform was also not undertaken for the same political reason.

(*f*) That the package should be 'owned' as an indigenous creation. Later, when the obvious similarity between the NEP and the SAP could not be concealed, the government fell back on the 'there is no alternative' (TINA) argument.

(*g*) That technocrat–bureaucrats with experience of working with the World Bank and other international organisations and known for their integrity should be made responsible for directing the reform, and not discredited politicians with axes to grind. In this case, the Finance Minister was picked from outside the arena of politics; both he and the Finance Secretary had had long associations with the World Bank and other international agencies.

(*h*) That the political leadership should be fully, and over a long term, politically committed to reform. In the first three years, NEP was implemented with little political resistance, ignoring the protest of the left-wing parties. The support from the business community was overwhelming, and share market activities took off dramatically.

Implementation: 1991–96

The first round of structural adjustment ran for five years up to 1996, when the Congress party was defeated in the general election. The new coalition government of secular and regional parties with some left-wing participation has pledged to continue 'reform', without specifying clearly what 'reform' constitutes.

Generally speaking, the five-year period under adjustment (1991–96) did worse than a comparable five-year period preceding its introduction in 1991 (1986–91), as the following account will show.

Export, import and trade balance

Exports did very badly to start with, but ended the period of five years with a bang, with growth averaging 20 per cent in the last three years. However, there were few new export items; growth came mainly in exporting engineering, textiles, gems and jewelry, cotton and yarn, and leather products. The expected surge in agricultural exports did not materialise. Despite some increase in rice, oil cakes, soyabean, cashew kernels and shrimp exports, agricultural exports do not give the appearance of a sector that can carry the load of the Indian economy on its back. Though with the Indian share of world trade so abysmally low—around 0.6 per cent compared with around 2.7 per cent at the time of independence—there is some space for increase without doing much; such increase cannot be sustained for long unless exports are diversified. Already there is some evidence of the export growth slowing down.

The cacophony around export growth drowns the figures for imports. Imports fell faster (19.4 per cent) than exports in the first year and then grew faster than exports in the subsequent years: 12.7 per cent, 6.5 per cent, 22.9 per cent and 26.9 per cent, respectively. The sharp curtailment of imports in the first year affected growth and exports, but in subsequent years, higher exports, because of their import intensity, compelled higher levels of imports. While the policy of constraining demand in the first two years helped to bring down the deficit from $9.4 billion in 1990–91 to $2.80 billion, $4.37 billion and $1.29 billion in the first three years, the control seemed to have slipped and the deficit mounted to $4.82 billion and $7.02 billion, respectively, in the last two years. Correspondingly, taking into account the 'invisibles'—

non-factor services, investment income, private transfers and official grants—current account balance declined from $9.68 billion in 1990–91 to $1.18 billion in the first year of reform and to only $0.32 billion in the third year, but then rose in the subsequent two years to end with a figure of $5.09 billion in the last year. The ratio of current account balance to GDP has, however, declined.

Foreign exchange reserve, direct foreign investment and foreign debt

India's foreign exchange reserve rose from around $1 billion at the beginning of NEP to nearly $21 billion in 1994–95 and then declined to $17 billion in October 1995, for reasons to be discussed in the following paragraphs. This increase did not come by way of trade surplus, but was largely a sum total of various types of foreign borrowing; from IMF, World Bank and other international agencies and foreign governments, from NRI deposits and unstable foreign portfolio investments. Only a small part was due to increase in FDI, $6 billion in seven years, during 1990–97, and a certain amount was due to the time-bound amnesty declared by the government to holders of black money, which, passing through several hands in the infamous hawala market, returned to India as foreign exchange. Despite its present volume, it is unstable and unreliable.

Total accumulated debt burden was of $99 billion in early 1996, and $92 billion in early 1997, making India the fourth largest borrower after Brazil, Mexico and China. The debt–service ratio, at 26 per cent, is much higher than China's 9 per cent.

Despite increasing convertibility of the Indian currency—first giving foreign exchange earners import entitlements, then allowing conversion of foreign exchange earnings partly in official and partly in market exchange rate, then making trade accounts (but not capital accounts) convertible—the exchange rate remained remarkably stable for a long time, at around Rs 31 per US dollar. In October 1995, the value of the rupee began falling, partly by design to compensate for domestic inflation and partly because the process went out of control. The exchange rate was eventually stabilised at around Rs 34 per US dollar, but at the cost of $3 billion of foreign exchange reserves needed to buy the Indian Rupee in the foreign market. The foreign exchange reserve stood at $17 billion at the end of the fifth year of reform.

Macro-economic management

GDP growth rate, after an initial setback—when it declined from 4.7 in 1990–91, to 1.1 per cent in 1991–92—recovered to 5.1 per cent and 5.0 per cent in the following two years. The following two years suggest better figures of 6.3 per cent and 7 per cent, respectively. Overall, the growth rate of GDP in five years is slightly less than the figure for the 1980s (Government of India, 1990–91 to 1996–97).

Gross domestic investment as a ratio of GDP steadily declined from 27.7 per cent in 1990–91 to 23.4 per cent and 24.0 per cent in the first two years, but then rose to 23.6 per cent, 26 per cent and 27.4 per cent, in the following three years. Earlier, the worry was that curtailment of public investment was also affecting private investment (Joshi and Little, 1995a: 39). Similarly, gross domestic saving as a ratio of GDP declined from 24.3 per cent in 1990–91 to 22.8 per cent and 22.1 per cent in the first two years, and then jumped to 23.1 per cent, 24.9 per cent and 25.6 per cent in the remaining three years. This very positive turnaround does not accord with the experience of structural adjustment elsewhere and needs to be analysed, though these investment-saving figures are still far away from the East Asian ones. Even now public saving is sluggish, while household and corporate savings are doing well (Joshi and Little, 1995a: 40).

As for the fiscal deficit, during the first two years it declined, from 8.3 per cent in 1990–91 to 5.7 per cent, in two years in 1992–93, but then rose to 7.4 per cent in the following year. The declared objective of pushing it down to 4.7 per cent in 1993–94 was not fulfilled, as fiscal deficit rose to 7.5 per cent and stabilised around 6 per cent (6.1 per cent and 5.8 per cent) in the following two years. The sixth year, however, indicated improvement as fiscal deficit declined to 5 per cent. Similarly, as with the fiscal deficit, inflation was brought down during the first two years: the Consumer Price Index (CPI) declined from 13.6 per cent in 1990–91 and 13.9 per cent in 1991–92 to 6.1 per cent in 1992–93. But in the following three years, prices went up again and the index hovered around the 9 per cent level, just below the double-digit figure.

During the first two years, a tight control over money supply and government expenditure helped to bring down fiscal deficit and inflation and to reduce trade deficit, but at the cost of growth and a drastic reduction in both export and import. Attempts in subsequent years to boost growth, by lowering the bank rate and offering various inducements, as also by further liberalisation of imports, brought inflation back as well as higher levels of fiscal deficit. Higher import levels helped to improve growth rates and exports, but only by upsetting the trade balance once again and adding to the already heavy foreign debt burden. The Indian planners have been unable to find a solution to this dilemma.

Another dilemma confronts the interest rates for bank deposits. The credit restraint measures to balance internal and external accounts, not only adversely affect growth by making investment less attractive, they do not necessarily encourage savings, the latter being more a function of income and growth than of interest rates. Higher interest rates also attract speculative capital from abroad, which inflates foreign exchange reserves and creates a misleading sense of complacency, while adding instability to the economy.

No less alarming is the 'internal debt' burden which, with the external debt, now equals the country's GDP. 'Interest repayments', a legal commitment consequent on public borrowing, is a serious drain on public fund, accounting for around 40 per cent of the country's non-plan expenditure, and thus limiting the scope for further economy on this front. This, along with expenditures on defence and subsidies, accounts for nearly three-fourths of the non-plan expenditure in India, while expenditure on planning as a proportion of total expenditure is a much smaller figure compared with that in the 1970s or the 1980s.

Industry and labour

The low, 2.5 per cent average industrial growth until 1993–94, was followed by a significant increase in the last two years—9.3 per cent and 12.4 per cent, respectively, according to 'quick estimates' of the government that need to be confirmed. Capital goods industry did very badly over the first three years, but recovered significantly over the last two. Overall, industrial growth in the five years under structural adjustment was lower than that for the 1980s.

During this period, employment in the public sector as also in the organised private sector virtually stagnated. Most of the employment growth was in the informal sector. The implementation of the 'exit policy' in case of the sick units—both public and private—was hampered by the inadequacy of the 'national renewal fund'. One major criticism, in case of the sick public sector units, was that the revival packages took several years to be formulated and approved by the appropriate cabinet sub-committee, and by the time these were put into action the condition of the factory or the enterprise concerned went beyond redemption. Lending from banks and other financial institutions stopped as soon as an enterprise was declared sick, and from then onwards, to keep the firm ticking until the revival package was decided upon was usually an uphill task.

The disinvestment process undertaken in India was less oriented towards improving public sector efficiency than reducing fiscal deficits. Rather than loss-making firms with little demand in the market, the tendency was to sell equity in the better performing public sector units in order to make money. There were also frequent allegations of sleaze and under-pricing of public sector equity and properties.

Agriculture

Despite a record eight successive good harvests, the performance of Indian agriculture was the worst among the main sectors of the economy. Food production increased from 168.4 million tons in 1991–92 to 179.5 million tons in 1992–93 and 184.3 million tons and 191.1 million tons, respectively, in the following two years. Then, in the fifth year, 1995–96, it dropped significantly to around 185 million tons. The overall growth rate, at less than 2 per cent, was far less than the growth rate exceeding 3 per cent during the 1980s, and led to a fall in per capita food availability. It also fell far short of a requirement of 3–4 per cent annual growth to conform to NEP expectations of agricultural exports carrying the load of Indian imports through its earnings. The performance was somewhat better in cases of cotton and jute, two major commercial crops, though the trend was towards a lowering of growth in cases of tea, coffee and rubber plantations. This poor performance has come, despite policy changes favouring agriculture, a significant increase in support prices, a massive increase in credit inflow and, as we have already noted, a favourable weather condition. If, despite all these the performance was so poor, one shudders to think what could have happened were the vagaries of nature to operate on the wrong side.

One can offer two major explanations for the failure of agriculture to take off despite these favourable factors. First, the withdrawal of subsidy on potassic and phosphatic fertiliser, that has reduced the rate of growth of fertiliser use and has distorted the mix of different soil nutrients in application, as proportionately more of nitrogenous fertiliser is now being used. Second, the massive curtailment of public investment, in order to bridge the fiscal deficit, has mainly fallen on irrigation, power and other related agricultural and rural needs (Dasgupta, 1997b).

As a consequence of this failure, the per capita daily availability of food has declined during these five years compared with the five years preceding the introduction of structural adjustment. The rate of growth in per capita consumption of clothes and sugar has declined, while that for edible oil and tea has gone up, compared with the preceding period. This period has also been associated with a deterioration of social life in terms of a number of other social indicators such as poverty, malnutrition, illiteracy and inequality (Dreze and Sen, 1995: 180–81).

Political constraints

In the last two years of this five-year period, forced by political compulsions, the government began soft-pedalling. 'Poor' was rediscovered, a series of 'lollipops' (small budgetary amounts for the old, women, disabled, and other weaker sections of the population) were declared, the process of dismantling of subsidies and disinvestment of public sector was slowed down, earlier decisions to end priority sector lending and interest subsidy were not implemented, and strengthening of the Public Distribution System was promised in place of its earlier resolve to prune it if not actually dismantling it. Though the private sector, mainly foreign, had been pressing for a change in labour legislation and to carry out labour market reform—particularly the part that denied the employers the right to hire and fire and to close down non-viable units—this too was shelved.

The following were some of the major reasons for such slowing down:

(*a*) The consensus among the business community in favour of reforms began to crack and a section began doubting the wisdom of the pace and magnitude of liberalisation and globalisation. This was largely because of the growing fear of MNC domination as multinationals began moving in and taking over Indian concerns and their imports began displacing Indian production. There was also a feeling that they and the MNCs were not playing on a level playing field, as the concessions were loaded in favour of the latter.

(*b*) The growing hostility among the peasantry against a sharp decline in public expenditure on agriculture and rural development, withdrawal of fertiliser subsidies, proposed increases in power, irrigation and other changes, increasing reliance on imported inputs, competition of agri-business firms in the market for a number of commercial crops and the fear about various adverse consequences of GATT agreement on Indian agriculture. These more than outweighed the possible benefit flowing from higher procurement prices for agricultural crops. Reform in agriculture has been, at best, half-hearted, for a variety of other reasons too (Pursell and Gulati, 1995).

(*c*) The growing opposition of the trade unions as formal sector employment froze, the government appeared reluctant to bail out 300,000 private sick industrial units as well as many sick public sector units, the 'national renewal fund' for helping the redundant workers with training and some funds proved inadequate, and clamouring by MNCs for dilution of labour laws began receiving increasing attention from the government.

(*d*) A succession of scandals, revealing corruption in high places and implicating more than half the ministers, including the Prime Minister himself, undermined public trust in the government and in its policies. The report of the Joint Parliamentary Committee on the 'share scam', which made 'unregulated liberalisation' in general, and four major foreign banks in particular, responsible for engineering illegal and unethical dealings in share markets, somewhat dampened enthusiasm among a good section of the middle class in the share market.

In short, the achievement in these five years fell short of the expectations generated at the very beginning of NEP. At the end, the potential and actual losers vastly outnumbered the potential and actual gainers. The opposition was consolidated from the third year onwards, in the wake of the Dunkel proposals during GATT negotiations and became formidable by the time the general election was held in May 1996. Forced by political opposition, the implementation of the SAP, in the last two years, was, at best, half-hearted.

While, generally speaking, 'liberalisation' up to a point has been accepted, opposition is stronger against 'globalisation' under the MNC or WTO umbrella. Any attempt to impose exclusive market rights (EMR) of the MNCs with patent rights in other countries is likely to be strongly resisted as also the WTO prescription for the opening of a mail-box for receiving patent applications. The Marakesh decision to recast various Indian laws in conformity with the GATT-prescribed international patent, investment, labour standard regimes is also unlikely to find favour with the constituents of the United Front. Subsidies in the public distribution system (PDS), in agricultural price support programmes, in interests in priority sector loans and in agricultural inputs will be continued and even augmented in some cases. The proposed entry of the multinationals in the insurance sector has become a major issue of public debate.

Poverty alleviation and fulfilment of basic minimum needs—mainly of food, shelter, drinking water, education and health—would be an important component of the economic programme. Some disinvestment of the public sector is being undertaken, but mainly to earn revenue, balance the book and reduce fiscal deficit.

Conclusions

In this chapter we attempted to bring together the macro-economic experiences of a cross-section of countries spread over three continents, many of which have been under structural adjustment for a decade or longer.

We began with the two city states of East Asia—Singapore and Hong Kong—both now classified as developed countries in the World Development Report. Without a land mass and an internal market, many of the policies followed by South Korea, Taiwan and Japan, such as import substitution or land reform, were irrelevant in their context. For them, there was no alternative to export orientation as only extensive trade could provide them with economics of scale. These two made the best possible use of their location, Hong Kong as an outlet for mainland China and Singapore overlooking the strait that provided a vital link between Japan and the Gulf. Using their skilled manpower, both went for an impressive range of high-quality knowledge-intensive industries such as banks and electronics, as also the traditional garment industry. In both, MNCs played important roles with their elaborate contacts throughout the world. In neither everything was left to the market. In Singapore, in particular, the state played a very active role, to mobilise saving and then to direct investment, and to set up factories for sale. In both, the government played a major role in the housing market, and efforts were made to use the neighbouring countries with a large landmass as markets and as reservoirs of low-wage skilled labour power.

Coming to the three successful southern tier countries, Thailand, Malaysia and Indonesia, which have recorded high growth rates in recent years, we have shown that their pattern of industrial development differed from the East Asian ones in several respects. Here capital, technology and management are mostly in the hands of MNCs, while the local subsidiaries act within OEM framework. There has been no transition to ODM, not to speak of using their own brand names. The local economy only provides labour power, some materials and the label as country of origin to evade Western trade restrictions. We have also shown that development here has been largely an offshoot of East Asian development, via the flying geese model or the neighbourhood effect or simply the diversion of East Asian capital under pressure from G7 countries.

While these economies have been much more open and liberal than the East Asian ones, our account shows that here too, policies fluctuated between import substitution and a more liberalised system in the course of their development. Though both Indonesia and Thailand have been taking Fund–Bank help from the early part of the 1980s, the relationship between them has been far from easy. Compared with East Asia, their macro-economic management is not beyond reproach, as these countries have incurred high levels of external debt and their debt–service ratios are quite high. Two of them have been rather unsuccessful in keeping inflation under control.

The question is, whether the high growth these countries have achieved can be attributed to liberalisation under the Fund–Bank management. Our answer is in the negative; because had this been the case, the Philippines, the fourth country in the region, with the longest and closest association with both the Fund and the Bank and with better initial conditions, rather than any of the other three, should have done the best. We therefore, examined the specific factors that have helped the development in these three countries.

Sub-Saharan Africa's sad experience shows how structural adjustment has made its countries poorer, as their per capita income has actually declined. Once in the Fund–Bank net, these countries have not succeeded in getting out. One loan after another has followed, with periodic interruptions following a political turmoil, but all these support measures have not helped these countries to move away from stagnation. On the contrary, the deflationary package, forcing equalisation of exports and imports at a low level of activity, with declining investment and saving, has caused widespread misery; poverty and unemployment are growing. Ghana, claimed to be a great success under a dynamic military leader, does not appear so in the light of more up-to-date data.

The three Latin American countries discussed here, Brazil, Mexico and Chile, belong to a different breed despite their occasional crises. The first two are among the upper-middle-income countries, while Chile belongs to the lower-middle-income category. Brazil's experience is discussed in two parts. The period from 1955 to 1980, operating under a strategy of self-reliance based on import substituting industrialisation, was one of rapid growth, despite a high level of inflation; the latter operating within a predetermined structure of mark-ups and wage indexation. In contrast, the period of the 1980s, when adjustment was tried, was one of no growth but with an even more alarming level of inflation. In Mexico too, adjustment failed to bridle price increase, and allowed unregulated foreign speculative capital inflow that led to a second crisis in 1995. Chile is the sole case of success, partly because the more extremist economic philosophy of automatic adjustment, sponsored by the Chicago boys that dominated the 1974–82 period, was discarded and public investment was augmented.

In the Indian study we examined two separate issues. First, why India failed though its policy in the pre-1991 period closely resembled the East Asian policy package based on import substitution? We have come out with some explanations and have rejected some given by others. The second question we have tried to answer is about the post-1991 experience under structural adjustment. We have shown that in the five years following 1991, the Indian economy has done no better than in the preceding five years, though, at least to start with, the new government more or less followed the guiding rules of NPE. Structural adjustment operated in full swing in the first three years, but then it lost momentum because of political opposition, and the programme was not taken to its logical conclusion, e.g., withdrawal of subsidy and PDS, and a more committed effort towards disinvestment and closing down of sick industries. Some would argue that, because the attempt was half-hearted, the outcome was not as bad as it could have been.

Taking all these country experiences together, at the minimum, there is no evidence that structural adjustment works. Even where the country concerned has shown political will and commitment, and has opened up the economy as fully as it is possible, there is no sign of high and sustaining growth rates, not to speak of distribution, employment and poverty alleviation, or even of control over inflation. At the other end, as the SSA experience shows, it has inflicted an irreversible damage and has become instrumental in transferring resources out of their rickety economies to the richest nations in the world.

eight

Conclusions

In this study on structural adjustment, we have examined the issue from a wide variety of standpoints. In Chapter 2 we have analysed its theoretical basis, the NPE, and its paradoxical conclusion that for economic liberalism to work a country needs its political obverse, authoritarianism. We have concluded that self-interest is not the sole motive behind human economic behaviour, and that authoritarianism does not guarantee economic progress.

On the whole, we have found NPE self-contradictory and ahistorical. Its adoption of self-interest as the motivating force for human action stands in contrast with its own view that it is possible to find a body of bureaucrats that will rise above self-interest and rent-seeking groups and would do what is good for the country. Similarly, the description of politicians as solely interested in remaining in power and as the fountain of rent-seeking behaviour does not tally with the expectation that they would allow the bureaucrats a large measure of autonomy and would allow them to take actions that might be opposed to their own interests. We have also been critical of the view that an authoritarian regime can remain insulated from interest groups and distributional coalitions and make the market operate autonomously. The world is full of such regimes and only a small number of these produce economically satisfactory results. If East Asia is a success story, that is not because of the authoritarian nature of its regimes, nor are its regimes incorruptible or impartial.

While unbridled state control can be wasteful, inefficient and corrupting, the human material being what it is in a class society, and cannot therefore be a recipe of success, we hold that open and competitive economy is a myth and it is sheer wishful thinking to assume that a no-control regime can deliver development to a poor country. Nor does the experience of various countries prove that an open economy is more capable of handling corruption; in some countries, liberalisation has been accompanied by wide allegations of sleaze and corruption in high places.

NPE seeks to make the agriculturist the ally of the adjusting government on the premise that the dismantling of import substitution and control would make imported agricultural inputs cheaper, help to raise agricultural prices now no longer subject to price control, and encourage exports. In practice, the governments working under BWI conditionalities have failed to befriend their agriculturists. This is largely because what they have gained in terms of higher output and lower import prices has been outweighed by two other factors: (*a*) a massive curtailment in public investment in agriculture, which has also brought down private investment, and has seriously affected irrigation, power and other infrastructure development, and (*b*) higher input prices resulting from withdrawal of subsidies, particularly on fertiliser. In many countries of Africa, an added factor has been the erosion of quality of service following the winding up of marketing boards and the transfer of their activities to private hands. One hardly comes across a country that has implemented, or is still implementing, structural adjustment, where agriculture is blooming. No less severe has been the cut in social expenditure, particularly in SSA countries.

In Chapter 3, we have pointed out that while the agencies sponsoring, financing and monitoring structural adjustment—the World Bank and IMF—are controlled by the rich G7 countries in terms of voting rights, paradoxically, they operate today only in the poor countries, and have no role to play in the world economy at large. The question that inevitably follows is whether in their decision to introduce and implement structural adjustment, these very rich countries have been prompted by an altruistic motive or whether their self-interest is involved in this exercise. More particularly, we asked, how far and to what extent the adjustment package had been introduced to rescue the international banking system from bankruptcy and/or to find markets for the MNCs of US origin in order to rectify the massive balance of trade deficit of the United States. In other words, whether structural adjustment is an instrument through which the burden of adjusting the trade deficit of the United States has been passed on to the fragile shoulders of the LDCs.

One of the major issues of debate, both in Chapter 3 and in Chapter 6, was about the respective roles of the state and the market. Here the debate was conducted in the context of the less developed semi-capitalist countries and the defined objective was to achieve transition to full capitalist development. Other issues such as what the development strategy should be for achieving socialism or whether, in the ultimate analysis, capitalism is good or bad, were not considered relevant in this specific context. Countries under focus in Chapter 6, those located in East Asia, have no socialist pretensions, and are unabashedly in favour of private capitalists. At the same time, their governments have been highly active in the economy, both in terms of the number and importance of state-owned enterprises in a wide range of fields as also in the way they have directed the private sector—through subsidies, concessions, and other means—towards certain activities.

One may argue that here the state is operating in the collective interest of the private capitalists, though its actions may, in some specific cases, come in conflict with those of some individual capitalists. The state also frequently acts as the referee in the East Asian context, to set the rules of competition between firms, to prescribe norms for the allocation of scarce resources, whether import licence or subsidised loan, or even not to allow a particular capitalist to overshadow others. The state is by no means neutral, it is favouring those who are operating in line with its policies and is deliberately discriminating against those whose policies and actions, according to the state, are not in conformity with its goal of industrialisation.

The main significance of state intervention in those states lies in its broad economic and political goal: that is, to engineer autonomous development of indigenous capitalism, as distinct from dependent development within the agenda set by BWIs or their G7 patrons. The role of the state is necessary because indigenous capitalists, on their own, would be unable to do everything necessary in their collective interest, or to win battles against foreign MNCs in a level playing field. Unless ground rules of competition are loaded in their favour, at least partly, and for a time, their weak, infant industries would be no match to their formidable rivals in the global market. These industries need some respite from foreign competition, almost the way young saplings are fenced off to protect them from invading cows and goats, but such fencings are no longer needed when these grow into mature trees. In East

Asia, as the economy has become diversified and mature, the process of liberalisation has been initiated, now that their firms are capable of taking on the best in the West in a level playing field. In India, a long period of import substitution, with all its faulty implementation, has given rise to a new, self-confident class of indigenous capitalists who hope to benefit from liberalisation. In other words, operation of import substitution as a part of a strategy of self-reliance for a certain length of time, produces growth, helps industrialisation and the eventual emergence of a class of indigenous capitalists equipped to look after themselves in a no-holds-barred ruthless competition. To put it simply, liberalisation follows growth, not the other way round.

Not all saplings grow to become mature trees, but some do, and those who do would probably not have grown to that size had there been no such initial protection. The fact is that indigenous capitalists are weak to start with and would not survive without state support. Whether those among the saplings which, for a variety of reasons, never grow, should continue to receive protection in the form of fencing for an indefinite time period is another question. A major explanation for East Asia's success with import substitution has been the capability of the countries of that region to implement it as a time-bound exercise (OECF, 1991: 8). Another distinguishing feature of the East Asian experience has been the way they have combined import substitution with export promotion. Their governments expected a firm to try out its products first in the home market, perhaps with government protection and subsidy, but with the understanding that eventually it would be ready to move into the wild where the 'survival of the fittest' is the rule.

In most developing countries, the choice is not between private sector and public sector or between the market and the government, but between domestic public sector and foreign private sector, or between MNC-dominated market-orientation and a state-led system that fosters domestic industries. There is no known case where a country has made the transition from backwardness to development without state support, and this applies to USA, UK, and every developed country of the world. As Stigliz pointed out in a recent statement, all the major successes 'involved heavy doses of government involvement', while, on the other side, there are few examples of success 'without government involvement'. In fact, Stigliz goes even further to state: 'There is a remarkable similarity between the government activities undertaken by the East Asian tigers and those undertaken by the United States in a comparable period of its development' (Stigliz, 1997: 2). The market alone has never delivered, while East Asia has succeeded because, as Stigliz, a key figure in the World Bank, admits, the 'government played a critical, catalytic role' (ibid., 1997).

That such statements are now coming from Bank stalwarts, though in less than formal occasions, is because the interventionist role of the state in East Asia can no longer be denied. Only 6–7 years ago it was fashionable to cite East Asia as a paragon of free trade economics. But this is no longer possible. When *The East Asian Miracle* was being drafted, a section within the World Bank, alarmed that its theology did not correspond with the concrete experience of these countries, deliberately manipulated and diluted conclusions of the original draft that made out a stronger case for state intervention. The Japanese themselves have challenged the concept of efficiency used for the purpose of resource allocation, saying that a distinction should be made between short-term and long-term efficiency and that economic efficiency alone should not be the goal. They have justified subsidised interests, opposed deregulation when (as in Sub-Saharan Africa) it is not likely to lead to a big wave of investment, have urged a dynamic view of comparative advantage, and have supported the case for state intervention in a whole variety of cases (OECF, 1991: 3).

On the other hand, as our study shows, market orientation forced on the LDCs through structural adjustment does not seem to have worked, excepting for one or two countries like Ghana or Chile. Though advertised as a short-term cure, adjustment (as also stabilisation) programmes have become permanent fixtures of the economies of many poor countries. Yet, adjustment has not led to sustainable growth, despite having been pursued, off and on, for 10 to 17 years. On the contrary, Sub-Saharan Africa has become distinctly poorer, and is still underdeveloping, under structural adjustment. The argument that, had adjustment been pursued consistently by fully committed governments, the outcome would have been different, right or wrong, is neither here nor there. This raises another relevant issue: Is structural adjustment politically feasible? We have shown that adjustment produced a net outflow of resources from their rickety economies for 10–15 years, at a time when they needed resources most. This, combined with stabilisation, severely deflated their economy, and might have caused irreparable damage to their productive capacity.

Over the past two decades many miracles have been projected, including Turkey and Mexico, but none has stood the test of time. Although the economic transformation of three Southeast Asian countries—Thailand, Indonesia and Malaysia—discussed in Chapter 7, is cited as an instance of success with structural adjustment, and without much state intervention, the first two of which having been under adjustment programme lending for reasonably long periods, this is a simplification. Other factors, such as domestic oil production and diversion of Japanese capital to this area because of the Louvre accord, appear to be more powerful explanations. Besides, the failure of the fourth country in the region, the Philippines, paradoxically the one with a longer, much closer Fund–Bank link and a more consistent record of implementation of their guidelines, shows that for the success of the former one should look for some other explanations. We have also noted that the basis of industrialisation in Southeast Asia is weak, dependent entirely as it is on OEM arrangement under MNC guidance, and having no industrial infrastructure comparable with East Asia. Further, unlike the East Asian countries, here, faulty macroeconomic management has led to inflation, a high order of external debt and accompanying high debt–service ratios.

Obviously, state intervention, to work, has to be judicious and balanced. Protection to infant industries cannot go on indefinitely. Tariffs exceeding 250 per cent rate, and a complex web of import and other controls do encourage rent-seeking behaviour on a big scale. Too many regulations and controls stifle initiative, and promote inefficiency and wastage, while corrupting officials and politicians. All these are valid points and such abuses need to be rectified. But from this to take the plunge in the exactly opposite direction, to dismantle all kinds of control and regulation, to open all windows, doors and ceilings, to give MNCs national treatment and to make them operate without local content requirements, would be to take a very high risk, and perhaps an irreversible step, that might perpetuate dependence and close the option of indigenous capitalist development.

In Chapter 4 we have referred to the conflict between the national objectives of a host government and the global objectives of the multinational firms. Such conflict can be manifested on various issues, in particular on the way the domestic production is valued in the world market, on the rate of utilisation of local mineral and agricultural resources, or on the political power exercised by the MNC supported by the government of its own country of domicile. There can be no doubt that MNCs, with their access to global resources, technology, production at all stages and marketing, impart a certain amount of flexibility: by matching domestic demand pattern with supplies, by undertaking production in difficult terrains and by finding export outlets all over the world. But such flexibility, range of operations and efficiency, while benefiting the MNC to optimise its profits at the global level, may or may not always be beneficial to the host country.

The conflict also arises from the narrow time frame that all private firms, including MNCs, use for making decisions. And also from their unwillingness to widen the concepts of profitability and viability by taking into account the consequences of their action on the rest of the economy and society. Project analysis tends to be time-bound and project-bound and based on private cost and benefit considerations alone. Our chapter on environment (Chapter 5) points to serious dangers implicit in such project analyses, which fail to internalise social costs and benefits and remain oblivious of the needs of the future generations. Environmental abuses arise from the reluctance to locate and assess a project or activity within a broader frame of time and space. The extent of damage caused by private action to society at large is not easy to assess since those responsible for such degradation often hold the key to information and have a vested interest in not divulging those.

While rational pricing of resources is an important safeguard against excessive use, we have noted that global prices do not usually emerge from a free interaction of market forces of demand and supply. The transfer prices of MNCs have no bearing on the demand for or the supply of a resource by one of its affiliates, and are usually determined by their headquarters with the objective of minimising the tax burden. The scarcity value of oil was not reflected in the prices ruling from the late 1940s to 1973. The drastic revision in oil prices, beginning with a fourfold increase in

1973, came about not by way of the operation of market forces but by the determined cartel action of oil producing countries.

As for the interesting Coasian solution in terms of rearrangement of identifiable private rights in resources, often by way of bargaining between parties and in exchange of payments, irrespective of who is polluting and who is the victim, while this can apply at small community levels, at higher levels, with major common resources at stake, with many parties in dispute spread over a very large area and with an uneven distribution of information, the transaction costs become too high to make it work.

The Bank view on environment fails to take care of such long-term issues and also those involving interdependence between the project in question and the rest of the economy and society. We have pointed out that even in the open economies of the developed countries, environmental protection comes mainly by way of administrative fiat and a greater understanding of the environmental issues among the general masses, thanks to the campaigns by voluntary groups. Popular participation is also reckoned as a major safeguard against environmental abuses. At the global level, individual countries have been generally reluctant to shed some of their sovereignty in the interest of global commons. While countries relying on timber trade have been unwilling to sacrifice that trade and save trees without some compensation, various proposals for global taxation, based on emissions of environment-degrading gases or the capacity to pay as measured by GNP or trade share, have not found favour, nor have the rich countries agreed to change their automobile-dependent lifestyle in the global interest. Further, concern for environment is being increasingly used as an argument to keep third world exports away.

This raises an important question, whether price-based solutions can work without appropriate institutions (Intriligator, 1997: 5). Land reform figures in our discussion on East Asia as a precondition for industrialisation and modernisation, and its non-implementation as an explanation for India's failure to industrialise despite following similar policies. Through land reform, property rights are rearranged so that control over land passes on from the parasitic groups interested in ostentatious living to those who produce. Recording of land rights, in place of oral contracts, and making arbitrary eviction difficult, makes it possible for the tenants and sharecroppers to get bank loans, to take interest in investment for land improvement, and to try out new crops and cropping practices. Cooperatives provide the small operators, collectively, with the economics of scale, while establishment of elected local level governments, as a part of a measure to decentralise administration, allows large-scale popular participation in many development decisions affecting them. Beneficiary committees looking after common resources—such as deep tubewells, water harvesting tanks, village roads—have been found to be enthusiastic and efficient in carrying out their tasks. In all these cases, popular participation in various forms allows information to be spread, transaction costs to be reduced and decisions on cropping and investment to be taken on the basis of more reliable data.

Chapter 4 on world trade shows how unequal global trade relations are, and how dominated it is by the rich country interests. We conclude that world trade is far from free and competitive and the prices ruling in the world market are trade-distorting, and, therefore, cannot be taken as bases for production decisions. Distortions are principally due to two factors: massive subsidies and protection given by the rich countries to their own production and exports and the fact that a large proportion of what passes as international trade is intra-company transfer by MNCs at book-keeping prices that have no bearing on demand and supply for the goods in question. We then discuss various forms of trade distortion practised by the rich countries themselves—such as VER, VIE, MFA, the blatant use of GATT safeguards, anti-dumping legislations and countervailing duties and Super 301, the last being a unilateral action undertaken by the United States to force a country to open its markets.

While the Western countries have been asking the poor countries to desist from erecting non-tariff barriers, they themselves have been strengthening these during the 1980s to keep the LDC exports out. Similarly, while theoretically the Western countries are opposed to subsidies, in practice they operate an elaborate system of subsidies. In case of agriculture, their astronomical subsidies, initially motivated by a concern for security, have transformed industrial countries with no comparative advantage in food production into main food exporters. These also reveal some other features of their double-speak: (*a*) that countries should conform to their own naturally and historically given comparative advantage, and (*b*) that countries should not seek self-reliance for security or other reasons; they should instead seek security via trade.

Coming to GATT, we show how some of the laudable principles have been subtly changed, e.g., from free trade to fair trade, and from non-discrimination to reciprocity, to create grounds for protectionist measures in the West, while in the negotiations that determined their trade future, the LDCs, bereft of the ability to give something to get something, have tended to play a peripheral role. At the same time, exemptions had been given from GATT provisions to domestic agricultural systems to suit US and European interests, and to powerful regional economic groupings. The GATT-inconsistency of MFA was never in doubt, still it was allowed to operate in order to protect the dying textile industry in the rich countries.

The Marakesh agreements, which followed the eighth, the Uruguay round of negotiations, particularly those on investment, services, patents and subsidies, would have the effect of opening up the markets of the LDCs and of integrating these more closely with the global economy. The powers hitherto exercised by the governments to regulate foreign investment, in terms of local content requirements, were taken away. But such mobility across the border was not permitted to labour, one of the three critical factors of production. This asymmetry in the treatment of capital and labour was noted by us as also the fact that the global patent regime would perpetuate the technological dependence of the LDCs on their rich counterparts.

Though the LDCs are being offered two large carrots—of markets in textiles and food in the rich countries—there is every likelihood of the fallacy of composition operating. As nearly all the LDCs would be chasing those markets, there is a real possibility of a glut in global production, which in turn is likely to further depress world prices in primary goods. As for textiles, a lion's share of that market is likely to be cornered by the East Asians (Development Committee, 1992: 96–97). This brings to the fore issues relating to comparative advantage and terms of trade; whether, given the adverse movement in terms of trade, the LDCs can gain much by producing primary goods and establishing light industries for exports, and whether a more dynamic view of comparative advantage a la East Asian countries, should be taken, of trying out a more diverse pattern of industrial production and exports under the leadership of an interventionist state.

Lastly, we discussed the political economy of NPE. If the bureaucrats are operating autonomously despite their political bosses, that is largely because of the role played by (*a*) the BWIs through conditionalities, and (*b*) the Western countries responsible for propping up these corrupt and authoritarian regimes. They together make the politicians in LDCs do what they would not have done otherwise solely on the basis of their own perception of self-interest. Such an interpretation, completely missing from NPE literature, would have given NPE the consistency it is lacking. But at the same time, such an interpretation would fly in the face of the concept of ownership, the idea that the LDC governments subjecting themselves to conditionalities incorporated in PFP would take those as an act of self-deception, as having been formulated by themselves. Or at least this is what they would claim in public. Ownership would give conditionalities a certain measure of legitimacy no doubt, from the point of view of the general public in these countries, but for how long? Where would that legitimacy stand when the visiting Fund–Bank team would refuse to release the next tranche on the ground that the performance criteria set out in PFP conditionalities have not been met?

The concept of ownership is, perhaps, one of the worst examples of double-speak in development literature. Here, the powerful BWIs are forcing a government to agree to a set of conditionalities and are merely asking the governments concerned to put their signature to a PFP incorporating these, yet they are pretending as if these represented the views of the country concerned. This also raises valid questions about the rationale of conditionalities. If a country really owns these, there would be no need for conditionalities. As we have noted, conditionalities are indeed few and their violations are tolerated in a large measure for those countries which share the Fund–Bank economic philosophy. But for those who do not, and are forced to accept them because otherwise funding would not be available, ownership is hypocritical and the adjustment programme is scrapped or diluted as soon as there is any hint of domestic trouble. The very high interruption and mortality rates of SAPs mainly result from this attempt to force conditionalities down the throat of reluctant governments.

No less interesting is the in-house BWI debate on whether any progress in a recipient country has been due to conditionalities and resultant policy changes or because of the finance these accompanied. Some have taken the view that conditionalities are more important and help to put the economy on the right track, while the finance that goes with it is given only in order to make them accept these conditionalities. There are others who feel that conditionalities, by restricting their choices, actually interfere with the functioning of these governments, while a more generous funding would have been more in their interest. A country facing economic crisis needs money, not advice.

What, then, are the main conclusions of this study? First, there can be no room for dogmatism or a theological approach. No standardised format can apply universally in all conditions when the LDCs vary widely amongst themselves in terms of initial conditions, size of internal market, natural and human resources, existing nature of relationship with other countries, level of development and so on. Countries like Brazil or India are better equipped for a strategy of self-reliance based on import-substituting industrialisation, than, say, resource-poor, small Somalia, while for small island countries such as Singapore or Taiwan only trade can give them the scale economics needed for industrialisation. How to balance import substitution with a complementary objective of export promotion is another issue where there would be room for variation among countries with varying internal market and export possibilities.

It should be recognised that economics as a science has not been able to answer all questions. It is still a mystery how Brazil managed to sustain a very high growth rate for 25 years, between 1955 and 1980, despite a very high level of inflation of around 40 per cent per year. In the case of South Korea too, inflation seems to have coexisted with varying rates of growth. Equally, it is a mystery how stabilisation policies mainly aiming at bringing inflation under control have repeatedly failed, and have, in the case of a number of Latin American countries, led to more inflation than they started with, but with less or no growth. When there is so much uncertainty about the cause–effect relationship, a prudent approach would be to allow policy diversity, in tune with biodiversity in the sphere of nature, to minimise the risk of catastrophic global changes.

Second, subject to what we have just stated, for indigenous capitalist development there appears to be no alternative to state intervention, but the extent and nature of such intervention is a matter of concrete conditions prevailing in a country. There is always a risk of such intervention becoming excessive, and of a tendency to erect an elaborate structure of rules, regulations, licences and what not. There would always be firms and individuals seeking rent from such controls, and unscrupulous officials and politicians looking for some unearned income. How to handle such situations, politically, is an important issue but is beyond the brief of this book. Similarly, what makes officials and politicians less self-serving and more patriotic is another very important issue that cannot be handled within the scope of this book. But to take the view that such problems would disappear in a market oriented economy where the state takes a back seat would be simplistic and flying in the face of accounts of corruption coming from countries such as India and Indonesia, as also highly developed countries like Italy, Japan and the United States.

Third, to allow the state to play the interventionist role, and to avoid the trap of BWI conditionalities, the least that an LDC should do is to follow a policy of prudent macro-economic management: low level of inflation, low level of debt, and high levels of saving and investment. There is no alternative to reliance on both domestic saving and domestic investment. Domestic saving ratio, as the East Asian experience shows, generally grows with economic growth, and is not highly responsive to interest rates. At the same time, a policy of import liberalisation, by permitting the entry of hitherto untasted luxury goods, may raise consumption propensity and reduce saving. While foreign saving can help in providing additional funds for investment, there is a limit to what a country can get from this source. Further, as our discussion on Latin America shows, foreign capital inflow of the speculative type may become a destabilising factor in the economy. FDI is a more acceptable form of foreign capital inflow, but this is usually concentrated in a small number of more advanced LDCs. A massive external debt, with its attendant high debt–service ratio, can become a serious drag on the economy, and a prudent management should do its utmost to avoid such a development.

Fourth, today's LDCs are more closely integrated with the global economy than they had been in the past, and, given this, the question arises how to handle such integration without sacrificing the national goal of indigenous capitalist development. With the adoption of global norms and legislation on a wide range of subjects in the Marakesh agreement, and with the establishment of WTO for monitoring their implementation, this is hardly an easy task. This task cannot be performed by any single LDC and the majority they enjoy in the WTO forum would not be enough to make their voices heard. We have noted in Chapter 4, that one of the major explanations for the LDCs getting a raw deal in the Uruguay round of GATT negotiations was their failure to unite and to remorselessly pursue their common aims. One reason why they could be so easily consigned to the periphery was the demoralisation that followed the collapse of the Soviet Union which reduced their bargaining power. Conditions are somewhat better now as efforts are being made to regroup and present common programmes on issues like labour standard, environment standard and investment and competition policies. Only through collective pressure and action would it be possible to undo the damage done by the Marakesh agreement.

This raises perhaps the most important of all questions: Do the governments of the LDCs have the political will to unite and stand together on major international issues? An answer to this question should take account of both the negatives and the positives. A major negative point is the diversity among LDCs, as we have already noted. The East and Southeast Asian countries are likely to do much better than others in improving their shares in textile trade after MFA ceases to exist. They are the ones with whom the rich countries prefer to trade, to whom the private banks prefer to lend, and in which the MNCs are more likely to locate their activities, while no one would touch SSA. What is the common cause that can unite them all? However, there are positive points too. One positive point that we have discussed, is the history of G77 countries, of NIEO, and of several such common actions, mainly in the 1970s. Another is the way the East Asian countries managed to assert economic independence even when politically and militarily they were (and still are) appendages of the Western alliance. On balance, what the probabilities are no one can say. But if they fail, the cost would be losing the option of independent capitalist development.

Epilogue

Since the manuscript of this book was delivered to the publishers in early 1997, there have been some important economic developments, the most important being the financial crisis that is facing the Southeast and East Asian countries now, at the time of the publication of this book. Further, two important recent publications on East Asian experience have come to the knowledge of the author which have important bearings on the debate on their development path. We propose to deal with those in this Epilogue, without disturbing the main text.

IMF reply to World Bank

Strangely, an IMF publication (Sarel, 1996) has been put under wide circulation that questions the Krugman–Young view that the growth in East Asia has been largely due to massive capital and labour accumulation and, therefore, cannot be sustained for long. It points to the difficulty of estimating the rate of growth of capital stock during this period, to the dubious assumptions involved while calculating total factor productivity, to the questionable methods used, to the difficulties of attributing to labour and capital their respective shares of national income, and then concludes: 'Because of these unanswered and perhaps unanswerable questions, the results of studies that emphasize the contribution to growth of capital and labour and depreciate that of technology should not be regarded as definitive. They should be viewed as interesting, but only suggestive' (Sarel, 1996: 6–7). It argues that the results that Young derived—of low Total Factor Productivity (TFP) in these four countries—were obtained by using a specific estimation period (1970–85) and taking 0.45 as the relative contribution of labour and capital, which was higher than the 0.33 that Sarel adopted in his exercise (Sarel, 1996: 10–11).

This study then carries out a 'growth accounting' exercise of its own for the 'four tigers', covering the period 1960–90, more or less on the lines suggested by Young. In this exercise, comparing the rate of the technological progress (TFP) of the tigers, during 1975–90, with that for the United States during the same period, it finds that the former far exceeded that of the latter. Further, three of the four (excluding Singapore) showed TFP figures higher than that for Japan during the same period. On the whole, the productivity was slightly higher than that for United States and Japan in Taiwan and Hong Kong and slightly lower in South Korea and Singapore. It concluded: 'Although the Four Tigers accumulated capital and increased labor participation at a much faster rate than other economies, the increase in these two factors far from fully explains their exceptional growth rates; growth in productivity attributable to innovative technology also accounts for a significant fraction' (Sarel, 1996: 10). It then says that the debate on the relative roles of labour and capital accumulation and of factor productivity remains inconclusive (ibid., 1996: 11).

This IMF publication then summarises three types of views about public policy and government intervention; (*a*) neoclassicists: those seeking to leave everything to the market, (*b*) revisionists: those, while seeking that the government gets the basics right, also advocate selective intervention to 'jump-start' the industrialisation process, and (*c*) agnostics: those taking a sceptical view on this issue, on the grounds that 'it is impossible to offer a realistic counter-factual scenario', that the direction of causality is not always clear (e.g., between export orientation and technological progress, or between growth and saving), and the public policy is far from homogeneous. While state intervention in favour of selective industrialisation may work in some cases, there are many others where it may not. The paper, however, supports selective support—by encouraging investments and exports, using instruments such as direct subsidies or preferential allocation of credit—in favour of 'good sectors', with beneficial spillover effects over the rest of the economy (ibid., 1996: 11–17).

The study also questions the World Bank view that openness via export orientation and investment were the 'engines of growth' in case of the East Asian countries. It showed, quoting Carroll and Weil (1994), that growth influenced saving, while saving alone had no impact on growth. The investment rates of the 'four tigers' in 1960 were quite modest in comparison with those for another 100 countries. Similarly, taking the share of imports and exports in GDP as a measure of openness, the study found that Taiwan and South Korea 'were not more open in 1960, either in absolute terms or relative to other countries of comparable size'. On the contrary, both openness and high investment evolved as the economy grew. Further, while the World Bank study ignored 'initial conditions', this IMF study did not, but was also sceptical about the conclusions of Rodrik, that a more equal land distribution and higher literacy levels were important determinants of East Asian growth (ibid., 1994: 18–21).

Though this paper does not come out with clear, unambiguous conclusions, this in itself is significant, coming as it does from IMF, the BWI twin of the World Bank. It is by all accounts a significant departure from erstwhile Fund–Bank theology, also because it does not accept the World Bank explanation of East Asian growth as valid. While, as we have noted in Chapter 3, 'turf battles' between the two were not unknown in their history, never in the past has any of the twins come out with such open criticism of the other on a highly sensitive issue. It remains to be seen whether this paper heralds a significant disjunction of outlook between the two BWIs.

Japan vs. United States: Divergent views on development path

This paper comes at a time when Japan has been showing increasing restlessness with the World Bank attempt to impose its own model as the universal one, completely disregarding the Japanese path of development led by the state. As Robert Wade's recent paper (Wade, 1996) shows, the conflict between the first and the second largest shareholders of the World Bank—the United States and Japan—had been brewing for quite some time; the former asking the state to retreat from economic management while the latter advocated state intervention and linking trade and financial policies to a wider industrial strategy (ibid., 1996: 6–10). In 1991, the conflict reached a new height when Japan's OECF brought out a paper that justified selective industrial support, directed credit and linking it with industrial growth strategy, opposed universal application of privatisation and acknowledged the role of the public sector, as also sought to keep regulations that contained foreign ownership (ibid., 1996: 10–12). In April 1992, MITI projected Japan's experience as more valid than that of the IMF in reindustrialising Russia, particularly its emphasis on selective industries (ibid., 1996: 12). The Bank saw in these ideas a serious threat to its own ideological position. It was already critical of OECF's aid and credit policies in Southeast Asia (ibid., 1996: 14–17).

In 1991 Japan pressed for a thorough study of the East Asian development experience by the World Bank, and the latter agreed after Japan offered $1.2 billion for this purpose, which eventually led to the Bank publication of *The East Asian Miracle*, as we have already noted. The study was headed by John Page, while several country case-studies were to be undertaken by consultants, each getting about $10,000 for this (ibid., 1996: 18). The draft, initially prepared by the team, was much stronger on the role of the state, but it went through various revisions, to make its conclusions less favourable to state intervention and to project Bank 'fundamentals'. The report was not allowed to stray beyond the accepted Bank perimeters, while taking care not to antagonise Japan. In this paper Wade shows how the art of 'paradigm maintenance' has been perfected—with more than 80 per cent of Bank's professional staff coming from USA or UK, and holding similar views, and with committee and editing systems ensuring that, beyond a point, nothing challenging the Bank orthodoxy is allowed to be printed in the Bank's name (ibid., 1996: 30–31).

In the preface of *The East Asian Miracle*, Lewis Preston, Bank President, had to perform a balancing act. He acknowledged, perhaps to appease Japan, his number two boss, that in some Northeast Asian countries selective state intervention had contributed to growth and highlighted the importance of the institutional context within which a policy operates, but then, as we have already noted, the rest of the preface, as well as the document itself, concentrated its fire against selective industrialisation (ibid., 1996: 22–23).

The Southeast Asian financial crisis

The most important development of this period is, of course, the financial crisis facing the high growth Southeast Asian economies such as Thailand, Malaysia and Indonesia, following heavy speculation against their currencies. Thailand had to be bailed out with a hefty $17.2 billion dollars, though the price the former paid was to subject itself to more stringent IMF conditionalities. For a country used to an 8 per cent rate of growth a year, the growth rate for 1997 is unlikely to exceed 2.5 per cent. In the case of Indonesia, the bill to save Indonesia was of the order of $12 billion, following a sudden depreciation of more than 30 per cent in the value of the rupiah. The peso of the Philippines, the least successful among the Southeast Asian four, had to be floated on 11 July, but the amount of support it has asked for from IMF, $1 billion, is peanuts compared with IMF's stake in Thailand and Indonesia. In the case of Malaysia, despite the deployment of a $20 billion fund for keeping its currency, ringgit, stable, the Kuala Lumpur stock market hit its lowest point for 22 months on 5 August 1997. Understandably, Japan, with its far-reaching industrial involvement in the region, has been the main financier of various IMF deals.

The crisis arose largely because some speculators began heavy selling of currencies of this region in the world market, thus bringing down their values and inducing an outward movement in capital from these countries to those considered safe by the investors. The devaluation of the Thai baht, by 20 per cent in response to the crisis, in July 1997, shook the region and panic quickly spread to other countries. The Prime Minister of Malaysia, Mahathir Mohammad has blamed 'rogue speculators', particularly George Soros, for undoing in two weeks what the country had achieved in 40 years. The foreign ministers of nine ASEAN countries have issued a joint communique blaming 'well coordinated efforts to destabilise ASEAN currencies', from some unnamed quarters, for their economic ills. On the other side of the argument, it is being said that these countries had been following imprudent policies for far too long; and though the danger signals had been there for all to see, no action was taken to repair the cracks in time.

These unfortunate developments fully vindicate our decision to treat the three major East Asian countries (Japan, South Korea and Taiwan) in Chapter 6, separately from the two other 'tigers', the tiny island countries, Hong Kong and Singapore, and the three fast growing Southeast Asian countries, 'the southern tier', Thailand, Malaysia, and Indonesia (in Chapter 7). They also justify our observation that development in the latter group of countries, with a virtually non-existent base of capital-intensive and knowledge-intensive large-scale capital goods industries, cannot be stable, as it is dependent almost entirely on foreign capital. The OEM arrangement, under which industry in these countries operates, involves foreign capital equipment, foreign technology, and foreign management, while the host countries mainly contribute labour and their names as countries of origin for taking advantage of the quota system in the West on behalf of the former. Where the East Asians graduated from OEM to ODM and then to their own internationally known brands in due course, such a transition did not occur in Southeast Asia. We made a clear distinction between the dependent industrialisation of the Southeastern variety and the state-led industrialisation in Japan, Korea and Taiwan where the public sector is large, the private sector operates under strong state direction, and the foreign enterprises are not allowed smooth passage into the domestic economy at the cost of the indigenous companies. The firm national objective of self-reliance, based on import substituting industrialisation, distinguishes these three East Asian countries from the Southeast Asian ones where politics and the corresponding package of economic policies periodically oscillate between the state and the market.

We have also noted another major difference between the two—a much more successful management of macro-economic variables in the East Asian countries while the Southeast Asian ones are beset with a large foreign debt, a high proportion of short-term obligations in total foreign obligation, high fiscal deficits and inflation, and a high current account deficit. Indonesia is among the largest five borrowers in the world, while Malaysia's current account deficit of 5.5 per cent of GDP in 1996, is high and dangerous by any standard.

A third, and perhaps, the most significant difference lies in their respective degrees of integration with the global market. The East Asian countries have adopted global integration in phases and on their own terms, never permitting the foreign enterprises an upper hand in the domestic economy, and permitting relaxation of controls and the licence regime only after their own enterprises had become good enough to take on the best in the world. In contrast, the Southeast Asian countries, as also Hong Kong and Singapore, had been more welcoming to foreign ventures. While the East Asians insisted on substantial 'local content requirements', up to 90 per cent in many cases, in cases of the Southeast Asian countries, these were non-existent or insignificant. This eagerness to placate foreign capital has been reflected, in their case, in making their currencies more easily convertible, and pegging these to a basket of currencies dominated by the dollar. The ease of conversion of currency has made these currencies more susceptible to speculation.

Coming so soon after the Mexican crisis of 1994–95, where also 'hot money' played an important role in, first, projecting a 'miracle' and, then, in destabilising the currency, these disasters sharply point to the vulnerability of countries relying substantially on foreign capital, particularly the speculative variety, as distinct from saving generated locally, for their development. The helplessness of these countries, despite impressive growth rates, against the onslaught of obsessive speculators, such as Soros, is a warning to other LDCs who are being goaded by the World Bank and IMF to take the express route to full convertibility of local currencies.

The crisis in Hong Kong

The financial crisis, once started in Southeast Asia, is now spreading to other parts of the globe, including some of the immediate neighbours—Hong Kong and South Korea. This year has witnessed the political transformation of Hong Kong from a British colony extolling the virtues of free enterprise to an integral part of China, a country committed to social ownership of production. However, China has pledged itself to what it describes as 'one nation, two systems', which implies that, in terms of economic policy, Hong Kong would be left where it is now, at least for some time to come. However, the recent developments in the region have cast a big shadow on Hong Kong, whose stock market underwent a mini-collapse in later October 1997 along with Australia. The share price index plummeted from more than 16,000 (with 1964 as 100) in July to slightly more than 10,000 in October in a matter of three months. This happened despite the island having a very large foreign exchange reserve of $85 billion, and the mainland, with which it is now politically integrated, having a massive $123 billion of reserves. This shows that, no matter how sound the internal economy and management are, economies closely integrated with the world market cannot fully protect themselves from a violent turbulence in the money markets in the neighbouring countries. A bigger question is, whether and how far such a crisis is likely to influence the course of development in the economy of the mainland itself. As Hong Kong, a part of China now but fully integrated with the West-dominated world economy, becomes more fully integrated with the bigger national economy in due course, such a crisis is bound to be transmitted to the latter, unless the Chinese policy-makers can find ways of neutralising those from the rest of the economy, which is still largely under social ownership and/or control.

The South Korean crisis

As for South Korea, by mid-December 1997, its economy, the 11th largest in the country, was tottering, as its currency, Won, slid alarmingly, losing 30 per cent of its value in a matter of days, and riot police had to be mobilised to discipline those seeking to sell their shares and bonds as panic gripped the nation. As expected, South Korea had to negotiate a $57 billion package to stabilise the currency and to reverse the outward flow of capital. But the feeling in the country is that even this record-breaking sum may not be adequate to handle the deep crisis facing the economy. Again, as one would expect from an IMF package of that order, stiff conditionalities are being imposed to hasten the process of liberalisation.

Paradoxically, it is probably this drive towards liberalisation that has landed South Korea in this financial mess. We have noted in Chapter 6 that, during their years of development, the East Asian companies mobilised their funds mainly from the state-led banks, and only a relatively small proportion came from the share and bond markets, while non-banking financial institutions were discouraged. While the interest rates charged were lower than what could have been, the market rate with free play of forces of demand and supply, the rate of repayment was satisfactory as the banks were cautious and conservative in their outlook. The banking reform started in the 1980s, under IMF pressure, when South Korea, facing adverse trade balance following oil crises, had to subject itself to them for a short period, and large-scale disinvestment in state-owned banks was undertaken, still the larger part of deposits were mobilised by state-led banks, and quite high statutory liquidity ratios were maintained.

But, over time, the discipline maintained by the banking system has been eroded, while the importance of the banking system as a whole has been undermined by the growth of non-bank financial institutions; from a share of mere 8.6 per cent in 1972 and 34 per cent in 1980 to 54.2 per cent in 1990. Nearly every one of the *Chaebols* and other large firms is overburdened with bank debt 'after an orgy of expansion' (*The Economist*, December 13–19, 1997: 23), while banks themselves raised billions in foreign currency and passed those on to firms as Won, the local currency. Another sin, never committed during the period preceding the current drive towards liberalisation, was to accumulate short-term external debts of the order of $100 billion. Apart from their sheer size, such short-term borrowings are difficult to manage, as nearly every day someone has to be repaid something.

Further, with increasing integration with the global economy, South Korea's convertible currency has become increasingly subject to global speculation and the immunity of the economy from outside shocks has virtually disappeared. At the same time, the fact that shares and bonds are playing a more important role than banks for funding investment, has made the economy that much vulnerable to perverse speculation. In this case, the virus of financial crisis in Southeast Asia could be easily transmitted to other countries as the barriers that were in place earlier have been dismantled. At the time of writing this Epilogue the virus has not yet entered Taiwan and Singapore, for reasons that need to be analysed.

It remains to be seen how South Korea copes with the new set of conditionalities, and whether they are going to make the economy even more vulnerable to such external shocks. Or whether, given its proven record of speedy recovery during the early 1980s, it would succeed in turning the tide in its favour, pay off IMF within a few years, dispense with the conditionalities and return to pre-liberalisation policies that protected it from such speculation-driven shocks in the past.

WTO: International standards on labour and investment

Before ending this Epilogue, let us also refer to the attempt by WTO to impose international standards on labour and investment in a ministerial level meeting in mid-1997. More significant than this attempt, a follow-up of the Marakesh agreement which was very much on the agenda ever since WTO was established, was the growing resistance to this move among the LDCs and its crystallisation in a meeting of 15 such countries (G15) in November 1997. Within the developed countries too, public opinion seems to be increasingly losing faith in the efficacy of the market as the recipe for curing all economic ills, while 'green' and 'human' issues, such as those relating to environment, poverty, unemployment, the plight of the aged, ethnic issues and social participation in decision-making are increasingly coming to prominence in dialogues on development.

Lastly, a word of apology. This otherwise more or less comprehensive critical review of structural adjustment, has missed out the gender related issues. Rather than a few casual observations, the author intended to insert a chapter on this subject in the book, but could not complete it before the deadline.

References and select bibliography

Adedaji, Adebayo, 1993. 'African Regional Perspectives on the Bretton Woods Institutions', North–South Roundtable Meeting, New York (mimeo), April.

Agarwal, Ashis, 1994. *GATT and the Developing Countries,* Mohit Publications, New Delhi.

Agarwal, Pradeep, 1995. 'Singapore: Export-Oriented Industrialization', in Agarwal, Pradeep et al. (eds), *Economic Restructuring in East Asia and India: Perspectives on Policy Reform,* Indira Gandhi Institute of Development Research and Institute of Southeast Asian Studies, Singapore, Macmillan and St Martin's Press, London and New York, Chapter 3, pp. 54–102.

Agarwal, Pradeep, Subir V. Gokarn, Veena Mishra, Kirit S. Parikh and **Kunal Sen** (eds), 1995a. *Economic Restructuring in East Asia and India: Perspectives on Policy Reform,* Indira Gandhi Institute of Development Research and Institute of Southeast Asian Studies, Singapore, Macmillan and St Martin's Press, London and New York.

———, 1995b. 'India: Crisis and Response', in Agarwal, Pradeep et al. (eds), *Economic Restructuring in East Asia and India: Perspectives on Policy Reform,* Indira Gandhi Institute of Development Research and Institute of Southeast Asian Studies, Singapore, Macmillan and St Martin's Press, London and New York, pp. 159–216.

———, (eds), 1996. 'Policies for Industrial Competitiveness: What India Can Learn From the East Asian Experience', Indira Gandhi Institute of Development Research, Project Report to International Development Research Centre, Ottawa, Canada, Bombay (mimeo).

Agosin, Manuel R., 1981. *Trade Policy Reform and Economic Performance: A Review of the Issues and Some Preliminary Evidence,* UNCTAD, Discussion Paper No. 41, Geneva.

Ahluwalia, Montek S., 1995. 'India's Economic Reforms', in Cassen, Robert and Vijay Joshi (eds), *India—The Future of Economic Reform,* Oxford University Press, Bombay, Chapter 2, pp. 13–29.

Ahmed, Yusuf J., Salah El Serafy and **Ernst Lutz** (eds), 1989. *Environmental Accounting for Sustainable Development,* World Bank, Washington DC.

Amsden, Alice H. 1988. 'Taiwan's Economic History: A Case of Etatisme and a Challenge to Dependency Theory', in Bates, Robert H. (ed.), *Toward a Political Economy of Development—A Rational Choice Perspective,* University of California Press, Berkeley, Chapter 4, pp. 142–75.

Amsden, Alice H. 1989. *Asia's Next Giant—South Korea and Late Industrialization,* Oxford University Press, New York and Oxford.

———, 1991. 'Comments', in Meier, Gerald M. (ed.), *Politics and Policy Making in Developing Countries: Perspectives on the New Political Economy,* ICS Press, San Francisco, pp. 127–32.

Anderson, Kym and **Richard Blackhurst** (eds), 1993. *Regional Integration and the Global Trading System,* Harvester–Wheatsheaf (Published for the GATT Secretariat, Geneva), New York.

Arestis, Philip and **Victoria Chick** (eds), 1995. *Finance, Development and Structural Change—Post-Keynesian Perspectives*, Edward Elgar, Aldershot.

Atkin, Michael, 1993. *Snouts in the Trough: European Farmers, the Common Agricultural Policy and the Public Purse,* Woodhead Publishing Ltd, Cambridge.

———, 1995. *The International Grain Trade,* 2nd edition, Woodhead Publishing Ltd, Cambridge.

Avramovic, Dragoslav, 1983. 'The Role of the International Monetary Fund: The Disputes, Qualifications, and the Future', in Williamson, John (ed.), *IMF Conditionality,* Institute for International Economics, Washington DC, Chapter 23.

———, 1989, *Conditionality: Facts, Theory and Policy,* World Institute for Development Economics Research (WIDER), Helsinki, United Nations University.

Avery, William P. (ed.), 1993, *World Agriculture and the GATT,* Lynne Rienner Publishers, Boulder and London.

Ayittey, George B.N., 1995. 'Why Structural Adjustment Failed in Africa', in Schydlowsky, Daniel M. (ed.), *Structural Adjustment—Retrospect and Prospect,* Praeger, Westport, Connecticut, London, Chapter 7, pp. 108–22.

Azam, Jean-Paul and **Christian Morrisson,** 1994. *Political Feasibility of Adjustment in Cote D'Ivoire and Morocco,* Development Centre Studies, OECD, Paris.

Bacha, Edmar L., 1983. 'Vicissitudes of Recent Stabilization Attempts in Brazil and the IMF Alternative', in Williamson, John (ed.), *IMF Conditionality,* Institute for International Economics, Washington DC, Chapter 14.

Bagchi, Amiya Kumar, 1987. *Public Intervention and Industrial Restructuring in China, India and Republic of Korea*, International Labour Organisation, Asian Employment Programme (ARTEP), New Delhi.

Balassa, Bela, 1981. 'Structural Adjustment Policies in Developing Economies', World Bank Staff Working Paper No. 464, John Hopkins University and the World Bank, Washington DC.

Barker, Cres and **Bill Page,** 1974. 'OPEC as a Model for Other Mineral Exporters', in *Institute of Development Studies Bulletine,* Vol. 6, No. 2, October (Special Issue on Oil and Development edited by Frank Ellis), pp. 81–90.

Barraclough, Solon and **Andrea Finger–Stich,** 1996. *Some Ecological and Social Implications of Commercial Shrimp Farming in Asia,* United Nations Research Institute for Social Development, Geneva.

Barraclough, Solon and **Krishna Ghimire,** 1990. *The Social Dynamics of Deforestation in Developing Countries: Principal Issues and Research Priorities,* United Nations Research Institute for Social Development, Geneva.

Barrat Brown, Michael and **Pauline Tiffen,** 1994. *Short Changed: Africa and World Trade,* Pluto Press with Transnational Institute, London and Boulder.

Bates, Robert H. (ed.), 1988. *Towards a Political Economy of Development—A Rational Choice Perspective*, University of California Press, Berkeley.

———, 1989. *Beyond the Miracle of the Market—The Political Economy of Agrarian Development in Kenya,* Cambridge University Press, Cambridge.

Bates, Robert H. 1991. Comments incorporated in 'A Critique by Political Scientists', in Meier, Gerald M. (ed.), *Politics and Policy Making in Developing Countries—Perspectives on the New Political Economy*, ICS Press, San Francisco, Chapter 10, pp. 261–71.

Baumol, W.M. and **W. Oates,** 1975. *The Theory of Environmental Policy*, Prentice Hall, Englewood Cliffs, NJ.

Beckerman, Wilfred, 1991. 'Global warming: A Sceptical Economic Assessment', in Helm, Dieter (ed.), *Economic Policy towards the Environment*, Blackwell, Oxford.

Behrman, Jere R., 1992. 'Comments', in Corbo, Vittorio et al. (eds), *Adjustment Lending Revisited—Policies to Restore Growth, A World Bank Symposium*, World Bank, Washington DC, pp. 64–66.

Berg, Elliot, 1991. 'Comments', in Thomas, Vinod et al. (eds), *Restructuring Economies in Distress: Policy Reform and the World Bank*, World Bank, Oxford University Press, Oxford, pp. 215–19.

———, 1995. 'African Adjustment Programs: False Attacks and True Dilemmas', in Schydlowsky, Daniel M. (ed.), *Structural Adjustment: Retrospect and Prospect,* Praeger, Westport, Connecticut, London, Chapter 6, pp. 89–107.

Bhagwati, Jagdish (edited by Douglas A. Irwin), 1991. *Political Economy and International Economics*, MIT Press, Cambridge, Mass.

Bhaskar, V., 1992. 'Privatization and the Developing Countries: The Issues and the Evidence', UNCTAD, Discussion Paper No. 47, Geneva.

Bird, Graham, 1992. 'IMF Lending: The Analytical Issues', Overseas Development Institute Working Paper No. 64, London.

———, 1993. 'IMF Lending: The Empricial Evidence', Overseas Development Institute Working Paper No. 70, London.

Blaikie, Piers and **Sally Jeanrenaud,** 1996. *Biodiversity and Human Welfare*, United Nations Research Institute for Social Development, Geneva.

Brandt, Willy (Chairman), 1980. 'Report of the Independent Commission on International Development Issues', *North–South: A Programme for Survival*, Pan Books, London.

Boratav, Korkut, 1993. 'Public Sector, Public Intervention and Economic Development—The Impact of Changing Perspectives and Policies During the 1980s', UNCTAD, Discussion Paper No. 61, Geneva.

Brautigam, Deborah, 1995. 'The State as Agent: Industrial Development in Taiwan, 1952–72', in Stein, Howard (ed.), *Asian Industrialization and Africa—Studies in Policy Alternatives to Structural Adjustment*, St Martins Press, London, Chapter 5, pp. 145–81.

Brown, Drusilla K., 1993. 'Modeling and Analysis of Agricultural Trade Liberalisation', in Stern (ed.), *The Multilateral Trading System: Analysis and Options for Change*, Harvester–Wheatsheaf, New York, Chapter 12, pp. 315–43.

Brundtland, Gro Harlem, 1993. *Population, Environment and Development*, UNFPA, New York.

Buchanan, James M., 1980. 'Rent Seeking and Profit Seeking', in Buchanan, James M. et al. (eds), *Towards a Theory of Rent Seeking Society*, Texas A and M University Press, College Station, Texas, Chapter 1, pp. 3–15.

Buchanan, James M., Robert D. Tollison and **Gordon Tullock** (eds), 1980. *Towards a Theory of Rent Seeking Society*, Texas A and M University Press, College Station, Texas.

Carroll, Christopher D. and **David N. Weil**, 1994. 'Saving and Growth: A Reinterpretation', *Carnegie–Rochester Conference Series on Public Policy*, Vol. 40, pp. 133–92.

Carson, Rachel, 1983 (1962). *Silent Spring*, Harmondsworth, Penguin.

Cassen, Robert and **Vijay Joshi** (eds), 1995. *India—The Future of Economic Reform*, Oxford University Press, Bombay.

Chen, Edward K.Y., 1979. *Hypergrowth in Asian Economies: A Comparative Survey of Hong Kong, Japan, Korea, Singapore and Taiwan*, Macmillan, London.

Chhibber, Ajay and **Javed Khalizadeh–Shirazi,** 1991. 'Public Finance', in Thomas, Vinod et al. (eds), *Restructuring Economies in Distress: Policy Reform and the World Bank,* World Bank, Oxford University Press, Oxford, Chapter 3, pp. 20–46.

Chiu, Lee-in Chen, 1995. 'The Pattern and Impact of Taiwan's Investment in Mainland China', in Croix, Sumner J. la et al. (eds), *Emerging Patterns of East Asian Investment in China: From Korea, Taiwan and Hong Kong*, An Eastgate Book, M.E. Sharpe, Armonk, New York and London, Chapter 9.

Cho, Yoon Je and **Deena Kahtkhate,** 1989. 'Financial Liberalisation: Issues and Evidence', *Economic and Political Weekly*, Vol. 24, No. 20, 20 May.

Cline, W., 1982. 'Can the East Asian Model be Generalised?', *World Development*, Vol. 10, No. 2, February.

Coase, R.H., 1960. 'The Problem of Social Cost', *Journal of Law and Economics*, Vol. 3.

———, 1988. *The Firm, the Market and the Law*, The University of Chicago Press, Chicago.

Cohn, Theodore H., 1993. 'The Changing Role of the United States in the Global Agricultural Trade Regime', in Avery, William R. (ed.), *World Agriculture and the GATT*, Lynne Rienner Publishers, Boulder and London, Chapter 2, pp. 17–38.

Colclough, Christopher, 1993. 'Structuralism Versus Neo-Liberalism: An Introduction', in Colclough, Christopher and James Manor (eds), *States or Markets—Neo-liberalism and the Development Policy Debate*, Clarendon Paperbacks, Oxford, Chapter 1, pp. 1–25.

Colclough, Christoper and **James Manor** (eds), 1993. *States or Markets—Neo-liberalism and the Development Policy Debate*, Clarendon Paperbacks, Oxford.

Commoner, Barry, 1972. *The Closing Circle: Confronting the Environmental Crisis*, Jonathan Cape, London.

Cooper, Richard N., 1983. Comments in a Panel Discussion, in Williamson, John (ed.), *IMF Conditionality*, Institute for International Economics, Washington DC, pp. 569–80.

Corbo, Vittorio and **Stanley Fischer,** 1992.'Adjustment Programmes and Bank Support—Rationale and Main Results', in Corbo, Vittorio et al. (eds), *Adjustment Lending Revisited—Policies to Restore Growth, A World Bank Symposium*, World Bank. Washington DC, pp. 7–20.

Corbo, Vittorio and **Patricio Rojas,** 1992. 'World Bank-Supported Adjustment Programs: Country Performance and Effectiveness', in Corbo, Vittorio et al. (eds), *Adjustment Lending Revisited—Policies to Restore Growth, A World Bank Symposium*, World Bank, Washington DC, pp. 23–39.

Corbo, Vittorio and **Sang–Mok Suh,** 1992. *Structural Adjustment in a Newly Industrialized Country—The Korean Experience*, World Bank, John Hopkins University Press, Baltimore.

Corbo, Vittorio, M. Goldstein and **M. Khan,** 1987. *Growth-Oriented Adjustment Programs,* IMF, World Bank, Washington DC.

Corbo, Vittorio, Stanley Fischer and **Steven B. Webb** (eds), 1992. *Adjustment Lending Revisited—Policies to Restore Growth, A World Bank Symposium*, World Bank, Washington DC.

Cornea, Andrea, Richard Jolly and **Frances Stewart,** 1987. *Adjustment with a Human Face*, Oxford University Press, Oxford.

Croix, Sumner J. la, Michael Plummer and **Keun Lee** (eds), 1995. *Emerging Patterns of East Asian Investment in China: From Korea, Taiwan and Hong Kong*, An Eastgate book, M.E. Sharpe, Armonk, New York and London.

Dailami, Mansoor, 1991. 'Korea: Successful Adjustment', in Thomas, Vinod et al., *Restructuring Economies in Distress: Policy Reform and the World Bank*, World Bank, Oxford University Press, Oxford, Chapter 18.

Dasgupta, Biplab, 1974. 'Large International Firms in the Oil Industry', in *Institute of Development Studies Bulletine*, Vol. 6, No. 2, October (Special Issue on Oil and Development edited by Frank Ellis), pp. 46–67.

———, 1976. 'Environment and Development', Report submitted to United Nations Environment Programme (UNEP), Nairobi (mimeo).

———, 1978. 'The Environment Debate—Some Issues and Trends', *Economic and Political Weekly*, Annual, February.

———, 1997a. 'The New Political Economy: A Critical Analysis', *Economic and Political Weekly*, Vol. 22, No. 4, 25 January.

———, 1997b. 'Indian Agriculture in the Global Context and Under Structural Adjustment', in Chaddha, G.K. and Aloke N. Sharma, *Growth, Employment and Poverty in Rural India: Change and Continuity*, Allied Publishers, Delhi.

———, 1997c. 'SAP: Issues and Conditionalities—A Global Review', *Economic and Political Weekly*, Vol. 22, Nos 20 and 21, 17–24 May.

Dasgupta, Biplab, Brian Johnson and **Hans Singer,** 1997. 'Environment and Development: A Conceptual Overview', Report submitted to United Nations Environment Programme, Nairobi.

Dasgupta, Partha, 1991. 'The Environment as a Commodity', in Helm, Dieter (ed.), *Economic Policy Towards the Environment*, Blackwell, Oxford, Chapter 2, pp. 25–51.

———, 1995. 'Economic Development and Environment: Issues, Policies, and the Political Economy', in Schydlowsky, Daniel M. (ed.), *Structural Adjustment—Retrospect and Prospect*, Praeger, Westport, Connecticut, London, Chapter 7.

David, Wilfred L., 1985. *The IMF Policy Paradigm: The Macroeconomics of Stabilization, Structural Adjustment and Economic Development*, Praeger, New York and Eastbourne.

Deardorff, Alan V., 1993a. 'Economic Perspectives on Antidumping Law', in Stern, Robert M. (ed.), *The Multilateral Trading System: Analysis and Options for Change*, Harvester–Wheatsheaf, New York, Chapter 6, pp. 135–54.

———, 1993b. 'Should Patents be Extended to all Developing Countries?', in Stern, Robert M. (ed.), *The Multilateral Trading System: Analysis and Options for Change*, Harvester–Wheatsheaf, New York, Chapter 15, pp. 435–48.

Deardorff, Alan V. and **Robert M. Stern,** 1993. 'Options for Trade Liberalisation in the Uruguay Round and Beyond', in Stern, Robert M. (ed.), *The Multilateral Trading System: Analysis and Options for Change*, Harvester–Wheatsheaf, New York, Chapter 5, pp. 113–34.

de Castro, Juan A., 1994. 'The Internalization of External Environmental Costs and Sustainable Development', UNCTAD, Discussion Paper No. 81.

Dell, Sidney, 1983. 'Stabilization: The Political Economy of Overkill', in Williamson, John (ed.), *IMF Conditionality*, Institute for International Economics, Washington DC, Chapter 2.

de Melo, Jaime, 1992. 'Sources of Growth and Structural Change in the Republics of Korea and Taiwan: Some Comparisons', in Corbo, Vittorio et al. (eds), *Adjustment Lending Revisited—Policies to Restore Growth, A World Bank Symposium*, World Bank, Washington DC.

Development Committee, 1984. *Trade Policy Issues and the Developing Countries*, Washington DC, No. 3, April, pp. 1–41.

———, 1985a. World Bank, Washington DC, No. 4.

———, 1985b. *Trade and Development*, (jointly by WB and IMF), Washington DC, No. 6, April.

———, 1987a. *Environment, Growth and Development*, World Bank, Washington DC, No. 14, April.

———, 1987b. *Market Prospects of Raw Materials*, World Bank, Washington DC, No. 15, April.

———, 1988a. *Environment and Development: Implementing the World Bank's New Policies*, World Bank, Washington DC, No. 17, September.

———, 1988b. *The Impact of the Industrial Policies of Developed Countries on Developing Countries*, Washington DC, No. 20, September.

———, 1989. *World Bank Support for the Environment, A Progress Report*, Washington DC, No. 22, September.

———, 1990a. *Problems and Issues of Structural Adjustment*, Washington DC, No. 23, April and September.

———, 1990b. *Funding for Global Environment*, Washington DC, No. 24, May.

———, 1992. World Bank, Washington DC, 44th meeting, September.

———, 1993a. World Bank, Washington DC, 46th meeting, May.

———, 1993b. World Bank, Washington DC, 47th meeting, September.

———, 1994. World Bank, Washington DC, 48th meeting, April.

Deyo, Frederic, 1996. 'State Industrial Restructuring and Human Resource Strategies: Thailand and the East Asian NICs', in Lele, Jayant and Kwasi Ofori-Yeboah (eds), *Unravelling the Asian Miracle: Explorations in Development Strategies, Geopolitics and Regionalism*, Dartmouth, Aldershot, pp. 66–80.

Dommen, Edward (ed.), 1993. *Fair Principles for Sustainable Development: Essays on Environmental Policy and Developing Countries*, Edward Elgar, UNCTAD, Aldershot.

Dornbusch, Rudiger, 1992. 'Comments', in Corbo, Vittorio et al. (eds), *Adjustment Lending Revisited—Policies to Restore Growth, A World Bank Symposium*, World Bank, Washington DC, pp. 114–16.

Dornbusch, Robert and **L.T. Kuenzler,** 1993. 'Exchange Rate Policy; Options and Issues', in Dornbusch, Robert and L.T. Kuenzler (eds), *Policy Making in the Open Economy—Concepts and Case Studies in Economic Performance*, Oxford University Press, Oxford.

Downs, Anthony, 1957. *An Economic Theory of Democracy*, Harper and Row, New York.

Dreze, Jean and **Amartya Sen,** 1995. *India—Economic Development and Social Opportunity*, Oxford University Press, Delhi.

Dutt, Amitava Krishna, 1995. 'Interest Rate Policy, Growth and Distribution in an Open Less-Developed Economy: A Theoretical Analysis', in Arestis, Philip and Victoria Chick (eds), *Finance, Development and Structural Change—Post-Keynesian Perspectives*, Edward Elgar, Aldershot, Chapter 1, pp. 3–26.

Easterly, William, 1995. 'Explaining Miracles: Growth Regressions Meet the Gang of Four', in Ito, Takatoshi and Anne D. Krueger (eds), *Growth Theories in Light of the East Asian Experience*, The University of Chicago Press, Chicago and London, Chapter 11, pp. 267–90.

Eckerseley, Robyn, 1996. 'Markets, the State and the Environment: An Overview', in Eckerseley, Robyn (ed.), *Markets and the State and Environment—Towards Integration*, Macmillan, London, Chapter 1, pp. 7–45.

ECA (United Nations Economic Commission for Africa), 1996. 'Evaluation of, and African Alternative Framework to, Structural Adjustment Programs for Socio-economic Recovery and Transformation', in Yansane, Aguibou Y. (ed.), *Prospects for Recovery and Sustainable Development in Africa*, Greenwood Press, Westport, Connecticut and London.

ECLAC (United Nations Economic Commission for Latin America and Caribbean), 1994. *Policies to Improve Linkages with the Global Economy*, Santiago, Chile.

Ecologist, 1972. 'A Blueprint for Survival', Penguin, Harmondsworth.

Edwards, Sebastian, 1991. 'Comments', in Thomas, Vinod et al. (eds), *Restructuring Economies in Distress: Policy Reform and the World Bank*, World Bank, Oxford University Press, Oxford, Chapter 21, pp. 489–93.

Ehrlich, Paul, 1971. *The Population Bomb*, A. Ballantine/Friends of the Earth, London.

Encyclopaedia Britannica, 1994. *1994 Britannia Book of the Year*, Chicago.

Faini, Riccardo, Jaime de Melo, Abdel Senhadji–Semlali and **Julie Stanton,** 1991. 'Macro Performance Under Adjustment Lending', in Thomas, Vinod et al. (eds), *Restructuring Economies in Distress: Policy Reform and the World Bank*, World Bank, Oxford University Press, Oxford, Chapter 11, pp. 222–46.

Feldstein, M. and **C. Horioka,** 1980. 'Domestic Saving and International Capital Flow', *Economic Journal*, Vol. 90, pp. 314–29.

Findlay, Ronald, 1991. 'The New Political Economy: Its Explanatory Power for Less Developed Countries', in Meier, Gerald M. (ed.), *Politics and Policy Making in Developing Countries—Perspectives on the New Political Economy*, ICS Press, San Francisco, Chapter 2, pp. 13–40.

Fischer, Stanley, 1995. 'Structural Adjustment-Lessons from the 1980s', in Schydlowsky, Daniel M. (ed.), *Structural Adjustment—Retrospect and Prospect*, Praeger, Westport, Connecticut, London, Chapter 2.

Fishlow, Albert and **Catherine Gwin,** 1994. 'Lessons from the East Asian Experience: Overview', in Fishlow, Albert et al. (eds), *Miracle or Design: Lessons from the East Asian Experience*, Overseas Development Council, Policy Essays, No. 11, Washington DC, pp. 1–12.

Fishlow, Albert, Catherine Gwin, Stephen Haggard, Dani Rodrik and **Robert Wade** (eds), 1994. *Miracle or Design: Lessons from the East Asian Experience*, Overseas Development Council, Policy Essays, No. 11, Washington DC.

FitzGerald, Garret, 1979. *Unequal Partners*, United Nations, New York.

Folmer, C., M.A. Keyzer, M.D. Merbis, H.J.J. Stolwijk and **P.J.J. Veenendaal,** 1995. *The Common Agricultural Policy Beyond the Macsherry Reform*, North Holland, Amsterdam.

Foroutan, Faezeh, 1993. 'Trade Reform in Ten Sub-Saharan African Countries: Achievements and Failures', Policy Research Working Paper 1222, World Bank, Policy Research Department, Trade Policy Division, Washington DC.

Friday, L. and **R. Laskey,** 1989. *The Fragile Environment*, Cambridge University Press, Cambridge.

Frankel, J.A. 1991. 'International Capital Mobility: A Review', *American Economic Review*, Vol. 81, No. 1, March, pp. 78–99.

Frankel, Richard M., Don F. Hadwiger and **William P. Browne** (eds), 1979. *The Role of US Agriculture in Foreign Policy*, Praeger, New York.

Frankel, Roberto, Jose Maria Fantelli and **Guillermo Rozenwurcei,** 1993. 'Growth and Structural Reform in Latin America: Where We Stand', UNCTAD, Discussion Paper No. 62, Geneva.

Friedland, William H., 1991. 'Introduction: Shaping the New Political Economy of Advanced Capitalist Agriculture', in Friedland, William H. et al. (eds), *Towards a New Political Economy of Agriculture*, Westview, Boulder, Chapter 1, pp. 1–34.

Friedland, William H., Laerence Busch, Frederick H. Buttel and **Alan P. Rudy** (eds), 1991. *Towards a New Political Economy of Agriculture*, Westview, Boulder.

Friedman, Harriet, 1991. 'Changes in the International Division of Labor: Agrifood Complexes and Export Agriculture', in Friedland, William H. et al. (eds), *Towards a New Political Economy of Agriculture*, Westview, Boulder, Chapter 3, pp. 65–93.

———, 1995. 'Food Politics: New Dangers, New Possibilities', in McMichael, Philip (ed.), *Food and Agrarian Orders in the World Economy*, Praeger, London, pp. 15–33.

Fukuda, Shin–ichi and **Hideki Toya,** 1995. 'Conditional Convergence in East Asian Countries: The Role of Exports in Economic Growth', in Ito, Takatoshi and Anne O. Krueger (eds), *Growth Theories in Light of the East Asian Experience*, The University of Chicago Press, Chicago and London, Chapter 10, pp. 247–62.

Gelb, Alan and **Patrick Honohan,** 1991. 'Financial Sector Reform', in Thomas, Vinod et al. (eds), *Restructuring Economies in Distress: Policy Reform and the World Bank*, World Bank, Oxford University Press, Oxford, Chapter 5.

Gijswijt, August, 1996. 'The Establishment of an International Regime: The Case for the Stratospheric Ozone Depletion', in Ester, Peter and Wolfgang Schluchter (eds), *Social Dimensions of Contemporary Environmental Issues: International Perspectives*, Tilburg University Press, Chapter 4, pp. 55–79.

Gokarn, Subir V., 1995. 'Korea: Industrial and Financial Restructuring', in Agarwal, Pradeep et al. (eds), *Economic Restructuring in East Asia and India: Perspectives on Policy Reform*, Indira Gandhi Institute of Development Research and Institute of Southeast Asian Studies, Singapore, Macmillan and St Martin's Press, London and New York, Chapter 2, pp. 22–53.

Gold, Bela, 1979. *Productivity, Technology and Capital*, Lexington Books, Lexington.

Goodman, David, 1991. 'Some Recent Tendencies in the Industrial Reorganization of the Agri-Food System', in Friedland, William et al. (eds), *Towards a New Political Economy of Agriculture*, Westview, Boulder, Chapter 2, pp. 37–64.

Government of India, for various years. *Economic Survey*, New Delhi.

Griffith–Jones, Stephany, 1992. 'The Return of Private Capital to Latin American Countries: The Facts, an Analytical Framework and Some Policy Issues', in Teunissen, Jon Joost (ed.), *Fragile Finance—Rethinking the International Monetary System*, FONDAD, The Hague.

Griffith-Jones, Stephany, 1993. 'International Financial Markets: A Case of Market Failure', in Colclough, Christopher and James Manor (eds), *States or Markets—Neo-Liberalism and the Development Policy Debate*, Clarendon Paperbacks, Oxford, Chapter 5, pp. 101–20.

Grindle, Merilee S., 1991. 'The New Political Economy: Positive Economics and Negative Politics', in Meier, Gerald M. (ed.), *Politics and Policy Making in Developing Countries—Perspectives on the New Political Economy*, ICS Press, San Francisco, Chapter 3.

———, 1996. *Challenging the State—Crisis and Innovation in Latin America and Africa*, Cambridge University Press, Cambridge.

Grindle, Merilee S. and **John W. Thomas,** 1991. *Public Choices and Policy Change—The Political Economy of Reform in Developing Countries*, John Hopkins University Press, Baltimore and London.

Grunberg, Isabelle, 1990. 'Exploring the Myth of Hegemonic Stability', *International Organization*, Vol. 44, No. 4, Autumn.

Gwin, Catherine, 1995. 'A Comparative Assessment', in Huq, Mahbub ul et al. (eds), *The UN and the Bretton Woods Institutions: New Challenges for the Twenty First Century*, Macmillan, London, pp. 95–116.

Hammond, Rosa and **Lisa McGowan,** 1994. 'Ghana: The World Bank's Sham Showcase', in Danahar Kevin (ed.), *50 Years is Enough: The Case Against the World Bank and the International Monetary Fund*, Southend Press, Boston, MA.

Hayami, Yujiro, 1991. 'Land Reform', in Meier, Gerald M. (ed.), *Politics and Policy Making in Developing Countries—Perspectives on the New Political Economy*, ICS Press, San Francisco, Chapter 6.

Hayek, F.A., 1949. *Individualism and Economic Order*, Routledge, London.

Healey, John, Richard Ketley and **Mark Robinson,** 1992. *Political Regimes and Economic Policy Patterns in Developing Countries, 1978–88*, ODI No. 67, London.

Helm, Dieter (ed.), 1991. *Economic Policy Towards the Environment*, Blackwell, Oxford.

Helm, Dieter and **David Pearce,** 'Economic Policy Towards the Environment: An Overview', in Helm, Dieter (ed.), *Economic Policy Towards the Environment*, Blackwell, Oxdord.

Helpman, E. and **P.R. Krugman,** 1985. *Market Structure and Foreign Trade*, MIT Press, Cambridge, Mass.

Hemmi, Kenzo, 1994. 'The Japanese Perspective', in Ingersent, K.A. et al. (eds), *Agriculture in the Uruguay Round*, St Martin's Press, New York, pp. 140–56.

Herrera, Amilcar O., Hugo D. Scolnik et al., 1976. *Catastrophe or New Society? A Latin American World Model*, Bariloche Foundation of Argentina, IDRC (International Development Research Centre), Ottawa.

Hillman, Jimmye S., 1994. 'The US Perspective', in Ingersent, K.A. et al. (eds), *Agriculture in the Uruguay Round*, St Martin's Press, New York, pp. 26–54.

Hindess, B., 1988. *Choice, Rationality and Social Theory*, Unwin–Hyman, London.

Hindley, Brian, 1987. 'Different and More Favourable Treatment—And Graduation', in Finger, Michael J. and Andrez Olechowski (eds), *The Uruguay Round: A Handbook on the Multilateral Trade Negotiations*, World Bank, Washington DC.

Ho, Samuel, 1981. 'South Korea and Taiwan: Development Prospects and Problems in the 1980s', *Asian Survey*, December.

Hobday, Michael, 1995. *Innovation in East Asia—The Challenge to Japan*, Edward Elgar, Aldershot.

Hoekman, Bernard M., 1993a. 'Multilateral Trade Negotiations and Coordination of Commercial Policies', in Stern, Robert M. (ed.), *The Multilateral Trading System: Analysis and Options for Change*, Harvester–Wheatsheaf, New York, Chapter 2, pp. 29–61.

———, 1993b. 'Trade Offs, Coalitions, and National Interests: Developing Country Options in MTN', in Stern, Robert M. (ed.), *The Multilateral Trading System: Analysis and Options for Change*, Harvester–Wheatsheaf, New York, Chapter 17, pp. 473–501.

Hoekman, Bernard M. and **Patricia Cremoux,** 1993. 'Perspectives for Multilateral Reductions in Agricultural Support Policies', in Stern, Robert M. (ed.), *The Multilateral Trading System: Analysis and Options*, Harvester–Wheatsheaf, New York, Chapter 11, pp. 277–307.

Hoekman, Bernard M. and **Michael P. Leidy,** 1993. 'Antidumping and Market Disruption: The Incentive Effects of Antidumping Laws', in Stern, Robert M. (ed.), *The Multilateral Trading System: Analysis and Options*, Harvester–Wheatsheaf, New York, Chapter 7, pp. 155–82.

Hoekman, Bernard M. and **Robert M. Stern,** 1993. 'International Transactions in Services: Issues and Data Availability', in Stern, Robert M. (ed.), *The Multilateral Trading System: Analysis and Options for Change*, Harvester–Wheatsheaf, New York, pp. 391–434.

Hoggard, Stephen, 1991. Comments incorporated in 'A Critique by Political Scientists', in Meier, Gerald M. (ed.), *Politics and the Policy Makers in Developing Countries—Perspectives on the New Political Economy*, ICS Press, San Francisco, Chapter 10, pp. 272–73.

———, 1994. 'Politics and Institutions in the World Bank's East Asia', in Fishlow, Albert et al. (eds), *Miracle or Design: Lessons from the East Asian Experience*, Overseas Development Council, Policy Essays, No. 11, Washington DC, pp. 81–108.

———, 1996. 'Democracy and Economic Growth', in Schydlowsky, Daniel M. (ed.), *Structural Adjustment—Retrospect and Prospect*, Praeger, Westport, Connecticut, London, Chapter 11.

Hopkins, Raymond F., 1993. 'Developing Countries in the Uruguay Round: Bargaining Under Uncertainty and Inequality', in Avery, William P. (ed.), *World Agriculture and the GATT*, Lynne Rienner Publishers, Boulder and London, Chapter 7, pp. 143–63.

Horton, S., R. Kanbur and **D. Mazumdar,** 1991. 'Labour Markets in an Era of Adjustment: An Overview', PRE Working Paper Series, WPS 694, World Bank, Washington DC.

Hudec, Robert E., 1990. 'Thinking About the New Section 301: Beyond Good and Evil', in Bhagwati, Jagdish N. and Hugh T. Patrick (eds), *Aggressive Unilateralism: America's 301 Trade Policy and the World Trading System*, University of Michigan Press, Ann Arbour.

Huq, Mahbub ul, Richard Jolly and **Paul Streeten** (eds), 1995a. *The UN and the Bretton Woods Institutions: New Challenges for the Twenty First Century*, Macmillan, London.

Huq, Mahbub ul, Richard Jolly and **Paul Streeten**, 1995b. 'Overview', in Huq, Mahbub ul et al. (eds), *The UN and the Bretton Woods Institutions: New Challenges for the Twenty First Century*, Macmillan, London.

Hymer, Stephen, 1972. 'Multinational Corporations and the Law of Uneven Development', in Bhagwati, Jagdish N. (ed.), *Economics and World Order: From the 1970's to the 1990's*, Macmillan, New York.

ILO, 1993. 'Structural Change and Adjustment in Zimbabwe', Interdepartmental Project on Structural Adjustment, Occasional Paper 16.

———, 1995. *Sectoral Activities Programme, Joint Meeting on the Impact of Structural Adjustment in the Public Services (Efficiency, Quality Improvement and Working Conditions)*, 24–30 May, Geneva.

Ingersent, K.A., A.J. Rayner and **R.C. Hine** (eds), 1994a. *Agriculture in the Uruguay Round*, St Martin's Press, New York.

———, 1994b. 'The EC Perspective', in Ingersent, K.A. et al. (eds), *Agriculture in the Uruguay Round*, St Martin's Press, New York, pp. 55–87.

Intriligator, Michael D., 1997. 'What Russia Could Learn from China in the Transition to a Market Economy', Paper presented at the ECAAR (Economics Allied for Arms Reduction), New Orleans (mimeo).

Irvine, Sandy and **Alec Ponton,** 1988. *A Green Manifesto: Policies for a Green Future*, Optima, London.

Islam, Nurul, 1991. 'Comments', in Thomas, Vinod et al. (eds), *Restructuring Economies in Distress: Policy Reform and the World Bank*, World Bank, Oxford University Press, Oxford, pp. 152–58.

Ito, Junichi, 1996. *Trade Liberalization of Agricultural Products and Conservation of the Environment*, National Resource Institute of Agricultural Economics, Ministry of Agriculture, Forestry and Fisheries, Japan, Tokyo.

Ito, Takatoshi, and **Anne O. Krueger** (eds), 1995. *Growth Theories in Light of the East Asian Experience*, The University of Chicago Press, Chicago and London.

Jackson, John H., 1993a. 'Safeguards and Adjustment Policies', in Stern, Robert M. (ed.), *The Multilateral Trading System: Analysis and Options for Change*, Harvester–Wheatsheaf, New York, Chapter 8, pp. 183–232.

———, 1993b. 'The Constitutional Structure for International Cooperation in Trade in Services and the Uruguay Round of GATT', in Stern, Robert M. (ed.), *The Multilateral Trading System: Analysis and Options for Change*, Harvester–Wheatsheaf, New York, Chapter 13, pp. 351–89.

Jacobs, Michael, 1996. 'Sustainability and the Market: A Typology of Environmental Economics', in Eckersely, Robyn (ed.), *Markets and the State and Environment—Towards Integration*, Macmillan, London, Chapter 2, pp. 46–70.

Jayarajah, Carl, William Bronson and **Binayak Sen,** 1996. *Social Dimensions of Adjustment: World Bank Experience 1980–93*, A World Bank Operations Evaluation Study, OED, Washington DC.

Jayawardena, Lal, 1995. 'The Keynesian Vision and the Developing Countries', in Huq, Mahbub ul et al. (eds), *The UN and the Bretton Woods Institutions: New Challenges for the Twenty First Century*, Macmillan, London, pp. 49–59.

Jha, Veena, Rene Vossenaar and **Simonetta Zarrilli,** 1993. 'Ecolabelling and International Trade', UNCTAD, Discussion Paper No. 70, Geneva.

Jilberto, Alex E. Fernandez and **Andre Mommen,** 1996. *Liberalisation in the Developing World: Institutional and Economic Changes in Latin America, Africa and Asia*, Routledge, London.

Johnston, R.J., 1996. *Nature, State and Economy—A Political Economy of the Environment*, Wiley, New York.

Joshi, Vijay and **I.M.D. Little,** 1995a. 'Macroeconomic Stabilization in India, 1991–1993 and Beyond', in Cassen, Robert and Vijay Joshi (eds), *India—The Future of Economic Reform*, Oxford University Press, Bombay, Chapter 2.

———, 1995b. 'Future Trade and Exchange Rate Policy for India', in Cassen, Robert and Vijay Joshi (eds), *India—The Future of Economic Reform*, Oxford University Press, Bombay, pp. 55–70.

Kanyenze, Godfrey, 1996. 'The Impact of Economic Stabilisation on the Wage Structure in Zimbabwe', in Harvey, Charles (ed.), *Constraints on the Success of Structural Adjustment Programmes in Africa*, Macmillan, London, Chapter 4, pp. 52–75.

Keohane, Robert O., 1984. *After Hegemony: Cooperation and Discord in the World Political Economy*, Princeton University Press, Princeton.

Kiguel, M.A. and **Nissan Liviatan,** 1992. 'Nominal Anchors, Stabilization and Growth: Some Thoughts on High-Inflation Economics', in Corbo, Vittorio et al., *Adjustment Lending Revisited—Policies to Restore Growth, A World Bank Symposium*, World Bank, Washington DC, pp. 99–116.

Killick, Tony, 1992a. 'Continuity and Change in IMF Programme Design 1986–92', ODI Working Paper No. 69, London.

———, 1992b. 'Explaining Africa's Post-Independence Development Experiences', ODI Working Paper No. 60, London.

———, 1993a. 'Issues in the design of IMF Programmes', ODI Working Paper No. 71, London.

———, 1993b. 'Improving the Effectiveness of Financial Assistance for Policy Reforms', in Development Committee, 1993b, World Bank, Washington DC, 47th meeting, September.

———, 1994, 'Conditionality and the Adjustment-Development Connection', ODI, London.

Kim, Si Joong, 1995. 'Korean Direct Investment in China: Perspectives of Korean Investors', in Croix, Sumner J. la et al. (eds), *Emerging Patterns of East Asian Investment in China: From Korea, Taiwan and Hong Kong*, An Eastgate book, M.E. Sharpe, Armonk, New York and London, Chapter 12.

Kim, Joon-Kyung, Sang Dal Shim and **Jun-Il Kim,** 1995. 'The Role of the Government in Promoting Industrialization and Human Capital Accumulation in Korea', in Ito, Takatoshi and Anne O. Krueger (eds), *Growth Theories in Light of the East Asian Experience*, The University of Chicago Press, Chicago and London, Chapter 7, pp. 181–96.

Kim, Kwan S., 1995. 'The Korean Miracle (1962–80) Revisited: Myths and Realities in Strategies and Development', in Stein, Howard (ed.), *Asian Industrialization and Africa—Studies in Policy Alternatives to Structural Adjustment*, St Martin's Press, London, pp. 87–143.

Kindleberger, Charles P., 1986. *The World in Depression, 1929–1939*, University of California Press, Berkeley.

Kinrade, Peter, 1996. 'Towards Ecologically Sustainable Development: The Role and Shortcomings of Markets', in Eckerseley, Robyn (ed.), *Markets and the State and Environment—Towards Integration*, Macmillan, London, pp. 86–109.

Knudsen, Odin and **John Nash,** 1991.'Agricultural Policy', in Thomas, Vinod et al. (eds), *Restructuring Economies in Distress: Policy Reform and the World Bank*, World Bank, Oxford University Press, Oxford, Chapter 7, pp. 131–58.

Krueger, Anne O., 1978. *Liberalisation Attempts and Consequences*, Ballinger Publishing Company, Cambridge.

———, 1990. *Perspectives on Trade Development*, Harvester–Wheatsheaf, New York. (In particular Chapter 7 on 'The New Political Economy of Rent-Seeking Society').

———, 1992. *The Political Economy of Agricultural Pricing Policy, Vol 5—A Synthesis of the Political Economy in Developing Countries*, A World Bank Comparative Study, Washington DC.

Krugman, Paul R., 1991. *Has the Adjustment Process Worked?*, Institute for International Economics, Washington DC.

———, 1996. 'Pop Internationalism', in Krugman, Paul R., *The Myth of Asian Miracle*, The MIT Press, Cambridge, USA, Chapter 11, pp. 167–87.

Krugman, Paul R. and **Lance Taylor,** 1978. 'Contractionary Effects of Devaluation', *Journal of International Economics*, Vol. 8, August.

Kwok, Reginald Yin-Wang, 1995. 'Hong Kong Investment in South China', in Croix, Sumner J. la et al., *Emerging Patterns of East Asian Investment in China: From Korea, Taiwan and Hong Kong*, An Eastgate book, M.E. Sharpe, Armonk, New York and London, Chapter 5.

Lal, Deepak, 1983. *The Poverty of Development Economics*, Institute of Economic Affairs, London.

Lal, Deepak and **H. Myint,** 1996. *The Political Economy of Poverty, Equity and Growth—A Comparative Study*, Clarendon Press, Oxford.

Lancaster, Carol, 1991. 'African Economic Reform: The External Dimension', Institute for International Economics, Working Paper No. 33, Washington DC.

Lateef, K. Sarwar, 1994. *The Evolving Role of the World Bank, the First Half Century: An Overview*, The World Bank, Washington DC.

Leeahtam, Pisit, 1991. *From Crisis to Double Digit Growth—Thailand's Economic Adjustment in the 1980s*, Doya Publishing House, Bangkok.

Leechor, Chad, 1991. 'Ghana—Ending Chaos', in Thomas, Vinod et al. (eds), *Restructuring Economies in Distress: Policy Reform and the World Bank*, World Bank, Oxford University Press, Chapter 15, pp. 309–27.

Lele, Jayant and **Kwasi Ofori–Yeboah** (eds), 1996. *Unravelling the Asian Miracle: Explorations in Development Strategies, Geopolitics and Regionalism*, Dartmouth, Aldershot.

Lesser, William H., 1991. *Equitable Patent Protection in the Developing World: Issues and Approaches*, Eubios Ethics Institute, Christchurch (New Zealand) and Tsukuba, Japan.

Levin, Jorgen, 1994. *Kenya—Two Steps Backwards and One Step Forward*, SIDA, Planning Secretariat, Stockholm.

Lewis, John P., 1995. *India's Political Economy—Governance and Reform*, Oxford University Press, Delhi.

Lim, Linda, 1995. 'Foreign Investment, the State and the Industrial Policy in Singapore', in Stein, Howard (ed.), *Asian Industrialization and Africa—Studies in Policy Alternatives to Structural Adjustment*, St Martin's Press, London, pp. 205–38.

Lipsett, S.M., 1959. 'Some Social Requisites of Democracy: Economic Development and Political Legitimacy', *American Political Sciences Review*, Vol. 53, pp. 69–105.

Little, I.M.D., Richard N. Cooper, W. Max Corden and **Sarath Rajapatirana,** 1993. *Boom, Crisis and Adjustment—The Macroeconomic Experience of Developing Countries*, World Bank, Oxford University Press.

Low, Patrick, 1995. *Trading Free—The GATT and the US Trade Policy*, A Twentieth Century Fund book, New York.

Lui, Tai-lok and **Samuel K. Chiu,** 1996. 'Interpreting Industrial Restructuring in Hong Kong: State, Market and Institutions', in Lele, Jayant and Kwasi Ofori–Yeboah (eds), *Unravelling the Asian Miracle: Explorations in Development Strategies, Geopolitics and Regionalism*, Dartmouth, Aldershot, pp. 40–65.

MacBean, Alasdair, 1978. *A Positive Approach to the International Economic Order, Part 1: Trade and Structural Adjustment*, British-North American Committee, Birn, Shaw & Co., London.

Mansfield, Edward D., 1993. 'Effects of International Politics on Regionalism in International Trade', in Anderson, Kym and Richard Blackhurst (eds), *Regional Integration and the Global Trading System*, Harvester–Wheatsheaf, New York, Chapter 9, pp. 199–217.

Marshall S., Jorge, Jose Luis Mãrdones S. and **Isabell Marshall L.,** 1983. 'IMF Conditionality: The Experiences of Argentina, Brazil and Chile', in Williamson, John (ed.), *IMF Conditionality*, Institute for International Economics, Washington DC, Chapter 14.

Maskus, Keith K. and **Denise R. Eby,** 1993. 'Developing New Rules and Disciplines on Trade-Related Investment Measures', in Stern, Robert M. (ed.), *The Multilateral Trading System: Analysis and Options for Change*, Harvester–Wheatsheaf, New York, Chapter 16, pp. 449–69.

Matthews, W.H., 1976. *Outer Limits and Human Needs: Resource and Environmental Issues of Development Strategies*, Dag Hammarskjold Foundation, Uppsala.

McCleary, William A., 1991. 'The Design and Implementation of Conditionality', in Thomas, Vinod et al. (eds), *Restructuring Economies in Distress: Policy Reform and the World Bank*, World Bank, Oxford University Press, Chapter 10.

McCutcheon, Robert, 1979. *Limits of a Modern World—A Study of 'Limits of Growth' Debate*, Butterworths, London-Boston.

McMichael, Philip (ed.), 1995. *Food and Agrarian Orders in the World Economy*, Praeger, London.

Mcnally, May M., 1995. *International Wheat Subsidies—Who Really Profits?*, Garland Publishing, New York.

Meadows, Donella H., Dennis L. Meadows and **Jorgen Randers,** 1972. *The Limits to Growth: A Report for the Club of Rome's Project on the Predicament of Mankind*, Pan, London.

———, 1992. *Beyond the Limits—Global Collapse and Sustainable Development*, Earthscan, London.

Meier, Gerald M., 1991. *Politics and Policy Making in Developing Countries—Perspectives on the New Political Economy*, ICS Press, San Francisco.

Mishra, Veena, 1995. 'Indonesia: Adjustment in the 1980s', in Agarwal, Pradeep et al. (eds), *Economic Restructuring in East Asia and India: Perspectives on Policy*

Reform, Indira Gandhi Institute of Development Research and Institute of Southeast Asian Studies, Singapore, Macmillan and St Martin's Press, London and New York, Chapter 4, pp. 103–33.

Mookherjee, Dilip (ed.), 1995a. *Indian Industry—Policies and Performance*, Oxford University Press, Delhi.

———, 1995b. 'Introduction', in Mookherjee, Dilip (ed.), *Indian Industry—Policies and Performance*, Oxford University Press, Delhi, Chapter 1.

Moon, Pal-Young and **Beng-Soon Kang,** 1991. 'The Republic of Korea', in Krueger, Anne O., Maurice Schiff and Alberto Valdes (eds), *The Political Economy of Agricultural Pricing Policies, Vol. 2—Asia*, A World Bank Comparative Study, John Hopkins University Press, Baltimore.

Moran, Christian, 1991. 'Chile—Economic Crisis and Recovery', in Thomas, Vinod et al. (eds), *Restructuring Economies in Distress: Policy Reform and the World Bank*, World Bank, Oxford University Press, Oxford, Chapter 21, pp. 468–93.

Mosley, Paul, 1991. 'The Philippines', in Mosley, Paul et al. (eds), *Aid and Power—The World Bank and Policy-Based Lending*, Vol. 2, Routledge, London, Chapter 12, pp. 39–71.

Mosley, Paul, James Harrigan and **John Toye** (eds), 1991. *Aid and Power—The World Bank and Policy-Based Lending*, Vols 1 and 2, Routledge, London.

Moyer, H. Wayne and **Timothy Josling,** 1990. *Agricultural Policy Reform: Politics and Process in the EC and the USA*, Harvester–Wheatsheaf, New York.

Muir, J.F. and **R.J. Roberts,** 1982. *Fisheries and Aquaculture*, Westview Press, Boulder, Columbia.

Mukherjee, Amitava, 1994. *Structural Adjustment Programme and Food Security*, Avebury, Aldershot.

Muzulu, Joseph, 1993. 'Real Exchange Rate Depreciation and Structural Adjustment: The Case of the Manufacturing Sector in Zimbabwe (1980–1991)', University of Sussex, IDS, Ph.D. thesis.

Nadal, A. 1997. 'Multinational Corporation and Transfer of Technology: The Case of Mexico', in Germidis, D. (ed.), *Transfer of Technology by Multinational Corporations*, OECD, Paris.

Nafziger, E. Wayne, 1995. 'Japan's Industrial Development, 1868–1939: Lessons for Sub-Saharan Africa', in Stein, Howard (ed.), *Asian Industrialization and Africa—Studies in Policy Alternatives to Structural Adjustment*, St Martin's Press, London, pp. 53–85.

Nash, John, 1991. 'Mexico: Adjustment and Stabilization', in Thomas, Vinod et al. (eds), *Restructuring Economies in Distress: Policy Reform and the World Bank*, World Bank, Oxford University Press, Oxford, Chapter 22, pp. 494–514.

Nellis, John R., 1991. 'Reform of Public Enterprises', in Thomas, Vinod et al. (eds), *Restructuring Economies in Distress: Policy Reform and the World Bank*, World Bank, Oxford University Press, Oxford, Chapter 6.

Nelson, Joan, 1988. 'The Political Economy of Stabilisation—Commitment, Capacity and Public Response', in Bates, Robert H. (ed.), *Toward a Political Economy of Development—A Rational Choice Perspective*, University of California Press, Berkley, Chapter 3, pp. 80–130.

———, 1991. Comments incorporated in 'A Critique by Political Scientists', in Meier, Gerald M. (ed.), *Politics and Policy Making in Developing Countries—Perspectives on the New Political Economy*, ICS Press, San Francisco, Chapter 10.

Nonneman, Gerd, 1996. 'Linkages Between Economic and Political Liberalization: Some Concluding Observations', in Nonneman, Gerd, *Political and Economic Liberalization, Dynamics and Linkages in Comparative Perspective*, Lynne Rienner Publishers, Boulder, London, Chapter 16.

North–South Roundtable Meeting, 1993. 'Report', Preparatory Meeting on 4–6 April, New York (mimeo).

OECD, 1972. *The Industrial Policy of Japan*, OECD, Paris.

———, 1992a. *Benefit Estimates and Environmental Decision-Making*, OECD, Paris.

———, 1992b. *Technology and the Economy—The Key Relationship*, The Technology/Economy Programme, OECD, Paris.

———, 1993. *World Cereal Trade: What Role for Developing Countries?*, OECD, Paris.

———, 1995. *Technological Change and Structural Adjustment in Agriculture*, OECD, Paris.

———, 1996a. *Nuclear Energy Agency and Information, Radioactive Waste Management in Perspective*, OECD, Paris.

———, 1996b. 'Competition Policy and Environment', Working Papers, Vol. 4, No. 5, OECD, Paris.

———, 1996c. *Subsidies and Environment—Exploring the Linkages*, OECD, Paris.

———, 1996d. 'The Agricultural Outlook: Trends and Issues to 2000', OECD, Paris.

OECF (Overseas Economic Coöperation Fund), 1991. 'Issues Related to the World Bank's Approach to Structural Adjustment—Proposals from a Major Partner', OECF Occasional Paper No. 1, Tokyo (mimeo).

Okuda, Kazuhiko, 1996. 'Japan's Perception of NAFTA', in Lele, Jayant and Kwasi Ofori-Yeboah (eds), *Unravelling the Asian Miracle: Explorations in Development Strategies, Geopolitics and Regionalism*, Dartmouth, Aldershot, pp. 171–83.

Olson, Mancur, 1968. *The Logic of Collective Action*, Schocken Books, New York.

———, 1982. *The Rise and Decline of Nations: Economic Growth, Stagflation and Social Rigidities*, Yale University Press, New Haven and London.

Pearce, D., A. Markandya and **E. Barbier,** 1989. *Blueprint for a Green Economy*, Earthscan, London.

Penrose, Edith, 1967. *The Large International Firm in Developing Countries: The International Petroleum Industry*, George Allen and Unwin, London.

Pigou, A.C., 1920. *The Economics of Welfare*, Macmillan, London.

Plant, Roger, 1994. *Labour Standards & Structural Adjustment*, ILO, Geneva.

Polak, Jacques J., 1994. *The World Bank and IMF—A Changing Relationship*, The Brookings Institution, Washington DC.

Pourgerami, A., 1991. *Development and Democracy in the Third World*, Westview Press, Boulder, Colorado.

Pursell, Gary and **Ashok Gulati,** 1995. 'Liberalizing Indian Agriculture: An Agenda for Reform', in Cassen, Robert and Vijay Joshi (eds), *India—The Future of Economic Reform*, Oxford University Press, Bombay, pp. 261–311.

Rafter, Kunibert and **H.W. Singer,** 1996. *The Foreign Aid Business: Economic Assistance and Development Cooperation*, Edward Elgar, Cheltenham, UK and Brookfield, US.

Ram, R., 1986. 'Government Size and Economic Growth', *American Economic Review*, Vol. 76, No. 1, March.

Ranis, G. and **J.C.H. Fei,** 1963. 'Innovation, Capital, Accumulation and Economic Development, *American Economic Review*, June.

Rapley, John, 1996. *Understanding Development—Theory and Practice in the Third World*, Lynne Rienner Publishers, London.

Redding, Gordon and **Simon Tam,** 1995. 'Colonialism and Entrepreneurship in Africa and Hong Kong: A Comparative Perspective', in Stein, Howard (ed.), *Asian Industrialization and Africa—Studies in Policy Alternatives to Structural Adjustment*, St Martin's Press, London, pp. 183–203.

Repetto, Rupert, 1995. 'Trade and Sustainable Development', in Schydlowsky, Daniel M. (ed.), *Structural Adjustment—Retrospect and Prospect*, Praeger, Westport, Connecticut, London, Chapter 8.

Rodrik, Dani, 1994. 'King Kong Meets Godzilla: The World Bank and the East Asian Miracle', in Fishlow, Albert et al. (eds), *Miracle or Design: Lessons from the East Asian Experience*, Overseas Development Council, Policy Essays, No. 11, Washington DC, Chapter 1, pp. 13–54.

Runge, C. Ford, 1993. 'Beyond the Uruguay Round: Emerging Issues in Agricultural Trade Policy', in William, P. (ed.), *World Agriculture and the GATT*, Lynne Rienner Publishers, Boulder and London, Chapter 9, pp. 181–234.

Runge, C. Ford and **Tom Jones,** 1996. 'Subsidies, Tax Disincentives and the Environment: An Overview and Synthesis', in OECD, *Subsidies and Environment—Exploring the Linkages*, OECD, Paris, pp. 7–22.

Sahasakul, Chaipal, Nattapong Thongpakde and **Keokam Kraisoraphong,** 1991. 'Thailand', in Mosley, Paul et al. (eds), *Aid and Power—The World Bank and Policy-Based Lending*, Vol. 2, Routledge, London, Chapter 13.

Sarel, Michael, 1996. 'Growth in East Asia: What We Can and What We Cannot Infer', *Economic Issues*, No. 1, International Monetary Fund, Washington DC.

Sarkar, Prabirjit and **Hans Singer,** 1992. 'Debt Crisis, Commodity Prices, Transfer Burden and Debt Relief', Institute of Development Studies, Discussion Paper No. 297, Brighton.

Schaeffer, Robert, 1995. 'Free Trade Agreements: Their Impact on Agriculture and the Environment', in McMichael, Philip (ed.), *Food and Agrarian Orders in the World Economy*, Praeger, London, pp. 255–75.

Schmiddt–Hebbel, Klaus and **Steven B. Webb,** 1992. 'Public Policy and Private Saving', in Corbo, Vittorio et al. (eds), *Adjustment Lending Revisited—Policies to Restore Growth, A World Bank Symposium*, World Bank, Washington DC, pp. 139–58.

Schott, Jeffrey J., 1990. *The Global Trade Negotiations: What Can Be Achieved?*, Institute of International Economics, Washington DC.

———, 1994. Assisted by Johanna W. Buurman, *The Uruguay Round*, Institute for International Economics, Washington DC.

Schramm, Gunter and **Jeremy J. Warford** (eds), 1989. *Environmental Management and Economic Development*, World Bank, Washington DC.

Schydlowsky, Daniel M. (ed.), 1995. *Structural Adjustment—Retrospect and Prospect*, Praeger, Westport, Connecticut, London.

Sen, Kunal, 1995. 'Thailand: Stabilization with Growth', in Agarwal, Pradeep et al. (eds), *Economic Restructuring in East Asia and India: Perspective on Policy Reform*, Indira Gandhi Institute of Development Research and Institute of Southeast Asian Studies, Singapore, Macmillan and St Martin's Press, London and New York, Chapter 5, pp. 134–58.

Shinohara, M., 1982. *Industrial Growth, Trade and Dynamic Patterns in the Japanese Economy*, University of Tokyo Press, Tokyo.

Shiva, Vandana and **Gurpreet Karir,** 1997. *Towards Sustainable Aquaculture: Chenmmmeenkettu*, Research Foundation for Science, Technology and Ecology, New Delhi.

Shiva, Vandana and **R. Holla-Bhar,** 1993. 'Intellectual Piracy and the Neem Tree', *The Ecologist*, Vol. 23, No. 6.

Silva, Eduardo, 1996. *The State and Capital in Chile—Business Elites, Technocrats and Market Economics*, Westview Press, Boulder and Oxford.

Simatupang, Batara, 1996. 'Economic Transformation and Liberalization in Indonesia', in Jilberto, Alex E. Fernandez and Andre Mommen (eds), *Liberalisation in the Developing World: Institutional and Economic Changes in Latin America, Africa and Asia*, Routledge, London, Chapter 3, pp. 51–71.

Singer, Hans W., 1994. 'Structural Adjustment Programmes: Evaluating Success', in Gunning, Jan Willem, Hank Kox, Wouter Tims and Ynto de Witt, *Trade, Aid and Development*, Macmillan, London, pp. 172–84.

———, 1995. 'An Historical Perspective', in Huq, Mahbub ul et al. (eds), *The UN and Bretton Woods Institutions: New Challenge for the Twenty First Century*, Macmillan, London, pp. 17–25.

Singh, Ajit, 1994. 'Policy-Based Lending: The Bretton Wood Institutions' Approach to Structural Adjustment in the Light of the East Asian Experience', Paper presented at The Conference on the Socioeconomic and Political Consequences of IMF and World Bank Policies, Karachi, 22–24 September.

———, 1995. 'The Stock Market, Economic Efficiency and Industrial Development', in Arestis, Philip and Victoria Chick (eds), *Finance, Development and Structural Change—Post-Keynesian Perspectives*, Edward Elgar, Aldershot.

Skladany, Mike and **Craig K. Harris,** 1995. 'On Global Pond: International Development and Commodity Chains in the Shrimp Industry', in McMichael, Philip (ed.), *Food and Agrarian Orders in the World Economy*, Praeger, London, pp. 169–91.

Snider, Lewis W., 1996. *Growth, Dent and Politics: Economic Adjustment and the Political Performance of Developing Countries*, Westview Press, USA.

Sorsa, Piritta, 1992. *The Environment—A New Challenge to GATT*, World Bank, WPS 980, Washington DC.

Srinivasan, T.N., 1991. 'Foreign Trade Regimes', in Meier, Gerald M. (ed.), *Politics and Policy Making in Developing Countries—Perspectives on the New Political Economy*, ICS Press, San Francisco, Chapter 5, pp. 123–47.

Stein, Howard (ed.), 1995a. *Asian Industrialisation and Africa—Studies in Policy Alternatives to Structural Adjustment*, St Martin's Press, London.

———, 1995b. 'The World Bank, Neo-classical Economics and the Application of Asian Industrial Policy to Africa', in Stein, Howard (ed.), *Asian Industrialisation and Africa—Studies in Policy Alternatives to Structural Adjustment*, St Martin's Press, London, pp. 31–52.

———, 1995c. 'Policy Alternatives to Structural Adjustment in Africa: An Introduction', in Stein, Howard (ed.), *Asian Industrialization and Africa—Studies in Policy Alternatives to Structural Adjustment*, St Martin's Press, London, pp. 1–29.

Stern, Robert M. (ed.), 1993. *The Multilateral Trading System: Analysis and Options for Change*, Harvester–Wheatsheaf, New York.

Stevens, Luis and **Andrés Solimano,** 1992. 'Economic Adjustment and Investment Performance in Developing Countries: The Experience of the 1980s', in Corbo, Vittorio et al. (eds), *Adjustment Lending Revisited—Policies to Restore Growth, A World Bank Symposium*, World Bank, Washington DC, pp. 117–38.

Stewart, Frances, 1993. 'Biases in Global Markets: Can the Forces of Inequity and Marginalisation Be Modified?', Paper presented at North–South Roundtable Meeting, New York, April (mimeo).

Stigliz, Joseph E., 1997. 'An Agenda for Development for the Twenty-First Century', Keynote Address to Ninth Annual World Bank Conference on Development Economics, Washington DC.

Stiles, Kendall W., 1980. 'IMF Conditionality: Coercion or Compromise?', *World Development*, Vol. 8, No. 7, July.

Streeten, Paul, 1995. 'The Political Economy of Reform', in Schydlowsky, Daniel M. (eds.), *Structural Adjustment—Retrospect and Prospect*, Praeger, Westport, Connecticut, London, Chapter 10.

Suh, Sang-Mok, 1992. 'The Economy in Historical Perspective', in Corbo, Vittorio and Sang-Mok Suh (eds), *Structural Adjustment in Newly Industrialized Country—The Korean Experience*, World Bank, John Hopkins University Press, Baltimore, Chapter 2.

Sunkel, Osvaldo, 1973. 'Transnational Capitalism and National Disintegration in Latin America', in Girvan, Norman (ed.), *Dependence and Underdevelopment in the New World and the Old, Social and Economic Studies*, Vol. 22, No. 1, Special Number, March.

Tan, Augustine H.H., 1991. 'Comments', in Meier, Gerald M. (ed.), *Politics and Policy Making in Developing Countries—Perspectives on the New Political Economy*, ICS Press, San Francisco, pp. 50–53.

Taylor, Lance, 1995. 'Policy Reform in the 1980s', in Schydlowsky, Daniel M. (ed.), *Structural Adjustment—Retrospect and Prospect*, Praeger, Westport, Connecticut, London, Chapter 3.

Teunissen, Jan Joost (ed.), 1992. *Fragile Finance—Rethinking the International Monetary System*, FONDAD, The Hague.

Thomas, Vinod, Ajay Chhibber, Mansoor Dailami and **Jaime de Melo** (eds), 1991. *Restructuring Economies in Distress: Policy Reform and the World Bank*, World Bank, Oxford University Press, Oxford.

Thomas, Vinod and **Peter Stephens,** 1994. *The Evolving Role of the World Bank—The East Asian Economic Miracle*, World Bank, Washington DC.

Thompson, Susan J. and **J. Tadlock Cowan,** 1995. 'Durable Food Production and Consumption in the World Economy', in McMichael, Philip (ed.), *Food and Agrarian Orders in the World Economy*, Praeger, London, pp. 35–52.

Tinbergen, Jan (coordinator), **Antony J. Dolman** (editor) and **Jan Van Ettinger** (director), 1976. *RIO—Reshaping the International Order*, E.P. Dutton & Co, New York.

Toye, John, 1991. 'Ghana', in Mosley, Paul et al., *Aid and Power—The World Bank and Policy-Based Lending*, Vol. 2, Routledge, London, Chapter 14.

———, 1993. 'Is there a New Political Economy of Development?', in Colclough, Christopher and James Manor (eds), *States or Markets—Neo-liberalism and the Development Policy Debate*, Clarendon Paperbacks, Oxford, Chapter 15, pp. 321–38.

Toye, John, 1995. *Structural Adjustment and Employment Policy—Issues and Experience*, ILO, Geneva.

Trela, Irene, 1975. 'Phasing out of the MFA in the Uruguay Round: Implications for the Developing Countries', London, Ontario (mimeo).

Trela, Irena and **John Whaller,** 1990. 'Unraveling the Threads of MFA', in Hamilton, Carl B. (ed.), *Textiles Trade and the Developing Countries: Eliminating the Multifibre Agreement in the 1990s*, World Bank, Washington DC.

Tsurumi, Yoshi, 1989–90. 'US-Japanese Relations: From Brinkmanship to Statesmanship', *World Policy Journal*, Nos 2–3, Winter.

Tullock, Gordon, 1980. 'Rent Seeking as a Negative Sum Game', in Buchanan, James M. et al. (eds), *Towards a Theory of Rent Seeking Society*, Texas A and M University Press, College Station, Texas, Chapter 2, pp. 16–36.

Tybour, James R., 1991. 'Industrial Performance: Some Stylized Facts', in Thomas, Vinod et al. (eds.), *Restructuring Economies in Distress: Policy Reform and the World Bank*, World Bank, Oxford University Press, Oxford, Chapter 8.

Typres, Rod, 1991. 'The Cairs Group Perspective', in Ingersent, K.A. et al. (eds), *Agriculture in the Uruguay Round*, St Martin's Press, New York, pp. 88–109.

Ufkes, Frances M., 1995. 'Industrial Restructuring and Agrarian Change: The Greening of Singapore', in McMichael, Philip (ed.), *Food and Agrarian Orders in the World Economy*, Praeger, London, pp. 195–215.

United Nations, 1971. 'Development and Environment', Report Submitted by a Panel of Experts Convened by the Secretary General of the UN Conference on the Human Environment (Founex report), Mouton, Paris.

———, 1972. *Report of the United Nations' Conference on the Human Environment*, Stockholm.

———, 1973. *Multinational Corporations in World Development*, New York.

UNCTAD, 1994a. United Nations Conference on Trade and Development, Trade and Development Report, 1994, UNCTAD, Geneva.

———, 1994b. *The Outcome of the Uruguay Round: An Initial Assessment*, UNCTAD, Geneva.

UNIDO (United Nations Industrial Development Organisation), 1975. *Lima Declaration and Plan of Action on Industrial Development and Cooperation*, United Nations, New York.

Vaitsos, Constantine, 1972. 'Patents Revisited: Their Function in Developing Countries', *Journal of Development Studies*, Vol. 9, October, pp. 71–97.

Vas, Rob, 1994. *Debt and Adjustment in the World Economy, Structural Asymmetries in North–South Interaction*, St Martin's Press in association with Institute of Social Studies, The Hague.

Vernon, Raymond, 1971. *Sovereignty at Bay—The Multinational Spread of U.S. Enterprises*, Longman, London.

Vivian, Jessica M., 1991. *Greening at the Grassroots: People's Participation in Sustainable Development*, United Nations Research Institute for Social Development (UNRISD), Geneva.

Vogler, John, 1996. 'Introduction: The Environment in International Relations: Legacies and Contentions', in Vogler, John and Mark E. Imber (eds), *The Environment and International Relations*, Routledge, London, Chapter 1, pp. 1–21.

Wade, Robert, 1990. *Governing the Market: Economic Theory and the Role of the Government in East Asian Industrialization*, Princeton University Press, Princeton.

———, 1994. 'Selective Industrial Policies in East Asia: Is the Asian Miracle Right?', in Fishlow, Albert et al. (eds), *Miracle or Design: Lessons from the East Asian Experience*, Overseas Development Council, Policy Essays, No. 11, Washington DC, Chapter 2, pp. 55–80.

———, 1996. 'Japan, the World Bank, and the Art of Paradigm Maintenance: The East Asian Miracle in Political Perspective', *New Left Review*, No. 217, May–June, pp. 3–36.

Walter, Ingo (ed.), 1976. *Studies in International Environmental Economics*, Wiley, New York.

Watkins, Kevin, 1992. *Fixing the Rules: North South Issues in International Trade and GATT Uruguay Round*, Catholic Institute for International Relations, London.

Weale, Albert, 1992. *The New Politics of Pollution*, Manchester University Press, Manchester and New York.

Webb, Steven B. and **Karim Shariff,** 1992. 'Designing and Implementing Adjustment Programs', in Corbo, Vittorio et al. (eds), *Adjustment Lending Revisited—Policies to Restore Growth, A World Bank Symposium*, World Bank, Washington DC, pp. 69–98.

Webb, M.C. and **S.D. Krasner,** 1989. 'Hegemonic Stability Theory: An Empirical Assessment', *Review of International Studies*, Vol. 15, pp. 183–98.

Wei, Sung Shou and **Lishui Zhu,** 1995. 'The Growth of Foreign and Taiwan Investment in the Xiamen Special Economic Zone', in Croix, Sumner J. la et al. (eds), *Emerging Patterns of East Asian Investment in China: From Korea, Taiwan and Hong Kong*, An Eastgate book, M.E. Sharpe, Armonk, New York and London, Chapter 7.

West, Edwin G., 1996. 'Adam Smith into the Twenty-First Century, The Shaftesbury Papers, 7', in Rawley, Charles K., *The Political Economy of the Minimal State*, The Shaftesbury Papers, Edward Elgar, Cheltenham, UK and Brookfield, US.

Williams, Maurice, 1993. 'Role of the Multilateral Agencies After the Earth Summit', in North–South Roundtable Meeting, New York, April (mimeo).

Williamson, John (ed.), 1983. *IMF Conditionality*, Institute for International Economics, Washington DC.

———, 1983b. 'The Lending Policies of the International Monetary Fund', in Williamson, John (ed.), *IMF Conditionality*, Institute for International Economics, Washington DC, Chapter 24, pp. 605–54.

———, 1992a. 'International Monetary Reform and the Prospects for Economic Development', in Teunissen, Jan Joost (ed.), *Fragile Finance—Rethinking the International Monetary System*, FONDAD, The Hague, pp. 86–96.

———, 1992b. 'Comments', in Corbo, Vittorio et al. (eds), *Adjustment Lending Revisted—Policies To Restore Growth, A World Bank Symposium*, World Bank, Washington DC, pp. 20–22.

———, 1995. 'Policy Reform in Latin America in the 1980s', in Schydlowsky, Daniel M. (ed.), *Structural Adjustment—Retrospect and Prospect*, Praeger, Westport, Connecticut, London, Chapter 4.

Winters, L. Alan, 1994. 'The LDC Perspective', in Ingersent, K.A. et al. (eds), *Agriculture in the Uruguay Round*, World Bank, St Martin's Press, New York, pp. 157–81.

WCED (The World Commission on Environment and Development), 1987. *Our Common Future* (The Brundtland Report), Oxford University Press, Oxford.

World Bank, of various years. *World Development Report* (WDR), Washington DC.

———, 1987. *Korea—Managing the Industrial Transition*, Volume I, Washington DC.

———, 1989. *Sub-Saharan Africa: From Crisis to Sustainable Growth*, Washington DC.

———, 1990a. *India: Strategy for Trade Reforms*, Washington DC.

———, 1990b. *Conserving World's Biodiversity*, Washington DC.

———, 1990c. *Adjustment Lending Policies for Sustainable Growth*, Washington DC.

———, 1992. *Adjustment Lending: An Evaluation of Ten Years of Experience*, Policy Planning and Research Department, Washington DC.

———, 1993. *The East Asian Miracle—Economic Growth and Public Policy*, Oxford University Press, Oxford.

———, 1994a. *Adjustment in Africa, Reforms, Results and the Road Ahead*, A World Bank Policy Research Report, Oxford University Press, Oxford.

———, 1994b. (Jeremy Watford, Adelaida Schwb, Wildfrido Cruz and Stein Hansen), *The Evolution of Environmental Concerns in Adjustment Lending: A Review*, World Bank, Environment Department, Washington DC.

Wortzel, L.H. and **H.V. Wortzel,** 1981. 'Export Market Strategies for NIC and Less Developed Countries-Based Firms', *Columbia Journal of World Business*, Spring number, pp. 51–60.

Yansane, Aguibou Y. (ed.), 1996. *Prospects for Recovery and Sustainable Development in Africa*, Greenwood Press, Westport, Connecticut and London.

Yansane, Aguibou Y.,1996. 'Are Alternative Development Strategies Suitable for Africa to Remedy Its Deepening Crisis?', in Yansane, Aguibou Y. (ed.), *Prospects for Recovery and Sustainable Development in Africa*, Greenwood Press, Westport, Connecticut and London, Chapter 1.

Young, Alwyn, 1994. 'The Tyranny of Numbers: Confronting the Statistical Realities of the East Asian Growth Experience', NBER Working Paper No. 4680, March.

Zaidi, S. Akbar, 1994. 'Locating the Budget Deficit in Context: The Case of Pakistan', Proceedings of the Conference on the Socioeconomic and Political Consequences of IMF and World Bank Policies, Karachi, 22–24 September (mimeo).

Zuckerman, Elaine, 1991. 'The Social Cost of Adjustment', in Thomas, Vinod et al. (eds), *Restructuring Economies in Distress: Policy Reform and the World Bank*, World Bank, Oxford University Press, Chapter 12.

About the author

Biplab Dasgupta, Professor of Economics, Calcutta University, and Director of its Centre for Urban Economic Studies, is also a member of the Upper House (Rajya Sabha) of the Indian Parliament. A Ph.D. in economics from the London School of Economics and an M.Sc. in Computer Science from London University's Institute of Computer Science, Professor Dasgupta was a lecturer at the School of Oriental and African Studies, London, and a Fellow-Reader in Economics and Statistics at the Institute of Development Studies, Sussex, for 15 years, before joining Calcutta University in 1980. In a long and distinguished career, he has been Visiting Professor at Jawaharlal Nehru University, Delhi, and the Institute of Social Studies, The Hague; Member, Governing Body, Centre for the Study of Social Sciences, Calcutta, Institute of Development Studies, Jaipur, Wild Life Institute of India, Dehra Dun, and the Regional Engineering College, Durgapur. He was also member of the Lower House (Lok Sabha) of Parliament for one term. He has undertaken assignments for various UN agencies such as ILO, UNRISD, FAO, UNEP and UNESCO and has travelled widely.

Besides numerous articles in academic journals, Professor Dasgupta has previously published a number of books including *The Oil Industry in India: Some Economic Aspects*, *Patterns and Trends in Indian Politics: An Ecological Analysis of Aggregate Data on Society and Elections* (with W.H. Morris-Jones), *The New Agrarian Technology and India*, *Village Society and Labour Use* and *Migration from Rural Areas* (jointly with three other authors).

Subject index

Author index